Latin America's Left Turns

Latin America's Left Turns

Politics, Policies, and Trajectories of Change

edited by
Maxwell A. Cameron
and Eric Hershberg

LYNNE
RIENNER
PUBLISHERS

BOULDER
LONDON

Published in the United States of America in 2010 by
Lynne Rienner Publishers, Inc.
1800 30th Street, Boulder, Colorado 80301
www.rienner.com

and in the United Kingdom by
Lynne Rienner Publishers, Inc.
3 Henrietta Street, Covent Garden, London WC2E 8LU

Library of Congress Cataloging-in-Publication Data
Latin America's left turns : politics, policies, and trajectories of change
/ edited by Maxwell A. Cameron and Eric Hershberg.
     p.   cm.
  Includes bibliographical references and index.
  ISBN 978-1-58826-714-6 (hc : alk. paper)
  ISBN 978-1-58826-739-9 (pb : alk. paper)
1. Latin America—Politics and government—1980–
2. Right and left (Political science) 3. Socialism—Latin America.
I. Cameron, Maxwell A. II. Hershberg, Eric.
  JL960.L375 2010
  320.98—dc22

                                            2010006847

British Cataloguing in Publication Data
A Cataloguing in Publication record for this book
is available from the British Library.

Printed and bound in the United States of America

∞ The paper used in this publication meets the requirements
          of the American National Standard for Permanence of
          Paper for Printed Library Materials Z39.48-1992.

    5   4   3   2   1

*To the memory of Donna Lee Van Cott,
friend, colleague, and passionate advocate
for social justice in Latin America*

Contents

Acknowledgments

A collaborative project such as the one from which this book has resulted involves the contributions of many individuals and institutions. Jon Beasley-Murray was as central as the coeditors to the initial conceptualization of the project, fund-raising, and recruitment of participants. We could not have completed the project without grants from the Peter Wall Institute for Advanced Studies (and we acknowledge in particular the support of Dianne Newell and Markus Pickartz) at the University of British Columbia (UBC) and from the Social Science and Humanities Research Council of Canada, which supported workshops in 2007 and 2008, respectively. The Latin American Studies Program at Simon Fraser University and the Department of Political Science and the Centre for the Study of Democratic Institutions at UBC also contributed generously. Jeanne Persoon and Suzy Hainsworth provided able administrative and logistical support, and useful rapporteurs' reports were prepared by Santiago Anria, Catherine Craven, and Valerie Duquette.

The workshops benefited immensely from the intellectual contributions of Andres Mejía Acosta, Victor Armony, Carmen Rosa Balbi, Cathy Conaghan, Elizabeth Friedman, Judith Adler Hellman, Tanya Korovkin, Gerardo Otero, Pablo Policzer, Freya Schiwy, Martín Tanaka, and Carlos Toranzo Roca. Many colleagues at UBC and Simon Fraser University were very supportive and gave of their time, including Alejandra Bronfman, Lesley Burns, Alec Dawson, Gastón Gordillo, Rita de Grandis, Anil Hira, Gerardo Otero, Phil Resnick, Pilar Riaño-Alcalá, Jason Tockman, and Hannah Wittman. Research assistance was provided by Rebecca Monnerat, Jorge Madrazo, and Amielle del Rosario. We regret the loss of Donna Lee Van Cott during the course of this project and dedicate our effort to her memory. The insights of two anonymous reviewers helped us to sharpen the argument and render the text more intelligible. Editorial staff at Lynne Rienner Publishers have been especially constructive, and we wish in particular to acknowledge the contributions of acquisitions editor Jessica Gribble, who shepherded the project from draft to finished form.

While we are pleased to acknowledge the contributions of many people other than ourselves, we must, as is customary, insist that any errors of omission or commission are strictly our own.

1

Latin America's Left Turns: A Tour d'Horizon

Jon Beasley-Murray,
Maxwell A. Cameron & Eric Hershberg

In the wake of a series of electoral victories often dubbed a "pink tide" by the media, there has recently been a resurgence of interest in the diverse movements, parties, and leaders that comprise the contemporary Latin American left. After three decades during which the region followed (more or less reluctantly, depending on the case) the imperatives of neoliberal economic restructuring, diverse forces on the left—from Argentina to Venezuela, Brazil to El Salvador—have now captured the imagination of vast swaths of the continent's population, taken hold of the reins of government, and promised change. Leaders such as Hugo Chávez, Evo Morales, Fernando Lugo, Mauricio Funes, and Luiz Inacio Lula da Silva have made bold claims about their determination to promote equality and to transform how power is exercised in Latin America. These claims, and the ambitions they reflect, have animated renewed interest in Latin America by progressive intellectuals and commentators around the world. The region can hardly be characterized, as one pundit recently posited, as "forgotten" (Reid 2007). Many disparate political and theoretical projects find inspiration or succor (or in some cases causes for anxiety) in what they claim to see happening in Latin America. Our aim in this book is to provide a wide-ranging but grounded and thorough analysis of these "left turns," to consider their future prospects, and to examine their implications for political theory in the wake of neoliberalism.

We are concerned with the antecedents, present practice, and implications of these Latin American left turns. The complex and diverse circumstances that have given rise to this phenomenon are one central focus of this book. Another has to do with how politics is practiced by different currents of the Latin American left. In the first instance, this has to do with relations between state and society that are being reinvented, sometimes in quite novel fashion, as well as with the operation of institutions. We are also interested in the policy ramifications of the striking shift in social and political dynamics in the re-

1

gion. That the left has been on the rise is incontrovertible. What it does once in power, however, is a subject that time is only now permitting us to answer, albeit in very preliminary fashion. Yet the prominence of the left is not solely a function of its presence in the halls of government. A key message of this book is not only that the Latin American political landscape has shifted leftward, but also that this shift emerges from and affects the underlying logics of political interactions that matter above and beyond what takes place inside the state apparatus. The long-term effects of the left turns, and their likely durability, can only be a matter of debate.

Latin America's pink tide in part manifests itself in the succession of elections in which leftist presidential candidates have either won or performed nearly well enough to take office. Hugo Chávez's 1998 victory at the polls in Venezuela marked a trend that continued with the leftward shift in the Concertación in Chile—the triumph of Socialists Ricardo Lagos in 2000 and Michelle Bachelet in 2006; the rise to power in Uruguay of Tabaré Vásquez and the Frente Amplio, and that of Néstor Kirchner during that same year (with Kirchnerismo prolonged with the 2007 victory of Cristina Fernández de Kirchner). Further advances included those of Evo Morales in Bolivia in 2005, Rafael Correa and Daniel Ortega in Ecuador and Nicaragua during the following year, Álvaro Colom's ascent to the presidency of Guatemala in 2007 and, in 2008, that of Fernando Lugo in Paraguay.[1] The Farabundo Martí National Liberation Front (FMLN) presidential candidate Mauricio Funes won the election that took place in El Salvador in March 2009 and (albeit in rather different circumstances) Honduras's José Manuel "Mel" Zelaya also attempted to shift his government toward the left before being overthrown in June 2009.[2] Furthermore, it is notable that Andrés Manuel López Obrador, Ollanta Humala, and Ottón Solís nearly won the vote in 2006 presidential balloting in Mexico, Peru, and Costa Rica, respectively, and that even where the left has failed to reach office at the level of the executive, it frequently has made important advances in legislative and subnational arenas. Such was the case in Mexico and Colombia in 2006 and 2007, respectively, to cite but two examples.

But well beyond cases where the left has occupied the corridors of government, we see an underlying trend toward the emergence and mobilization of social and political currents variously protesting against the current political order, affirming or seeking recognition for subaltern groups, and demanding social and cultural change as well as political citizenship (Schaefer 2009; Schiwy 2008). Not only are popular movements making new demands, but as Benjamin Arditi maintains in his contribution to this book, they are doing so with greater efficacy than at any other moment since the arrival in Latin America of the third wave of democratization. In part this can no doubt be attributed to the cumulative effects of a quarter century of democratic politics, as well as to widespread dissatisfaction with what Peter Smith has termed "the glacial pace of social progress" (Smith 2005:297), but it also testifies to the growing capacity of progressive sectors to recruit new adherents and to motivate followers to enter (or disrupt) the public sphere. Especially noteworthy is the degree to which, in reaction, the dominant discourse has incorporated key features of the left's agenda, another phenomenon emphasized by Arditi.

It is tempting to assert that today's left-wing governments have unprecedented room for maneuver. Their ideological adversaries are discredited; some were even forced from power in the face of massive popular protests. Although the right has by no means disappeared and retains considerable political as well as economic influence, left-wing presidents currently enjoy greater electoral legitimacy, as well as the solidarity of their peers in the hemispheric neighborhood. Moreover, the geostrategic context could hardly be more propitious: the United States, bogged down in a costly and protracted "war against terror" elsewhere, buffeted by an economic crisis of enormous magnitude, and governed as of 2009 by Democrat Barack Obama, is unlikely to commit significant resources to intervene against even the most radical of social experiments to its south. No less important, the boom in commodities prices between 2003 and 2008 boosted government revenue in most South American countries, opening opportunities for significant investments aimed at promoting greater equity. Even where the current crisis is taking its toll on local economies, the past few years of rapid growth has more often than not provided an important buffer against external shocks, as Eric Hershberg suggests in the concluding chapter to this volume, opening opportunities for countercyclical spending to mitigate the impact of economic slowdown. Hence arguably the left's worst enemy can only be itself, should it fail to take advantage of this historic conjuncture. Yet the Latin American left faces daunting challenges—and it is in part because of its diverse responses to these challenges that we stress that these are left turns in the plural. We do not suggest that the left turns are irreversible, or that they constitute the final word for progressive politics in the region, although the conditions that have created them are unlikely to disappear in the short term and they have gone some way toward fulfilling some of their expectations.

The often tumultuous protests that in many cases brought left governments to power express social needs and demands that have accumulated since the debt crisis of the early 1980s and the ensuing period of economic adjustment and restructuring, to say nothing of the historic injustices that linger from the region's colonial past and its protracted periods of conservative authoritarian rule. The lefts that came to power on the back of these protests must make good on their promise to bring tangible change, even as global economic storm clouds gather. Unless they manage to alleviate the misery and poverty still endured by many millions, the pink tide may fade in an undercurrent of disillusionment (Luna and Filgueira 2009).[3] The stakes are higher than electoral fortunes alone. More broadly, can movements and parties work together, outside and inside government, to articulate and implement visions for the future? Can such visions be translated from rhetoric and diplomatic grandstanding into specific policies, sustainable programs, and concrete results? And can this be achieved within a renewed commitment to a more meaningful understanding of democratic politics and the republican ideal?

The last point is especially critical. A widely recognized failure of neoliberalism lay not only in the flaws of its policy recipes—not all of which were without merit—but also in the manner of its execution and the lack of a commitment to democratic accountability and deliberation. There was little or no attempt to seek agreement or approval for the terms of the Washington Consensus; indeed, if it was ever a consensus, it was only so inside Washington. Market-driven and almost viscerally antipolitical, the neoliberal leaders of the 1980s and 1990s substituted technocratic formulae for democratic debate (Hershberg 2006). The lefts cannot repeat this mistake. If they are truly to change, even revolutionize, the continent's social, economic, political, and cultural landscape, they must maintain and deepen their links with the social forces required to put their policies into practice and turn their visions into reality. Part of the lefts' challenge, therefore, is political: left-wing movements and the political parties and leaders that aspire to channel their energies into the political order have to reimagine the very constitution of a possible democratic society.

A central contention of this book is that the "left turns" are best described as a multiplicity of disparate efforts to reopen or refound the constitutional order or social pact. Indeed, even in its tamest versions, the Latin American left manifests what Laura Macdonald and Arne Ruckert (2009), coinciding with Emir Sader (Sader et al. 2008), and John French in Chapter 3 of this volume, have termed "post-neoliberalism in the Americas." Even in countries where the disjuncture from the past seems most attenuated, such as Chile, what is in play is more than another of the swings of the political pendulum for which the region is notorious. Some have argued, for instance, that the Chilean experience since the rise to power of Ricardo Lagos in 2000 is best understood not merely as a prolongation of neoliberalism but rather as a pursuit of what Richard Sandbrook and colleagues (2006) have labeled social democracy in the global periphery. In this view, superficial continuities mask underlying departures from orthodox conceptions of citizenship, which were premised on the incorporation of individuals, as producers and consumers, into markets. What are emerging instead are openings to agendas that privilege collective rights and solidarities and aspire to achieve universal social citizenship. In so doing, they signal a fundamental rethinking of state-society relations, to a greater or lesser extent according to the case. More fundamentally still, the electoral victories that have attracted such attention can often be seen as symptoms of a deeper change in which insurgent social movements, from the Mexican Ejército

Zapatista de Liberación Nacional (EZLN) to the Argentine *piqueteros,* have forced a reexamination of the fundamental constitutional tenets of Latin American republics. At times hydralike and almost anarchic in their diversity, these movements of what Jon Beasley-Murray (in Chapter 7 of this volume) conceives of as the "multitude" have also provoked experimentation with new forms of community and new modes of politics. Social movements have exposed the fictitious nature of mechanisms of representation behind which lay ethnic marginalization, urban disorder, and abysmal social gaps. Another challenge for left-wing political parties, then, is to renew the constitutional order, while also sustaining a creative constituent process of democratic experimentation and innovation. It may be that the fate of the left turns hangs on the extent to which they can achieve this delicate balancing act.

In short, the future of the current left turns, indeed the future of Latin America as a whole, will be defined by the relationship between publics and politics, society and state, movements and parties, and constituent and constituted power. Will Latin America turn toward the rule of the many, concretely affirming the res publica, or will leftist governments simply play for time and thereby perpetuate the rule of the few?

Policy Challenges

Few observers of Latin America's recent history would dispute the contention that states in the region are plagued by weaknesses. Starved of resources, deficient in institutional capabilities, and lacking widespread legitimacy, Latin American states predictably fail to coordinate processes of economic development, to engage the populace in the construction of universal citizenship, or even simply to respond to demands from below in any adequate form. State weakness is not merely a feature of the contemporary landscape. Quite the contrary, the "limits to state autonomy" were the focus of social scientists studying the region well before the lost decade of the 1980s and the ensuing experiment with neoliberalism (Hamilton 1982). The latter no doubt exacerbated matters, contributing to what Sandbrook and his colleagues (2006) have labeled the "historical burden" confronting developing countries worldwide, but the problem predates the era of globalization that Latin America encountered following the international debt crisis of the 1980s. Developmental states have been notable for their absence in Latin America. Even where developmentalism made its greatest advances, states lacked both the embeddedness and autonomy needed to fulfill the full range of functions associated with sustained and equitable development (Evans 1995).

Yet as the region experiences an unprecedented wave of electoral victories by forces on the left of the political spectrum, no task is more urgent for incoming governments than that of configuring states that promote generalized prosperity and create mechanisms for citizen engagement with the res publica. If Latin American states are to survive their current crisis of legitimacy, then they need to be better funded, more efficient, and more reflective of public preferences than those that prevail in the region at the time of this writing or that have existed in the past. It is not a simple matter of reconstructing what was in place at some Golden Age. Rather, what today's leaders and, indeed, the entire political class confronts is the challenge of refounding the Latin American state. Any progressive alternative in the task of state management must enhance its capacity to distribute resources, to oversee effective institutions, and to represent the citizenry democratically. The first entails boosting historically limited taxation capacity and greater progressivity in revenue generation; the second requires bureaucratic reforms; and the last requires greater transparency and accountability. That the state is at the core of the challenge for the organized left merits emphasis. Brazilian social scientist Emir Sader is also one who asserts that the left's task is to reconstruct the state so as to overcome the deterioration sparked by the combination of authoritarian regimes and neoliberal policy prescriptions of the past quarter century (Sader 2008). What this formulation elides, however, is that the gaps leftist governments must overcome are rooted much further back in history. Even during the heyday of developmentalism, the region lacked institutions conducive to the sustained provision of social welfare and democratic accountability: mid-twentieth-century populism, for instance, was not a manifestation of state strength, but rather evidence of its weakness. Similarly, the empirical record shows that the limited extractive capacity of Latin American states predates the neoliberal era.

The policy challenges and possibilities for Latin America's lefts extend across multiple domains: ensuring competence in domestic macroeconomic management, advancing toward a redistribution of assets, sustaining productive international alliances, and achieving stable internal governance are but several of the most pressing sets of issues on the agenda. Left-wing governments have initiated innovations in all these areas, but the specific strategies adopted have varied widely and overall there is as yet little consensus as to what is to be done or what can be achieved. Each domain is still a site of dialogue, disagreement, and contestation internal and external to the left. In what follows we aim simply to enumerate core issues that confront progressive forces as they engage these distinct but interrelated challenges.

Priorities for national macroeconomic management include fostering growth and reducing vulnerability to external forces. Advocates of the so-called Washington Consensus assigned priority to maintaining macroeconomic stability and keeping inflation at bay. To a large degree these goals remain central to policymakers throughout the region: Brazil and Uruguay provide examples from among countries that have embarked on a leftward turn. Elsewhere, however, there appears to be some slippage, linked in part to attempts to stimulate growth and certainly in the interest of boosting consumption. The otherwise quite different cases of Venezuela and Argentina exemplify this trend. Similarly, as Paul Haslam documents in Chapter 11 of this volume, there have been varying approaches to foreign investment and to relations with multinational corporations and international financial institutions. Whether any of this has an effect on relationships with the global financial system remains to be seen, as does the related and perhaps more important issue of the sustainability of any departures from orthodoxy. The challenge will be to determine the conditions under which alternatives to mainstream macroeconomic prescriptions emerge, the degree to which different approaches shape relations with the global economy, and the capacity of different formulae to stimulate sustainable growth with steady improvements in equity.

Efforts to reduce the region's intolerably unequal distribution of income and assets highlight rival approaches to poverty alleviation but also go well beyond that to encompass underlying visions for the extension of social citizenship rights. Relevant considerations in this domain include fiscal policies (both revenue and expenditures), social welfare and insurance, and approaches to the provision of health and educational services. Here again there is growing variation in both proposals and policies, yet so far there has been limited comparative analysis of the immediate impact on welfare or the durability of the identifiable short-term trends. Debates about distribution inevitably raise questions about the implications of *asistencialismo*, the persistence of populism, and the potential for crafting socialist or social democratic alternatives in the region, all of which speak to the question of how today's lefts will differ from their competitors and from their predecessors during earlier phases of Latin American development.

Under neoliberalism, protectionist economic policies were radically cut back and Latin America now finds itself inserted into a global political economy that until recently, at a moment of high demand for the region's commodities, offered opportunities for prosperity but that today as much as ever presents competitive challenges that tax the capabilities of states and firms throughout the region. What sorts of industrial policies are conducive to stimulating competitiveness? Where is productive upgrading taking place, and how can it be diffused across the economy? To what extent can productivity-enhancing measures—whether in primary, secondary, or tertiary sectors—be consistent with the imperative of increasing both the levels and quality of employment?

Domestic governance is a problem for the left as much as for the right, however much the latter tries to make "law and order" its particular mandate. Most Latin American states have lost whatever capacity they once had to provide security for the population, and the left requires a vision and policies to ameliorate the climate of violence that undermines the quality of life in city and countryside alike. But problems of governance and security are not solely about everyday violence; they also indicate pervasive deficits in accountability. These range from failures to secure justice for human rights violations, present as well as past, to a lack of transparency in the distribution and deployment of public funds. Corruption remains an Achilles' heel of Latin American democracies just as it was of the dictatorships that preceded them. Only at their peril will left governments ignore its noxious consequences for their legitimacy and durability.

Three issues cut across the above policy domains. First, effective ideas about policy emerge from epistemic communities, which are sometimes highly technocratic, yet their successful implementation requires appropriate social coalitions. The age of technocracy is over: good ideas that do not resonate widely and good policies that lack sociopolitical underpinnings are ultimately useless. Second, the nation-state is no longer the sole territorial or political unit of relevance to social, political, and economic change. National governments define countries' macroeconomic policies and their international relations, but they are constrained by globalized markets and traversed by transnational social movements. At the same time, subnational institutions and publics increasingly manage distribution and fashion novel forms of participation and accountability. Third, left-wing governments differ from one another and from their competitors in their approaches to politics itself. They have distinct modes of symbolic politics, the discursive and other means by which they recognize distinct constituencies and open the political sphere to their concerns. And they differ also in the extent of their encouragement of participation, their transparency, and their responsiveness to demands articulated by different social forces. Any discussion of the left, then, must move from an analysis of policies to a consideration of political organization and modes of representation.

Social Democracy and Socialism, Populism and Post-Liberalism

In the past, the options for Latin America were often defined in terms of reform versus revolution, and a major point of contention was the extent to which political forces of the left were willing to submit themselves to the democratic rules of the game. But submitting to the democratic rules of the game meant, in addition, accepting the legitimacy of the interests and values of other forces, not all of which were necessarily democratic—including business, social elites, and even, as in Chile, the armed forces. As a result, the democratic transitions that began in the late 1970s and gathered momentum through the 1980s were seen as conservative: the left was required to accept that in return for transitions from authoritarian rule, it would have to moderate its demands and both accept the basic parameters of a capitalist market economy and leave certain entrenched social inequalities alone.[4]

The left turns unfolding in the region are as heterogeneous in their politics as they are in their policies, but all accept democracy, at least in principle; similarly, nowhere is the left pursuing a radical statist project that is inimical to the interests of the business community as a whole. Even in Venezuela, where the public sector has historically taken a lead role in the oil-driven economy, the private sector is deeply fearful but on the whole takes up a larger share of the economy than it did before Chávez came to office. Nevertheless, attitudes toward democracy, understandings of what democracy means, vary considerably, and so does the extent to which the lefts in government are willing to pursue a more interventionist strategy in the economy. The challenge is to characterize these differences accurately and to capture the underlying tensions that give rise to them.

In contrasting the range of approaches to politics inherent in the diverse left-wing forces in the region, there is a tendency to identify and differentiate political projects through dichotomization. Often these dichotomies are re-workings of the distinction between liberalism and socialism, reframed in the Latin American context in terms of social democracy and populism. The most noteworthy, but hardly the only, example is provided by the works of Jorge Castañeda (Castañeda 2006; Castañeda and Morales 2008).[5] Our book takes issue with Castañeda's view that the left is divisible into one or another of two categories, social democracy or populism. The "two lefts" thesis is tendentious—a way of nodding in favor of moderate social democracy while shunning radical populism (Barrett, Chavez, and Rodriguez-Garavito 2008). And the line drawn by Castañeda between the two types of lefts is slippery and may shift: while Venezuela's Chávez and Bolivia's Morales, for instance, are usually cast as populist radicals, and Chile's Bachelet or Uruguay's Vásquez as social democrats, the position of, say, a leader such as Brazil's Lula may depend on which elements of their political styles are emphasized. Moreover, some of those frequently dismissed as populist claim explicitly to be spearheading a socialist project for the twenty-first century. The validity of such assertions merits careful consideration rather than perfunctory dismissal.

We argue against the tendency to conflate socialism and populism, not because we doubt there are convergences between the two, but because this conflation is too often a maneuver to suggest the futility of radical left alternatives in order to promote what may be, in some contexts, an illusory social democracy. Dichotomizing the left into radical populists and social democrats conveniently reproduces the old cleavage between revolution and reform within the new context of democracy and globalization. That is, it says that the radical left may not be pursuing anticapitalist revolution, but neither is it acting responsibly within the context of electoral democracy and the market economy. It may not be totalitarian, but it is illiberal—or so the argument goes. Meanwhile, social democracy is held out as the alternative to be pursued by responsible reformers. Yet social democracy in the current Latin American context may turn out to be another liberalism, and one that, in Latin America, conceals an inhuman face.

Liberalism, although not always an explicit point of reference, thus lurks near the surface of this debate—and our effort to make this clear is a central contribution of this book. At first sight, liberalism is central to the debate on left turns because social democracy takes it for granted—that is, social democracy builds on liberal institutions—while populism ostensibly rejects it. Social democracy assumes the validity of liberal procedures, such as parliamentary representation, codification of citizenship rights, and the separation of powers; it also assumes that equality before the law and rights of citizenship can be leveraged for the material advancement of the working classes. Finally, social democracy rejects the claim that the inherent contradictions of capitalism must lead to polarization and crisis.

In contrast to social democracy, populism and socialism are antagonistic to liberalism, but for different reasons. Populism claims to bypass bureaucracy and constitutional mechanisms, understood as instruments of exclusion and oligarchic control, and seeks to express the will of the people directly and spontaneously. Populism is endemic in Latin America, and it has often, as in the case of Argentine Peronism, served as the shock force by which political inclusion has been achieved, albeit sometimes at the expense of secure civil rights or the rule of law. Yet populism is a Janus-faced creature, to be found as much on the right as on the left: for instance, though sometimes anti-imperialist, it is also frequently linked to virulent forms of nationalism, and its charismatic leaders have often used, some would say betrayed, popular struggles for personal gain and the strictly partisan.[6]

Socialism, like populism, rejects liberal features of institutional order, but for reasons of class, not national interest: at the level of production, socialists argue that the inherent contradictions of capitalism are insuperable; at the level of political institutions, socialists doubt the possibility of advancing the interests of subaltern classes within a liberal constitutional order whose supposed neutrality is seen as a means to safeguard economic profit and social exploitation.

Liberalism often functions as the normative ground upon which these options are assessed, all the more so at a time when traditional versions of socialism have lost intellectual traction or political persuasiveness. Yet the Latin American lefts have persisted, in spite of the crisis of socialism, by redirecting their critical slings and arrows not at capitalism but at the ideas associated with global capitalism in the Latin American context—that is to say, the policy recipes of neoliberalism. With the exception of the Zapatistas, today's Latin lefts speak more of neoliberalism than of capitalism and they question the performance of democratic governments more than the principles of democracy. Even in the World Social Forum, the tendency is toward communitarianism (for instance, participatory budgeting or a recovery of supposed indigenous values of reciprocity) rather than communism, at least as that has been traditionally conceived. Perhaps better, they seek new ways of being in "common" than those suggested by traditional communism and, as such, break with long-held conceptions of anticapitalism. In some ways they even build on some aspects of neoliberalism, not least the way in which it emphasized fluidity and connectivity over the rigid borders and fixed conduits between state and society stressed by state socialism and traditional conceptions of communism alike.

Yet the failure of neoliberalism to generate sustainable and broadly shared material improvements, combined with the precariousness of liberal institutions, especially in the context of booming commodity prices for much of the present decade, gives rise to a convergence between radical populism and current articulations of socialism. It is even harder to separate populism and socialism in a context in which all parties in the struggle accept some version of democracy. Radical populists, socialists, liberals, and social democrats all agree that popular sovereignty is foundational, and that it can and should be expressed in government, directly or indirectly, through the mediation of elections. This is the fundamental source of legitimation for contemporary left-wing governments: that the political parties and leaders of the left, whether they be socialists, social democrats, or radical populists, best represent the interests and desires of the vast masses of the people. But who are "the people"? Crucially, they are not the same as "the citizenry."

In Latin America, liberalism and related ideas of citizenship are terms often opposed to the people, the popular sectors, or *lo popular*. Liberalism has seldom been securely embedded in Latin American societies; it is an ideology often associated, at least in the tropics, with its apparent antinomies such as the dispossession of indigenous peoples or the rule of oligarchic elites. Neoliberalism reinforced the association between liberalism and exclusionary economic and social policies. Radical in its hostility to the state, neoliberalism was deeply conservative in its technocratic and elite-driven approach to policymaking. Neoliberal technocrats extolled the virtues of the market, but had little patience with the public sphere. They were content to operate within the parameters of liberal institutions provided these did not constrain the radical restructuring of state-society relations necessary to liberate markets.

Social movements, in opposition to this trend, not only rejected neoliberalism, but also exhibited ambivalence and impatience toward liberalism. Liberalism's weakness in Latin America reflects the inability of successive models of capitalist development, most recently neoliberalism, to create shared and sustained prosperity, and the limits of the advancement of the interests of the popular sectors within precarious and often exclusionary legal and institutional orders. Hence the increasing salience of what Benjamin Arditi has designated "post-liberalism": not the rejection of capitalism or liberal citizenship per se, nor complacency with the human misery that results from neoliberal policies imposed in conductions of precarious citizenship, but an affirmation of "something outside liberalism, namely, an excess of politics vis-à-vis the liberal scheme" that "loosens the connotative link between electoral and democratic politics" (Arditi 2008:73).

The notion of post-liberalism helps us understand the wave of constitutional reform that has accompanied the rise of left-wing governments. Claudio Lomnitz calls this "foundationalism," a desire to refound the republic and revive nationalist and popular projects that have been thwarted in the past, but also to reconsider the nature of political representation itself (Lomnitz 2006). Some of this vogue for constitutional reform arises from the perception that neoliberalism (especially in the form of trade agreements, as well as rules on intellectual property rights, investment, and services) has had a constitutionalizing effect. In Mexico, the Zapatista uprising followed changes to the constitution that were undertaken as part of neoliberal reforms to complement the North American Free Trade Agreement (NAFTA). In this sense (and others), it is important to note how the left turns build on as well as react against developments that took place under neoliberalism.

In short, to answer (1) whether it is meaningful to speak of social democracy in Latin America; or (2) whether populism—as opposed, say, to socialism—is the unavoidable form that protest against the status quo takes; and (3) whether shifts to the left are due to failures of neoliberalism, we must ask why the lefts often articulate a political outlook that exceeds or bypasses liberal institutions. Left-wing parties' political challenge is to rebuild states so that they provide more robust mechanisms for transforming urgent demands for change into alternative policies, in the process creating more open, participatory, and just societies. At the same time, post-liberalism suggests that this transformation will forever remain both incomplete and excessive and that social movements will always press against the new borders and refined hierarchies that inevitably result from such institutionalization. Can parties and movements, nonetheless, negotiate the institutional void created by the insufficiencies of liberalism in the Latin American context?

Surely this addresses only one aspect of the question of social democracy, for Latin American countries typically lack the socio-institutional underpinnings of social democracy as traditionally understood. In their ideal-typical European form, social democracies resulted from cohesive labor movements allied with programmatic political parties that entered into a social compact with capital through which property rights are maintained while redistributive policies are pursued through state intervention in markets. Skepticism about the relevance of social democracy for the region is in part a reflection of doubt concerning the organizational basis for such a project, on the one hand, and the willingness of Latin American capital to enter such pacts, on the other.

Political Parties and Insurgent Movements

Rather than dichotomize the left, we would do better to ask: why is liberalism insufficient in Latin America? What is it that makes social democracy so elusive, keeps populism so pervasive, and ensures that socialism is always somewhere on the horizon? The apparent "illiberalism" of some left-wing leaders and governments, such as Chávez in Venezuela, Correa in Ecuador, and Morales in Bolivia, reflects the collapse of political parties and representative institutions, as well as deeper social cleavages and inequalities. These deeper cleavages and inequalities could not be contained by conservative transitions that placed certain basic questions outside the agenda for public contestation. Moreover, a series of resurgent social movements, some increasingly organized and others less so, have in recent years put the question of political organization and constitutionalism back on the agenda. Political parties have been forced to respond to these movements and their disparate demands and, in doing so, to reconceptualize the role of parties and representational institutions.

Perhaps nowhere are the insufficiencies of liberal discourse more apparent than in the arena of indigenous politics, a topic that is almost completely neglected by those who would transplant social democracy into a Latin American context. The demands of indigenous peoples may appear to be revolutionary, yet at another level they are both deeply conservative (in the sense of conserving tradition) and in some ways surprisingly liberal. The idea of inclusion—that the indigenous peoples should have the right to participate in democratic self-government and to share in the economic opportunity to exploit natural resources—is only radical from the perspective of a status quo in which basic liberal rights and freedoms are denied within the context of market economies incapable of satisfying basic human needs. The specific demands, however, may be limited to redistribution of power and life chances rather than to a fundamental revolutionizing of all social relationships. Or they may demand revolutionizing social relationships through the fulfillment of long-denied liberal promises, such as full rights of citizenship. These seemingly radical projects have, moreover, arisen from institutional decay, and they lead to governments that operate not in the context of enduring institutional bargains, wherein programs may be easier to implement and sustain as well as constrain, but in contexts of policymaking that offer wide room for change but little hope of institutionalization. At the same time, indigenous movements can also tend toward an affirmation of subalternity that imperils the status of the nation itself and challenges the liberal ideals of hegemonic universality. In some ways it is this tension, between liberal inclusion pursued through illiberal means and/or subaltern autonomy justified via liberal arguments, that characterizes Bolivia's ongoing constitutional crisis.

So the insufficiencies of liberalism are also inherent in the paradoxical processes of constitutional reform that have swept the nations where representative institutions are most tenuous. The new politics of constitutional reform appeals to a power that exists prior to existing laws and institutions: a constituent rather than constituted power. We acknowledge that there lurk here a series of dangers; there are very different modalities of what Arditi terms postliberalism, and it would be wrong simply to affirm them en masse. But we also know that liberalism has often served authoritarian and disciplinary ends in Latin America, whether through the imposition of notions of private property on collective lands and communities or through the insistence on forms of indirect representation and electoral competition that often marginalize other forms of popular participation. At the same time, the left is in some ways less illiberal than it once was. Many of Latin America's lefts no longer champion armed revolution—or even the conquest of state institutions. They remain, however, the "torchbearer of the Cinderella values of the French Revolution" by means of a radicalization of democracy, whether or not that passes through the state (Arditi 2008:62).

It is in this sense that the commitment to constitutionalism is a novel feature of some left turns, most notably in the Andes, but it is a commitment that may be hard to sustain or to make stick in countries where constitutions are often seen as scraps of paper. Constituent power opens politics and expands the horizon of the possible, but will it address poverty, inequality, economic underperformance, or social exclusion? Will it take on the task of reforming state institutions, or should it be seen as a movement against or (perhaps better still) despite the state? To what extent will constituent power be expressed within constitutional channels and accept elements of checks and balances between branches of government as it seeks to overcome the resistance of established interests, be these within the state itself or in the broader society? The pitched battles under way from the end of the first decade of the twenty-first century in Venezuela and Bolivia highlight the importance of these questions. They also show that there are different modes of excess, different forms of post-liberalism (Beasley-Murray 2008).

There is also a tension between social movements and political parties. Social movements have an ambivalent relationship with the left governments and parties they accompany in the struggle for power. For, on the one hand, these movements underpin and enable the lefts' electoral successes; without their support, the lefts would still linger in the political wilderness. Yet on the other hand, movement radicalism undercuts the authority of the governments that it has implanted. Parties also represent a threat to social movements. When left-wing parties come to power, social movements are often coopted or incorporated into public office and policy programs in ways that may deflate their capacity for mobilization. Put simply, if movements incarnate constituent power that parties subsequently channel and represent as constituted power, what is at stake is the extent to which this representation is a negation of the energies that drive the left turns and the extent to which state institutions can fulfill their promises and desires.

For this reason, a major focus of comparison in this volume is the contrast between Venezuela under Chávez on the one hand and Evo Morales and the Movimiento al Socialismo (MAS) in Bolivia on the other. These are the two cases that we believe deserve the most attention. There are several reasons. First, they are the two cases that have inspired the most heated debate and controversy, not only among progressive forces but among observers everywhere. Second, they provide the best examples for thinking about the issues of constituent power, the multitude, liberalism, and democracy that form the heart of this volume. Third, they are often lumped together by observers as examples of the populist left—for reasons as obvious as they are shallow. For those who see the left in old Cold War terms, the two represent a sort of axis of anti-imperialism. Such a perspective is blind to issues of pluriculturalism, which are central to understanding Bolivia, inattentive to the different ways the left has come to power and governed in both cases, and neglects the crucial relationship between parties and movements that we see as defining the range of options for the Latin American lefts. Finally, understanding the differences between the experiences of Bolivia and Venezuela helps to place other Latin American left-wing parties, movements, and leaders in a different perspective. Although a fully blown comparative analysis of all the experiences of the left in Latin America is beyond the scope of this book, our contribution has been to help sort out the similarities and differences between two of the most critical cases.

A Roadmap for What Is to Come

This book begins with three chapters that encourage readers to think in new ways about the contemporary Latin American lefts. Juan Pablo Luna uses the idea of constituent power to challenge the two lefts thesis that has carried such influence in the conventional literature. He suggests that the success of leftist parties in contemporary Latin America is built upon a broad electoral movement that opposes neoliberal reforms and represents the losers in the economic model implemented during the 1990s. There are both similarities among disparate left-wing parties and governments as well as important differences within both the putative populist and social democratic camps. Luna proposes a typology based on the programmatic content of left-wing leaders and parties and the constraints they face, both exogenous and endogenous. This enables him to contrast pairs of cases that typically are placed in the same camp—Chile and Uruguay, Venezuela and Bolivia—by advocates of those who perceive the contemporary landscape in terms of two lefts, divided typically into "good" and "bad."

Another recurring theme is post-*neo*liberalism. Chapter 3, by John French, criticizes the juxtaposition of the social democratic against the populist lefts as a disciplinary move by neoliberals (Beverley 2009). French shows that by postulating a politics of expertise and enlightenment, neoliberals exalted reason, rationality, and objectivity (the "cold" and disinterested) over a lesser sphere of emotion, passion, and "personalism" (the "hot" and blindly partisan, if not corrupt). French shows that regardless of how Venezuela's Chavez and Brazil's Lula have practiced politics in different ways, both are post-neoliberal (rather than post-liberal).

The contribution by Maxwell Cameron and Kenneth Sharpe begins with the observation that Latin American left turns have occurred within the framework of electoral democracy, and that the concerns about the illiberalism of the left (or indeed of some Latin American democracies generally) are belied by a remarkable commitment to constitutionalism on the part of precisely those leaders who have emerged in countries where liberal and republican institutions have historically been most weak: the Andes. Yet the commitment to constitutionalism can limit the possibilities for fundamental reform. Cameron and Sharpe see the allure of constituent power as a formula for attempting foundational change without revolutionary violence, but also stress the dilemma that such change must, they argue, of necessity be negotiated with other political forces that retain electoral resources and legitimacy—and thus are also entitled to their share of constituent power.

We then turn to two critical case studies, of Venezuela and Bolivia, respectively. Chapter 5, by Jennifer McCoy, sees dangers inherent in a regime based on constant mobilization. She addresses the contradictions within Chávez's Bolivarian Revolution as it moves beyond liberal democracy to a participatory, or "protagonistic," democracy based on the idea of constituent power. McCoy notes that Chávez has relied on a politics of mobilization: Like Morales, and not unlike classical populism, Chávez constantly evokes an "us" versus "them." But unlike the populists of old, not only does Chávez use the "constituent power" of the multitudes to alter the rules of "constituted power" under the old regime, he also seeks to change the underlying locus of power. McCoy acknowledges that the Venezuelan project represents the same demand for change and social inclusion, without ideological definition, in reaction to the unmet expectations from the promises of market opening and democratic restoration since the 1980s, and she seeks to assess whether the Bolivarian Revolution can indeed create a more participatory and equitable society.

Santiago Anria's account in Chapter 6 of Bolivia under the administration of Evo Morales highlights the simultaneous workings of top-down and bottom-up logics of governance and frames these in terms of different forms of accountability. Whereas the rural roots of MAS gave rise to grassroots control over the leadership, its extension into urban areas fostered the reemergence of patterns of rule reminiscent of earlier experiences of populism. At the same time, his analysis reveals the degree to which, even while MAS has managed to remain true to many of its campaign promises, opposition forces have been able to constrain the Morales government in ways that are not evident in Venezuela. In part this reflects the persistence of liberalism alongside pressures for the creation of new mechanisms of participation and representation.

The next two chapters focus on alternatives to liberalism, the tension between constituent and constituted power, and the role of the multitude in politics in the context of Bolivia and Venezuela. Jon Beasley-Murray begins Chapter 7 with Arditi's observation that the ballot box should be neither the point of departure nor the exclusive focus of any discussion of left turns—a phrase he sees as problematic. Left turns are symptoms of broader movements that cannot simply be reduced to electoral dynamics or processes of representation and deliberation within the framework of liberalism. Beasley-Murray emphasizes how events like the Caracazo—the eruption of protest and looting that occurred in the capital of Venezuela in 1989—mark the rupture of hegemonic social pacts and present an opportunity for the expression of constituent power. He criticizes Chávez's government, which he argues is exemplary of the so-called left turns as a whole, for the way it continues to assert the transcendence of constituted over constituent power. Yet he recognizes a double tension: on the one hand, constituted power is always dependent on the constituent power that it claims to supersede, but, on the other hand, and for all its creative drive to novelty, constituent power needs also to give rise to new habits and routines, new practices and institutions, with all the dangers that such routinization presents.

Benjamin Arditi suggests in Chapter 8 that there is a close connection between post-liberalism and the politics of the left. Arditi describes post-liberalism as "something outside liberalism or at least something that takes place at the edges of liberalism." As a democratic politics that transcends liberal mechanisms of representation in the electoral arena, it encompasses a series of radical and populist forces demanding both participation and redistribution. A central tension that emerges from the idea of post-liberalism is the need to reconcile demand for change, justified by appealing to the original, constituent power of the people to make their own institutions of self-government, and the victory of the electoral left within existing constitutional, legal, and democratic institutions. The very idea of "the people" implies subjects with wills, yet the people often irrupt into politics not as a coherent or stable subject but as an inchoate multitude. While this line or argument is developed most notably by Jon Beasley-Murray, post-liberalism, constituent power, and the multitude are recurring themes in this volume.

The final set of chapters examines policy challenges facing the contemporary lefts, taking as a point of departure the erosion in the capacity of historically weak states to provide for the public good under neoliberalism. Luis Reygadas and Fernando Filgueira address this deficit in the context of inequality and social incorporation. They analyze its evolution over time as well as different models of social policy and welfare state development. They go beyond the conventional treatment of income inequalities by considering inequalities along lines of gender, race and ethnicity, rural and urban settings, and information. With regard to the latter, they devote special attention to the character and significance of the digital divide, an issue that most governments on the left have failed to address.

Juan Carlos Moreno-Brid and Igor Paunovic review the macroeconomic development strategies of left-wing governments in Latin America. Although they acknowledge that the left has not put into practice a coherent alternative to the Washington Consensus, they find that the left does govern with different policy priorities in three major areas: (1) macroeconomic policies (fiscal stance, exchange rate, and monetary policy); (2) sectoral policies (distinctive elements of industrial and competitiveness policies); and (3) social policies. These are features of the current regional landscape that Hershberg addresses in the concluding chapter, which focuses on the intersections between domestic conditions and trends in the broader global order.

One area where the left has made a big difference is foreign direct investment (FDI). Paul Haslam gives particular attention to the modes of bargaining that characterize relations between states and private corporations. Focusing on Argentina, Bolivia, Chile, and Venezuela, Haslam finds that significant shifts have taken place, and that FDI is now confronted by new regulations and pressures that depart from the Washington Consensus ideal. Rather than entirely novel arrangements, however, the past decade has witnessed a revival of patterns of bargaining characteristic of relationships between foreign investors and the state that were typical of the import substitution period.

The final chapter, by Eric Hershberg, moves beyond the conventional focus on internal dynamics to consider how crucial features of the external context may shape the prospects for different currents of the Latin American left. Encompassing the characteristics of the region's ties to the global economy, the evolution of diplomatic relations within Latin America and the waning influence of the United States, as well as the region's exposure to ideational shifts with regard to forms of democratic politics and the appropriate components of development policies, the chapter identifies much that is distinctive about the current conjuncture alongside enduring features of the landscape. Hershberg concludes that the international context matters, and crucially, but that the ways it will impact developments will be mediated by domestic institutions and sociopolitical coalitions. A central task for the Latin American lefts will be to forge institutions and coalitions that enhance capabilities for pursuing policies that redistribute power and resources in ways that are consistent with the expansion of citizenship.

Although we do not purport to cover the full range of issues necessary for a reconsideration of the significance and likely fortunes of the contemporary lefts in Latin America, we hope that this collection of essays will help to identify avenues for further analysis, highlighting the diverse forces and trends that make up the shifts to the left in the region and offering critical elements for a prognosis for their potential to fulfill the promise of transformation in a region of the world that cries out for meaningful change.

Notes

An earlier version of this essay introduced a collection of articles published in *Third World Quarterly* 30, no. 2 (March 2009). That collection, like this volume, resulted from a project undertaken at the University of British Columbia and Simon Fraser University designed to illuminate the origins, nature, and implications of Latin America's left turns. We are grateful to the Social Science and Humanities Research Council of Canada and the Peter Wall Institute at the University of British Columbia for funding that initiative.

1. Whether to include Nicaragua as part of the pink tide is controversial, since Ortega led an "orthodox" faction of the FSLN against reformists and reached office thanks only to an alliance with some of the country's most reactionary politicians. His policy positions on such matters as abortion further call into question his left credentials. Yet, opposition to abortion rights is substantial in pink tide cases—witness Tabaré Vásquez's veto of a liberalization law in 2008—and Nicaragua's international alliances are strongly within the left camp.

2. The Honduran case suggests a number of twists to our account that, for reasons of timing, this book is unable to consider. His deposition may come to be seen as some kind of watershed, and it is undoubtedly the sternest challenge faced by the Latin American left in recent years. It is worth noting, however, both that Zelaya did not originally present himself to the Honduran electorate as a candidate of the left and, also, that social mobilization in his support followed rather than preceded what we might characterize as his own personal "left turn."

3. Indeed, evidence presented by Luna and Filgueira (2009) highlights the degree to which the performance of incumbents determines their prospects for remaining in office. Having said that, we would not agree with Hagopian and Mainwaring (2005) and others who speculate that the survival of democracy will hinge on regimes' capacity to deal successfully with exclusion and security. The *quality* of democracy will reflect its success in confronting these challenges; its *survival* may be less in doubt.

4. The classic formulations of this dilemma can be found in the four volumes published as part of the Transitions from Authoritarian Rule project, organized by Guillermo O'Donnell, Philippe Schmitter, and Laurence Whitehead, and published by Johns Hopkins University Press in 1986.

5. Analogous arguments are put forth by Reid (2007) and Weyland (2006), among others. Additional recent works on the Latin American left include Arnson (2009);

Sader and Consejo Latinoamericano de Ciencias Sociales (2008); Los colores de la izquierda (2008); Barrett, Chavez, and Rodriguez-Garavito (2008); and Macdonald and Ruckert (2009).

6. That populism of the right remains a salient category in Latin America is evident in contemporary Colombia, where Álvaro Uribe has personalized politics, presenting himself as a charismatic leader responsible for taming guerrilla forces and providing "democratic security."

Part 1

Thinking About the Left

2

The Left Turns: Why They Happened and How They Compare

Juan Pablo Luna

Compared to five or ten years ago, the political map of Latin America today contains significantly more political movements and governments that call themselves leftist or are classified as such by external observers.[1] What explains these left turns? Has the region shifted left? If so, how do we analyze convergence and divergence within the left turns?

Current scholarship on the rise of the left provides relatively homologous answers to the first question, but seems inadequately equipped to address the remaining and perhaps more pressing ones. Theoretical perspectives focus almost exclusively on analyzing leadership style, political discourse and rhetoric, and short-term institutional developments. Empirically, there is a lack of fieldwork on how these political parties and leaders built their electoral coalitions over time, how these coalitions are structured today, and what means were employed and challenges faced (especially distributive dilemmas) by contemporary leftist governments in seeking to promote socioeconomic change in Latin America while institutionalizing their power.

Moreover, some aspects of our conventional view of ruling leftist governments could hinder our exploration of these additional questions. A case in point is the established dichotomy of the "good" (social-democratic) and "bad" (populist) left, which needs to be challenged. These classifications are excessively driven by reactions to distinctive leadership styles and rhetoric and are usually based on short-term analyses of the conditions that enabled the emergence of those leaderships. In a nutshell, as in biology, anatomy should precede taxonomy.

In this chapter I first sketch the emerging scholarly consensus on the rise of the left. I then propose an alternative approach to analyzing current leftist governments, illustrating its potential usefulness with a cursory analysis of two "social-democratic" governments (Chile and Uruguay) and a much briefer examination of two other cases (Bolivia and Venezuela).

The Left Turns: Why and How?

Four statements synthesize the conventional wisdom on the rise of the left in Latin America:

1. Parties and individual leaders self-proclaimed as left, center-left, or progressive made significant electoral inroads in the recent wave of elections. This means that today approximately 60 percent of Latin Americans are currently being governed by the left (Arnson 2007).

2. Citizens' disenchantment with the state of affairs in their countries could be said to be the lowest common denominator explaining the rise of the left. This disenchantment is twofold: On the one hand it stems from the failure of market reforms implemented during the 1990s to fulfill their promise of delivering solid economic growth and social progress, instead creating new vulnerabilities, with the aggravating factor of a recession that was sparked by the 1998 Asian financial crisis. On the other hand was the political discontent with traditional parties or more generally with the political system representing the status quo; this usually emerged in the midst of governance crises and/or corruption scandals linked to political arrangements that consolidated in the aftermath of each country's transition to democracy. This discontent was rooted in weak and poor-quality democratic institutions and by major failures of political representation (Mainwaring, Bejarano, and Pizarro 2006).

In sum, the leftist governments currently in office in Latin America seem to have won recent elections on the basis of a minimum common denominator composed of three elements: (1) opposing incumbents (in almost every case traditional parties or traditional politicians) by mobilizing economic and political discontent during the 1998–2002 regional economic crisis; (2) being able to bring together a broad, socially heterogeneous electoral constituency in the context of fragmented civil societies, usually drawing on highly segmented mobilization and electoral strategies to attract different types of (disenchanted) voters; and (3) having a charismatic leader who was able to bring together the broad constituency needed to unseat incumbents. This formula seems not only to apply to so-called populist cases but also to situations in which an institutionalized leftist party reached power, aided at least in part by strong leaders who were able to broaden the electoral appeal of their parties (e.g., Lula, Vázquez, and Bachelet).

3. Leftist governments freshly arrived into office were until recently enjoying extended periods in power during the economic bonanza created by the commodity boom. This boom has helped to sustain and strengthen the shift to the left in contemporary Latin America and provided some room for policy shifts regarding the region's development model.

4. Apart from the three commonalities listed above, significant divergences exist among governments that have recently been elected in the region. Available analyses have largely attributed these divergences to political-institutional fac-

tors, such as the nature of the party system in which the party/movement competed before taking office (Castañeda 2006; Lanzaro 2007).

Although the normative overtones of J. G. Castañeda's classification are obvious (Weyland 2007), both K. Weyland and J. Lanzaro essentially coincide with Castañeda's clustering of leftist governments into two different groups: a populist left (i.e., those led by Hugo Chávez in Venezuela, Néstor Kirchner in Argentina, Evo Morales in Bolivia, Rafael Correa in Ecuador, and Daniel Ortega in Nicaragua) and a reconstructed radical left that originated in the revolutionary movements and leftist fronts of the 1960s and 1970s (i.e., those headed by Lula da Silva in Brazil, Ricardo Lagos and Michelle Bachelet in Chile, and Tabaré Vásquez in Uruguay).[2] According to this view, while the reconstructed or social-democratic left prioritizes social policies while embracing liberal democracy and a market economy, the populist version is characterized by weak ideological underpinnings and a basic desire to maintain its popularity at any cost, even when this results in economic mismanagement, the erosion of democratic values, or harsh anti-US rhetoric.

Among others adhering to the "two lefts" thesis, Castañeda (2006) and Lanzaro (2007) coincide in explaining these divergent configurations in terms of political institutions. In this regard, Weyland's focus on the preeminence of state rents (oil, natural gas) in populist cases is an exception that is especially important for explaining how different leaders attempted to institutionalize their electoral coalition once in office.[3] In general, though, the authors offer a similar causal account: while social-democratic or reconstructed lefts originated in the context of an institutionalized party system and underwent a long process of partisan adaptation (renovation, moderation) to compete efficiently in that system, populist variants are prototypical of inchoate party systems in which charismatic leaderships emerge rapidly to fill a power vacuum left by the collapse of an outgoing party system.

While it is true that this type of explanation provides important insights into the nature of these political parties and movements, it also suffers from some blind spots that reduce analytical leverage. Specifically, available narratives fail to identify and explain the important political and policy divergences that occur within each type, not distinguishing between cases pertaining to different leftist types and to crucial intragroup divergences. The next section discusses these limitations and proposes an alternative analytical approach.

Unpacking Leftist Types: "Anatomy" and Its Implications for Government Action

I argued above that the nature of the recently arrived heterogeneous leftist governments in Latin America, and what they do once in office, is contingent upon each country's long-term development. Although that long-term trajectory plays out in the type of leadership, party, and social base of the left that is present in each case, it also introduces other types of constraints that are relatively independent from the type of leadership and party (where those exist) that it creates. To drive this point home, a brief discussion of the typology recently put forth by S. Levitsky and K. M. Roberts (forthcoming) seems worthy.

Levitsky and Roberts's (forthcoming) proposal adds a second dimension to the institutionalization-based classification of leftist types, which they capture by classifying leftist parties as "established parties vs. new political movements." The second point they consider is the "degree to which political authority is concentrated in the hands of a dominant personality," which translates into either top-down (usually "autocratic") exercises of power or into processes that allow leadership accountability to the "broader interests of parties and or movements," making possible instances of political mobilization from below. This dimension contributes significantly to our understanding of the left in Latin America by taking into account the predominant type of linkages that exist between the party or leader and its constituents. This enables, for instance, the unpacking of the "populist, wrong left" group into three analytically different types: a populist machine (established party organization and concentrated power) such as is present in Kirchner's Peronism, the Alianza Popular Revolucionaria Americana (APRA), and the Frente Sandinista de Liberación Nacional (FSLN); "a populist left" (new political movement, concentrated power) present in the cases of Chávez, Gutiérrez, and Correa; and a "movement left" (new political movement, disperse power) represented by the Bolivian Movimiento al Socialismo (MAS). The remaining group corresponds to the "institutionalized, good left" type, collapsing the Partido dos Trabalhadores (PT) in Brazil, the Socialist Party in Chile, and Frente Amplio (FA) in Uruguay as "electoral-professional left."

By enriching our understanding of these parties' organizational patterns, this typology does a lot in terms of illuminating the nature of electoral mobilization occurring in each case and some very relevant characteristics of the current leftist governments in Latin America. The typology I propose is more focused on trying to understand how these different lefts govern and, eventually, how that knowledge will help predict which types of policymaking will occur under each leadership type. In particular, I am interested in policymaking that relates to eventual shifts in each country's development model. For that reason, structural constraints and opportunities for seeking and institutionalizing those shifts should be brought into the analysis. While some of those constraints and opportunities derive from the type of party in power and the relative autonomy it has from civil society, others relate to path-dependent configurations that are left out of the picture if we focus too stringently on party leaderships.

This different emphasis is also consequential for case selection. Levitsky and Roberts (forthcoming), while dealing with the Chilean case, analyze the

Socialist Party. Instead, given my interest in the analysis of leftist governments, in Chile's case I will refer to the government of the Concertación, which also includes nonleftist parties such as the Christian Democrats, the Radicals, and at least some leaders of the Partido por la Democracia, and not solely the Socialist Party. In short, the actions of governments in which leftist parties take part are obviously related to those parties' organizational patterns and mobilization strategies. However, different partisan constraints and a series of nonpartisan ones should be more centrally considered to understand what those governments actually do while in office.

Second, in terms of partisan constraints, my typology lends more attention to distributive and programmatic conflicts occurring within the partisan organization and social base of the left in government. Although I concur with Levitsky and Roberts's general classification of organizational/ mobilizational strategies, I suggest these might not be predominant strategies (perhaps with the exception of the populist left type). Socioeconomic and interest group fragmentation in contemporary Latin America makes it difficult for political parties to craft a winning electoral coalition on the basis of only one type of linkage to their electorates. Usually, as argued above, leftist parties have won elections by putting together a diverse electorate, sharing relatively high levels of discontent with the status quo as a minimum common denominator. Beyond this minimum common denominator, leftist party social bases are heterogeneous and bring together distinct electoral bases with different and, in some cases, opposing stakes regarding eventual policy shifts. In those cases, distributive conflicts are stark and governing leftist parties face the challenge to reconcile divergent and frequently competing interests, while simultaneously seeking to implement reforms and maintain their electoral appeal.

The diversity of leftist party social bases and the potential distributive conflicts that might run within each party's electorate should then be consequential for analyzing government action and cannot be completely grasped by only looking at the institutionalization and concentration of power present in different cases. In short, the distributive struggles created by the necessary combination of different linkage types with alternative constituencies might introduce, for government action, constraints that are more consequential than those yielded by the predominant (or more visible) linkage type. This type of constraint might be called "endogenous," as it still deals with the nature of the electoral mobilization vehicle and its relationship to civil society.

Third, though they partially translate into the trajectory of each party (institutionalized vs. new) and into the endogenous constraints I just described, nonpartisan factors also introduce significant "exogenous" constraints into government action. In short, two leftist governments sharing similar programmatic agendas might govern differently and might seek different policy outcomes not only due to endogenous (partisan) constraints, but also due to the influence of structural (exogenous) ones. For instance, in each case state institutions and sociostructural configurations flowing from each country's long-term trajectory and from a country's specific ways of integrating into the global economy introduce a different set of constraints. At least in the cases I analyze below, exogenous and endogenous constraints seem to be largely collinear, which justifies collapsing both types of constraints into a single dimension distinguishing between high or low constraints on government action. However, for the sake of clarity, I claim it makes sense to keep endogenous and exogenous limits to government action as analytically distinct constraints.

In this section I show how taking these nonpartisan and noninstitutional (exogenous) constraints into consideration produces a different classification of country cases than those already available. In particular, it yields the unpacking of the social-democratic type that has so far been treated as a single current by those who have discussed Castañeda's influential two-group classification and proposed more than two types (Levitsky and Roberts, forthcoming; Lanzaro 2007; Roberts 2007b; Schamis 2006). All these alternative classification attempts cluster social-democratic governments (Brazil, Chile, and Uruguay) together, while introducing distinctions within the populist left. The unpacking of the social-democratic type also justifies the greater attention I pay to what follows in the cases that have been, for the moment, treated as a single group. In this chapter, I focus only on Chile and Uruguay among cases typically included in the social democratic camp. To clarify the argument, I also provide a cursory discussion of Venezuela and Bolivia.

Table 2.1 classifies the currently governing lefts in Chile, Uruguay, Venezuela, and Bolivia into two dimensions: the programmatic orientation of the leftist project carried by the governing party or leader and the level of (endogenous and exogenous) constraints that each government faces regarding government action. Regarding the first dimension structuring the typology—the orientation of the governing party or leader's project—I argue that current left turns in Latin America represent a contemporary manifestation of the region's perennial struggle to pursue political and socioeconomic inclusion simultaneously.[4]

Table 2.1   A Leftist Government Typology: Nature of Change Sought
and Levels of Endogenous (partisan) and Exogenous
(nonpartisan) Constraints on Government

Nature of Change Sought by Leftist Project	Levels of Endogenous and Exogenous Constraints	
	Low	High
Ameliorationist/Institutional	Chile	Uruguay
Radical/Constituent	Venezuela	Bolivia

Within contemporary left turns it is possible to identify two different programmatic currents attempting to iron out conflicting goals. The first seeks gradual sociostructural change (i.e., greater equality) within the contours of liberal democracy and a market economy. Given these features, it could be labeled a social-democratic project that seeks reforms to ameliorate social conditions and reduce the friction between liberal democracy and a market economy.[5] This does not mean, however, that the project is driven by and implemented through the type of sociopolitical coalitions of the kind observed in social-democratic Europe. In Table 2.1, this programmatic current is labeled "ameliorationist/institutional" and will be referred to as such in the remainder of this chapter.

The second current represents a more radical programmatic inclination, one that has been labeled—mistakenly in my view—as a "populist" or "neopopulist" project. These labels are both too normatively biased and analytically obscuring, in part because those approaches usually conflate political phenomena (an unmediated, top-down relationship between a leader and an amorphous *pueblo*) and policy output (irresponsible policymaking) (see Weyland 1996).

Programmatically, this second current is characterized by its willingness to seek alternatives for political and economic inclusion that might go beyond liberal democracy and a market economy. In this sense it entails a predisposition toward what Arditi (2008) calls a "post-liberal" attempt at promoting a new sociopolitical arrangement. This implies the search for a foundational project. Therefore, following Beasley-Murray, Cameron, and Hershberg's introductory chapter to this volume, I label this current "radical/constituent."

In analyzing cases within this second current, we should not underestimate the possibility that foundational attempts could significantly depart from the ideals of liberal democracy and a market economy. In a nutshell, foundational movements might either crystallize into illiberal or radical democratic regimes, which both represent attempts to solve the political incorporation crisis. In turn, initiatives for socioeconomic incorporation could range from a full-blown socialist attempt to the massive clientelistic redistribution of state rents in the short run. Interestingly, in either of these two possibilities, these regimes might achieve greater social incorporation and, therefore, enjoy broader popular support than their predecessors. In short, massive social inclusion—at least in the short run—could and does frequently occur in the context of political regimes that might not fulfill our academic checklist of a liberal democracy. In a way, these regimes exemplify the sometimes overlooked contradictions that the pursuit of radical social democratization might entail when attempted through liberal-democratic means and in the context of highly unequal social structures.

Dismissal of these endeavors as merely "populist" means we lose much of their apparent analytical significance. Instead, we need to understand and analyze these political movements as attempts, quite possibly doomed attempts, to craft a new compromise between a political regime and a socioeconomic development model. Drawing insights from the historic interaction between capitalism and democracy in currently advanced capitalist democracies (see, e.g., Moore 1966; Skocpol 1979; Rueschemeyer, Stephens, and Stephens 1992), it is possible to expect these processes to entail sociopolitical and/or economic violence.

What basically characterizes this second current is its rejection of a compromise between a market economy and a liberal democracy and its apparent search for something new. This search is particularly intense in places where failures in political representation and social exclusion in the 1990s created a political vacuum that leftist leaders are now attempting to fill through constituent reforms. Beyond their minimum common denominator, which I propose to use as a demarcating criteria and that combines the rejection of both past policies and traditional political arrangements, it would be wrong to view such attempts as a unified and programmatically cohesive current.

In summary, the first dimension (nature of change sought by the leftist leader/party) I propose using to analyze current leftist governments distinguishes between ameliorationist/institutional and radical/constituent programs. Beyond conceptual specifications, this dimension produces a classification that is largely collinear with those already available (good vs. bad left, social-democratic vs. populist left), which place Chile, Uruguay, and Brazil in one group and Venezuela, Bolivia, and Ecuador in the other.[6] From an explanatory perspective, these classifications might also resonate well with conventional wisdom, which sees the social-democratic left as having emerged from long-standing leftist parties that pursued a gradual process of ideological moderation, and the foundational left as the offspring of deeper crises of political representation and the collapse of traditional party systems.

* * *

Different insights into conventional wisdom can be gained from introducing a second dimension, that is, the presence of low or high levels of constraint on leftist governments' ability to carry out their programmatic agendas. In the low-constraints category I place governments that enjoy greater autonomy from organized civil society, that control partisan organizations from above (in this respect this is collinear to Levitsky and Roberts's category), and that have at their disposal a more autonomous state apparatus. In contrast, highly constrained cases have stronger autonomously organized civil society and institutionalized linkages to the governing party or social movement; partisan organizations have greater resources to constrain leadership; the leftist social base is strained by distributive conflicts tied to the country's economic development model; and the governing elite lacks complete access to an autonomous state bureaucracy, either because the state apparatus is too weak or because it is powerful but largely autonomous from the executive power. Therefore, in low-constrained systems public policy is largely implemented through top-bottom processes, while in highly constrained systems public policy results from a much more complex interaction between top-bottom and bottom-up processes.

In arguing the use of this second dimension of analysis, I would like to draw a short comparative sketch of the populist lefts of Venezuela and Bolivia that closely parallels the analysis of Roberts (2007b) and that of Levitsky and Roberts (forthcoming). In Venezuela, Chávez came into power through a power vacuum created by the collapse of the *partidocracia*. His rapid rise meant that he lacked more organic ties with organized social interests, which gave him a high degree of autonomy once he took office. On this basis, and drawing on massive cash inflows, Venezuela's president was able to institutionalize his support from above by creating a "dependent civil society" (Roberts 2006; Hawkins and Hansen 2006).

In contrast, MAS in Bolivia originated from a very well-organized social movement that was very active in the demise of the country's traditional party system during the 1990s and early 2000s. Moreover, the country's ethnic and regional cleavages converged with opposition to the implementation of neoliberal policies (Van Cott 2005; Yashar 2005). Evo Morales, therefore, came into the president's office with a much clearer mandate from organized civil society, which translates into significantly less autonomy than Chávez in government action. As a result, Morales's government faces the challenge of keeping a hold on its moderate middle-class vote while simultaneously fulfilling the more radical demands of its original social base in MAS and organized civil society. Exogenous constraints (like those imposed by the organizational capacity and power resources of the opposition and by central state weakness) seem also higher in this case.

I now turn to a more thorough narrative of the cases of Chile and Uruguay. This comparison might yield additional support for a typology that, by considering constraints in a broader sense, looking beyond partisan factors, is able to unpack the social-democratic type.

In Chile, the combination of radical economic reforms under Pinochet, the renewal of the Chilean left in exile following the forced ending of Allende's government, and the exclusion of the Communist Party from the Concertación effectively unraveled the organic ties between the Socialist Party and organized popular sectors (Garretón 1989; Oxhorn 1995; Roberts 1998). Today, the relationship between organized labor and the Concertación is marginal, creating low levels of endogenous constraints.

Meanwhile, since the transition to democracy, ideological linkages between parties and the citizenry have generally been determined by the authoritarian/democratic cleavage or by pro- versus anti-Pinochet identification (Tironi and Agüero 1999; Torcal and Mainwaring 2003). Moreover, mass alienation from politics and the party system has grown steadily, leading to a significant decrease in voter turnout (Altman 2006) and invalid voting (Carlin 2006). In 2004, when asked to position themselves as "left," "center," "right," or "independent," more than 40 percent of Chileans did not position themselves in any category or chose "independent" (Centro de Estudios Públicos, CEP Survey, annual average, www.cepchile.cl). In 2006, roughly 75 percent of Chileans did not sympathize with any particular political party and only 9 percent considered a candidate's party to be the most important factor (vis-à-vis individual candidate traits) in deciding their vote (LAPOP 2006).

As a corollary to these trends, office-seeking politicians from all camps face strong incentives to compete on nonprogrammatic linkages for the support of an increasingly ideologically dealigned electorate. At the national level, candidate-centered appeals seem to explain the electoral allegiance of dealigned voters. The recent presidential candidacies of Joaquín Lavín in 2000 and Bachelet in 2005 were the most successful in obtaining the vote of non-ideological voters; particularly in lower strata, both candidacies were significantly better in generating electoral support among independents and dealigned voters than their opponents.

It is therefore possible to conclude that a sizable group of voters who supported the candidacy of the radical right in 2001 switched in 2005 to favor Bachelet's presidential bid. In spite of their obvious differences, both candidacies represented a strong renovating swing, campaigning against the old politics of the Concertación and promising a new, closer-to-the-people governing style. Finally, while Bachelet's candidacy emerged from her high popularity ratings in public opinion polls and in contrast to the Concertación's rank and file, the candidate did not systematically pursue links with labor unions or other social movements representing popular sectors. Therefore, apart from the need to discipline the Concertación's congressional delegation, Bachelet's administration enjoys considerable autonomy from the parties that supported her candidacy and from civil society in general.

In contrast to the Chilean left, Uruguay's FA is portrayed as a party with mass appeal that emerged and won office by opposing neoliberal reform attempts in the context of redemocratization. FA's original support base was the organized working class and progressive sectors of the middle classes and the intelligentsia. During the 1990s, these groups solidified their link to FA as the party opposed subsequent reform attempts that were only marginally successful. Later on, drawing on public discontent with traditional parties, FA won over the unorganized poor, a segment historically coopted by traditional parties, while retaining its strong links to its historical constituency. As a result, today roughly 55 percent of Uruguayans align themselves with a political party, and 65 percent of these partisan sympathizers are *frenteamplistas* (LAPOP 2006).

In short, the Uruguayan leftist party is broadly supported by the citizenry and has a dual support base that includes strong ties to organized groups. Moreover, distinct fractions of the party have privileged relations with different segments of its social base.

In other cases—those historically characterized by the presence of clientelistic linkages between traditional parties and voters—the erosion of oligarchic parties' ability to provide nonprogrammatic side payments to their constituents led to party-system collapse (e.g., in Venezuela), increasing voter alienation (e.g., in Colombia and Costa Rica), or the recrafting of nonprogrammatic cooptation patterns by incumbents (e.g., in Peru and Argentina, and Venezuela under Chávez). Uruguay's case is distinguished by the different social coalitions of import-substitution industrialization (ISI) beneficiaries and their tacit alliance with the FA, which systematically helped to contain popular discontent while at the same time enhancing interest aggregation levels in Uruguayan society, and the significance of programmatic linkages for party competition in the system.

Moreover, the enduring strength of traditional partisan subcultures and the gradual nature of the reforms (and economic decay) cushioned electoral dealignment and laid the foundation for a programmatic realignment, through which FA became the interpreter of popular discontent with reform attempts of the 1990s and their aftermaths. The divergent pattern observed in Uruguay is therefore related to a specific causal configuration centered on a well-institutionalized and "uncontaminated" party with longstanding friendly ties with interest groups, good territorial organization, consolidated leadership, programmatic appeal, and governing experience at the municipal level. In turn, this partisan and social base configuration translates into higher levels of endogenous constraints than in Chile. A brief excursion into the political management dilemmas faced by the Vázquez administration might serve to illustrate this point.

In the electoral debacle with traditional parties in 2004 when the FA took office, the party's main challenge was to remain unified to ensure effective governance and maintain a working majority in Congress. Thus it was essential to align mainstream FA fractions with the executive. To accomplish this, Tabaré Vásquez appointed the heads of the Senate lists of each major fraction to his cabinet; they also were the most prominent fractional leaders.

By filling up the executive branch with powerful FA leaders, Tabaré Vásquez sought to circumscribe potential conflicts to the council of ministers, where they could be solved while avoiding harsher and more decentralized confrontations in Congress. Once issues were settled in the executive, congressional majorities would be secured through fractional discipline. For difficult issues, Vásquez allowed his ministers, who represented different fractional views on controversial issues, to discuss their discrepancies openly, even in the press, up to the point where the continuity of a minister was threatened. On those occasions the president stepped in to arbitrate the conflict, establishing the final position and sometimes compensating the losing side, either symbolically or through tangible side payments. When congressional approval was needed, fraction leaders were then made responsible for securing discipline in Congress.

Frente Amplio's government has also confronted difficult times with labor unions. While the reinstatement of tripartite collective bargaining and the passing of a new statute protecting union activities solidified the links between FA and the Plenario Intersindical de Trabajadores–Convención Nacional de Trabajadores (PIT-CNT), recent state reform proposals have triggered labor mobilizations opposing the government. After the approval of reforms that had been part of the party's historical platform—such as the creation of a direct income tax and a new health insurance system—the party's main challenge, according to one top government official, is "to prevent interests groups [i.e., pension beneficiaries, civil servants, banking system unions] from perforating those reforms" through the approval of ad hoc exemptions and subsidies conceded in response to social and fractional mobilization.[7]

To sum up, the anatomy of the FA government translates into significant political management dilemmas that imposed salient tradeoffs during the first half of the presidential term. In this example, different patterns of linkage to specific social bases yield important differences that are especially useful for analyzing the actions of Latin American leftist forces currently in power. For instance, distinct distributive dilemmas could be derived from each leftist party's historical trajectory and current social base configuration. However, the salience and shape of such distributive struggles also depend on the interaction between politico-institutional factors (endogenous constraints) and social and state structures (exogenous constraints). Although both types of constraints seem to be largely collinear for classification purposes, they are analytically distinct. Again, a cursory comparison of Chile and Uruguay seems useful to illustrate this claim.

In Uruguay, the ISI model was only partially dismantled in the 1990s. From a sociological perspective, this reformist pattern gave rise to "three Uruguays," each of which roughly encompassed a third of the population: (1) a privatized, market-oriented sector represented by upper social segments; (2) a corporatist Uruguay dependent on state rents, mainly composed of the middle classes; and (3) a socially marginalized group unable to compete in the market and that has lost, or never had access to, state protection (Filgueira et al 2006). In a loosely schematic way the second group represents FA's traditional constituency and the third group the party's emerging one.

The challenge is that while the FA's traditional constituency might become alienated by reformist attempts and possesses the organizational capacity to block them (essentially by mobilizing fractional support), the party's emergent constituency—the one most likely to benefit from such reforms—lacks this degree of organizational capacity, its recent allegiance to the FA being especially motivated by economic and political discontent with the status quo. The emerging constituency might therefore become alienated from the party if tangible improvements (i.e., job creation) are not forthcoming. However, such improvements would depend in part on implementing reforms that are politically costly for the party, especially to certain FA fractions with strong ties to organized labor. These ties are not only salient vis-à-vis state employees, but are also prominent in the case of unions that would have an important say in any reforms that were introduced in areas such as pensions or education.

*   *   *

We turn now to Chile, where state and market reforms have yielded a dual social configuration that assigns a much greater role to market allocation and a much lesser one to the state and ISI-related corporations. Here, the weakening of organized interest groups has its counterpart in individualized access to finance and mass consumption. Finally, while upper and upper-middle sectors purchase social protection (pensions, health, and education) on the private market, lower social segments have access to targeted, state-supplied social assistance of significantly lower quality. The municipalization of health care and education has further fragmented and weakened the organizational capacity of unions tied to these sectors (Castiglioni 2005).

As a result of this configuration, popular sectors and public servants' organizations have significantly weakened, while business interests and private companies responsible for providing health care (Instituciones de Salud Provisional, or ISAPREs), pensions (Administradores de Fondos Previsionales, or AFPs), and education (private corporations running educational establishments) have grown stronger (Castiglioni 2005). Due to this trajectory the Concertación lacks organic ties with the labor movement.[8]

This state of affairs translates into lower constraints for the Concertación, which in turn means that progressive policy change, while not impossible in Chile, will likely depend on top-down political agency. Indeed, two recent examples—the approval of Plan AUGE (Acceso Universal con Garantías Explícitas en Salud) under the Lagos government, which significantly contributed to reducing social inequity in health care provision (Dávila 2005), and the present administration's introduction of a noncontributory universal pension that would also improve social welfare in Chile—were proposals that originated among the political elite and in the absence of interest groups pushing for their implementation. This low-constrained configuration is not only the result of partisan (endogenous) factors. Pinochet regime's dismantling of the ISI model translated into elite autonomy after the transition to democracy by weakening or simply wiping out interest groups tied to previous policies. This places Chile in sharp contrast with Uruguay, where any reformist attempt must confront and accommodate interest groups tied to the benefits of previous policies and to the FA itself.

The different configuration of constraints that these governments face could also explain why the Concertación in Chile has confronted increasing levels of social inequality but has excluded a progressive tax reform from its agenda, while in Uruguay a progressive income-tax reform was implemented by Frente Amplio after only two years in office. Moreover, while the FA resurrected collective wage bargaining immediately after taking office (which rapidly translated into a further strengthening of the labor movement), the Concertación's agenda has been more oriented toward further liberalization in labor. Meanwhile, the divergent trajectory of these two political forces could also explain why FA decided not to sign a free trade agreement (FTA) with the United States (after Vásquez and his finance minister actively pursued it) in the midst of fractional and activists' confrontations, while the Chilean government under Lagos signed one without facing any significant opposition from civil society or partisan activists.

To further argue the role of exogenous constraints into government action it could be useful to assume for a moment that pursuing a "social-democratic" model is both feasible and satisfying. Chile and Uruguay confront very distinct challenges and opportunities in their path toward "social democracy." In Chile, the state should take a more active role in reregulating the economy and in providing greater decommodification of social welfare. To do so it has a leaner and more autonomous state bureaucracy and political leadership that has gained increasing autonomy from popular sectors, which in turn have gradually become alienated from political mobilization in exchange for individualized market consumption, access to targeted social assistance, and/or plain social anomy. However, powerful business sectors here are likely to block those reforms and have the political clout to do so.

In Uruguay, crafting a more competitive and profitable insertion into the global economy while improving social welfare involves a complex combination of deregulation and reregulation in state and social policy reforms. Both business sectors and marginalized social groups would benefit from strategically induced productive investments that enhance both profits and employment. However, to provide better investment conditions (including social capital), state and social policy reforms should be undertaken. Such reforms would inevitably undercut the current incomes and benefits of ISI beneficiaries, who are the FA's historical social base and have organic ties with some of the party fractions.

In short, to pursue such reforms, the FA is constrained by the lack of political and institutional autonomy, which results from its social base configuration, a state with much less autonomy and institutional capacity than its Chilean counterpart and a more difficult insertion into the global economy. In terms of state structures, and paraphrasing Peter Evans's famous formula of the state's need for "embedded autonomy" (1995), it could be argued that while the Chilean state has autonomy and lacks embeddedness, the Uruguayan state is socially embedded but not autonomous.

This section has not sought to provide a systematic analysis of leftist politics and policies in contemporary Chile and Uruguay, but rather has attempted to illustrate some of the insights that can be gained from paying more attention to leftist government features that go beyond leadership style and partisan organization. Specifically, I have argued that greater attention should be paid to structural variables and state structures that interact with those politico-institutional variables in a path-dependent sequence, creating leaderships that, beyond the programmatic current they pertain to (ameliorationist/institutional vs. radical/constituent), are more autonomous or more constrained due to both partisan (endogenous) and nonpartisan (exogenous) configurations. While such path dependence is not deterministic, the scope, shape, and political management of future policy shifts will inevitably entail substantially divergent processes and outcomes in each case. To close, Table 2.1 places the four cases briefly analyzed in this section within the two-dimensional typology I have proposed for future analyses of Latin America's left turns.

Conclusion

Leftist parties and leaderships swept into office on the promise of solving what Luis Reygadas and Fernando Filgueira (Chapter 9, this volume) aptly call the region's "second incorporation crisis." This second (social and political) incorporation crisis parallels the first, which resulted in popular sectors being enfranchised and partially incorporated through different sociopolitical arrangements under import-substitution industrialization (Collier and Collier 1991; Filgueira 1999, 2007). The emergence of this second crisis after the exhaustion of ISI brought Latin American countries into disequilibrium, providing leftist and progressive leaders the opportunity to make recent electoral inroads by promising a more inclusive socioeconomic and political regime than those of the 1990s.

The relative durability (conjunctural vs. structural) of the leftward shift in a given country depends on the current government's capacity to solve Reygadas and Filgueira's second incorporation crisis effectively, pursuing both viable political and socioeconomic inclusion. In doing so, these governments could induce a new and more stable socioeconomic and political equilibrium. However, available options for change are limited because of a country's relative social, institutional, and productive endowments. The presence of highly fragmented civil societies and weak states are two contextual factors that complicate the eventual solutions to a second incorporation crisis. In short, while current leftist governments face the challenge of providing greater social and political inclusiveness while crafting a viable developing model, path-dependent trajectories will shape specific opportunities and constraints in each case.

Therefore, to analyze these left turns in terms of government action, it is necessary to complement institutional approaches and leader/party-centered accounts with the incorporation of a longer-term perspective and sociostructural variables. Moreover, beyond party system institutionalization, the nature of party linkages with different social bases, each with its own level of organization and specific, often competing, interests in the country's current development model, needs to be brought into the analysis. In other words, to better understand the left turn and its eventual implications for democracy, the analysis of political regimes should be reembedded into the socioeconomic and state structures in which those regimes operate (Cullel 2004; O'Donnell 2004).

By the same token, analyses of economic policies or of the broader development model that leftist governments might pursue should pay more attention to the social, political, and institutional variables in which those models are necessarily embedded, as well as to the sociopolitical coalitions that make them workable (or not) in the long run. In a highly simplified way I have called this the "anatomy" of leftist governments, which translates into high or low levels of constraints. Those constraints are at least as important as the programmatic projects that seem to inspire the actions and rhetoric of each leftist party or leader currently in office.

Notes

1. This refers only to the electoral left (parties and leaders that have contested, and in most cases won, recent elections in Latin America). Therefore, while meaningful for analyzing the rise of the left and its broader implications, "other lefts" such as those found in cultural movements and civil societies in the region fall beyond the scope of this chapter.

2. More recently, Lanzaro (2008); Levitsky and Roberts (forthcoming); and Roberts (2007b) have proposed unpacking the populist left, splitting the cases of Alianza Popular Revolucionaria Americana (APRA) in Peru and the Peronist Party in Argentina from the other populist cases in which a historical populist party is lacking (Venezuela, Ecuador) or where the populist leader has an organic social-movement base (Bolivia).

3. Obviously, the Chilean case is an exception to this pattern; Weyland accommodates this disparity by referring to the Chilean state's historical autonomy from political leadership.

4. For simplicity's sake I am emphasizing policies related to each country's socioeconomic development model and downplaying other policy domains that might be both useful and pertinent for drawing alternative distinctions.

5. Although labeling this project as social-democratic could be questionable, see Panizza (2005a) for a lucid argument in defense of this particular terminology.

6. Argentina and Peru might pertain to a third "messy" category (as argued by Roberts 2007b).

7. Personal conversation with an official from the Oficina de Planeamiento y Presupuesto, October 2007.

8. Congress members from the Concertación and the Alianza alike point to business interests and lobbies as the most active groups in agenda setting and policymaking in Chile. In the Uruguayan case, pensioners and the PIT-CNT are identified by congress members as the dominant civil society actors shaping congressional policymaking (personal interviews 2002–2003).

3

Many Lefts, One Path?
Chávez and Lula

John D. French

❝ ❝ ▌never know where to begin [when] speaking in events as beautiful as this," Hugo Chávez told an overflowing crowd in the Caracas Poliedro on 27 January 2006. The Venezuelan president began his address to the polycentric VI World Social Forum (WSF) by citing "the grand emotion" he felt facing an audience "overflowing with passion." In a speech full of references to past heroes, Chávez delivered a message to "Mr. Danger," the term he selected for a US president he would label the devil in his speech to the UN General Assembly in September 2006. On occasions like this rally, he observed, "I always come with the desire . . . to reflect on issues and ideas. And there lies the perpetual dilemma—passion vs. reason—but both are necessary." While citing martyrs, condemning crimes, and promising inevitable retribution, Chávez attacked those who failed to understand that the Latin American lefts that had come to power were all moving "along the same path, in the same direction." It is here that the Empire has shown itself to be very intelligent, he went on: "intellectuals of diverse origin and the media have spent two years promoting the divisive idea that . . . several lefts exist: Fidel and Chávez are the crazies—and now they include Evo [Morales] too; and others, like Lula, Lagos, Tabaré, and Kirchner are 'statesmen'; but Chávez and Fidel are crazy, the 'crazy left.'" Having weighed in on the key debate about Latin America's left turns, Chávez went on with vigor to discount such labels: "call us what they will, but we are going to give the right the greatest defeat ever on this continent, which will be remembered for 500,000 years" (Chávez 2006, 2008).

As if following up on Chávez's remarks, the May–June 2006 issue of the US journal *Foreign Affairs* published an article by Mexican intellectual Jorge Castañeda. Castañeda is well known among academics in the United States as author of an influential 1993 book on the twentieth-century trajectory of the Latin American left and its subsequent crisis in the late 1980s (Castañeda 1993).[1] Yet the appearance of "Latin America's Left Turn" in the journal of the

US foreign policy establishment was not surprising. In the 1990s, Castañeda had broken with his Mexican comrades to support the candidacy of conservative businessman Vicente Fox, who won a landmark 2000 presidential election that ended one-party rule in Mexico. Rewarded with the position of foreign minister, Castañeda's *Foreign Affairs* article has been widely cited and debated in both the ivory tower and along the Washington–New York corridor.

Castañeda's article opened with a backward glance that took on the air of a fairy tale: just over a decade ago, Latin America seemed poised to begin "a virtuous cycle of economic progress and improved democratic governance. . . . The landscape today is transformed" with the region "swerving left" in a backlash "against the predominant trends of the last 15 years." Dating this shift back to the 1998 election of Chávez in Venezuela, Castañeda described "a veritable left wing tsunami" in which "a wave of leaders, parties, and movements generically labeled 'leftist' have swept to power." Yet he was quick to sharply distinguish a "good left," which was "modern, open-minded, reformist and internationalist," from a Chávez left, "born of the great tradition of Latin American populism," that was "nationalist, strident, and close-minded" (Castañeda 2006:28–29). Far less balanced than his 1993 book, his 2006 article attacked populism as "a bizarre blend of inclusion of the excluded, macroeconomic folly" and "virulent strident nationalism" (Castañeda 2006:34; Castañeda 1993:39–40, 43–45).

This chapter takes up this heated political and academic debate regarding the twenty-first century turn toward the left in Latin America. Most broadly, it rejects the dichotomous categorization of the contemporary Latin American left championed by Castañeda, former Mexican president Ernesto Zedillo, and many political scientists. Embracing the notion of many lefts but one path, the article uses Hugo Chávez's discussion of Lula to better understand the lived politics of Latin America's plural lefts. The key to the unity that exists within the left's diversity, it is suggested, can be found in the notion of the left as a space of convergence across difference based on a common antineoliberal politics. Finally, it argues that leadership—understood as a unity, as in the case of Chávez—can be distinguished from Lula's praxis of convergence but that this divergence need not endanger the shared left terrain that has provided the basis for the unprecedented success of this generation of Latin American leftists.

Populism or Social Democracy?
Rejecting Dichotomous Visions of the Left

The vigor of Castañeda's disdain reflected how badly things had worked out for the neoliberal "social democratic left" he had believed was the wave of the future in the early 1990s. Indeed, Castañeda was forced to admit in 2006 that he had been "at least partially wrong" to have believed that the Latin American governments carrying out free market reforms in the 1990s would have to adopt "social democratic" policies as the necessary complement to the modernizing reforms vigorously denounced as neoliberal by the "old, radical, guerilla-based, Castroist, or communist left" (a category to which he had long consigned Lula and the PT) (Castañeda 2006:31, 37). In the 1990s, the most successful examples of Castañeda-style social democracy were the post-Pinochet Concertación in Chile, a coalition built around a Socialist–Christian Democratic alliance, and the government of Fernando Henrique Cardoso, the neo-Marxist creator of dependency theory who served as Brazil's president from 1994–2002. Yet a decade later, Castañeda noted ruefully, only Chile had succeeded and few Latin Americans recognized Chile as the "true model for the region" (Castañeda 2006:35). As for Brazil, the 2002 election had seen a poorly educated former manual worker from the "bad" left beat José Serra, an extremely competent administrator with a US Ph.D. who had been chosen by Cardoso's Brazilian Social Democratic Party (PSDB).

The sequence of sweeping electoral victories that marked the left's arrival in the first decade of the twenty-first century sprang from precisely the hard-core left of the past that had condemned the Castañeda-Cardoso brand of politics as neoliberal betrayal (Castañeda 2006). In positioning himself vis-à-vis the new governing leftist leaders, the former Mexican foreign minister was reduced to miraculously rechristening swaths of the old "bad" left he had opposed as newly "social democratic," and thus part of what he now called the "right left" in Latin America. Castañeda was full of praise for Tabaré Vásquez and the Frente Amplio in Uruguay, for example, but he was most eager to claim Brazilian President Lula for a renovated left that existed largely in his head. Yet his "support" for Lula was tinged with resentment and his attempt to coopt Lula for the "right left" was marked by clear uncertainty. Despite evidence of Lula's moderation, he claimed only that the PT had "*largely* followed him [Lula] on the road *toward* social democracy" (emphasis added), while admitting that it still maintained a "lingering emotional devotion to Cuba," as did Lula.[2] To illustrate the mixed nature of the Brazilian developments, he cited the fact that "when Lula welcomed Bush" to Brasília in November 2005, there were demonstrators from Lula's own party burning "the US president in effigy" across the street from the presidential palace. As he summed it up, "the conversion is *not complete*" (Castañeda 2006:37, emphasis added).

So far, I have traced the roots of dichotomous treatments of the Latin American left in the contemporary political dialogue between two Latin American politicians, each with their eye on Washington, D.C. (if for different reasons). Yet this type of simplified hierarchized difference does not necessarily disappear when we move from the heated sphere of political antagonism into the more ethereal arena of academic social science. As political scientist Kenneth Roberts recently observed, "political diversity within Latin America's 'left turn' is sometimes reduced to a core differentiation between social democratic and populist alternatives. This dichotomy is too quick to attach familiar labels to new phenomenon in different contexts," not to mention, one might add, the multiplicity of meanings that the term "social democratic" occupies historically within the Western European context, much less its transformations over the last two decades.[3] The second difficulty with this dichotomy, Roberts goes on, is that it "lumps together too many disparate cases under the populist concept," which is transformed into a "residual category" and "political epithet" used to "demarcate the 'good' or 'responsible' left from the demagogues and 'idiots' (in Alvaro Vargas Llosa's contemptuous parlance)." In doing so, an effort is made to "delegitimize socioeconomic alternatives that depart from neoliberal orthodoxy" while "artificially reducing Latin America's options to one or another variant of populism or neoliberalism" (Roberts 2007b:5).

The political ploy described by Roberts was dramatically illustrated by a commentary on Lula's election by Ernesto Zedillo, a Yale economics Ph.D. who served as the last Partido Revolucionario Institucional (PRI) president before Vicente Fox. Appearing in the US business magazine *Forbes*, the article began by calling populism "the most pervasive political ideology [*sic*] in Latin American politics for nearly a century [*sic*]." He also noted, and by no means approvingly, that populism had proven "extremely effective at attracting mass support" by using "a socially divisive rhetoric" that promised "a better life for their people simply by wishing for it—never as a result of discipline, thrift, and hard work." Having sternly invoked a particularly disciplinary version of Weber's Protestant ethic, the director of Yale's Center for the Study of Globalization reported himself hopeful that Lula might prove less than "a traditional die-hard populist." It may be, he went on, that in addition "to being a charismatic politician, [Lula] may have evolved into a responsible one." If so, the new president will rightly "disappoint his now-enthusiastic grass-roots supporters" by dosing "his country with even more bitter medicine than that prescribed by the International Monetary Fund" in August 2002. If he refuses, however, the result will be "quite simply hell" for the economy and people of Brazil, and this will leave populism discredited. And if President Lula does perforce act "responsibly," he might—with generous US financial support—"become the unwitting hangman of Latin American populism" (Zedillo 2002:55).

As I have demonstrated, the sharp juxtaposition of social democracy and populism originates in the policing efforts by the neoliberal establishment in Latin America. "Liberalism, though not always an explicit point of reference, thus lurks near the surface of this debate" and serves as the covert norm (see Chapter 1 in this book by Jon Beasley-Murray, Maxwell Cameron, and Eric Hershberg). This is abundantly clear in one recent article, which defines the key challenge facing the region's "social democratic" left as follows: "to overhaul the culture and informal institutions of currently existing liberal democracy" since progress will only be made "upon the foundations of strong representative and properly accountable institutions." It is also possible to detect below the surface an underlying concern about extra-institutional mobilization and popular majoritarianism, as shown by the author's unease about unruly *piqueteros* being used by radical minorities in Argentina. The article also contains an especially emphatic warning about the "risks incurred by attempts at instituting a *political ground zero* in complex modern societies," that is, anxiety about the "refoundationalism" characteristic of what is dubbed the non–social democratic left in Latin America (Panizza 2005a:100–101, emphasis added).[4]

In practice, many social scientists prove almost as uncomfortable with the charismatic, the demagogic, and the excessive (emotion, not reason) as Michael Reid, an English journalist who has served since 1996 as the Latin American bureau chief for neoliberalism's most ideologically rigorous publication, *The Economist*. While Reid skipped the Europeanizing "social democratic" label favored by Castañeda, his 2007 book described "the battle for Latin America's soul" as pitting "democratic reformism" against "populist autocracy, as personified by Hugo Chávez"; herein lies "the populist challenge to liberal democracy. . . . Strip away the verbiage, and Chávez looks a lot like a typical military caudillo and his project an updating of populism" consists of a charismatic and messianic savior directly bonding with the masses through the media, combined with a lack of restraint, unsustainable redistribution, and a polity made up of *clienteles,* not citizens (Reid 2007:xiv, 13, 12, 79–80).

Reason, Passion, and the Question of Social Democracy: The 1990s Birth of "Left" Neoliberalism

"A holy alliance is trying to exorcize the ghost of populism," Carlos de la Torre recently noted, but it is possible to "identify important debates over the meanings and interpretations of democracy . . . behind the smokescreen" (Torre 2007:385). In truth, the question of social democracy has less to do with Latin America than it has to do with Latin American and Latin Americanist intellectuals across lines of ideology and politics. The emergence of this regionally esoteric term, with its current valences, dates to the late-1980s evolution of part of the 1960s generation that cut its teeth on the populism debate that marked the emergence of the Latin American New Left (Mackinnon and Petrone 1998). Across the subsequent decades, a vast amount of research has been conducted on how to best understand the mid-twentieth-century populist leaders, movements, governments, culture, and regimes. Very little of this, however, has penetrated the world of those who refurbished a revolutionary version of antipopulism as social democracy, while effectively—perhaps inadvertently—converting the new Latin American social democracy into "a recipe for the consolidation of neoliberalism in practice" (Cammack 1997:241).

Those who set out to create a Third Way were aware that their effort seemed "unrealistic" and "incongruous" (Vellinga 1993:3; Touraine 1993:297). As Cardoso noted, this new social democracy emerged in a region "besieged by apparently triumphant neoliberalism and weakened by the criticism and death of real socialism," while facing "a political tradition," populism, that was "unfavorable to it" (Cardoso 1993:274–275). Indeed, the term itself was "not viewed very positively" in Latin America and the region hardly seemed "the most ideal breeding ground" for social democracy (Vellinga 1993:4, 12; Touraine 1993:304). Of the voices heard in Menno Vellinga's 1993 programmatic collection entitled *Social Democracy in Latin America*, soon-to-be-president Cardoso was clearest in identifying the practical neoliberal tasks ahead: to criticize past lefts, reduce the state, restrict redistribution associated with corporatism (such as wage increases), and move away from nationalist flag waving, usually by leftists (Cardoso 1993:284–286, 289). What needs to come to the fore, Cardoso said, was a concern for efficiency while attending to "the rational aspects of accumulation, productivity, and investment" so often missed in the regressive critique of wealth associated with the "egalitarian utopia" of Catholic socialism (Cardoso 1993:284–285). For the Argentine Marcelo Cavarozzi, the PT was "the most dramatic example" of the "grassroots left" linked to liberation theology, labor, and mass protest, which he criticized for its "Manichean view" that perceived "political representation, at its best, as a distortion of true and real democracy, which . . . is associated with modalities of direct participation" (Cavarozzi 1993:154–155).

Despite the fragility of their project, Latin America's self-styled "social democrats" in the 1990s did aspire to something truly utopian. The goal was not to refound a nation or grace it with a new constitution, but to erase its history, politics, and popular culture as part of putting an end, once and for all, to the "era of populism" (as Cardoso put it in 1994). The likelihood of success can be measured by the array of past presidents Castañeda identified with populism in his 2006 *Foreign Affairs* article: it included such twentieth-century giants as Mexico's Lázaro Cardenas, Argentina's Juan Perón, Brazil's Getúlio Vargas, and Bolivia's Victor Paz Estenssoro! The irony, of course, is that you cannot erase or even refound a country's past, only rethink its future in light of that past. The oddity of the utopian aspiration of Castañeda and Cardoso was not completely missed by intellectual architects of the new social democracy of the 1990s.[5] Alain Touraine noted that state action on behalf of redistribution and a lessening of inequality did not differentiate social democratic "policies from the old national populist ones" (Touraine 1993:303). Vellinga recognized that several of the established social democratic parties in Latin America, such as APRA in Peru and Acción Democrática (AD) in Venezuela (members of Socialist International), were "tied up" with populism and founded by commanding caudillos like Haya de la Torre and Rómulo Betancourt (Vellinga 1993:13). Such fine points, however, are routinely passed over by those who fail to distinguish between social democracy as a flattering self-conceit, an alternative political economy, a set of principles and values, a discourse, or a facade. In truth, social democracy in Latin America tracks most clearly with liberal values held dear by the intelligentsia: abstraction and rationality, civility and controlled emotions, distance and irony, and a positivist obsession with North Atlantic modernity in one form or another.

By contrast, populism and the popular, with which it is still often confused, are coded quite differently and therein lies their singular strength. It took an English journalist with neoliberal politics to recognize most forthrightly that populism today "has become a loaded, normative term, rather than an analytical one." Reid's 2007 book even recognized that populism was often "a creative political response to inequality and the dominance of powerful conservative groups . . . [and served as] the political vehicle through which many Latin American countries entered into the modern era of mass politics" (Reid 2007:12). It was, as Miguel Centeno and Fernando López-Alves have noted, "perhaps the region's first 'homegrown' regime model. While clearly influenced by both the Popular Front Left and fascism, Latin American corporatist populism had indigenous ingredients and sought to formulate answers clearly linked to the nature of the [local] economic, political, and social problems they were meant to solve" (Centeno and López-Alves 2001:5–6).

Even Castañeda's 1993 book *Utopia Unarmed* did not ignore the many positive features and lasting legacies of populism. While decrying its timid reformism and frequent resort to authoritarianism, this Mexican leftist en route to a social democratic version of neoliberalism nonetheless emphasized that "the national-populist tendency undoubtedly belongs on the left of the political spectrum. . . . These movements' original leaders, together with the historical periods of collective consciousness and popular enfranchisement, are symbols of . . . the inclusion of the excluded. . . . Finally, the populist epoch was a golden age of national self-assertion. It was a time when Latin American countries stood up to the rest of the world, gained attention and respect, and defended their pride, dignity, and many of their true interests" (Castañeda 1993:39–40, 42, 43, 44).

To understand twenty-first century left turns in Latin America demands that we move beyond excessively narrow temporalities while taking into account the historical roots of contemporary politics, both in term of legacies and that which is new. The region's variety of lefts must also be disaggregated into the diverse historical trajectories that impacted these plural lefts within the ebb-and-flow of end-of-the-twentieth-century Latin American and global economics and politics. And above all, we must attend to the social and the cultural as much, if not more, than the political, institutional, and economic. As Torre has noted about populism, politics "cannot be reduced to the words, actions, and strategies of leaders. The autonomous expectations, cultures, and discourses of followers are equally important in understanding the populist bond. In order to comprehend the appeal of populism serious attention should be paid to the words, communications, and conversations between leaders and followers" (Torre 2007:392). It requires, in other words, that we attend to lived relations between flesh-and-blood individuals and groups, while analyzing politics as embodied work done with words by individuals in their relations with others.

As we do so, Luis Reygadas reminds us, we need to pay special attention to the gaps between our analytical vocabularies and the discursive realm of the subaltern who have emerged as a central force in Latin American polities over the past century. Reygadas notes that intellectuals, and the documents and manifestos they write, often prefer a language of liberal "citizenship, equality, inclusion, and intercultural dialogue." Yet these weak narratives, he suggests, cannot yet substitute for the "them-us" logic that structures "subaltern discourses of inequality [that] go back to a long history of plundering, discrimination, and exclusion." These images and tropes are not, he insists, "a simple reflection of that history. On the contrary they are active constructions that interpret the Latin American condition from the perspective and the interests of the excluded" (Reygadas 2005:504).

Chávez, Lula, and the Politics of Latin America's Left Turns

Now we can return to the Caracas WSF speech by a politician far more successful than Castañeda or Cardoso. Those "who have lifted the flags of revolution," Chávez thundered, are on "a victorious offensive against the Empire" with battles looming in Latin America, Asia, and Africa. "Representative democracy," he went on, "always ends up being a democracy of the elites and therefore a false democracy." We want a new model, a revolutionary and "people's democracy, [one that is] participatory and protagonistic" not one defined by "an elite that represents the 'people.'" (Chávez 2006). This forceful anti-imperialist, antiliberal, and socialist rhetoric suggests less a revival of Latin American populism, the eternal bête noire of the enlightened, than a rebirth of the tricontinental third worldism of the Cuban Revolution that inspired the "radical, guerilla-based Castroist, or communist left" of the 1960s (Castañeda 2006).

Chávez's radical words do in fact stand in stark contrast to the moderation of the rhetoric of his Brazilian counterpart, which would seem to support the notion of a Chávez radical left and a Lula one (however labeled), at least at the discursive level. Before discussing this, however, we might consider that the Venezuelan president, in the very same speech, directly criticized leftists who unfavorably compared the words or actions of Lula to those of his own government. "Nobody can ask me to do the same as Fidel does, the circumstances are different; like Lula cannot be asked to do the same as Chávez, or Evo cannot be asked to the same as Lula." He recalled the Porto Alegre WSF the previous year, where he had been more enthusiastically received by a largely Brazilian audience than Lula. As he observed in Caracas, "I told my *compañeros* and brothers of Brazil," at the 2005 WSF *Gigantinho*, that Lula "is a great man and that they have to work with Lula and support Lula" who was facing reelection in 2006 as was Chávez (both won with 61 percent of the final vote, Chávez on the first round) (Chávez 2006).

In Caracas, Chávez was speaking to an audience favorable to a more resolute and consequential "leftism" than was characteristic of the Lula government. Despite the moral authority derived from his in-your-face leftist posture, Chávez drew a significantly different boundary between left and right than might be expected given the political genealogy invoked in his speech. Yet do Chávez's efforts to cast the left's net so widely, even promiscuously, make any sense at all? Perhaps it merely reflects his personal friendship with Lula, which goes back to before 1998, or his admiration for Lula's past history of struggle that links both men as insurgents. It might even be an expression of a "big man" theory of history in which peoples have states, states have rulers, and high-level hemispheric and global politics is the game that powerful men play with each other. This latter possibility seems unlikely, however, since the volatile Chávez has routinely violated diplomatic protocol with harsh comments about the presidents and politicians of other Latin American countries. There is little reason to believe he would hold his tongue if he felt betrayed or disappointed by Lula.

Yet we need not take at face value the Venezuelan president's claim of a single left on the march. Perhaps it was merely opportunistic statecraft that led him to minimize his differences with Lula? And is it really possible for Lula to have the "warm personal friendship with Chávez" of which he boasts, while simultaneously being on excellent terms with the US president denounced by Chávez as the Devil? In other words, perhaps the claim that President Lula is of the left stems solely from Chávez's need to curry the favor of Lula and his government. A not entirely dissimilar calculus might be said to drive Bush's favorable stance vis-à-vis Lula, which allowed Lula's government to retain the advantages of apparently incongruous alignments, while refusing to allow either of the parties in conflict to force the country into a definitive position. In this fashion, the Lula government becomes an indispensable point of convergence—between the volatile Chávez and less enthusiastic Latin

American governments as well as between Chávez and a US government eager to see him out of power.[6]

That Chávez recognizes his own dependence upon Brazilian support leads him to emphasize that Lula is not Cardoso and Lula and his government have not betrayed the left. Although he might prefer a Lula who was more forthright, Chávez is confident that Lula will not harm him or his government; otherwise, he would be first to denounce him. In truth, Lula's Brazil has repeatedly served as a vital guarantor of Venezuela's Chávez in the face of his enemies, just as it has emerged as a support for the government of Evo Morales, despite that government's abrupt nationalization of the Bolivian properties of the Brazilian state-owned oil enterprise Petrobras. And President George Bush, dealt these cards, had no choice but to return over and over again—as recently as 2007—to a man he described as a friend and ally. Moreover, Venezuela's twice freely elected president is well aware that Lula attracts support in sectors of global politics that are unenthusiastic about his policies and discourse. In this sense, Chávez, Morales, and Bush all occupy a place within the space of *convergence* constructed around Lula, each at various distances to his left and right but all intertwined in the net.

The pro-Lula position assumed by Chávez further clarifies the meaning to be accorded to the idea of the left in Latin America during the twenty-first century conjuncture of neoliberal globalization. Here we can return to a story that Chávez recounted in his 2006 speech to the Caracas WSF. After hailing Schafik Handel of El Salvador, a legendary communist and one-time presidential candidate of the Frente Farabundo Martí de Liberación Nacional (FMLN), the Venezuelan president gave an account of the first time he met his fellow revolutionary at the VI Encuentro of the Foro de São Paulo (FSP) held 26–28 July 1996 in San Salvador. The FSP began with a conference of the region's leftist parties and organizations that was held in São Paulo at the initiative of the PT in July 1990. The FSP Encuentro in San Salvador was the sixth such meeting (São Paulo 1990, Mexico City 1991, Managua 1992, Havana 1993, Montevideo 1995) of a group whose meetings have grown in the twenty-first century (Montivideo 2008, Mexico City 2009). So Chávez and his compañeros decided in 1996 to attend.

> We went just after being released from jail, and a strange thing happened . . . the leftists of Latin America looked on us with trepidation, they kicked us out of the assembly. They had their reasons: "A colonel who led a military coup. A *caudillo*." . . . There we were, and I remember that I was not allowed to address the assembly by majority decision by the Forum organizers. I told them: That's fine; I didn't come here to talk to the assembly. I came to see what this is all about, to learn, to learn about movements, political parties, and leaders, to listen to speeches, to take good notes, to learn to integrate myself. (Chávez 2006)

Chávez's story revealed fissures that separated his biographical trajectory from those of the party left, which predominated in the forum, with the leading roles accorded the PT (Brazil), the Cuban Communist Party, the FMLN (El Salvador), Partido de la Revolución Democrática (PRD) (Mexico), the FSLN (Nicaragua), and the Frente Amplio of Uruguay. At the same time, it also highlighted the legitimacy that the ex-prisoner and disgraced military man accorded the FSP as the representative body of the Latin Americas pluralistic left (however defined), and what he believed their recognition might offer to him.

Two years into his presidency, in 2000, the "singular political process" in Venezuela was hailed in the final declaration of the IX FSP Encuentro in Managua and Chávez himself would attend the Havana FSP Encuentro of 2001 as a head of state (Lula was also there, having already met Chávez earlier). Yet Chávez's words in Caracas remind us that the ties that bind him to the FSP are not only ideological or strategic but personal. Indeed, this is precisely why Chávez chose to discuss a slight from 1996 that might otherwise have been a source of bitterness. As Chávez recalled with warmth, it was the former communist party guerrilla Schafik who had "the delicacy, the firmness, the courage, the spirit to approach me . . . and he invited me to the table he had coordinated, and offered excuses for the debate that resulted from my surprise appearance in the Assembly" (Chávez 2006).

And these personal ties, built up one-on-one and in meetings like the FSP, are a deeper part of what tie the two presidents together. This is illustrated by an earlier speech by Chávez to fifteen thousand people who gathered on 30 January 2005 to hear him address the WSF in Porto Alegre, Brazil. Having cited that speech to his Caracas listeners a year later, the Venezuelan president ended his two-and-a-half hour Porto Alegre speech with a declaration that, in being so human, was all that much more deeply political. While acknowledging that some in his Brazilian audience might heckle, he declared: "I love Lula. I appreciate him. Lula is a good man with a great heart. He is a brother and *compañero* and I leave him my embrace and my appreciation" (Chávez 2005).

Convergence as Praxis: Neoliberalism, the Forum of São Paulo, and the World Social Forum

While shaped by personal ties and trust, the political foundation that defines the contemporary politics and practice of the Latin American left was laid during a process of convergence over the last twenty years. The Forum of São Paulo (FSP) was founded in a darkly pessimistic period for the left and its key role was to serve as a space of convergence marked by a pluralism of traditions, ideologies, forms of struggle, and styles of leadership. In its convocation and conduct, the FSP reflected the style of leftist organizing that characterized

Lula, the PT, the Brazilian left, and its allied social movements. Addressing the 15th anniversary Encuentro in 2005, President Lula recalled 1990 "when we were few, discredited, and we talked a lot. . . . The Forum of São Paulo, in truth, taught us to act like *companheiros*, even in our diversity." After all, those involved "did not think in the same manner [*jeito*], didn't believe in the same prophecies, but did believe that the Foro de São Paulo could be a path. . . . In the beginning, . . . some parties didn't wish to participate, because they thought we were a bunch of crazies [*malucos*]. . . . Meetings were not easy, [but] difficult; many times the divergences were greater than the agreement but there was always a group that played midfield to contemporize, to seek the right word" (Lula 2005:2, 4–5).

Across its Encuentros, the central opponent was invariably defined as neoliberalism and, to a somewhat lesser degree, US imperialism. In the 2007 words of another founder, the FSP encompassed "the entire ideological spectrum of the left. With an anti-imperialist and antineoliberal definition, the FSP represents a space where the different member organizations can meet each other, a space for debate, and a mechanism for communication, coordinating, and solidarity" (Regalado 2007:249).[7] The founding of the FSP came a year after Lula's first presidential campaign in 1989, which he lost by only 6 percent of the national vote. At the time, Brazil had seen the rise of mass antisystemic social movements, a radical and militant grassroots-oriented "new unionism," and a party whose radicalism placed itself outside the boundaries of even a refounded Brazilian democracy (the refusal to vote for Tancredo Neves in indirect elections in 1985; the refusal to sign the democratic constitution of 1988). In many ways, the PT represented the ideal case to address the relationship between popular insurgencies, social movements, and a radical leftist political party pledged to socialism. Based on a "logic of difference" in the words of Mimi Keck, the PT was a movement uneasily turned party that exemplified the tension between rejection and participation while its party documents took a militantly leftist stance, except for its rejection of the Soviet model (though sympathetic to Cuba and Sandinista Nicaragua) (Keck 1992; Cavarozzi 1993).

As the first election after a twenty-one-year military dictatorship, the 1989 campaign was a tense and polarizing one. It was in this charged context, at the most radical moment in the PT's history, that Lula was asked in a radio interview how he intended to save Brazil from "savage capitalism" and take it toward socialism. He replied: "I never liked the nomenclature 'savage capitalism.' I always thought such savage capitalism doesn't exist; I know of a capitalism that bites and that doesn't bite, that which is bad and that which is good. I think that there has been a retrograde mentality on the part of Brazilian businessmen, the government, and the dominant class. As I've said, when it comes to earning money, Brazilian businessmen are as modern as the Europeans but, when it comes to paying wages, they are backwards like the English of a century ago. So what I think is that we need a new dynamic, not just economic but cultural, so that those people begin to understand that it is essential to distribute income." Having used his words to deflect impressions of radicalism, Lula went on to offer an accurate preview of the objectives of his future presidential administration—thirteen years before its inauguration: "I would say that we are elaborating a program of government that will prioritize some things in the social camp. I would not say that we're going to make socialism" (Heródoto 1989:6–7).

The point is not that Lula was a social democrat before his time or to repeat earlier criticism of the scholarly utilization of stylized European categories that obscure the actual complexity of any given left. Today's attempts to baptize Lula and the PT in their faith reflect a failure to understand the specificities of the Brazilian as well as Latin American context. As French and A. Fortes observed in 2005, "the PT was a pluralistic party that included Marxist-Leninist revolutionaries, practitioners of liberation theory, and New Deal–style social reformers," even social democrats and liberals. It eschewed ideological definitions, idealized a bottom-up participatory politics and was constructed as "a point of *convergence* characterized by an absence of doctrinal rigidity and a high social density" (French and Fortes 2005:14, 18).

The PT was founded on an event, a personality, and an image and was characterized, by one Marxist *petista* (a member of the Partido dos Trabalhadores) in 1987, as a "heterogeneous organization" with a "hybrid outlook" based on a "remarkable—and probably unstable—ideological identity." What "distinguished the PT from the outset was a unique compound of two outlooks that would normally be regarded as incompatible": a "potentially sectarian workerism" and what Emir Sader called "an uncritically received liberalism" (Sader 1987:100, 97–98). The ability to maintain this heterodox confluence of forces, tendencies, and ideologies depended upon the forging of bonds of group-belonging, the crafting of a shared story, and a partisan *petista* identity if not project. Lines needed to be drawn, but its strengths lay in its leader (which was usually ignored out of leftist orthodoxy), and the open-ended terrain of the PT functioned best as a space of convergence that tolerated difference and even internal factions. The presiding inspiration was well put in Lula's remarks to the VI Encuentro of the FSP in 1996: "We must place much less importance on our ideological differences and much greater emphasis on united action. We must abandon the sectarian spirit that so often has dominated and divided us. That means ending the traditional arrogance that has characterized the left" (XIII Foro De São Paulo 2007:18).

In the 1990s, the PT stood with those sectors of Latin American politics that consistently criticized the neoliberal policies of the center-right government led by Cardoso. Yet what was gained in strategic political terms by the left's deployment and popularization of the term neoliberalism? If opposition to neoliberalism, not capitalism, marks the fundamental boundary of the contemporary left, as I would argue, the terminology could be said to obscure the essential capitalist and imperialist enemy if viewed in orthodox Marxist terms. Yet the emphasis on neoliberalism is especially appropriate to Latin America, where autonomous or semi-autonomous national development (be it capitalist or socialist) has long been a shared goal across the political spectrum. While anticapitalism has had its place in the discourse of the region's left, the practical emphasis has more often been on the incapacity of capitalism to achieve the autonomous national development being sought, while the bourgeoisie was long criticized for failing to spark a bourgeois democratic revolution or deliver prosperity to the masses.

As first popularized in Latin America, neoliberalism brilliantly delineated a vague and shifting opposing camp that correctly frustrates those who favor the political forces associated with the Washington Consensus of 1989. The *Economist* bureau chief in São Paulo in the late 1990s, for example, is especially irritated by the slipperiness of the term. In his 2007 book, Reid recognizes that the Washington Consensus is now "indeed an irrevocably damaged brand." Yet a frustrated Reid rightly notes that its "central tenets—of macroeconomic stability and open, market economies—have [now] become an enduring part of the scenery in many countries in the region. That this is not more widely perceived," or convertible into political capital, "owes much to the baleful influence of a meaningless term: 'neoliberalism.'" While recognizing neoliberalism ties to the discredited Pinochet and Menem, Reid seeks to rescue its policies from the obloquy to which neoliberalism is currently subjected: "neoliberalism" is widely used by its critics either simply to describe an open capitalist economy or as a term of abuse. While citing the Chilean Concertación as the best example, Reid then dubs Lula a "social democrat" and "a convert to this consensus" although, he adds, "in some way an ambivalent one" (Reid 2007:10–22). In offering the same caveat as Castañeda, Reid thus confirms that the neoliberal camp is aware that Lula's leftism falls short of being fully assimilable.

With the passage of time, the PT and Brazilian left creatively developed the language and practice of antineoliberalism so that they were prepared, by the dawn of the new millennium, to take it to the global level. The WSF Charter was the product of dialogue between Brazilian social movements, mostly but not entirely hegemonized by the PT, and the Association pour une Taxation des Transactions Financières pour l'Aide aux Citoyens (ATTAC) group in France in the late 1990s. In its basic principles, the charter defines a very broad *space of convergence* (my term) that disregards past ideological disputes or current rivalries within the left. The goal is a space in which a vast array of forces, projects, and currents can come together around a lowest common minimum. Indeed, the first point of the 2001 charter of the nonparty World Social Forum was to bring together "groups and movements of civil society that are *opposed to neoliberalism* and to *domination of the world by capital* and *any form of imperialism*, and [who] are committed to building a *planetary society directed towards fruitful relationships among humankind and between it and the earth*" (WSF 2004:70, emphasis added).

The WSF is not defined—nor is the contemporary Latin American left—necessarily by opposition to capitalism per se but to neoliberalism. It is not defined by opposition to all capital but to "domination by capital," and, while unequivocally opposed to "any form of imperialism," it does not assert that all capitalist countries are necessarily imperialist. As a result, the WSF process would come to encompass, over subsequent years, countless celebrities, French cabinet ministers, Nobel Prize–winning economist Joseph Stiglitz formerly of the World Bank, and the international financial speculator George Soros. In ideological terms, it attracted anarchists, socialists, communists, social democrats, and liberals, not to mention the unaffiliated and a vast array of labor, environmental, women's, and indigenous groups. Under such circumstances, those obsessed with defining the left in terms of "revolution" or "social democracy" are caught up in a mid-twentieth century past whose relevance is fading in the face of today's challenges.[8]

Comparing the Men and the Words:
Chávez's and Lula's Distinctive Styles of Leadership

Chávez's refusal to label Lula a neoliberal does not mean that the Venezuelan president likes Lula's policies. Nor does it indicate his acceptance of the model of politics implied by the new global thinking on the left represented by the WSF. In hosting the WSF, Chávez clearly accords status and legitimacy to this Brazilian-identified global convergence, but his speech also illustrates the difference between his politics and those of Lula, the PT, and the largest current within the World Social Forum. The Venezuelan president not only positions himself to the militant Marxist left of the WSF but explicitly criticizes the WSF's self-definition as a process, not an organization: as "an open meeting place for reflective thinking, democratic debate of ideas, formulation of proposals, [and the] free exchange of experiences" (WSF 2004:70). Rather than constituting the WSF as a new leftist international, the forum aspires to serve as a pluralistic space of encounter by civil society, a movement of movements, with stress on horizontality and autonomy (its particular strengths).

While affirming his government's respect—in "an almost sacred way"—for "the autonomy of the social movements" represented in Caracas, the Venezuelan president showed little patience for rules that preclude formal

WSF manifestos and plans of action. While making abundant use of military metaphors (offensives, victories, battles, retreats), Chávez insisted on the need for "the perfect strategy for the coming years. . . . We have to link up all our causes, [we need] unity, unity, unity." The WSF, he warned, runs the risk of becoming simply a "folkloric tourist encounter" unless it can "agree to a united work plan, a united universal plan of action" for the upcoming battles so "vital for the future of the world." Otherwise, "we would just be wasting our time." While mentioning respect for diversity and autonomy once, the word *unity* appears a dozen times in this section of Chávez's remarks. After doing so, he immediately offers a revealing "clarification": "no one is planning to impose anything on anyone, only coordination, unity [i.e., an imposition]." A brief reference to vital pending battles then ends abruptly with, "Look, Karl Marx coined the phrase: 'Socialism or death'" (Chávez 2006).

Chávez is clearly critical of what he takes to be the WSF's diffuseness and excessively cautious politics, indeed he is more openly critical of the WSF than of Lula himself. And these remarks demonstrate why his presence at the WSF sparked controversy, as did Lula's second appearance in 2005 but for different reasons. Although welcome in a personal capacity under the charter, both men are elected heads of state as well as charismatic leaders whose rise is based upon a relationship—constituted through identification, emotion, and imagination—with a mass base of tens of millions. Both are men of passion as well as reason, with anger being most starkly identifiable in Chávez while Lula is known for his smiles, humor, and moments of empathy that call forth his tears. While their discursive repertoire and use of metaphor and symbolism differ to a degree, the greatest difference is to be found in how they position themselves in relationship to their listeners. While Lula touches a "deeply messianic nerve of Brazilian popular imagination," the former metalworker does so as one of the subaltern who had "succeeded through his experience of the common" and whose individual success is presented as "expressly collective" (Holston 2008:5–6).

As a former military man from a lower-middle-class family of teachers, Chávez, by contrast, rose to middling success within a core institution of the state as an officer, not a subaltern. Unlike Lula, his persona was not constructed through a sequence of combative mass struggles in dialogue with 150,000 followers. Rather, his political activism originated in a clandestine politics of small groups and his rise from obscurity came as a revolutionary conspirator and a failed leader of a 1992 military coup d'état against an elected government. The process of identification and the forging of imagined relations with Chávez began with his famous three words on TV after his first coup attempt in 1992.[9] After a second failure, Chávez discovered his true talent: as a politician, with a way with words, who would rise to power through electoral means. Not surprisingly, Chávez has a very different relationship to the national imaginary and the structure of feeling surrounding his success is quite different than in Lula's case where "one of us" has succeeded.

While Chávez initially aspired to a military seizure of power, the twists of history led him to revolutionize his country through successive elections in a tumultuous sequence of struggles, near defeats, and triumphs as president. Yet the "most potent weapon" of Chávez, noted by Venezuelan literary critic Yolanda Salas in a 2004 interview, was his use of language. "He is someone who is skilled at wielding discourse and fascinating the [deprived and excluded] masses. . . . I call him the great storyteller of Venezuelan politics. He's always got a great narrative, a great story, something great to say, something that seduces. . . . And if anyone knows the popular imaginary, it's Chávez who has stolen it [*sic*] from us, because he uses it, he controls it, he manipulates it" (Rojas 2005:328).

In her anguish, Professor Salas speaks for others like herself and shows a critical self-awareness of the punctured illusions that had too long characterized the intelligentsia. *Chavismo* laid bare the exclusions that underlay the "myth of democracy" and the fantasies that Venezuela had attained "an advanced stage of development, that we were cosmopolitans." Chavismo revealed another Venezuela whose collective consciousness was characterized by "certain profound traditional images. Just when we thought we were no longer a rural country, Chávez comes along and capitalizes on a popular symbology which is rural in origin." Those on the top, she concluded, had missed those Venezuelans and hadn't seen them "as real human beings, hadn't recognized them"; even the intellectuals' treasured discourse about "civil society" didn't reach them (Rojas 2005:328–329).

The emerging *chavista* discourse called for an end to the "pillaging, appropriation and extermination" of the *pueblo pobreza,* which originated with the conquest but continues to this day under a squalid corrupt oligarchy backed by foreign exploiters (Hawkins 2003:1147). The dialogue between Chávez and subaltern representations of inequality analyzed by Reygadas are striking. These representations, he observes, "synthesize complex social processes into simple dramatic images with emotional and ethical elements" through resorting "to the archives of historical memory to recuperate easily identifiable images: the abuse of colonial powers, the mistreatment of indigenous populations, black slavery. On this basis they [subalterns] interpret contemporary grievances" through anachronistic images "of another era with little correspondence to the present. . . . These temporal imbalances have symbolic and political efficacy: they settle accounts with the ghosts of the past and . . . should not be interpreted as [signs of] immobility or immutability," but rather as products of "a continuous reconstruction that reclaims many elements of previous configurations, but is also open to contingency and change" (Reygadas 2005:502–504).

In this world of subaltern representations, Reygadas emphasizes, "the intentional aspects of inequality are generally underscored," whether through actions or inactions, and all guilt is attributed to the powerful. Material, moral, and psychological suffering is not represented as the result of the disembodied processes and abstractions favored by intellectuals of all political outlooks (market failures, globalization, capitalism). And the government and its leaders are considered the most responsible for poverty and suffering, with the expectation that they will "be the chief component in its resolution" (Reygadas 2005:502–504) and will do so in a direct, immediate, and visible way. It is here that we arrive at the grandiose and direct identification between leader and nation, between leader and *pueblo pobreza,* between *comandante* and follower in chavismo (Hawkins 2003:1154). But for this to occur requires concrete results, not mere words (whose power is often overestimated).

In a sense, the role of pedagogue that thrilled Chávez early in his military career has been scaled up as president, but he is still on center stage talking down to often adoring audiences. In a July 1977 letter to his parents, the young Chávez described giving a patriotic lecture to an audience of five hundred high school students in the name of the nation. "When I was standing on the stage before beginning, the school choir sang the National Anthem. I felt a great emotion, I felt the blood surge through my veins, and my spirit burned so much, and I gave one of the my best presentations. . . . At the end, the students couldn't stop applauding . . . [and] it seemed to me that I was carried away to a future time . . . [and] that it might be that I would achieve what I desired and become happy" (Zago 1992:25, as cited in Hawkins 2003:1147).

Two years earlier, Lula had been elected president of the metalworkers union as an apparent patsy for its former president. Having rarely spoken publicly in his early years in union leadership, Lula nervously fingered something written for him by the union attorney but, preempted by the former president, ended up not saying a word. For Lula, as with the poor and subaltern, there first had to be a fight to gain voice in a society characterized by subalternizing hierarchies and despotic rule both politically and in the factory. Putting aside the individual Lula, it is vital to better understand how the world looked to these workers at midcentury. To use Brazilian parlance, the common people (*povo*) had few illusions about the power realities they faced, although they had an acute awareness of their own misery (*miseria*), combined with a deeply engrained sense of being unjustly treated (*injustiçado*) at the hands of the more powerful. The result was that manifest discontent coexisted with high levels of dissimulation within a mass consciousness permeated by a sense that the world was stacked against the poor, the weak, the colored, and the uneducated.

Another defining feature of the consciousness of these working folk was their perception of themselves as small and weak; hence, the cultivation of guile and cunning as their weapon of choice vis-à-vis the powerful. *Malicia* or *astúcia* (cunning) was also admired in those who wished to be leaders, as with Lula, who proved a master of being everything to everyone. To make these possibilities real required a leader capable of maneuvering within existing power relations to take advantage of small rifts among the superordinate, without being reduced to them. Since defiance of superiors was immediately punishable, to be a leader required the ability to relate to and manipulate those antagonistic to your interests and desires—all the more so if committed to a transformative or struggle-oriented practice. At the same time, the price of such maneuver was the suspicion of the led so it was essential that they believe in your integrity, commitment, and loyalty. Here, I return to my proposed formula that leadership is a relationship and politics is an *embodied work that is done with words*; hence, the fundamental importance for mobilization of a leader, in this case one of your own, who you come to judge as reliably worthy of *depositing your faith as part of a pact of reciprocity*.

The central thrust of my overarching argument about the nature of politics is that leadership, understood *as process and relationship* (two-way even if asymmetrical), is the causal link between *mass consciousness* and *mobilization*. As in all mass charismatic electoral phenomenon, Lula's practice of leadership shares much with that of Hugo Chávez. The key differences between the two are (1) Lula's strategy of drawing people into a space for convergence across difference, which I argued is a key contribution to a twenty-first-century left; (2) Lula's central focus on organizing the popular sectors on a more enduring and autonomous basis; and (3) Chávez's preference, in attracting diversity into a following around him, to act as their "representative," their epitome, their condensation—while conducting a relation between leader and led on a more top-down basis, characterized by individualism and a resort to "unity" (command), not convergence (persuasion).

Keeping an eye on society as much if not more than the polity, we need a broader working definition of politics as embodied work that is done, with words, by individuals in their relations with others. In valorizing the social, cultural, and discursive, such an anthropological approach can capture the distinctive style of political leadership that together constitute the twenty-first-century turn toward the left in Latin America. In the case of Lula, the last three decades in which he rose from trade unionism to the presidency have been based on *a transformative politics of cunning* characterized by *an additive politics*, executed through the *creation of spaces of convergence* across difference, and carried out through *an embodied work that is done with words*. Most importantly, this notion of convergence has much to contribute to the politics of a twenty-first-century left that seeks to build a post-neoliberal world: the creation of spaces of convergence across difference in pursuit of common values and an unknown post-neoliberal (not post-liberal) future.

In this deeper sense, we can better understand the central point made by Hugo Chávez in his 2006 address in Caracas. That the left's struggle in Latin

America must be understood *as a process* in which presidents and countries have "their [own] circumstances, but we *walk the same path, in the same direction* and that's what's important" (Chávez 2006:10, emphasis added). The common path of these many lefts in Latin America is defined by their historic repudiation of the neoliberal ideas that marked the unparalleled US hegemony and military supremacy that peaked in the 1990s. This common antineoliberalism need not imply identical public policies, similar styles of political mobilization, or adherence to a single discourse in favor of or opposed to liberal democracy across the region. It does, however, express a powerful conviction—echoed in the slogan of the XIV Forum of São Paulo in Montevideo (2008) and reiterated again in Mexico City in August 2009—that "we are not only in an epoch of changes but in a change of epochs" as we make our common future in a post-neoliberal world (*Declaración Final. XIV Encuentro del Foro de São Paulo* 2008; *Declaración Final. XV Encuentro del Foro de São Paulo* 2009:1).

Notes

This is an updated, revised version of an article that appeared in *Third World Quarterly* 30, no. 2 (2009).

1. Jorge Castañeda, "Latin America's Left Turn," *Foreign Affairs* (May/June 2006): 28–43. See my appreciation of the book in French (2000), p. 289.

2. For a fascinating personal account of the relationship between Fidel and Lula since their first meeting in 1980, see the recollections in Castro (2008).

3. Those writing about Latin America routinely use "social democratic" as if it were a known and unchanging category, when this very issue has been the subject of immense debate within Western Europe since the 1980s: Sassoon (1996); Moschonas (2002); Eley (2002).

4. See also Chapter 1 in this book. For a more detailed critique of Panizza, see French (2008).

5. On the difficulty of coming to terms with populism in the 1950s, see French (2006:304, 206).

6. See Lula's adept handling of this challenge in a 24 February 2006 interview (*Economist* 2006: 2–3).

7. Regalado is a member of the Cuban Communist Party Central Committee.

8. For a contemporary Cuban Communist perspective that emphasizes revolution and armed struggle, see Regalado (2007:222, 232).

9. See Naim's account of the impact of "unfortunately, for now" in Hawkins (2003:1148).

4

Andean Left Turns: Constituent Power and Constitution Making

Maxwell A. Cameron & Kenneth E. Sharpe

The popular mobilizations in Venezuela and Bolivia under President Hugo Chávez and President Evo Morales have reshaped the politics in these two countries in ways that have angered and inspired citizens, observers, and foreign governments. Conservatives see demagoguery and the "revolt of the masses" that so worried Spanish philosopher José Ortega y Gasset (1932). The masses are a threat not only to the existing order, but to order and civilization itself. Existing constitutions have been torn down, rewritten by constituent assemblies and replaced in referenda where these masses swelled to the polls. Liberal democrats share these concerns but put their accusations differently: they see Chávez and Morales as populist, rabble-rousing leaders who have mobilized vast swaths of the population to dismantle a constitutional system that once tamed the passions of the people. They emphasize how important it is to channel popular participation through orderly voting in a system of representative—not direct—democracy, where checks and balances (the courts and legislature) can tame populist demagogues, and political parties and responsible elites can settle conflicts by bargaining and compromise. Jennifer McCoy (Chapter 5 of this volume) argues persuasively that Chávez has used the rhetoric of constituent power to polarize and politicize Venezuela in ways that open the door to the abuse of power and arbitrariness, actually taking power from the people and centralizing it in his own hands.

Some writers on the left have offered a similar critique, but with a different twist. They worry that too much control is being exercised over popular forces by strong presidents. In this view, Chávez is criticized for creating a hegemonic system based on an emotional appeal (a system that he continuously manipulates through the media) and for masquerading as the agent of deeper social forces. Many in the Latin American left share the concerns about unchecked power—military rule, dictators, corrupt and abusive populist leaders, and clientelist politics are very much a part of their historical memory. But

61

at the same time, the popular mobilization and new leadership in Venezuela and Bolivia held out the hope of more popular participation, less exclusion from politics, and the promise of substantial social and economic reforms—a more effective and meaningful democracy—that neoliberalism and pacted democracies had choked off. Those on the left favorably disposed to such popular mobilization—or, some might say, popular democracy or grassroots participation—speak positively of "constituent power," a term used by analysts and actors alike (see Negri 1999; Kalyvas 2001; Chávez in Blanco Muñoz 1998). And from this perspective, it is only right and proper that constituents have the power to participate, to make decisions, to rewrite constitutions, to transform society. This is not a dangerous revolt of the masses; it is not a threat to democracy; it is the essence of democracy and the necessary condition for more just societies.

In the heat of debate about governments like those of Chávez and Morales—and about constituent power—what is sometimes overlooked are the institutional arrangements that are created to govern, to mediate between the charismatic leadership of a Chávez or a Morales and their constituents. Perhaps the most important arrangements are the new constitutions themselves. In Venezuela and Bolivia, constituent power was used to "constitute" new constitutions, and constitutions in turn shaped which constituents would exercise what kinds of power. And what is further overlooked is the way these constituents also shaped—and may have even limited—the power of the presidents themselves.

Who Has the "Constituting Power" and What Do They Use It For?

Across the Andes, a struggle is raging over the content and process of changing constitutions. There have been numerous efforts to change constitutions in the past, but the current wave of constitution making began with the election of Hugo Chávez and his Fifth Republic Movement (Movimiento Quinto Republica, or MVR) in 1998. This was followed by similar efforts to "refound" republican institutions in Bolivia and Ecuador. These efforts differed from the constitutional changes of the previous decade (notably in Peru in 1993 under Alberto Fujimori, and in Colombia in 1991 under César Gaviria) in that they were deliberately construed as processes in which the people—that is, a popular majority—would exercise their constituent power.

Chávez's first order of business, a central promise of his election campaign, was to call a referendum on constitutional change. Once he received a mandate, he convened a constituent assembly to rewrite the constitution and submit it to a referendum. Very significantly, and we will return to this point when we compare Venezuela with Bolivia, he designed the constituent assembly to displace the existing congress, so that the new assembly, and later a subset of its members, the so-called *congresillo,* emerged as both a constitution-making body and an ordinary legislature. He then initiated a process that he called "relegitimation" through "mega elections": every single elected official in the country had to submit to popular election. By 2000 he had emerged as a president with substantially greater powers. President Evo Morales and his Movement Toward Socialism (Movimiento al Socialismo, or MAS) were elected in 2005 to rewrite the constitution. The call for constitutional change among Bolivia's indigenous activists pre-dated the rise of Hugo Chávez, so it would be wrong to suggest that Bolivia was following the model of Venezuela; moreover, Evo Morales never disbanded the sitting congress, nor did Bolivia's constituent assembly legislate. In the case of Ecuador, however, Rafael Correa, elected in 2007, appears to have taken Venezuela as his model. He too called a referendum to convene a constituent assembly, and, when the opposition parties opposed this measure, fifty-seven of them were stripped of their seats by the Supreme Electoral Tribunal. The new constituent assembly, dominated by Correa and his allies, dissolved congress and assumed lawmaking powers.

Critics of these constitutional reforms have strenuously argued that they provided a pretext for stacking the deck against established elites and traditional political parties. Others see constitutional reform as a matter of inclusion of voices that have been silenced from time immemorial and of creating a more participatory democracy. They point to the adoption of mechanisms of direct democracy in the new constitutions and suggest that such reforms will always encounter intense resistance from elites. There is an important truth in both positions. The use of constitutional reform to include previously excluded voices *has* challenged the power of established elites and traditional parties. At the same time, the idea of democracy as wielded by Chávez, Morales, and Correa draws on a potentially revolutionary idea inherent in the very etymology of the word itself: the power of a people to govern itself by changing the form of government, if necessary. Thus, some on the left appeal to what has come to be called the constituent power of the people, whose rallying cry is often *que se vayan todos* (away with them all!). In this view, undertaking wholesale remaking of the political order along new and more participatory lines is democracy in action.

Constituent power is the power to make a constitution, the power not only to legislate or produce ordinary statutory law, but to create the institutions that make laws; it is a power that is predicated upon the notion that democracy implies not only the ability to periodically choose a government but also the right to determine the form of government by which a people, the constituents, will be governed. Thus, the appeal to constituent power by the Latin American left is also based on impatience with the previous delegation of authority and a desire to create more direct mechanisms of democratic participation such as referenda, including recall. This enables long-excluded popular sectors to by-pass or reconfigure institutional constraints, including, in principle, constitutional rules. This idea of constituent power thus involves two meanings. One is the power of constituents to rewrite a constitution, which changes the rules of the game and thus the distribution of power. The second is the new power created for constituents by the changed legal and constitutional mechanisms, for example, direct participation to be exercised regularly by means of referenda, recall, citizen initiatives, community councils, participatory budgeting, or other forms of popular participation.

Such struggles over constitution making are not new. When constitutions are in place for a while it is easy to identify them with order and the rule of law. To say an act or law is "constitutional" is to praise and legitimize it; to say it is unconstitutional is to criticize it and imply the need to correct the wrong-doing; and a threat to the constitution can come to seem like a threat to the rule of law and the constitutional order itself. But constitutions always represent the efforts of the powerful actors that created them to establish a particular kind of order to protect certain kinds of interests by turning them into rights that will be protected by laws. The large landholding revolutionaries who wrote the US Constitution, Charles Beard argued, designed it to protect property rights by setting up mechanisms to limit and diffuse popular democracy (Beard 1913). The worry here was not that citizens would seize private property or that the government would nationalize it, but that majorities of the poor would vote such high taxes on the rich as to threaten their interests. Politicians like Madison argued for checks and balances, representative democracy, and a diffusion of power between the federal and state governments exactly to diffuse constituent power (Dahl 1956).

After the Mexican revolution, it was the victorious coalition around Venustiano Carranza (dominated by powerful nationalist economic interests in the Northwest Group) that was the constituting power, but he had to compromise with labor and peasant groups—despite his defeat of Villa and Zapata—in writing the 1917 constitution. Its unusually progressive provisions on state control of natural resources, a commitment to land reform, and on labor rights reflected the balance of power at that moment. It made provisions for an elaborate bill of rights, federalism, and a separation of powers. And it was these constitutional forms that, tragically, were then used for over seven decades by the ruling party (the PRI) to create a political system that made a mockery of the very purposes for which these provisions were intended. It is not surprising that such revolutionary regimes write new constitutions. And it is always important to understand who the constituting power is (it is often not "the constituents") and whose participation and interests are favored by the new constitution (again, it is often not the constituents), and whether the new framework is honored in rhetoric or in fact.

Not all constitutional change is born of revolution; there are four other common patterns: (1) imposition by an external power following war or conquest; (2) imposition of constitutions by military dictatorships or authoritarian regimes (for example, the military regime under Pinochet wrote a constitution and submitted it to referendum in 1980); (3) regime transition or pact (the Venezuelan 1961 constitution was written after the establishment of the Punto Fijo pact, which created a system of power sharing between Venezuela's major parties, excluding the communists); and, more or less, (4) legal change within a given legal order (amendments to the constitutions following the rules set by the constitutions, as in Colombia in 1991).

War and revolution involve violent and wholesale changes in the state and its relationship with society. Under these conditions entirely new states may emerge, as in post-revolutionary France, Mexico, China, Russia, Cuba, or Nicaragua. The other patterns typically occur by less violent means, but they also involve changes in the nature of the state and its relations with society. Many of the current Latin American constitutions were written during periods of transition from authoritarian rule, and they often involved pacts among outgoing authoritarian political actors and new political forces demanding political opening.

Liberal critics may be right in pointing out the illiberal aspects of the new constitutional arrangements—they do sometimes weaken representative democracy and strengthen direct democracy; they do weaken traditional checks and balances (although in Venezuela and Bolivia these checks were often honored in the breach); and they do centralize more power in the hands of the new chief executives. But dismissing these constitutional changes as dictatorial power grabs or threats to democracy can blind us to a more careful and nuanced analysis of what is going on. Viewed in historical perspective, the changes in Bolivia and Venezuela (and to a lesser extent in Ecuador) look different than simply a revolt of the masses, or a power grab by a charismatic populist leader: constitution making is always about power struggles to "constitute" a new constitutional order that reshapes the power, participation, and interests favored by the older order. The constituents exercising the power to remake constitutions may be different than those who created the previous constitution, and the constituent power enabled by the new constitution may be different too. But a significant feature, important to understand and often overlooked, is that the left in Venezuela, Bolivia, and Ecuador is pursuing its agenda *through* constitution making, not through revolt, violence, or revolution. It is not pursuing its agenda extralegally but by changing the basic legal structure.

This may not calm the critics any more than critics would be calmed by how the PRI or Pinochet used their new constitutions to promote authoritarian regimes. But if the left is trying use constituent power to remake the constitutional and legal system, and to promote constituent power through those new constitutions, we need to understand the dynamics of this process. We need to understand what this kind of constituent power means and why we are seeing it now. We need to understand the kind of constitutional order that these actors are trying to build: to whom is power being redistributed and to what extent? Does the centralization of executive power encourage or discourage popular participation in policymaking and the distribution of national resources? Whose participation has been encouraged and whose discouraged? What kind of participation is it—what is the balance between local initiatives and top-down control, between local decisionmaking and centralized manipulation? Which rights have been strengthened and which weakened? What, if any, will be the long-term impact of these constitutional changes when the current leaders are gone (an issue Chileans are still struggling with decades after the fall of Pinochet left in place many aspects of the constitution he wrote)?

The Venezuelan Case

Hugo Chávez was elected in 1998 on the promise of rewriting Venezuela's constitution and ending what he regarded as the collusive and oligarchic pact of Punto Fijo. As Jennifer McCoy observes (in Chapter 5, this volume), the actual content of the changes Chávez proposed was vague and has only been revealed over time. The president proved to be a formidable organizer with a great capacity to mobilize constituents in favor of his reforms. His first campaign was a referendum to convene a constituent assembly, which he won by a wide margin. Elections were then held to rewrite the constitution, and, favored by an electoral formula that disadvantaged the opposition, Chávez's supporters won an overwhelming majority of the constituent assembly. The assembly dismantled the congress elected in 1998 and assumed full legislative powers. A new constitution was then approved in a referendum in 1999, and all elected officials were then required to submit to "relegitimation" (that is, they had to be elected again). In this context Chávez was reelected.

The new constitution eliminated the senate (weakening federalism) and relaxed civilian control over the armed forces. It contained a very progressive chapter on human rights and a provision for presidential recall at midterm. But more than the specifics of the constitution itself, the process of rewriting the constitution enabled Chávez to strengthen his hand vis-à-vis his adversaries. The constituent assembly that replaced the Congress elected in 1998 displaced the opposition parties and they never recovered from this blow. These parties and the traditional elites were, for all practical purposes, excluded from participation in writing the constitution: the rules were stacked so that the new assembly was dominated by Chávez and his followers. A boycott of the 2005 legislative assembly elections by the opposition gave the government a supermajority in the

National Assembly (over two-thirds). The weakening of the traditional parties that had constituted representative democracy in the previous regime was reinforced by the banning of some prominent opposition leaders from running for office. The judiciary's low level of independence before 1998 (the parties had a big role in picking the judges) was further weakened in the transitory period between the old and new constitutions, which created opportunities for reinforcing Chávez's political control over the judiciary. Yet Chávez's success depended in large measure on the widespread repudiation of what was widely seen as a corrupt and unresponsive political system and the class of political operators who had monopolized power under the Punto Fijo pact. By dealing a heavy blow to these elites, Chávez responded to the ill-defined but intense desire for change that had overwhelmingly elected him in the first place.

As the traditional mechanisms for party representation were weakened by the new constitutional processes, new mechanisms for participation were created—albeit within relatively top-down and hierarchical structures (see McCoy in Chapter 5 of this volume)—by Chávez's constant mobilization of his rank-and-file supporters. First, Bolivarian circles were created, followed by units for electoral battles, and local community development groups. It is tempting to categorize such popular organizations as either clientelistic groups organized and controlled by the Chávez government or his party, or as local, autonomous groups controlled and directed by local citizens—an instance of grassroots participatory democracy or "constituent power." But the reality is that there is tension between these new forms of local representation and the Chávez government and party. Michael McCarthy, who has studied grassroots water committees called Mesas Técnicas de Agua (MTAs), shows how these groups were promoted by pro-Chávez officials in Hidrocapital, the capital region water utility, so that they would help improve water distribution in ill-served communities. The government made funds available to improve water service, but to access these funds and bring projects to their communities, MTAs (headed by local activists) needed to organize the local citizens, do a detailed census of water users, map out the existing infrastructure, and diagnose the problems—and then put their case to Hidrocapital officials and press their case. These were local organizations, urged by the state to organize and press for state funds. The state had some control—it distributed the funds, it set up a structure to channel participation, it provided some technical assistance—but the state did not control the organization and activities of the MTAs (McCarthy 2009).

Other kinds of local organizations have been created under the Chávez government. *Misiones*, for example, were organized to address basic human needs like literacy, health care, communications, and housing. These social programs bypassed bureaucratic structures, reaching directly into local communities and providing needed goods and services. But perhaps the most significant recent innovation in democratic participation in Venezuela has been the community councils. These councils, which were reported to number in the thousands—26,000 in 2008 according to J. E. Machado (2008:5), although not all were continuously active—were designed to be the backbone of popular, protagonistic, participatory democracy.

According to Michael McCarthy, the councils have a lot in common with the MTAs that are now being urged to affiliate with them—they are "instances of local democracy which are led by an elected grassroots elite and execute projects in a commune-style self-management. They are not social movements. They are precarious forms of locally organized democracy" (McCarthy personal communication, 5 November 2009). Community councils are typically structured around an assembly, an elected executive, a credit cooperative, a social control unit, and working groups. They are created by means of a constituent assembly (Article 19, Communal Councils Law) and, according to one survey, in 85 percent of the cases a local initiative led to their formation (Machado 2008:22). The same survey concludes that the councils have a pluralistic membership (26)—eight out of ten councils have members with different political viewpoints—and that most of the disagreements within the councils are settled with dialogue or discussion, not imposed externally (30). But the councils are not totally independent of the state: they depend on public funding and they are chartered by the state—they fall under the jurisdiction of a presidential commission—though the capacity of the state to actually regulate their activities is unclear. In principle, they are legally autonomous and accountable to their own membership. Moreover, even though they rely heavily on funding from the center, the fact that so many have been organized suggests a good deal of grassroots initiative.

Yet how representative, participatory, and bottom-up such constituent groups are is constantly being negotiated. These groups may value their relative independence, yet they depend on state funding. Further, Chávez has made efforts to politicize state institutions (such as Hidrocapital) into pro-Chávez agencies and to politicize popular organizations, to make them sources of political support, by increasing his control over them. One example is the way Chávez has tried to create his own party and tie these groups to it.

The constitution is silent on the role of political parties, but, following his reelection in 2006, Chávez formed the United Socialist Party of Venezuela (Partido Socialista Unido de Venezuela, PSUV) in an attempt to create an official party under his control. After the party was formed, Chávez began to look for ways to turn the community councils into a reliable base of party support. For example, says McCarthy, "the Ministry of Comuna has created a Sala de Batalla Social to help prepare community councils for the next stage of popular power: Socialist Councils. In that space, multiple community councils are meant to deliberate macro issues among themselves and solicit responses from the state in a united fashion as a *chavista* community." Further, says McCarthy, "in spaces where the opposition is in power at the state or mayoral level, the central government appears to be using the Sala de Batalla, which groups together at least four chavista-leaning community councils to provide a chavista-based finance instrument and make life harder for the opposition powers" (personal communication, 5 November 2009). It remains to be seen whether such politicization will work. For example, if institutions like Hidrocapital do not deliver, local MTAs might not be willing to accept the revolutionary dedication of state officials in lieu of the water they need (McCarthy 2009:26). In short, the struggle over Venezuela's constitution involves considerable experimentation with new mechanisms of popular participation, and the nature of that constituent power is contested.

Another participatory innovation of the 1999 Bolivarian Constitution was recall referenda. This mechanism of citizen initiative was used by the opposition to seek to remove Chávez after it failed to do so by nonconstitutional means in 2002–2003. Critics of Chávez complain that the recall process underscores the nondemocratic character of the regime. The government made it nearly impossible to submit the necessary signatures, forced citizens to verify their signatures and made this information public (thereby enabling retribution and intimidation), and, finally, it spent massive sums of petrol dollars through the misiones to mobilize support. These objections are well founded. But it is also important to see the impact of the constitutional structure: by institutionalizing a recall mechanism as a way to hold a sitting president accountable, it channeled opposition away from coups and extralegal protest (and perhaps even socialized the opposition into operating within constitutional rules). And for all the levers of power Chávez was able to use to tilt the recall in his favor, this constitutional mechanism provided a degree of accountability and pressure on the regime that would otherwise have been absent. Our point is not that Chávez was a good democrat, but that both he and his opponents had to adapt to new constitutional rules.

One way to understand constituent power and constitution making under the Chávez regime is to compare his motives, base of support, and the actual constitution making in Venezuela with the situation during President Fujimori's *autogolpe* in Peru in 1992. Whereas Chávez sought to both centralize his own power and mobilize constituent power, Fujimori centralized executive power without mobilizing or organizing his social base. Fujimori won public support for closing congress, suspending the constitution, and ruling by decree because he made the case that these measures were necessary to achieve crucial state objectives: above all, counterinsurgency against the Sendero Luminoso (Shining Path) and vital economic reforms. In the process, he used a referendum to alter the constitution and expand executive powers. The novelty of the Fujimori *autogolpe* lay in its hybrid nature: it combined elements of constitutional reform by legal means with changes that typically occur during a regime transition. It did not entirely rupture the legal order, yet it violated certain laws and constitutional articles (acts that were subsequently ratified by plebiscitary means): the congress was closed, but an elected president remained in office; the constitution was only suspended and later modified, rather than discarded completely.

Perhaps the most important difference between Chávez and Fujimori is this: Although Fujimori provided a set of plausible public justifications for his concentration of executive power, he also had a secret ambition: to guarantee impunity for criminal actions taken by agents of his own government. The Peruvian *autogolpe* had both offensive and defensive goals. The new powers in the hands of the executive enabled the government to take the initiative in the war against the Shining Path insurgents, but it also allowed the government to cover up its human rights crimes and its corruption. The regime justified its exceptional measure on the grounds of the need to confront a regime enemy that posed an existential threat to the state, but its hidden rationale was always impunity. Fujimori needed to hang on to power because it was the only place he was safe; he knew that any legal system with integrity would find him criminally responsible for wrongdoings, as indeed the Peruvian justice system did in 2009 when it sentenced him to twenty-five years in prison for human rights atrocities.

Chávez did not face the security threat of a movement like the Shining Path, nor did he need to cover up past crimes. His earlier coup attempt in 1992 had been paid for with a prison sentence (later commuted). In both cases, the process of constitutional reform enabled the executive to massively expand its powers and to subordinate other agencies of government in ways that undermined the separation of powers. The difference is that Fujimori took these measures to the point that it was no longer possible to hold free and fair elections, so that the outcome of the 1992 *autogolpe* was, ultimately, an authoritarian regime, albeit one based on elections. By contrast, the regime created by Chávez in Venezuela remained an electoral democracy, however imperfect, and one with a strongly mobilized social base.

Chávez and Fujimori both tapped into constituent power by means of referenda and constituent assemblies, and both created constitutions with plebiscitary features (though Fujimori later used his control over the legislature to ensure that the opposition was unable to use referenda against his government). Moreover, both did so in an explicit attempt to disrupt the monopoly that traditional political parties had on political representation (what is sometimes called "partyarchy"). Both aimed to concentrate more power into their own hands. The difference is that Fujimori was virulently antiparty and ran for election on ephemeral electoral "alliances" that had little real presence between elections. He did not want to empower his supporters, and he assiduously avoided mobilizing them in ways that would restrain his own power. Chávez, on the other hand, exhibited a much greater interest in building lasting political organizations, above all, grassroots organizations. Belatedly, he recognized the need for a party, which he began to organize only after his reelection in 2006. The primary elections in the PSUV were completed in June 2008, and 2.5 million people (of 5.7 million members) participated. At various moments, especially in April 2002 and the recall referendum in 2004, the regime's constituents have come to its defense. They also constrain Chávez's power, which is based on continuous mobilization. The grassroots base of chavismo has the power to halt the government in its tracks, as it did in December 2007 when many voters simply refused to turn out to support a package of constitutional measures that Chávez had not adequately justified. While it is true that Chávez turned around and held another referendum in 2009, which he won, he nevertheless was forced to modify his proposals. The 2009 referendum eliminated term limits not just for the president, as in the 2007 referendum, but in a nod to the political aspirations of legislators, governors, and mayors, for *all* popularly elected officials.

The Bolivian Case

Morales was elected in 2005, but his rise to power was preceded by social movements mobilized in opposition to privatization of water, the sell-off of Bolivia's oil and gas, and the eradication of coca crops. These protests culminated in the overthrow of Morales's predecessor, President Gonzalo Sánchez de Losada. Morales was a creature of social movements, without which he would not have emerged as a political leader. At the same time, Morales's policies, especially land reform and the nationalization of oil and gas, provoked real opposition. The opposition was spearheaded by the prefects (governors) from the "crescent moon" departments, wealthier lowland areas, remote from Morales's base among the highland indigenous groups, whose landed and business interests wanted to resist Morales's reforms. Although Morales's supporters often dismissed the opposition as representatives of the old oligarchy, the fact was that the prefects had material resources, institutional leverage, and electoral appeal. The clash between the central government and the crescent moon departments thus pitted two sides against each other, both of which enjoyed electoral legitimacy, and neither of which monopolized the spirit of constitutionalism. Nevertheless, their conflict was largely channeled through constitutional arrangements.

Morales, notwithstanding a reputation for hard bargaining, proved to be willing to play by the existing constitutional rules of the game. Here, again, the contrast with Fujimori's *autogolpe* is instructive, as is the comparison with the strategy adopted by Chávez. Morales did not have the supermajority in congress necessary to change the constitution without the support of opposition members. Yet he did not summarily close the existing congress, as Fujimori did. Nor did he follow Chávez's more subtle strategy of supplanting the existing congress with a constituent assembly. Instead, he legally convened a constituent assembly, as promised in his election campaign, and he agreed that, in accord with Bolivian law, a vote of two-thirds of the constituent assembly would be required to modify the existing constitution. Since he did not win a supermajority in the constituent assembly that was convened to rewrite the constitution, a standoff developed that resulted in months of protracted disputes over how to proceed with constitutional reform. A major sticking point was the demand of the prefects to move the capital from La Paz to Sucre, something MAS would not accept. In the end, MAS rammed through its own vision of the new constitution, dismissed the proposal to change the capital, and called for a final vote that was boycotted by the opposition.

For a while it appeared that neither side would give and that Bolivia would be unable to reform its constitution, but a solution was found that involved another participatory mechanism: the recall referendum. A consensus formed between key political leaders of the opposition (both national and subnational) and the executive that both the president and the prefects would need to submit themselves to recall. The outcome was a victory for MAS when, in August 2008, Morales survived the recall and a number of the prefects did not. This changed the balance of power in Bolivia, forcing his opponents to negotiate a new draft text in the congress to be submitted to a referendum. There were many objections to the legality and constitutionality of Morales's actions, but the constitutional text was, at the end of the day, negotiated with the opposition. The government could claim that its actions were, by and large, consistent with the nation's legal order. Moreover, the process of constitutional reform did not result in Morales's entirely coopting or controlling other branches of government as happened in Venezuela.

Just as important, Morales repeatedly appealed to supporters to back his constitutional reform process. As the negotiations unfolded in congress over revisions to the constitution drafted by the constituent assembly, throngs of protesters marched two hundred kilometers to converge on the capital city La Paz for the announcement that a referendum would be held. This not-so-subtle use of mass protest to bring pressure to bear on the congress was part of Morales's strategy of working both inside and outside Bolivia's institutions to push his opponents to make concessions (Andean Democracy Research Network 2008).

The text of the constitutional draft that was approved by the congress blended indigenous with creole influences, direct and indirect democracy, and combined participatory with liberal and republican forms of representation (www.bolpress.com/art.php?Cod=2008110415). The constituent assembly originally eliminated any reference to the Bolivian nation from the constitution, but congress insisted on its reinscription. The constituent assembly described the separation of powers in ways that suggested the branches of government must work together cooperatively, while the congress reinforced the language of judicial independence and the rule of law. Mechanisms of direct democracy and participation were highlighted in the original text, while opposition members of congress stressed that the power of the people can be delegated to representative institutions. Finally, the draft modified by congress gave greater scope for departmental autonomy. "As I read this amazing new document, which is truly utopian," writes Nancy Postero (forthcoming: 22), "I am struck again by the efforts the authors made to balance cultural and economic justice, on the one hand, and rights-based notions of equality, on the other—the old tensions underlying liberalism." On 25 January 2009, the constitution was approved by over 60 percent of the electorate.

In short, the messy and irregular process of constitutional reform in Bolivia appears to have produced a document that represents a novel and unprecedented attempt to find a synthesis between the multiplicity of traditions and cultures that constitute Bolivian society. Of course, the new constitution may turn out to be another attempt to "plough the sea," to use Simón Bolívar's plaintive metaphor (quoted in Harvey 2000:72). Nevertheless, the Bolivian constitution appears to reflect a genuine attempt to combine indigenous with liberal and republican concepts of self-government. This result is due to a constituent assembly process, in contrast with those of Venezuela and Ecuador, which were controlled by overweening executives, in which Morales could neither command nor exploit a temporary political advantage to impose a hegemonic order.

Bolivia and Venezuela are markedly different in a number of respects. First, Morales has captured a very different kind of constituent power. He owes his power not to successful maneuvering through smoke-filled backrooms, or to the confidence of colleagues who selected him because of his instinct for power in the daily verbal combat of parliamentary politics—he was, after all, expelled from congress in 2002. Morales owes his power to years of organizing social movements and accompanying them in their struggles to control land, water, and gas, and to oppose the forced eradication of coca crops. It is true that Morales leads a party, but the misnamed Movement Toward Socialism is more of a "political instrument" for rural and indigenous movements and unions than a real political party (Hochstetler and Friedman 2008:9).

Second, Morales did not control the agenda and impose his vision of the constitution in the way that Chávez did. He either did not have the power, or did not seek to arrogate to himself the power, to close the existing congress. The constituent assembly that was elected did not supply MAS with the kind of majority that would obviate the need to work with the opposition. In the end, the draft submitted to referendum was a compromise that was hammered out with the sitting congress after the work of the constituent assembly was done. It was not simply the result of constituent power understood as popular mobilization, but was a result of compromises with other interests and groups. It blended elements of delegative and direct power both in content and in the process by which it was written.

Finally, there is a difference in the way the new constitution *created* constituent power. Morales embodies a political movement in which the role of the leader is not to monopolize power but to "rule by obeying" (*mandar obedeciendo*). He rose to power as a leader of social movements seeking to represent a plurinational country that affirms the rights of indigenous people as equal to creoles (those of European descent) and *mestizos*. Indigenous concepts of governance are, according to F. Schiwy, "anchored in the cultural memories of indigenous peoples" (Schiwy 2008:2), rather than in precepts of European political thought. For example, "rule by obeying" implies that the people can force from office those who fail to implement the decisions of the people. Recall is one institutional mechanism that reflects this philosophy. Seemingly anarchic and spontaneous expressions of popular power also serve as successful strategies of resistance, and are directed at Morales no less than at previous leaders. In addition, through a host of symbolic acts, the Morales government has sought to instill a sense of pride and dignity in subaltern groups, their culture and languages, which is crucial to their ability to exercise real power.

Many of Chávez's actions can rightly be labeled as illiberal (and that term is appropriate to describe Fujimori too) but it would not be right to describe Morales and MAS in these terms. They represent something more complex and hybrid. Noting their commitment to human rights, participatory democracy, tolerance, popular sovereignty, and, very centrally, constitutionalism and constituent power, Mark Goodale (2009:178) has described Morales and MAS as "twenty-first-century liberal revolutionaries" along the lines of Mexico's Benito Juárez. Postero (forthcoming: 7) puts the argument nicely when she says that MAS is "'vernacularizing' liberalism," making it "more democratic and more relevant to Bolivia's indigenous populations." MAS, by embracing liberal politics, holds a mirror up to Bolivian society and finds that it has failed to live up to its own ideals.

As Schiwy notes, liberalism, at least in Bolivia, has been associated with creole dominance, with the loss of communal land, forced labor, and other abuses of power. Liberal constitutions imposed European "imaginary communities" (Anderson 1991) based on concepts of nation and citizenship that were antagonistic to indigenous forms of collective life and organization, notably the *ayllu* and the patterns of reciprocity and self-government with which it is associated. In the words of Germán Choque Huanca, Bolivia's "constitution destroyed and denied indigenous authorities and forms of government" (quoted in Schiwy 2008:21). MAS represents another liberalism, one that is popular and emancipatory rather than disciplinary and repressive. From the standpoint of pure liberalism, the new constitution uses customary practices to undermine the rule of law, creates spaces of autonomy wherein the indigenous peoples will not have to pay taxes or obey the constituted authority, and shields and protects a sexist and collectivist culture. It is not that these complaints are mere fantasy; but it is striking how liberalism begins to sound remarkably disciplinary and punitive in the face of the assertion of indigenous rights and power.

Constitution Making and the Dilemma of the Left

We can get a different perspective on the debates over constituent power and constitution making in countries like Venezuela and Bolivia if we see them as part of a long-standing tension between advocates of constitutionalism and advocates of popular sovereignty, and add to this the particular conjuncture the Latin American left finds itself in today. There has always been a tension between constitutionalism and popular sovereignty, and it is not surprising that the popular democracy that has long been a banner for the nonviolent left in Latin America would be antagonistic to liberal constitutionalism. We will look briefly at that antagonism to set a context for the somewhat surprising turn of events we have examined in Venezuela and Bolivia: the left's embrace of constitutionalism. We suggest that this turn to constitutionalism is a partial solution to the dilemma the Latin American left has found itself in during the last few decades.

In the liberal constitutionalist view, popular sovereignty—or today's constituent power—must be limited or it is not constitutional at all. Instead it is a form of unlimited despotism in the name of "the people." Constitutions may be amended, which implies a nod toward the constituent power of the people, but amendments must be made only according to established rules. Similarly, mechanisms of direct participation, such as referenda and recall, can be tolerated within a liberal constitution provided that they are not used to bypass the existing constitutional order and the laws. The right to operate outside the constitution, to rebel against authority, must be reserved for those situations in which the government has broken the constitutional and democratic order and is governing despotically.

The idea that there are rules governing constitutional change, and hence limits on constituent power, raises the hackles of certain critics of liberalism who wish to appeal to the radical origins of the idea of democracy, to "the people" or some notion of popular sovereignty, or, in the realist argot, to a political decision by a constitution-making power (see Negri 1999; Schmitt 2008; Kalyvas 2001). In this view, the very act of constitution making implies the existence of a political will or decision that must be prior to the constitution itself. For radical democrats, constituent power outside the mechanisms of legal and representative institutions can better express a free and unrestrained democratic will. The danger here is obvious. Such appeals to the constituent power of the people share the same risk that power will be systematically abused as do the antidemocratic (even crypto-fascist) appeals to the prerogatives of executive powers to save the nation: both are prepared to free a society from the constraints imposed by constitutional and legal guarantees, from checks and balances, from the separation of powers.

Conflicting views of the rule of law lie at the heart of this debate. The apparently irreconcilable contradiction between constituent power (or popular sovereignty) and liberal constitutionalism manifests itself concretely in the fight between those who believe that the people must be free to remake their government from time to time, unrestrained by constitutional or representative institutions, and those who insist that bypassing the constitutional order is merely a step toward disorder and, ultimately, violent confrontation. In one view, law provides the foundation for the realization of democracy; in the other, it is a potentially antidemocratic obstacle to the expression of the will of the people. It is easy to confuse the rule of law with the imperative to enforce whatever statutes and laws are on the books. The political right in Latin America often insists on the rule of law ("the law is the law, and must be enforced" cried bankers when President Alan García attempted to nationalize the banks in Peru in 1987), which in practice means exhorting society to live up to the formal rules that have been created to protect its privileges. Thus, said Martha Harnecker in a public forum a few years ago, when asked about the abuses of power in Cuba: "we want a rights-based state (*estado de derecho*) yes, but not a state of the right (*estado de la derecha*)."

In the defense of existing law, liberalism becomes complicit with the status quo and loses its potentially progressive character. Thus the oft-made remark that Latin America never experienced a French Revolution (see Ugarteche 1998). The problem is all the more dramatic because of the liberal tendency, evident in the thought of Bolívar as much as contemporary liberal reformers, to see little upon which to build a legal and democratic order in a region of the world that is so prone to anarchy and disorder.

This basic tension between constitutionalism and popular sovereignty sets the context for the current dilemma of the left in Latin America. The transitions from authoritarianism to democracy in the last few decades have meant that the left has inherited constitutional arrangements that were often the result of pacts made by militaries or elites or other powerful interests exactly to restrict the political and economic reforms the left sought.

Let us be clear about what the central problem of the left is *not*. It is not quite the same as the issues facing social democrats in Western Europe. In that context, labor-based parties became social democratic when they entered electoral politics. Since workers do not constitute an electoral majority in any advanced capitalist society, socialism has never appealed to more than a minority of voters (Przeworski and Sprague 1986). As a consequence, wherever labor-based parties have entered electoral politics they have made compromises that have resulted in a watering down of their socialist programs; the result is social democracy. In Latin America, as Carlos Vilas (2006) rightly notes, socialist and communist parties have never monopolized progressive politics, and progressive politics has tended to encompass a wider range of nationalist and populist forces struggling for inclusion and redistribution. The greatest challenge for the "left"—if by that term we wish to encompass all these forces—has been the achievement of enough electoral support to construct a governing coalition. That is never easy, as Allende's Chile demonstrates; but the central difficulty has been to overcome the entrenched power of minorities in extremely unequal societies, interests often backed by substantial material resources and coercive power. This is the context in which the use of constituent power to transform constitutions has become important.

Conclusion

The use of constituent power to create constitutions that expand constituent power is a different kind of attempt to use constitutionalism than the "democratic road to socialism" of the Allende era (though Allende, too, considered calling a referendum to resolve his impasse with the opposition in congress). The left today is not simply trying to take power inside a constitutional democracy to bring about reforms. It is also pursuing an agenda different from the revolutionary agenda of the past because it acknowledges democracy as the only legitimate political regime, however much the content of democracy is contested. That agenda involves peacefully and (more or less) legally transforming the system so that progressive change can be brought about in and through a constitutional order in which citizens have more power. New leaders like Chávez and Morales are criticized across the political spectrum (especially by the right and the center) because their promotion of constituent power seems an abuse of authority. But these new leaders find themselves bound by the rule of law under the new constitutions and restricted in their arbitrary use of power.

The power of Chávez and Morales is also constrained, to varying degrees, by the strength of grassroots popular organizations, which can sanction, hold accountable, even remove leaders from power (Hochstetler and Friedman 2008:7). These are noninstitutional (or at least informal), societal mechanisms of accountability, but they are very important in regimes that depend on broad and sustained popular mobilization. The heavy reliance on referenda creates the need to mobilize constituents on a regular basis, between election campaigns, and the ability to sustain such mobilization depends on winning over "soft" supporters, negotiating with local and regional power brokers, and keeping adversaries off balance through strategic concessions or vigorous political campaigns. To date, we see little indication of the successful emergence of the sort of corporatist mechanisms that in authoritarian regimes (like the PRI in Mexico) blunted the power of the grassroots by coopting and controlling popular organizations. Chávez's PSUV party does not yet exercise this kind of control, although this possibility cannot be ruled out in the future.

It is far too soon to know how the new constitutionalism of Chávez, Morales, and other "left turn" governments will develop. Some might turn down an antidemocratic path and become increasingly authoritarian or corporatist as they restrain, coopt, or repress their popular base along with the traditional elites. Some might be ousted legally, or overthrown. But it is also possible that these new left governments will provide models of how to break free from the limits imposed by neoliberalism and the straitjacket of pacted constitutional arrangements the left inherited from the past. And they might accomplish this in ways that create new forms of accountability, different checks on the abuse of power, and new patterns of democratic participation and representation.

Note

Thanks to Eric Hershberg, Jennifer McCoy, and Jason Tockman for comments on earlier drafts of this chapter.

Part 2

Politics Beyond Liberalism

5

Venezuela Under Chávez: Beyond Liberalism

Jennifer McCoy

Venezuela initiated the current electoral turn toward the left in Latin America with the election of Hugo Chávez in 1998. He campaigned on a platform of radical change and a constitutional refounding of the Venezuelan state, to correct the dysfunctions of what he characterized as a corrupt, elitist, undemocratic political system. He specifically ventured the notion of constituent power, a core concept in this volume, when he said: "In France in 1789 constituent power exploded. This is the power to constitute a people against what is constituted, that simple. But this transformative power, as against the established, constituted power, has to be very great" (quoted in Blanco Muñoz 1998:530).

Chávez led a "peaceful revolution," elected to power rather than arriving by force, but with a mandate for radical change.[1] The mechanism for change began with an "originating" constituent assembly, elected by popular vote, which would have power above all other branches of government, including the president. He carried out this notion in the first months of his presidency when a popular referendum ratified the idea of such a constituent assembly, even though it was not envisioned in the then-current constitution, and the newly elected assembly subsequently took over legislative power, intervened in the judicial system, and attempted to dismiss elected governors and mayors. A similar originating constituent process was adopted a decade later in Ecuador under President Rafael Correa, while a constitutional refounding without originary power was carried out in Bolivia under President Evo Morales.[2]

The actual content of the radical change demanded by the Venezuelan people and promised by Hugo Chávez during the campaign of 1998 was vague. Early characteristics of what came to be known as the Bolivarian Revolution or the "process" included notions of nationalism, participatory democracy, redistribution of oil wealth, and regional integration, but its economic policy in particular was not spelled out. A decade later, we can begin to more confidently characterize and assess chavismo and the radical change it has attempted to carry out.

Two characteristics of this process of change stand out. First, it is operating within the rules of electoral democracy, not revolutionary force. This imposes significant constraints that need to be assessed. Second, it is a process that has relied on constant mobilization of the people, invoking an "us versus them" rhetoric in plebiscitary and electoral campaigns as well as street protests, to confront vested interests and eliminate or replace institutions. In this sense, it has attempted to use the "constituent power" of the multitudes to confront the "constituted power" of the previous political regime, not only in the form of the established constitutional rules, but also in the form of the loci of power.

The danger of any constant mobilization and politicization of society by privileging constituent power has been aptly characterized by Andreas Kalyvas: it resists any form of stabilization and institutionalization, and "opens the door to discretion and arbitrariness. . . . A limitless constituent power not only verges on dictatorship and arbitrariness, it also threatens its own existence by flying away from all determinations and figurations implying a degree of restraint and limitation" (Kalyvas 2001:417). Another risk, posited by Max Cameron, Jon Beasley-Murray, and Eric Hershberg (Chapter 1 in this volume), is that in a leader-driven process, constituent power may come to rest in the person of the charismatic leader rather than the people themselves.

The debate over the Venezuelan case is centered on the interpretation of these risks and possibilities. The case illustrates the apparent contradiction between constitutional democracy and popular sovereignty described in the introduction to this volume. Characterized alternatively as a plebiscitary authoritarian regime running roughshod over liberal principles, or as a participatory and protagonistic democracy privileging popular sovereignty, Chávez's Venezuela is normally analyzed within the debate between liberal democracy and radical democracy. Yet, the Venezuelan case may be instructive in answering the question of whether there is a solution to the apparent contradiction between rule-based democracy and mass-based popular sovereignty; in other words, is it possible to create institutions to channel the constituent power of the people without eroding its creative potential? Has Venezuelan constituent power succumbed to the risks of arbitrariness, or has it found a way to institutionalize and protect its power?[3] What is the prognosis for achieving a more equitable and just society, the purported aim of the left turn in Venezuela and elsewhere in Latin America?

Roots of Venezuela's Left Turn

Venezuela's democratic history prior to the democratic transition of 1958 was virtually nonexistent, with only a short-lived democratic experiment from 1945 to 1948. That experiment was crucial, however, in the lessons learned by political leaders, leading to the Punto Fijo power-sharing pact among three of the major political parties and a moderate reformist policy stance.[4] Through a series of economic and political accords, Venezuelan economic and political elites, the military, and the labor unions agreed on a political and economic model based on the distribution of externally derived rent (oil revenues), consensus-seeking mechanisms, and centralized political control under a strong presidential system.

After a decade of insurgency and military uprisings in the 1960s, the country consolidated a two-party dominant party system that penetrated all social organizations and operated in a centralist, hierarchical fashion. Social peace was kept with steady economic growth and rising incomes through the petroleum boom of the 1970s. Nevertheless, dependence on petroleum revenues, lax regulatory power, and increasingly rigid decisionmaking structures made the political regime vulnerable to falling oil prices, plummeting incomes, and visible corruption in the 1980s.

Social protest grew in the 1990s, beginning with the 1989 riots known as the Caracazo protesting neoliberal measures enacted by an aloof technocratic state under the Pérez administration. The turmoil continued through two 1992 coup attempts, the first of which was led by Lt. Col. Hugo Chávez, who was jailed, but then pardoned by a subsequent president. Continually sliding oil prices contributed to a near tripling of the poverty rates, from 25 percent in the mid-1970s to 65 percent in the mid-1990s, and real per capita income in 1998 had dropped to 1963 levels—a one-third drop from the 1978 peak (McCoy and Myers 2006:267). Such a severe social dislocation led to popular rejection of the traditional political parties beginning with the 1993 elections and culminating in the 1998 elections, when all of the major candidates were independents.

Venezuela, then, was experiencing a twin crisis: a distribution crisis resulting from a weakened capacity of the public bureaucracy to administer the state, extract revenues through sources other than externally derived rent, and distribute those resources effectively; and a representation crisis in which citizens lost confidence that their political leaders would represent collective interests over private interests, and chafed under the lack of access to centralized decisionmaking structures for subnational leaders and newer social and economic groups (McCoy and Myers 2006).

The rise of Hugo Chávez must be seen in this context—he epitomized the demand for change and won the election based on a promise of radical change in the polity and economy, but with vague ideological content. This was not a vote for a leftist ideology, but a vote of frustration and anger and a tossing out of the old political class that was perceived to be corrupt and incompetent. Chávez received 56 percent of the vote in an election endorsed by the Organization of American States (OAS) and the Carter Center. That vote was not only from the poor, however: while 55 percent of the poor voted for him, so too did 45 percent of the nonpoor (Canache 2004). Chávez was able to mobilize large sectors of the lower classes who felt excluded by established parties and did not possess institutionalized forms of political expression, but he also attracted middle-class and some upper-class support.

Hugo Chávez came to office blaming "corrupt and inept" political leaders for squandering the oil wealth and promising to change the scenario of poverty and inequality in a country perceived by its citizens to be still rich with oil revenues.[5] He named his Bolivarian Revolution after Simón Bolívar, the South American independence leader of the early 1800s, and referred to the new constitutional order as the "Fifth Republic," replacing the Fourth Republic of the forty-year representative democracy known as the Punto Fijo political system and based on the 1961 constitution.

Constituent Versus Constituted Power in the Bolivarian Revolution

Foreshadowing similar changes in Bolivia and Ecuador almost a decade later, Venezuelans supporting Chávez sought a fundamental change in the balance of social relations and the distribution of economic resources through the use of political rights (elections) and constituent power (constitutional change). It is a twenty-first-century version of change, reflecting profound disillusionment with the failure to achieve the improved living standards promised by market opening and liberal democracy of the last quarter of the twentieth century. The process of change itself has been conflictive, embodying elite displacement, redistribution of economic and political resources, concentration of power, and experimentation with new forms of participatory democracy. The demand for change also reflects the need for a new stage of incorporation of excluded citizens, this time focusing on the urban poor, in contrast to the incorporation of organized labor in the mid-twentieth century.[6] Such incorporation implies the negotiation of a new social contract or democratic bargain, yet the 1999 constitution did not achieve this renegotiation. Instead, the hurried nature and the dominant role of the executive in the constitution drafting thwarted an opportunity to negotiate a new, more inclusive contract that could have won the support of previously dominant sectors of society. The subsequent implementation of the constitution and imposition of laws through executive decree generated extreme political polarization that a decade later has yet to be resolved.

The 1999 constitution both reassured and alarmed various sectors of Venezuelan society as it did not radically change the constitutional foundations of the state, but did bring important changes, particularly to executive power. The constitution essentially followed the statist approach of the 1961 constitution, protecting private property while giving the state responsibility for social welfare, but also rolling back some of the liberalizing reforms in the labor market and pensions. The constitution deepened human rights and citizen participation mechanisms, but also strengthened an already centralized, presidentialist system, weakening the recent decentralization reforms.

In broad terms, the Bolivarian Revolution is an attempt to reformulate the political economy to be more inclusive of those who perceived themselves to be excluded in the latter half of the Punto Fijo period (which included large numbers of urban poor, middle-class civil society organizations, intellectuals, and junior ranks of the military). It is full of contradictions: nationalistic and integrationist, top-down and bottom-up change, centralized and participatory. It seeks to move beyond representative, liberal democracy to achieve a new form of "participatory, protagonistic democracy," which in its utopian form allows for empowered citizens to hold the state accountable without intermediary institutions (Ellner 2008). It follows the inspiration of South American liberator Simón Bolívar, composed of both a Latin American integrationist dream and a centralization of domestic power. Foreign policy is fundamental to Chávez's vision, with its goal of counterbalancing US global and regional hegemony with a more multipolar world. Like its domestic version, Venezuela's foreign policy is confrontational and conflictive.

The Bolivarian Revolution thus actually retains many of the basic traits of Punto Fijo politics: dependence on oil revenues; highly centralized decisionmaking structures, with a new set of privileged actors displacing the traditional elites; reliance on the distribution of oil rents; and failure to restore the regulative and administrative capacities of the state (though there is increased tax collection capability). The changes lie in the centralization of decisionmaking in one person (Chávez) rather than two hierarchical political parties; emphasis on class divisions rather than cross-class alliances; emphasis on confrontation and elimination of opponents to achieve change rather than consensus seeking to achieve stability; dismantling of traditional representative institutions and erosion of the separation of powers in favor of new forms of participatory democracy and accountability; change in petroleum policy from one of increasing market share to one of controlling production in order to raise prices; and a shift from market capitalism to twenty-first-century socialism.

Polarization and Confrontation

The Chávez government sought power in order to redistribute resources. It came to power as the result of a wave of popular grievances and frustration expressed in spontaneous protests throughout the 1990s. Yet its own origins were as a clandestine military group disgruntled with the Punto Fijo political system of the 1980s and 1990s. Chávez formed an electoral movement for the 1998 campaign, but this movement was fundamentally influenced by its military origins. Distrusting political parties and government bureaucracies, early in his administration Chávez turned to the military for development functions and later created parallel social service delivery mechanisms through the *misiones*. The chavista method of bringing about change and meeting the needs of the dispossessed was essentially populist—it was a top-down mobilization of the masses directed by a charismatic leader, bypassing mediating representative and bureaucratic institutions. It included a permanent campaign mode in which the leader called for political loyalty and devotion of his followers to counter the influence of the "enemy"—whether the Venezuelan "oligarchy" or the US "imperialists." Even new participatory organizational methods were determined by the leader, from the early Bolivarian Circles to the more recent community councils. The extent of true democratic transformation thus requires further analysis, returned to below.

Chávez and his inner circle saw the route to political change as requiring confrontation and defeat of the old order. This view contradicted the requirements of compromise and coexistence of an electoral democracy, and the resulting tension produced a fundamental struggle for political power to control the state apparatus and the oil industry, vital in a petro-state. The struggle extended, however, to other important sectors and institutions as well—the military, the media, popular sectors, civil society organizations, business, labor unions, and the public institutions of the courts, national assembly, electoral authority, and accountability mechanisms.

Representing some of the sectors traditionally excluded from power by the Punto Fijo elites, the new chavista government elected in 1998 approached its search for power in a systematic fashion, beginning with the writing of a new constitution, moving to control over political institutions, and eventually to different sectors, using a very aggressive and ideological discourse. In turn, the traditional social and business elites, ecclesiastic hierarchy, and the leaders of the large political parties reacted to the advance of these new emerging sectors, trying to protect their own interests. They incorporated large social middle sectors by raising fears and discrediting the government.

The confrontation was thus established, generating two polarized sectors identified as chavistas and antichavistas. The dynamics of the struggle for power, using strong emotional and divisive narratives, created a polarization that masked and subjugated other aspects of reality. As M. Lozada (2004) eloquently expresses it, polarization "makes social conflict invisible; generates a restricted representation of political conflict; privileges certain actors in the management of the conflict and its solution; and limits the representation of positions to the hardcore actors (violent groups, coup mongers), while omitting social movements or diverse groups. The more this dynamic penetrates the social fabric, the more cohesive elements of daily life become broken, with its consequent social damage, as those elements are mediated by what political elites say is the conflict" (Lozada 2004:201).

There were thus underlying questions related to the identity of the groups and the way they perceived their own social position compared to that of others. For chavistas, there was a feeling of retaliation and a need to end their "invisibility" and be recognized as equal human beings. For the opposition, there was a feeling of fear coupled with negation and absence of recognition of the "other." For this reason, at yet another level, the conflict represented different values and visions for the country, with some ideological content. Those who opposed the Chávez administration characterized his regime as threatening to the democratic values of individual liberties and private property. These groups generally represented the displaced traditional decisionmaking groups. Those supporting the Chávez administration characterized his government as one that finally would address the fundamental problems of poverty, inequality, and corruption in the country. Promoting a new participatory democracy, the Chávez government resonated with the dispossessed, empowering and giving hope to the poor in an unprecedented way, but at the same time fueling fears and prejudices among large sectors of the middle class. This apparent conflict in values became enshrined in the struggle over the nature of the democracy, "representative" versus "participatory," and the struggle over petroleum strategy—a commercially run enterprise increasing market share and reinvesting in the industry versus a politically run enterprise increasing price to raise revenues to invest in the "revolution."

In these ways, the struggle for power and control produced a zero-sum game between the main actors, while the clash of values pushed protagonists on both sides to perceive themselves in a fundamental struggle for the very future of the country, with irreconcilable differences. Possibilities for reconciliation and coexistence seemed very remote to these groups. Their own propaganda machines painted two opposing "virtual realities" of the country, and fomented division and conflict rather than unity and shared values. Each group felt the mere existence of the other put their own identity at risk, which justified the need to eliminate the other. (McCoy and Díaz, forthcoming).[7]

The specific form of the conflict evolved over time through cycles of conflict. Initially, with the new political rules in place in the 1999 constitution, Chávez confronted each of the organized interests that he portrayed as representing the old order—labor unions, the Roman Catholic Church, some nongovernmental organizations (NGOs), economic elites, and the private media. He conflicted with the Church over education and abortion, with the private sector over decree laws impinging on their interests, with NGOs and labor unions over his attempt to set up parallel, government-linked organizations, with the media over its increasingly critical views of the government, and with factions of the military over his politicization of promotions and military mission. Institutionally, the government controlled the new accountability entities created in the 1999 constitution, made new appointments to the supreme court and electoral authority, and won majorities in the legislature and local offices. The independence of institutions capable of checking executive power was thus weakening as early as 2000.

The catalyst for the greatest turmoil, however, was Chávez's replacement of the president and board of directors of the national oil company, Petróleos de Venezuela, S.A. (PDVSA), in February 2002 in an attempt to gain more political control over the independent board and its spending decisions. A subsequent strike and massive march resulted in violence and a short-lived coup removing Chávez from power for forty-eight hours in April 2002. The mass outpouring of his supporters in the streets and the actions of his supporters within the military, however, represented a victory of constituent power in returning Chávez to office.

Over the next two years, the opposition continued to try to remove Chávez from power, using a number of strategies. They carried out a devastating two-month petroleum strike in late 2002, a military sit-in seeking to galvanize popular rebellion, and eventually a recall referendum to remove Chávez from office. The president's defeat of each strategy by his opponents to remove him actually ended up strengthening him.

After Chávez's victory in the 2004 recall referendum, the government increased its hegemonic control of the key public institutions, expanding the supreme court, reinforcing control of the National Electoral Council, and receiving control of the National Assembly after an opposition boycott. From that position of strength, the government enacted several laws restricting the rights and prerogatives of various social sectors considered to belong to the opposition.[8] The opposition, demoralized and fragmented after the recall defeat and the strategic blunder of subsequent election boycotts, could do little to stop the advance of the government.

Constituent Power Revitalized?
A Second Constitutional Reform

Chávez's reelection with 63 percent of the vote in 2006 apparently encouraged him to propose even more radical change in a second constitutional proposal in 2007. This time, however, the reforms were drafted in secret by a presidential commission and imposed by the president on the National Assembly. Although the National Assembly (at this point still composed solely of government allies after the 2005 election boycott) did add some reforms to the presidential draft, this hardly represented a bottom-up process of constituent power. Instead, in an ironic twist, Chávez's own supporters asserted themselves for the first time against their leader by withholding their support for reforms they did not agree with, did not understand, or resented being imposed on them. Not willing to actually vote against Chávez, many of these supporters simply stayed home. The proposed reforms were defeated due to this abstention combined with active opposition from two new sources: a student movement reactivated for the first time since the 1990s, and the active opposition of a former chavista minister of defense and retired general. The outcome was a narrow defeat for the president (1.5 percent), his first electoral defeat in a dozen contests since 1998.

Institutionally, the 2007 failed constitutional reforms would have deepened the executive control of the political system, concentrating power to an extraordinary degree. They would have created a system of direct executive-community relationships and new regional vice presidencies parallel to (and thus weakening) popularly elected regional and local officials. They would have given the executive further control over the Central Bank, weakened due process under states of emergency, and allowed for continuous reelection of the president.

The vote was interpreted by the government as a punishment for poor government services; indeed dissatisfaction was rising over serious problems of governance, including growing food shortages, alarming crime rates, rising inflation, and unemployment. Abstention was also the product of chavista governors and mayors refraining from mobilizing their own electoral machines in reaction to the constitutional reforms that would have gutted their own power. Finally, the appearance of new actors opposing the reforms, but not tied to the traditional opposition, helped to galvanize voters to defeat the proposal.

The episode thus demonstrates that Venezuelan voters can and will provide a restraint even on a popular leader who steps over the line. It can be interpreted as constituent power emerging to confront what had become the new constituted power—the concentration of power in the executive. At the same time, the vote reasserted the constituted power of the 1999 constitution, which had more authentically been the product of constituent power at that time.

Nevertheless, the Chávez government was able to use its control of the National Assembly to progressively implement several of the rejected constitutional reforms through the legislative process in 2008 and 2009. It also reintroduced the concept of indefinite reelection in a popular referendum in February 2009. With public opinion still opposed, the president expanded the question to include all elected officials; with this twist, the referendum was approved, allowing Chávez to run again for president in 2012 for a third six-year term.

Inclusion and Representation in a Participatory Democracy

The left turns in Venezuela and Latin America more broadly are a product of the demand for change and social inclusion, in reaction to the unmet expectations from the promises of market opening and democratic restoration since the 1980s. They include a demand for governments to perform in delivering services (including vital personal security) and to be more responsive to citizens. In Guillermo O'Donnell's terms, it is a demand for expanded civil and social rights (equitable access to justice and improved standard of living) to follow the political rights already won (O'Donnell 2004). Marginalized Latin Americans are using those political rights to change leadership through the ballot box. The question is whether they will be able to achieve the expansion of civil and social rights in the face of limited state capacities and backlash from privileged sectors.

To what extent are these demands, and the state's response, "leftist"? If we follow Cameron's definition (2009) of a commitment to egalitarianism, a willingness to use the state to balance market forces, and an emphasis on popular participation, then demands of the Venezuelan people and the response of the Bolivarian Revolution, along with many other recent Latin American political dynamics, can be considered left. Yet, following the logic of a petro-state, the state's response in Venezuela has also been more classically populist: Inclusion of the marginalized is achieved in material terms through greater political control by the executive of oil revenues and its distribution through social programs (*misiones*). The Venezuelan case also has strong elements of nationalism, a politicized military, and concentration of power more reminiscent of classic populism in Latin America than the leftist characteristics described above. In political terms, however, inclusion is provided for through new direct democracy mechanisms such as the constitutional provisions for revocatory and legislative referenda, as well as more clientelistic mechanisms of community-based organizations directly linked to the executive.

Nevertheless, the perception of social inclusion, political representation, and personal empowerment and hope provided by Hugo Chávez to the impoverished majority of citizens is a powerful factor often underestimated or ignored by critics. The most important achievement of the Bolivarian Revolution—least understood by Chávez's opponents—is the sense of human dignity that Chávez's leadership and social missions have given to the poor and marginalized.

The challenge for scholarly analysis is to assess the nature and extent of transformation occurring in Venezuela in terms of the elements outlined above: commitment to egalitarianism, use of the state to balance markets, and deepened political participation. The remainder of this chapter assesses this transformation from the point of view of both political and policy change.

Political Representation

The relationship between social movements, civil society organizations, and political parties in Venezuela is complex. The 1999 constitution was written in a sociopolitical context in which political parties were completely discredited and social inclusion was a priority. The constitution thus does not contain the term "political party" and instead promotes citizen initiative through revocatory and legislative referenda, civil society participation in the nomination of important positions including all of the mechanisms of accountability (electoral council, comptroller, attorney general, ombudsman), and the nomination of electoral candidates by individuals and associations. The lack of specificity over terms like "civil society," however, subsequently spawned a vigorous debate about who exactly would constitute civil society and who do civil society organizations really represent? In Punto Fijo democracy, the political parties penetrated most civil society organizations, from university elections to professional associations and labor unions. In Bolivarian democracy, the government first attempted to create an "officialist" version of civil society organizations, including labor unions, and, failing that, proposed a law that would allow the state to regulate foreign funding for NGOs.

One of the hallmarks of the Bolivarian Revolution has been the experimentation with various forms of citizen organization and community-based political organization, from the early Bolivarian Circles to the Election Battle Units to local Water Committees to the more recent Community Councils (an estimated 30,000).[9] Social movements and self-help organizations in poor areas, as well as neighborhood organizations in middle-class areas, existed prior to the Bolivarian Revolution. But most civil society organizations, including university student elections and professional associations, labor unions, and other NGOs were penetrated by the political parties and highly partisan during the Punto Fijo years.

The president himself has proposed many of the organizational forms for community-based political movements, and some of these have been linked to more autonomous, organic movements (many with historical roots) within the *barrios*. Although more systematic evaluation is needed, preliminary studies of the effectiveness of these experiments in terms of bringing citizen empowerment, technical expertise, autonomy, sustainability, and their ability to hold the government accountable show mixed results.[10] Grassroots social movements within the barrios have attained a certain level of autonomy, even while dependent on state resources. Citizens, especially in poor neighborhoods, do appear to feel empowered by such mechanisms and have effectively used the community councils to bring state resources for needed neighborhood projects in many instances (author interviews). In addition, in recent years local groups have challenged the government party's imposition of electoral candidates and criticized the government's failure to meet community needs. These factors all lend credence to the optimistic view about the empowerment of local citizens.

On the other hand, the fact that the organizational ideas have often come directly from the president and that the organizations themselves mostly depend on state resources controlled at the executive level have led to questions about the ability of these organizations to be truly autonomous of the state, to be able to hold the government accountable, and to avoid clientelistic practices of resources being awarded on the basis of political loyalty and partisanship. In addition, delays in receiving the funds and mixed reports about oversight of the funds give some indication of inefficiency and corruption.

Another challenge for Venezuela today is to recreate a functioning party system that can provide effective representation. Yet this is also a point of contention in the debate over the definition of democracy and representation within Venezuela. The electoral need for a party led to the creation of the Movimiento Quinto Republica (MVR) party in 1998, but political ambitions of its members as well as coalition members distressed the president and in 2007 he moved to create an official party more under his control—the Partido Socialista Unido de Venezuela (PSUV). That attempt failed when several coalition parties refused to join, and one openly opposed his constitutional reforms. When the PSUV finally organized the election of its national directorship in 2008, the results surprised many as delegates rejected the military men who had been part of Chávez's inner circle and instead elected traditional leftist politicians and media personalities. Chávez tried to unite all of the progovernment parties for the 2008 gubernatorial and mayoral elections, but some dissident parties insisted on running their own candidates.

The opposition parties are now led by Primero Justicia (a relatively new party of young professionals), Un Nuevo Tiempo (based in oil-rich Zulia state and founded by Zulia's former governor and 2006 presidential candidate Manuel Rosales), and Movimiento al Socialismo (MAS, one of the few remaining parties from the Punto Fijo years). The two dominant parties of the Punto Fijo period—Acción Democrática and Copei—have virtually disappeared. In addition, Podemos (a division of MAS that joined the president's coalition early in the revolution) carved out a new role for itself as a potential center party between the government and the opposition, when it refused to join the PSUV and opposed the constitutional reforms in 2007. Nevertheless, party identification remains low in Venezuela, with only 9 percent of citizens identifying with the opposition parties and 24 percent identifying with the government's party, while more than half of the population call themselves independents (Datanalisis 2009).

Dissatisfaction with government performance resulted in the governing party's loss of the largest states and cities in the 2008 regional elections. The most striking results were in the Caracas urban areas, where the official candidates lost in the races for mayor of the greater metropolitan area as well as mayor of the eastern half of Caracas, which includes the largest poor neighborhood of the country. This was the first time the government had lost these votes, and it happened despite running some of the president's closest confidants as candidates and the president campaigning personally on their behalf. Though not necessarily a rejection of Chávez personally, the vote reflected the frustration of the people with the inability of the government to solve the pressing problems of soaring crime rates, lack of water and paved roads, unemployment, and inflation.

Whether the opposition would be able to use these victories to deliver better government services and thus launch competitive bids for national-level offices would depend, however, on national revenue sharing and the cooperation of the federal government. The Chávez administration had already rolled-back some of the decentralization reforms of the previous decade and decreased the autonomy of municipal and state governments. Soon after the regional elections, the administration took measures to transfer control of the ports and airports in states with opposition governors, and a number of public spaces and buildings in the cities won by the opposition, to central government authority. In an even more blatant move usurping the authority of the newly elected mayor of the Caracas metropolitan area, the government created the Capital District and appointed a head, displacing the elected mayor from his office both literally and figuratively.

Political Participation

The utopian ideal of a participatory and protagonist democracy, espoused by the Bolivarian Revolution as a means of transforming democracy to one in which citizens themselves are empowered to make decisions and hold the state accountable without the distorting effects of mediating, representative institutions, has yet to prove itself in Venezuela. One of the primary mechanisms developed is the recall and legislative initiative referenda provided for in the 1999 constitution. Venezuelans have voted in at least five significant referenda: one to convene the 1999 constituent assembly, three to approve constitutional reforms (one approving the 1999 constitution, one rejecting the 2007 constitutional reforms, and one approving the 2009 indefinite reelection reform), and one defeating a presidential recall effort in 2004.

These direct democracy mechanisms provide the capacity for the electorate to either propel forward or constrain the change led by the president. The rejection of the 2007 constitutional reforms indicates that the people are willing to, and can, put the brakes on the executive, as well as propel him forward. In general, however, Chávez is still driving the train. Cabinet ministers are loath to make any decisions or indicate any preferences without first consulting the president. Policy decisions are announced personally by Chávez in his weekly television and radio program, *Aló Presidente,* which usually lasts several hours. Cabinet ministers attend and receive instructions from the president during the show; the president floats new ideas and announces major new initiatives through this media; he also hires and fires people on the show. His implementation through legislation of some of the reforms defeated in the 2007 constitutional referendum further demonstrates his ability to carry out the changes he is intent upon through his control of public institutions (constituted power).

The Policies of Twenty-First-Century Socialism

The Chávez administration proposed the concept of twenty-first-century socialism in 2006, without clearly defining it. It seems to be a mixed economy with multiple definitions of property rights (the 2007 constitutional reform proposals included social property, collective property, cooperative property, and private property). It allows for foreign investment, but in strategic sectors only, through joint ventures with the majority control by the Venezuelan state. It provides for social welfare through executive control of oil revenues—both reinvestment decisions and massive spending on social programs for the poor. It is stridently antineoliberal, but not anticapitalist.

Chávez's own ideology evolved over time, and began as a nationalistic, participatory project without a clearly articulated economic plan. His government has reflected a great degree of pragmatism as it has adapted to changing international economic circumstances and responded to domestic political challenges. With oil prices at a historic low at $9/barrel in 1999, the Chávez administration's initial economic policy followed the austerity programs and even completed some privatization initiatives begun in the previous administration. When prices started to rise in 2003 and peaked in 2008 at $150/barrel, the administration shifted to greater social expenditures through the missions and petrodiplomacy abroad, offering discounted oil programs to the Caribbean and Central America, free fuel oil to US neighborhoods, bonds purchases to help a financially struggling Argentina, and barter, aid, and investment plans with Bolivia, Ecuador, Nicaragua, and Cuba. The sudden drop in oil prices in late 2008 curtailed this foreign aid program, at least temporarily.

The Chávez administration's attempts to create a more efficacious and responsive government were largely unfulfilled, however, after a decade in office. Public dissatisfaction with the performance of the government on personal security and police behavior were above 80 percent in mid-2009. Additional areas in which dissatisfaction outweighed satisfaction included control of corruption, employment, promotion of private investment, social security, public hospitals, and housing. On the other hand, nearly 60 percent of the population expressed satisfaction with health and education services (Datanalisis 2009). Throughout the decade-long Chávez administration, government promises to address long-neglected needs lacked a clear strategy to accomplish those objectives or to improve the efficiency of the national government.

Weak state capacity, long-deteriorating public services, political instability, and a continual climate of campaigning plague the government's ability to respond to the needs of the populace through effective governance. Venezuela's public services have been deteriorating since the 1970s, causing much of the dissatisfaction with the prior Punto Fijo regime and increasingly with the current regime. Both regimes have relied on external petroleum rents to finance a distributive policy and failed to develop effective regulatory policies. Venezuela's oil booms have historically fueled a paternalistic state as well as petrodiplomacy in foreign policy, and the criticism of Chávez's programs as unsustainable populist giveaways have been directed to past governments as well.

The government gained greater political control over the petroleum industry in 2003 after the two-month oil strike, and has since used the rise in oil prices to fund the missions. The government has not only maintained the proportion of central government spending spent on pro-poor programs, but has added direct social spending by the petroleum industry. Thus, the percentage of pro-poor spending as a proportion of GDP has increased under Chávez (Rodriguez 2008a and 2008b; Weisbrot 2008).[11] Nevertheless, no serious international assessment of the extensive social programs has been conducted to be able to measure the effectiveness of these antipoverty programs, in contrast to the studied (and lauded) conditional cash transfer programs in Brazil and Mexico.[12] There is a general consensus that poverty and unemployment have dropped, while access to drinking water and school enrollments has increased.[13] The impact of programs such as the adult literacy mission and the Cuban doctors in the neighborhoods, on the other hand, are difficult to measure and debated. Housing shortages continue to be a major problem. Likewise, conclusions about the impact of the social programs on income inequality depend on which statistical source one uses. A truly adequate evaluation of the impact of Venezuela's social programs requires transparent data with consistent measures.

Overcrowded and dangerous jails, pretrial detentions, and high crime rates have long plagued Venezuela. The national homicide rate, however, has doubled during the Chávez administration from 20 per 100,000 inhabitants to 45 per 100,000 inhabitants—one of the highest in the region—and personal insecurity is now the number one problem in the country (*The Economist* 2008; Provea 2007; and Datanalisis 2009). The numbers of incarcerated individuals remain constant, with about half under pretrial detention (Provea 2007).

In addition to personal insecurity, inflation, and unemployment, a pressing new problem emerged in 2007 and 2008 in public opinion polls: food shortages (Datanalisis 2008). A combination of foreign exchange controls, price controls, rising consumer demand, and lack of producer confidence created serious shortages in milk, oil, sugar, eggs, and meat. With worldwide demand and food prices rising, Venezuela's traditional reliance on imported food became a real vulnerability for the government. The rise in social spending also contributed to inflation rates of 25 to 30 percent annually in 2007 and 2008. In 2009, drought and production problems led to shortages of water in Caracas and of electricity in the interior of the country.

The Chávez administration has been effective in increasing tax collection capacity, and impressive economic growth rates from 2004 to 2008 stemmed not only from the oil economy, but importantly, from the non-oil economy. Poverty was reduced to 30 percent in 2006 (ECLAC 2007a). Even income inequality improved under the Chávez administration. Nevertheless, the sharp fall in oil prices to $30/barrel for Venezuelan crude in December 2008 put enormous pressure on the government and society. With its 2009 budget originally based on $60/barrel oil prices (with about half of government revenues typically financed by oil revenues), the government was forced to cut back in international and domestic spending plans. Just as the 1990s fall in oil prices resulted in a sharp spike in both poverty and inequality, so too a prolonged period of low prices after 2008 would risk a reversal in the recent progress on these two scores. By late 2009, even with a moderate increase in oil prices to $70/barrel, GDP growth was predicted to fall 2 percent for the year.

Prognosis

Despite the issues discussed here, perhaps surprisingly, satisfaction with democracy in Venezuela rose consistently since 2002 and was the second highest in Latin America in 2007 with 59 percent, while the average for the region was 37 percent.[14] By 2008, satisfaction with democracy was still the second highest following Uruguay, but the Venezuelan percentage had dropped to 49 percent, while the regional average remained at 37 percent (Latinobarómetro 2008). In addition, despite defining democracy primarily in terms of liberty, Venezuelans gave a higher ranking of the "democraticness" of their country than did the citizens of any other country in the region except Uruguay and the

Dominican Republic (Latinobarómetro 2008).[15] These numbers reveal that Venezuelans, compared to the rest of the region, have a generally positive perception of their democratic system.

Returning to the questions posed at the outset of the chapter, we can assess whether Venezuelan constituent power has succumbed to the risks of arbitrariness and abuse identified by Kalyvas, or has it found a way to institutionalize and protect its power? Second, what is the prognosis for achieving a more equitable and just society, the purported aim of the left turn in Venezuela and elsewhere in Latin America?

Constituent power in Venezuela has brought about significant change in Venezuelan political dynamics since the Caracazo first erupted in 1989. Expressions of frustration, alienation, and desire for change occurred both in social protests and in electoral realignment, leading to the end of the political arrangements known as Punto Fijo democracy and the rise of a new set of arrangements known as the Fifth Republic, the Bolivarian Revolution, or chavismo. Venezuelan politics have thus been in flux, with previously excluded sectors bringing new social forces to political power, a new "Bolibourgeosie"[16] emerging to displace the traditional political and economic elites, and a new distribution of economic resources. The old social pact based on distribution of oil revenues, state-led promotion of private sector interests, and class compromise has been broken, while a new one has yet to be forged. The government has viewed change as possible only through confrontation and displacing the traditional elite, while the traditional elite came to believe that coexistence with Chávez would not be possible.

Yet in curious ways, Venezuela under Chávez exhibits many continuities with the prior era. Reliance on oil revenues to satisfy the demands of important constituencies and finance an internationalist foreign policy and politicization of institutions continues. The constituent power emerging in the uprisings against the Pérez Jiménez dictatorship in the 1950s produced a new democratic regime that subsequently institutionalized itself into a constituted power. That constituted power, however, became rigid and inflexible, failing to continue to adapt to the emergence of new social sectors. In turn, a reemerging constituent power in the 1990s produced an upheaval that brought new social and political forces to power. The past ten years have been in one sense a continual experiment with new forms of popular participation that had the potential to be institutionalized to channel constituent power in a positive direction. Yet, the process has been driven by one person to such a degree that it is difficult to conceive of it as revolutionary in the sense of a people-driven process of change, as Chávez first described constituent power.

In fact, the single greatest vulnerability of the Chávez era is the *failure* to institutionalize the gains of the attempted revolution. Rather than creating autonomous institutions and political spaces for empowered popular participation, and agreed-upon rules that can provide mutual guarantees for various actors and sufficient predictability for material progress, chavismo has produced a system dependent on the popularity, charisma, and vision of a single individual. As Cameron (2009:342) said, Chávez has embodied the constituent power in himself. And, of course, that entails enormous vulnerabilities—not only are there few checks on potential abuses of power, but also there is little prospect that the process will continue beyond him. Chávez has acknowledged and reinforced this dilemma in his own call to amend the constitution to remove presidential term limits, asserting that the revolution requires him personally to lead it if it is to survive.

The willingness of so many citizens to accept such a concentration of power in exchange for the empowerment they feel from the president's recognition of them and giving them visibility, as well as the material benefits they are receiving, illustrates the grievances and deep desire for political change over the last decade. Yet recent votes have shown the willingness of Venezuelan people to stand up to Chávez when they believe he and his government have crossed the line. And they demonstrate the constraints on aspiring revolutionary leaders coming to power, and maintaining power, through electoral democracy. The rejection of the 2007 constitutional reforms and the results of the 2008 regional elections discussed above are two such cases. The National Assembly elections scheduled for September 2010 are another opportunity to bring more pluralism to public decisionmaking or to reinforce the dominance of the governing party.

Finally, the abrupt decline of oil prices in the wake of the 2008 worldwide financial crisis reminds us of the vulnerabilities of a petro-state to external shocks, whether governed by the left, right, or center. Although the Chávez government included as a major part of its strategy the revitalization of the Organization of Petroleum Exporting Countries (OPEC), thus helping to engineer the cuts in production and rise in prices of the 2000s, the inability of OPEC to control the price free fall in late 2008 put in stark relief the vulnerabilities of oil dependence.

Notes

1. Jimmy Carter used this phrase to describe the election results the night of 4 December 1998 after monitoring the elections with the Carter Center. Chávez subsequently referred to the phrase many times to describe his goals and methods.

2. In contrast to Venezuela and Ecuador, Bolivia's constituent assembly did not assume legislative powers; it simply drafted the constitution within the framework of the previous constitutional rules. Nevertheless, there was controversy over the implementation of the decision rule of two-thirds of the constituent assembly, and the year-long

process of drafting and approval of the new Bolivian constitution was much more conflictive and drawn out than in Ecuador or Venezuela.

3. See the analytical discussions in Cameron (2009) and Kalyvas (2001) about this question.

4. The Punto Fijo pact was named after the house in which it was signed in 1958, in which three of the four major political parties (the Communist Party was excluded) promised to share power after elections following a civic-military coup against the Pérez Jiménez dictatorship in early 1959. Thus was born a new democratic system popularly called the Punto Fijo regime, based on a new constitution in 1961. Although the power-sharing arrangement in the form of shared cabinet posts did not last beyond the 1960s, the representative democracy guided by a two-party dominant political party system of Acción Democrática (AD) and Partido Social Cristiano de Venezuel (COPEI) survived until the political and economic turmoil of the 1990s.

5. Venezuela's income inequality, as measured by the GINI index where 0 is equality and 1 is inequality, worsened between 1990 and 1999, from a score of .47 to .50. See ECLAC (2007a).

6. For discussion of the conflictive nature of attempts to draw a new democratic bargain in twenty-first-century Latin America, and the outlines of what such a bargain might look like, see McCoy (2006) and McCoy (2008a).

7. In their forthcoming volume, McCoy and Díaz provide an extensive analysis of the Venezuelan political conflict and the role of international actors in mediating the conflict. We can compare the Venezuelan experience of conflict and change with that of Bolivia and Ecuador during their more recent constitutional refoundings. In the case of Bolivia, both the structural constraints on the government and the formation of Evo Morales produced a style of greater negotiations and compromise, even though it was still quite conflictual. Like Chávez in his first year, Morales did not control a majority in the Senate, nor did he control the hydrocarbon revenues (produced in the "media luna" states in the eastern half of the country and dominated by the traditionally powerful social sectors). Unlike Chávez, however, Morales did not win a two-thirds majority in the constituent assembly, and his syndical background led him to use more of a negotiation style than continual confrontation. So even though he attempted and won greater central government control over hydrocarbon revenues, he did so in the context of making significant concessions to his opponents and never attempting to close congress. In Ecuador, President Correa came from a university background and was backed by the middle class, who were fed up with traditional elites and corrupt power structures. He was thus able to dominate his constituent assembly, close congress, and shape the outcome of the constitution in a manner similar to Chávez. Yet Ecuador has not seen the level of conflict and polarization that Venezuela did.

8. These included the Law of Social Responsibility in Radio and Television, reforms to the Penal Code, and the Land Law.

9. The Bolivarian Circles were early neighborhood organizations organized in political support of the president (see Hawkins and Hansen 2006); the Election Battle Units were organized at the neighborhood to mobilize turnout in the 2004 recall referendum; Water Committees were another attempt to provide for citizen participation in decisionmaking (see López Maya 2008); the Community Councils were organized in 2006 to receive government funding from the executive office for local infrastructure and economic projects.

10. See special edition of *Revista Economía y Ciencias Sociales*, no. 1 (2008), articles by Maria-Pilar Garcia, Margarita López Maya, and Dorothea Melcher.

11. Although Rodriguez would not agree, I have drawn this conclusion based on figures provided by Rodriguez and Weisbrot.

12. The Venezuelan programs use a mixture of cash transfers, general subsidies, block grants to neighborhoods, and technical assistance to individuals and groups, in addition to providing services in health, education, and vocational training.

13. In addition to the debate between Rodriguez and Weisbrot, see recent studies by D'Elia and Cabezas (2008), Patruyo (2008), and Penfold-Becerra (2005).

14. Latinobarómetro, cited in *The Economist*, "A Warning for Reformers," 15 November 2007, www.economist.com/world/la/displaystory.cfm?story_id=10136464 (accessed 1 April 2008).

15. *Latinobarómetro Report 2005* reports that the three primary meanings of democracy for Latin Americans are liberty, elections, and an economic system that provides a dignified income, though the relative weight of each of these factors varies by country. For example, in Brazil, a dignified income ranks the highest, while in Venezuela liberty ranks the highest, followed by elections. www.latinobarometro.org.

16. This is the popular term given to the new Bolivarian economic elite emerging under the Chávez administration.

6

Bolivia's MAS:
Between Party and Movement

Santiago Anria

In the national elections of December 2005, Evo Morales Ayma obtained an un-precedented 53.7 percent of the popular vote.[1] It was the first time in Bolivian history that an Aymara peasant was elected president of the country, and the first time in Bolivian democratic history that a candidate reached the presidency without going through a congressional runoff.[2] Compared to other left-of-center figures who in recent years have been elected to office in Latin America, Morales and his Movement Toward Socialism (Movimiento al Socialismo, or MAS) gained government by successfully articulating the heterogeneous demands of groups disenfranchised by neoliberalism into a powerful electoral coalition, which among others included coca-producing indigenous peasants, laid-off miners and other sectors of organized labor, peasant groups with land claims, and indigenous movements with indigenous rights and cultural claims. The peculiarity of the Bolivian case is that this coalition building occurred amid a spiral of mass protests and widespread crisis of representation, in which the social movements, under the MAS banner, managed to move beyond mass demonstrations and enter into the electoral democratic terrain.

Only ten years after its emergence, MAS has spread to the cities and become the country's dominant political force. Although Morales has concentrated a great deal of power in his hands and has often bypassed institutional channels to accomplish his goals, for which he is frequently labeled a "populist" and equated to Hugo Chávez or Rafael Correa, his command of MAS is rooted in years of peasant grassroots mobilization. This, in effect, constitutes an antithesis of populism in its various conceptions (Roberts 2007a, 2007b). For authors like Levitsky and Roberts, moreover, what makes Morales different from many other leftist leaders is that his political leadership is spawned by, and remains accountable to, autonomous popular movements organized from below (Levitsky and Roberts, forthcoming). According to these authors, mobilization from below does, in fact, impose real constraints on Morales's leadership. However, there is still little work showing how these accountability mechanisms function on the ground. This chapter shows that political accountability structures operate in multiple dimensions, both inside and outside MAS, and that MAS is neither exclusively bottom-up nor solely top-down, but a complex combination of both schema. The chapter also shows that as a hybrid post-liberal organization (see Arditi in this volume), MAS has different organizational logics and linkage patterns with rural *and* urban constituents. How are these articulated? How does this inform our understanding of the Bolivian experiments with post-liberal politics? And, ultimately, what does it tell us about the broader Latin American left turns?

The goal of this chapter is to provide a detailed description of the inner workings of the Bolivian MAS. By dissecting its organizational features and analyzing its practices in two major cities, La Paz and El Alto, it analyzes the degree to which MAS is constituted by newer, more egalitarian and participatory forms of leader-mass linkages or, conversely, whether it is illustrative of the same illiberal populism that has characterized older national-populist parties in Bolivia and elsewhere in the region. Although MAS has adopted illiberal practices from older national-populist parties like, say, the Nationalist Revolutionary Movement (Movimiento Nacionalista Revolucionario, or MNR) and Conscience of the Fatherland (Conciencia de la Patria, or CONDEPA), I suggest that what is unique to its experience is its rural roots in the coca-growing Chapare region, where it works under bottom-up and more decentralized and egalitarian schemes of participation. Its illiberal features are most prominent in urban settings, where MAS replicates top-down patron-client logics of participation. My larger aim is to properly situate MAS in comparative politics and determine how much its experience is distinctively Bolivian and, conversely, how much it pertains to broader phenomena in the region.

MAS was born of social movements in the rural areas of the Chapare region. Today, however, to deem it uncritically as a peasant party is to ignore its organizational flexibility and the broader coalition of interests that it represents, as it has successfully expanded itself to Bolivia's largest cities and surged to the forefront of national politics. MAS has articulated itself by building a powerful electoral coalition amid a "great protests cycle" (Ibarra Güell 2003), which was initiated as a popular resistance to neoliberalism and intensified during the Bolivian resource wars. In alluding to these, I refer to the Water War in April 2000, which started as a collective rejection of increases in the water tariff in Cochabamba and entailed a struggle between its residents and the US company Bechtel over the privatization of water. I also refer to the Gas War of October 2003 in the highlands of El Alto, which sparked as a collective reaction against President Sánchez de Lozada's intention to export natural gas to the United States through Chilean ports. Protests faced state repression, leaving dozens dead and forcing the resignation of the president. The high levels of agitation that characterized this period culminated with Morales's rise to power, with social movements playing leading roles in the country's liberal democratic institutions, and with an opportunity for deepening democracy. MAS's rise to power has signified the possibility for popular-based movements to "move beyond the framework of liberal participation" (Arditi, Chapter 8 in this volume). In other words, resistance to neoliberalism and a crisis of representation provided popular organizations with the opportunity to innovate in matters of political representation and participation. Social movements in Bolivia have done so through the creation of a "political instrument," MAS, a hybrid organization through which they have embraced post-liberal politics by participating in representative institutions without abandoning nonelectoral street politics.

When Morales assumed office in 2006, he called for a "sociocultural" and "democratic" revolution while announcing that he would rule by obeying the people (Movimiento al Socialismo 2006:43). Once in power, he addressed the demands set forth during the above mass mobilizations; thus he declared nationalization of natural gas and oil resources, proclaimed an agrarian reform, and called for a constituent assembly through which popularly elected delegates would seek to refound the republic along deeper egalitarian grounds (Cameron and Sharpe, Chapter 4 in this volume). Those long-held demands were fulfilled by centralizing power in the presidency, bypassing institutional channels, and often disrespecting checks and balances, reasons for which Morales has received harsh criticisms (Toranzo Roca 2008; Molina 2007). Notwithstanding such criticisms, one could argue that the above policies are examples of Morales's positive accountability to his social base: he did what he had promised to the people.

This chapter is divided into four parts. The first part lays out the conceptual groundwork for this chapter. The second part provides a brief background on contemporary Bolivian politics and discusses the origins and contemporary structure of the MAS organization, as well as Morales's government. I briefly explore MAS's emergence in rural areas of Bolivia, arguing that this "genetic coding" (Panebianco 1988) has indelibly shaped its organizational features even as it became a ruling force. Drawing on fieldwork conducted in La Paz and El Alto, the third part of this chapter explores how MAS operates in these cities, which are bastions of its electoral support. The chapter concludes by discussing how the Bolivian case can be situated in the broader context of Latin America's "left turns."

Conceptualizing MAS

Before turning to an account of the birth and operations of MAS, it is necessary to clarify some conceptual issues. How can we define MAS? If a political party, for instance, is "any group that presents at elections, and is capable of placing through elections, candidates to higher office" (Sartori 1976:64), then MAS is a political party. However, due to the conditions of its emergence as a coca-eradication resistance movement and its peculiar rise to state power amid a cycle of mass protests, it has become clear that MAS transcends the minimalist definition of a political party, although it has adapted itself to that institutional form in order to participate in liberal democratic institutions of representation. Conversely, it cannot be defined simply as a social movement because, through its participation in these institutions, it goes beyond that notion.

MAS's leaders define the organization as a "political instrument" of the peasant indigenous movements, rather than a conventional political party. They categorically associate parties with institutions that divide rather than unite popular forces—organizations that, it should be noted, excluded a broad segment of society from political participation and that underwent a legitimacy crisis in the early 2000s. The instrument is, following their view, a political extension of a group of social organizations that triggered its creation as a tactical move whereby participation in the electoral process could contribute to complete self-representation in the existing liberal democratic institutions. This idea, which implies a sort of continuity between the social movement and the electoral institution, was advanced by Álvaro García Linera (Linera, León, and Monje 2004:448–455).[3] While appealing, this notion is imprecise. On the one hand, it is true that the lines that separate the party and the founding organizations are diffuse (Núñez 2008). On the other hand, MAS is more than an electoral appendage of the peasant organizations in the Chapare, and it is more than the political extension of a social movement, as it now represents not only those who founded the instrument but a broader coalition of forces.

For J. Komadina and C. Geffroy (2007), MAS is a "political movement" because it "operates between the boundaries of civil society and the political arena in a double direction: it codifies and projects both the mobilizations and the representations of diverse social organizations toward the institutionalized political arena. It does so by participating in electoral processes, even while it aspires to transform the rules of the political game" (Komadina and Geffroy 2007:20). As a ruling force, it has sought to transform those rules by means of constitution making (Cameron and Sharpe, Chapter 4 in this volume). The novelty of MAS is that it has one foot in the political-institutional context of a democratic regime and the other in the social sphere. It is a hybrid organization that combines two forms of political action and organization—participation in liberal electoral institutions and nonelectoral contentious bargaining—and, in doing so, it permeates the boundaries of the two spheres.

In a recent contribution by Bolivian journalist Fernando Molina (2007; see also Molina 2006), we find a systematic critique of MAS from a liberal perspective that is relevant for the present study. According to this author, MAS has adopted the liberal logic of representation and competition, but has done so only to gain state power, that is, without honest faith in democratic institutions and procedures. Molina sees this as detrimental to Bolivia's representative democracy, as MAS, he claims, uses liberal electoral politics instrumentally, as a means and not as an end in itself. Following this argument, MAS's ultimate goal is simply the pursuit of power for the radical transformation of society as it sees fit, be it with or without respect to the rule of law. However, this author fails to acknowledge that since its origins MAS has, in fact, embraced liberalism and has sought to correct the limitations of the previous restricted democracy by promoting novel forms of popular participation and inclusion of those previously excluded from political participation—groups that, empowered by the decentralization reforms of the 1990s, organized MAS and sought to change the given through combining their participation in liberal democratic institutions and nonelectoral politics. According to N. Postero (forthcoming), moreover, MAS can be seen as "profoundly liberal," as it uses "liberal institutions to enact a substantive new state model that can more effectively engage its citizens and provide for their welfare." By promoting broader participation and inclusion through liberal democratic institutions (through lawmaking in the congress, by appealing to the public in direct referenda, and by calling a constituent assembly with broad popular participation), MAS seeks to transform liberalism "to make it more democratic and more relevant to Bolivia's indigenous populations" (Postero, forthcoming). The Bolivian left, as represented by MAS, is more post-liberal than antiliberal.

Background and a Brief Evolution of MAS

More than a product of political engineering, MAS is the result of Bolivia's singular historical trajectory and how this course has affected the configuration of social forces as well as the incorporation of new actors into the larger political order. The formation of MAS and its rise to power have been influenced by the implementation and crisis of neoliberalism, which created losers that would then resist the hegemonic aspirations of this model; resistance to coca eradication and state violence, which acted as a unifying force in the emergence of powerful resistance movements; a permissive institutional context that facilitated the incorporation of new actors into the political system through direct popular participation; and the crisis of the state and representational institutions that became evident during Bolivia's commodity wars. Because the evolution of MAS is inseparable from recent developments in contemporary Bolivian politics, this section addresses these two things jointly.

Bolivia adopted a draconian neoliberal program during the mid-1980s, whose consequences are critical to understanding MAS's rise. Neoliberal reforms paved the way for the closure of most state-owned and -operated tin mines, mining being the economic activity that had long dominated politics and society of the country. The closure of mines, in turn, coincided with a rapid increase of the coca and cocaine economy; as prices of drugs rose, thousands of miners and peasants were forced to relocate (Gill 2000). Some of these miners found a new home in the *cocales* (coca fields) of the Chapare and many found jobs in the profitable coca economy. Relocated workers, in particular miners, took with them their strong class consciousness and history of militant struggle and solidarity; as many had been involved with leftist and national-populist parties, they brought along considerable "militant capital" to the *cocales*. These workers influenced the coca growers' discourse by introducing elements of nationalism and Marxism that they had learned at the mines (Michel 2008). As a paradox of "relocalization," the move of miners to coca production contributed to the emergence of a powerful movement that opposed neoliberalism and the US-sponsored "War on Drugs." This movement formed a political instrument, advanced gradually through elections, and now controls the state.

Although political mobilization from peasant and indigenous communities was intense since Bolivia's return to democracy in 1982, it was with Law 1008 that such groups were able to unify their demands and gain strength. This law, which was promulgated under US pressure in 1988 as an effort to fight the cocaine economy, provided the legal framework for the eradication of coca crops. Its promulgation was followed by intense state repression and the Chapare region quickly became an unregulated territory, as this period was characterized by heated clashes between coca growers and the military. The political consequences of Law 1008 were, at the time of its promulgation, difficult to foresee; however, in retrospect, state repression worked as a catalyst for the coca-growers' movement that prompted its participation in the formal political system by constituting a relatively united political front with other peasant and indigenous organizations. MAS's core social bases and constituency are the *cocaleros* in the Chapare, which, in addition to other peasant organizations, today claim ownership over the political instrument.

The first electoral victories came in the mid-1990s, after Bolivia embarked on a decentralization process. The reforms included the 1994 Popular Participation Law and the 1995 Law of Administrative Decentralization, which, taken together, involved the creation of more than three hundred municipalities throughout the country and instituted unprecedented direct municipal elections. They unleashed a process of "ruralization of politics" (Zuazo 2008), as the reforms recognized peasant and indigenous communities as agents of participation at the municipal decisionmaking level and extended new citizenship rights to indigenous peoples (Postero 2007). In other words, the reforms opened channels of participation. Peasant and indigenous organizations, such as the coca growers of the Chapare, formed their political and electoral organizations and began participating in municipal elections, advancing gradually from the municipal level to the national one, yet combining this participation with nonelectoral politics. Unanticipated by neoliberal reformers, the losers of neoliberalism formed MAS and, taking advantage of the new opportunities to participate in local politics, sought to gain power in order to counter the thrust of neoliberalism (Van Cott 2005).

Having established an anchor in the Chapare, the challenge became winning majorities at the national level. This process would be facilitated by the cycle of protests initiated in the early 2000s. The spiral of social agitation started in Cochabamba during April 2000, when urban and rural social movements, as well as independent residents and middle classes, initiated mobilizations against the privatization of the water utility in what came to be known as the Water War. Local mobilizations in Cochabamba, as well as others in the highlands of La Paz and El Alto in September, strengthened the social movements and spawned an ideational shift against the hegemonic aspirations of neoliberalism, which had effects countrywide. While the escalation of social unrest reflected an acute crisis of the state and displayed the limits of neoliberal governance, it also provided a strong blow to traditional political parties as dominant representational institutions. The crisis facilitated the incorporation of new political formations into the larger political order.

MAS used this cycle to its advantage, and it moved strategically. In expanding from local to national levels (and from rural to urban) its leadership pursued a "supraclass strategy" of electoral recruitment (Przeworski and Sprague 1986). As a part of its repertoire, MAS opted for a simple vote-maximizing strategy that consisted of incorporating public intellectuals into its structure and turning for support to urban middle sectors. Appealing to the urban middle classes while participating actively in protest activities proved beneficial from the electoral point of view. And MAS saw an impressive electoral performance in the 2002 general election. In the end, however, MAS did not become government in 2002 as the conservative former President Gonzalo Sánchez de Lozada was able to craft a coalition that allowed him to return to the presidency. Despite this outcome, MAS emerged as the principal force "fighting neoliberalism both in the halls of Congress and on the streets" (Hylton and Thomson 2007:171).[4]

Reaching into the middle sectors to generate votes, however, involved a set of tradeoffs for the peasant organizations, as the recruitment of allies generated ideological and organizational transformations to the political instrument that, in turn, elicited derision from its core constituency. One example of such tradeoffs was related to the masista parliamentary brigade, which had "functions, positions, hierarchies, legislative imperatives" as well as "broad autonomy vis-à-vis the union structure" (Linera, León, and Monje 2004:433). MAS had managed to place twenty-seven deputies in the lower chamber in

2002 and thus accumulate some degree of institutional capital. While some of these deputies were representatives from the Chapare and had been selected by the bases through mechanisms of horizontal democracy (and thus became largely accountable to these bases), others were directly invited by the leadership, had no history of militancy in MAS, and had little checks from below. Unlike peasant representatives, however, many of the invited leaders had had parliamentary experience; thus they quickly became the voice of MAS, as they related to the media very effectively and knew how to play the institutional game. For Komadina and Geffroy (2007:99), the emergence of this parliamentary brigade brought forth an "*oligarchization* of the party leadership, which subsequently takes decisions different than the popular mandates, usually culminating in a sort of confiscation of the representation" (emphasis added). I will come back to this notion below.

The cycle of protests reached a peak in October 2003 with the Gas War that forced the resignation of President Sánchez de Lozada; it reached another peak in May–June 2005, leading this time to the resignation of President Carlos Mesa Gisbert and the call for early elections. Combining contentious bargaining with an electoral strategy proved to be beneficial for MAS. Due to Morales's participation in protest activities and his ability to articulate a broad cross-class coalition against the political establishment and neoliberalism, his popularity gradually increased until he finally won the presidency. Shortly after he assumed office, moreover, MAS conquered a majority of the electorate in the elections for the constituent assembly, whose mission was to write the country's new constitution. Because MAS gained barely above 50 percent of the seats for the assembly, it did not have the supermajority necessary to change the constitution without the support of opposition forces—forces that, in turn, were intransigent and not willing to compromise (Cameron and Sharpe, Chapter 4 in this volume). This, it should be noted, was a highly contested process and it reflected the regional dispute between the west and the east: MAS's agenda ignited opposition from the prefects in the affluent, predominantly white and mestizo, eastern departments dubbed the *media luna* (Santa Cruz, Beni, Tarija, and Pando), as they saw their interests threatened by the indigenous-led government and the new constitution. Because these departments have the largest gas reserves and the most fertile lands in the country, local business and landed elites quickly reacted against Morales by articulating an active right-wing countermovement that has henceforth opposed the constitution, demanded regional autonomy, and voiced its opposition to the central authority in La Paz (Eaton 2007).

In the end, the outcome of the constituent assembly was a text approved by progovernment delegates only. The text, in turn, needed to be submitted to the verdict of the people, which required that the congress sanction a law specifying the schedule and other details for the constitutional referendum. As MAS controlled the lower chamber but not the senate, this bill was blocked in congress until the events that followed the recall referendum of August 2008 shook the political arena. While Morales and MAS emerged victorious in this referendum, opposition prefects were overwhelmingly ratified in the media luna. These prefects did not wait to intensify their demands for autonomy and claimed its incorporation into the new constitution. In September 2008, groups demanding autonomy clashed with MAS supporters in the northern department of the Pando, leaving several *masistas* brutally massacred. Seeking to find a solution to the crisis, the government and regional autonomy leaders engaged in deliberations in congress, where the text of the constitutional draft was negotiated and modified, this time with inputs of opposition forces and with compromise from both sides. The text then became law with the constitutional referendum of January 2009, and it "appears to reflect a genuine attempt to combine indigenous with liberal and republican concepts of self-government" (Cameron and Sharpe, Chapter 4 in this volume). A year after its ratification, however, it remains to be seen how the constitution will be implemented.

Accountability Under the Government of Evo Morales

Becoming a ruling force altered the internal dynamics of MAS. This occurred as the notion of a "government of the social movements" became a real possibility. The process of becoming a ruling force involved the articulation of alliances with a wide array of social organizations; and this, in turn, involved the negotiation of spaces of power for these organizations, as many exchanged loyalty for spaces within the public administration. As a result, today, members of the organizations that spawned MAS perceive, not without reason, that a clique of new members has taken prominent roles within the government and the political instrument. For Román Loayza, who was one of the founding members of MAS and is now a dissident, "we [indigenous peasants] saw that leaders of social organizations that did not struggle like we did soon became spokespersons of MAS and they tried to utilize MAS for their own interests. We were upset as we watched this happening" (Loayza 2008).

It is here where the iron law of oligarchy (Michels 1962) clashes with the principle of "ruling by obeying." For Freya Schiwy (2008), "governing by obeying means that if the organizations and social movements that brought Morales to power find him failing to pursue their decisions, they are likely to force the president to step down." This, it should be noted, is just a part of the story, as one could add another equally important component: the embrace of this practice also implies an active participation of the social bases in the formulation and the correction of policies of redistribution. Where Morales has experimented with new participatory channels that deepen the liberal framework of participation, such as the recall and the constitutional referendums, and thus proved his commitment to the first component, the second component seems to be just one of the many discursive tools set forth as MAS qualitatively shifted from being a social movement to being the government. It is based on the necessity to maintain bonds between MAS and the groups that facilitated its rise to power, and on the need to demonstrate that this government seeks to correct the failures of previous "pacted" democracies. But as will be shown, this works more on a rhetorical level than in practice.

The challenges facing MAS can be illuminated by the recent work of George Lakoff (2008) on how progressive and conservative political actors make sense of accountability. For progressives, "it means accountability to the public on the part of those in charge" (2008:185); thus, progressives think of accountability as something that constrains their power and authority. For conservatives, in turn, accountability is seen as a constraint, imposed by authority, on those who are in subordinate positions. This distinction is akin to Guillermo O'Donnell's (1994) suggestion that accountability has two basic dimensions: (1) horizontal and (2) vertical. The first dimension relates to the operations of the system of checks and balances among different branches of government and speaks to the workings of the separation of powers. The second dimension, in turn, focuses on elections and is based on the premise that the populace can oversee and sanction elected officials through the exercise of the suffrage. Building on O'Donnell's typology, C. Smulovitz and E. Peruzzotti added another dimension, (3) societal accountability, which is a "nonelectoral, yet vertical mechanism of control that rests on the actions of a multiple array of citizens' associations and movements and on the media, actions that aim at . . . activating the operation of horizontal agencies" (Smulovitz and Peruzzotti 2000:150). Taking this scheme even further, one could add dimensions of accountability that operate *within* organizations; thus it is possible to identify two additional types of accountability that are inherently hierarchical. The first type could be labeled (4) "vertical top-down," whereby those in charge control underlings and hold them accountable to the internal norms of the organization (or, at times, to his or her will). The second additional type, in turn, could be labeled (5) "vertical bottom-up," whereby members of an organization hold those in charge accountable. While the remainder of this section briefly addresses 1, 2, and 3, the rest of this chapter examines 4 and 5 at some length.

As noted above, Morales has centralized power in the executive and wields that power through his frequent use of direct public referenda. This, by the same token, highlights Morales's commitment to mechanisms of direct democracy, mechanisms that seek to deepen the liberal format of politics. Regarding vertical accountability, Bolivian voters have supported MAS in the elections for the constituent assembly of 2006, in the recall referendum held in August 2008,[5] and in the referendum for the approval of the new political constitution that took place in January 2009. With regard to horizontal accountability structures, on the other hand, recent studies have shown that there has been a weakening of congress with regard to its role as an agent of control of the executive, which, it should be noted, is nothing new in Bolivian democracy and is today aggravated by the crisis of the party system and the lack of consolidated opposition parties. As for the mechanisms of societal accountability, organizations related to MAS have utilized contentious protest repertoires to activate horizontal agencies; for instance, they have often mobilized against opposition forces in congress, have surrounded the legislature, and have blocked the entrance of opposition members during critical moments, including during the negotiations that resulted in the draft of the new constitution. This, in turn, highlights one of the key peculiarities of MAS as it experiments with post-liberal politics: as a ruling force, it operates with one foot in the liberal democratic institutions and another in the noninstitutional nonelectoral terrain.

Accountability from Within:
MAS as an Informal Organization

"We don't have a structure," party leaders often repeat. However, MAS does indeed have one, or even two (Komadina and Geffroy 2007). A close examination of how these structures operate will shed light on how some of the accountability mechanisms work within the organization. As will be seen, Morales has centralized power within MAS, even though, at times, his authority has limits.

There have been some fruitful attempts at explaining how MAS operates internally. A study by Moira Zuazo (2008) shows that, in rural areas, there are horizontal decisionmaking mechanisms for the selection of authorities to run for congress. These mechanisms vary for each organization and each region, are not codified in a single written norm, and are rooted in indigenous customs and traditions. As noted by Arditi (Chapter 8 in this volume) post-liberalism welcomes the interactions between uses and customs on the one hand and liberal democratic institutions on the other. The most important decisions regarding the selection of national-level authorities usually happen in national congresses, which are typically "largely crowded meetings where the multitude, composed of a great number of social organizations, decides [who is going to run] by public acclaim" (Peredo 2008). According to Ramiro Llanos, however, "this is a partial truth" as, in the end, "the selection of candidates ultimately depends on Morales's approval or, at a minimum, is conditioned by Morales" (Llanos 2008). As a result, whereas there are many representatives in the congress who were selected directly by their social bases, others, the so-called invited, have become authorities "without the support of any social or popular organization" (Peredo 2008).[6] While the former are subject to pressures from their social bases, to which they are largely accountable, the latter enjoy a greater degree of autonomy and are not accountable to organized groups but to Morales.

Despite the decentralization in the selection of candidates, the locus of authority in MAS is currently Evo Morales. Formal leadership bodies such as the *direcciones* were created and formalized in the statutes as an attempt to extend the territorial reach of MAS. But even though those bodies do exist on paper, they lack independent authority vis-à-vis Morales. This perception is shared by José Antonio Quiroga, who states "for Evo it is hard to delegate, to share the power . . . he is very perceptive about what social leaders tell him. He is in constant contact with his bases and he does listen to them. But there is not an organic linkage between that and his decision. It is true that he listens, but that he rules by obeying is far from reality" (Quiroga 2008).[7] In the absence of effective formal channels of accountability, Morales remains the ultimate decisionmaker within the organization.

MAS maintains close linkages with various social organizations that brought it to power. Since its origins in the Chapare, its strongest and closest bonds have been to coca growers and these linkages have been formalized in its statutes. However, as MAS grew and expanded to urban areas and to the national level, it established alliances with preexisting urban organizations, linkages that have not been formalized. In their accords, urban social organizations have guaranteed for themselves a degree of participation in the government structure, be it as a representative at the congress or in the executive. Such is the case of Jorge Silva, a representative for urban artisan organizations, who claims that "this lets us [artisans] propose laws that facilitate and give more opportunities to the sector" (Silva 2008). These alliances, however, do not involve an organic participation in MAS's structure and this stands as a source of tension between organizations, which compete to control spaces of power, and also between organizations and MAS, which has not yet been able to incorporate the demands of these groups into its program. It remains to be seen what mechanisms MAS can implement to solve differences within as well as to formalize the channels of participation.

Insofar as such mechanisms are absent, Morales "is a referee and no one challenges his decisions" (Silva 2008). However, Morales is not the owner of the political instrument and he does not have absolute control over it. According to Román Loayza (2008), this is related to the features that shape a "political instrument," features that contrast with conventional understandings of political parties. In his words, "that MAS is a 'political instrument' means that social organizations appropriate MAS for themselves; there is no big boss, but a leader and that leader is now Evo Morales. . . . His bosses are the social organizations." This testimony exemplifies the belief in the mechanisms of bottom-up accountability within the organization. Interestingly, however, Loayza has recently renounced MAS, claiming that these structures have been coopted by Morales and his "neoliberal" surroundings, which, in his view, now control MAS. Loayza was accused of betrayal and expelled from MAS in April 2009 (*La Razón*, 30 April 2009b).

Although Morales has concentrated power in his hands, that is not to say he can do as he pleases, as there are accountability structures that are shaped by the nature of MAS's internal organization. It is precisely its informal features and the absence of a bureaucratic structure that leave maneuvering room for the social organizations that shape MAS. This heterogeneous network, at the same time, remains vastly decentralized, as each organization has its own internal structure and individual features. In many cases, popular organizations are not integrated into the statutes and they are autonomous from MAS, mobilizing both for *and* against the government and placing limits on Morales's leadership. In other words, while the lack of formal and democratic channels for participation allows Morales to occupy the central role in MAS, his leadership may be challenged by what occurs at the level of the social movements (Do Alto 2007). For example, events in Huanuni during October 2006 demonstrated how this may work. During that month, cooperativist and wage-earner miners clashed in Huanuni over the control of mining activities in the Posokoni hill.[8] The conflict left sixteen dead and more than sixty-eight wounded (*El Deber*, 7 October 2006a and 2006b), and led to the expulsion of Walter Villarroel, a leader of the National Federation of Mining Cooperatives, from the ministry of mining (*El Deber*, 7 October 2006b). On this occasion, the presence of cooperativist miners in the government structure did not impede this sector from expressing an autonomous position against government policies and from spurring on social conflict (see Zegada, Tórrez, and Cámara 2008). Although the strike was crushed by the government and did not force policy change, it demonstrated that Morales cannot fully control popular organizations from above.

Another example relates to the crisis of Cochabamba in January 2007, when groups related to MAS violently asked for the resignation of Manfres Reyes Villa, who was then the democratically elected prefect of Cochabamba. According to Do Alto (2007), although these organizations were close to MAS, they ignored Morales's desires to deactivate the protest and mobilized autonomously. This last example also illustrates how MAS embraces post-liberal politics, by doing politics with one foot in the institutional terrain and the other in the streets. The absence of formal channels of participation within MAS leaves maneuvering room for the social organizations that comprise it; when these mobilize with autonomy vis-à-vis the government, they can hold Morales accountable and place boundaries on his authority.

MAS in the Cities of La Paz and El Alto

Judging from its origins in the Chapare, some still insist that MAS is a peasant organization. The success of MAS, however, is due only in part to peasant mobilization. It is also "owed to members of the urban and informal economy, to popular, working-class, and middle-class rejection of the neoliberal governance in Bolivia that made their lives more difficult" (Albro 2007:314). Although MAS's strongest social bases are the coca growers in the Chapare, it can no longer be considered a peasant organization. To treat it as such is to overlook its organizational flexibility and the broader coalition of interests that it currently represents, as it has expanded itself to urban areas and became a ruling force.

The conurbation of La Paz and El Alto consists of an area with more than 1.5 million people. La Paz is Bolivia's principal city and its administrative and political capital and, together with El Alto, it comprises the biggest urban area of Bolivia, making both cities decisive players in national politics (Arbona and Kohl 2004; Albó 2006). These cities are often seen as critical to winning national elections and to ensure governability. Although MAS has broadened its constituency to urban sectors and won the hearts of Paceños (residents of La Paz) and Alteños (residents of El Alto), this process has not been accompanied by the consolidation of a structure that incorporates the interests of these urban populations. Fearing that one day MAS can lose the hearts of these sectors, party authorities believe it is imperative to "start building organically" (Torrico 2008).

MAS's experience in the cities of La Paz and El Alto is relatively recent and was influenced by a series of factors that facilitated its entrance into them. In the first place, this relates to the protest activities that took place in September–October 2000 in the department of La Paz. In September 2000, the conflicts that initiated in Cochabamba with the Water War spread to the highlands of La Paz as Aymara peasant leader and then leader of the Unique Confederation of Rural Laborers of Bolivia (Confederación Sindical Unica de Trabajadores Campesinos de Bolivia, or CSUTCB), Mallku Felipe Quispe,[9] led a series of indigenous social mobilizations and road blockades against the Bánzer government. The crowds of people demanded that the government fulfill a series of agreements it had celebrated with peasant workers (Espósito and Arteaga 2006). Although Quispe later formed his own party, the Pachakuti Indigenous Movement (Movimiento Indígena Pachakuti, or MIP), and rejected being associated with MAS (Van Cott 2005), his mobilizations acted as a blow to traditional political parties in the country. In a context of disenchantment with neoliberal governability and rejection of parties associated with corruption and ineffectiveness, Paceños and Alteños would then welcome MAS as a viable alternative.

In the second place, it is only possible to understand the urbanization of MAS in the context of a partisan dealignment, as its consolidation in La Paz, for instance, was only possible once CONDEPA started to lose influence in cities. Founded by Carlos Palenque in 1988, CONDEPA had emerged at the end of the 1980s to represent popular sectors that were "affected by adjustment policies and unrepresented by the established parties" (Mayorga 2006:154). This party was built around the charismatic leadership of Palenque, and its political practices combined the extensive use of clientelism, paternalism, plebiscitary appeals to the masses, unmediated relationships to constituents, and a strong antisystemic discourse (Revilla Herrero 2006; Alenda 2003). In part because CONDEPA failed to consolidate party structure and to forge organic linkages with its constituency, once the charismatic leader died in 1997 the party practically died along with its founder.[10] This party's loss of political power, however, "opened the doors of La Paz so that MAS could incorporate itself into the city" (Michel 2008). MAS entered the city and occupied vacated spaces that were created by the retreat of CONDEPA. And along with CONDEPA's evanescence, there was a transfer of their political practices to MAS. This occurred as ex-CONDEPA operators and leaders quickly became *masistas*.

MAS emerged as Bolivia's leading electoral force in the municipal elections of 2004, which consolidated the voting trend initiated in 2002. The 2004 elections were deeply affected by the first Gas War and its aftermath. While it would be inaccurate to say that Morales and MAS were the chief instigators of these contentious episodes (Lazar 2006), it quickly became clear that after the popular uprisings of October 2003 MAS came out as *the* political force able to incorporate popular discontent into a coherent political project. Although it won almost every municipality in the country, it could not win the municipal governments of La Paz and El Alto.

Evo Morales and MAS participated actively in the rebellions of May–June 2005, which forced the resignation of Carlos Mesa. However, the blockades and other pressure mechanisms were not well regarded by urban middle sectors, particularly in the city of La Paz, and Morales and MAS suffered a clear decline in popularity during these events, particularly in urban areas; however, they were still *the* referential force for the rest of left-wing forces. Recognizing this, after Mesa's June 6 resignation, some urban forces attempted to configure a broad front as a mechanism to incorporate a coalition of progressive forces into MAS in order to develop a comprehensive long-term program of government and as a collective effort to democratize MAS. The attempts to configure a strategic broad front failed, as MAS insisted on the "zero alliances" formula (Quiroga 2008). But perhaps as a sign of political opportunism, some of these forces—particularly the Movement without Fear (Movimiento Sin Miedo, or MSM)—decided to reach an accommodation with MAS and negotiated informal alliances that guaranteed spaces of power for their own candidates. Hours before the presentation of lists to the National Electoral Court (Corte Nacional Electoral, or CNE), the MSM placed some of its candidates on MAS's lists. These two parties never formalized their accord before the CNE and their linkages remain loosely structured. As some of the MSM candidates performed fairly well in the elections, this situation generated discontent in the *masista* urban bases.

The Importance of Territorial Representation

MAS was initially resisted by residents of La Paz and El Alto. But as the crisis of representation became more evident, demands for participation increased in an inverse relationship to the crisis. When MAS pushed the rural base into these cities, it sought to articulate a local organization throughout the territory, and it rapidly managed to do so. In La Paz, this process was facilitated by the retreat of CONDEPA, which had left militants and leaders *a la deriva* (adrift). But on the other hand, it was complicated by the presence of the MSM, which, since the late 1990s, has been the dominant force in the city. This pushed MAS leaders to negotiate a strategic alliance with MSM, which, according to Román Loayza, was detrimental to MAS as it forced it to adopt MSM political practices and to include its militants in the public administration (Loayza 2008).

The articulation of MAS in El Alto was even more complicated, as a series of clientelist parties had long dominated that city's political life, and because this city was particularly shaken by the events of 2003—events that revealed a profound crisis of representation and that opened structures for the entrance of new parties. Before October 2003, leaders such as Bertha Blanco[11] and Cristina Martínez[12] sought to build a territorial structure in the city in the late 1990s and managed to gain some votes in the municipal elections of 1999. But during those days such efforts were timid, as "Alteños did not like MAS. Further, El Alto neither was important to Evo nor to anybody, as it was [dominated by] CONDEPA" (Blanco 2008). Led by a populist leader, CONDEPA's structure in El Alto was built around the exchange of concrete benefits for the loyalty of its members. In 1999, after what some consider the "lost decade" of CONDEPA's rule (Revilla Herrero 2006; Alenda 2003), the Revolutionary Left Movement (Movimiento de la Izquierda Revolucionaria, or MIR) returned to power with José Luis Paredes as the highest municipal authority. This party entered into a terminal crisis during the October events, and Paredes resigned while forming his own civic association, with which he won the municipal elections of 2004. Although by this time MAS had already built a precarious structure in the city, it managed to win only two *concejalías*.

MAS was not an organic product of these cities, but was inserted as something foreign. As such, it has faced obstacles as it has sought to organize a structure of its own on top of political configurations that already existed. Along with this organizing, MAS incorporated militants and party operators that had previously militated in other parties. These incorporations were accompanied by a transfer of political practices that are now characteristic of MAS in these settings. But before examining these practices of MAS, I will outline how the party is organized at the local level.

Local Party Infrastructure

MAS's local infrastructure takes a pyramidal form, where the territorial districts constitute its base. This organizational pattern highlights the importance of territorial politics and representation. Although districts are not stipulated in the party charter (Movimiento al Socialismo 2004), they are the only local branches recognized by party authorities. The higher-level bodies prescribed in the statute are the *direcciones regionales*, but they only exist on paper. For national senator Antonio Peredo, "there aren't *direcciones regionales* in these cities. But they should exist, as this is established in the party charter. And they existed not too long ago. But how could districts configure a regional direction when [districts] are internally divided?" (Peredo 2008). The reasons why these regional bodies ceased to exist, however, are more complex than Peredo's explanation. As Elvira Parra put it, "we used to have regional directions, but since authorities kept fighting for political spaces and jobs, we no longer have these bodies" (Parra 2008).

Lacking *direcciones regionales* and regional leaderships, militants and leaders of urban districts interact with each other at the *dirección departamental*. This body channels all the activities and politics of MAS in these cities, and it is there where a horizontal linkage is being forged, as it provides local authorities the opportunity to relate with their counterparts of other districts. It is composed of executives of territorial districts in the department, and it is also composed of departmental executives of social organizations. This body has the capacity of imposing discipline on local branches and leaders, and these usually rely on the *departamental* to solve the problems that emerge within the districts.[13] As its president, Samuel Guarayos, put it, "if there happens to be a problem, we try to solve it. We have to struggle so that these local structures remain united" (Guarayos 2008). One problem, however, is that this unity is usually enforced and maintained from above and *a punta de palos* (by coercion) (Llanos 2008). It should also be noted that the absence of *direcciones regionales* means that local subunits find it hard to hold higher-level authorities accountable (Peredo 2008).

A Closer Look at the Urban Districts

The failure to incorporate territorial districts into the party charter creates a legal vacuum that shapes the entire life of the local branches. Despite the legal vacuum, districts exist and carry out the bulk of MAS's mobilizational work in the cities, yielding immense benefits to the party. And because these are autonomous from the party leadership and are self-financed, they have considerable room for establishing their own agenda.

The internal organization of the districts replicates the hierarchical structure of higher-level bodies of MAS. Therefore, each district has an elected president, a vice president, as well as a number of commissions and secretariats. Being president of a district allows one to be elected to a regional, departmental, or even national leadership position.[14] But in the absence of *direcciones regionales* in the cities of La Paz and El Alto, there is a crisis of leadership at the regional level. Local authorities perceive this as an unfortunate "loss of political and participatory spaces" (Ticona and Apaza 2008), as a regional body would give districts broader spaces of representation in higher level bodies.

Districts have little say as to how departmental authorities are selected, and they lack effective mechanisms of control over higher-level authorities. As a local leader put it, "the territorial representations have, in theory, the capacity to select and control departmental authorities. But this time, for example, this process has been reversed. The departmental president has been elected first, and now he oversees the organizational problems in the districts." The same authority lamented that the vertical accountability structures between the districts and the departaments are strictly top down. In his words, "what occurs at the departmental level does not respond to a socialist structure that we believe we're participating in. This is not a bottom-up approach to politics" (Guzmán 2008).[15]

The party statutes also fail to prescribe a detailed set of procedures through which local authorities ought to be elected (Movimiento al Socialismo 2004). As a result, career paths for urban militants do not follow clear rules and procedures. For example, when the *dirección departamental* organizes a congress to select the authorities of a district, competing candidates can lobby the organizing body for the voting mechanism of their preference. Based on interviews with presidents of districts and with authorities in the departamental, two of the most common voting mechanisms seem to be the secret vote and public acclaimation. The latter mechanism favors the candidates who can mobilize the largest number of militants and it usually benefits the candidates who are more likely to promise more political spaces and job opportunities to their followers. In other words, the inexistence of fixed rules and procedures often leaves room for a sort of Darwinian "rule of the strongest," as aspiring authorities who are able to mobilize large numbers of constituents manage to choose their preferred voting mechanism to the detriment of competing authorities (for a parallel argument, see Do Alto 2006).

The lack of fixed rules and procedures to climb the hierarchical ladder within the MAS organization also leaves room for top-down control, causing organizational problems as well as frustrations at the level of the rank and file.

These organizational problems are related to the lack of opportunities in terms of public sector jobs. For example, urban militants perceive that their mobilizational strength has been critical to MAS's rise to power, but that their access to legitimate jobs in the public administration has been quite limited. As an authority in district number six of La Paz put it,

> Almost two and a half years of Morales's government and we [urban militants] are still living under the chains of the traditional system. We feel we are antisystemic in a party that claims to have new "open door" channels of participation. And when we don't find spaces for participation, who do we complain to? This reflects what is going on with the state apparatus and in the president's governability: almost 90 percent of those around him are "invited." (Quispe 2008)[16]

Beyond Territorial Representation: A Network of Social Organizations

In addition to the territorial structure, MAS has structured a broad network of alliances with urban social organizations. Although urban organizations and MAS had been growing closer since 2002 and amid a scenario of national crisis, their strategic alliance truly materialized with the 2005 general election campaign. Organizations representing artisans, microenterprises, pensioners, cooperative miners, and other urban sectors perceived the alliance with MAS as a unique opportunity to achieve parliamentary representation. In Jorge Silva's words, "one of the ways to guarantee the advancement of the social organizations of small producers that I represent was to have representatives in the congress; and now I am here [in the congress] as a result of the accord we reached with MAS" (Silva 2008). From MAS's perspective, this strategic move has provided the "political instrument" with a voting mass that has generated electoral majorities since 2005.

In El Alto, the main social organizations are El Alto Federation of Neighborhood Boards (Federación de Juntas Vecinales, or FEJUVE) and El Alto Regional Labor Federation (Central Obrera Regional–El Alto, or COR).[17] Although the statutes of these organizations prohibit their leaders from participating as officials of political parties, that prohibition has never stopped party operators from attempting to infiltrate these entities. This is because, as a rule, the control over these organizations serves to seduce the overall electorate and guarantees a degree of political stability in the city (Linera, León, and Monje 2004; see also Alenda 2003). MAS is not an exception to the rule and has not innovated much in these matters. Infiltrating the leadership levels of these organizations, which channel most of the political life in the city, allows political parties to extend their influence and control throughout the territory and to recruit leaders that mobilize large numbers of people.

Social organizations of La Paz and El Alto do not have any formal ties to MAS. But the party has configured an umbrella of informal alliances with key leaders and authorities of these urban organizations in an effort to insert the party into the cities and thus expand its social base. It is important to clarify that party operators have frequently worked with a top-down patron-client approach, as their strategy has consisted of seducing leaders of organizations in exchange for jobs in the public administration (or the promise of a job). From the outset, this approach has not consisted of building organic ties with the organizations as such. As Bertha Blanco put it, "when we were constructing MAS, we needed to find candidates. We didn't have candidates in the city, and nobody wanted to be associated with MAS. And what did we do? We went to find persons within the organizations, for example in the COR. And there we talked directly with the authorities" (Blanco 2008). However, what initially began as an effort to find candidates in these cities later evolved into a penetrating strategy aimed at controlling social organizations from the top. As a *masista* deputy for El Alto openly put it, "we can't deny we do that. We aim for our people to become leaders in these organizations. It is an effort to control the social organizations from the top" (Machaca 2008). Along these lines, as a former delegate to the constituent assembly explained, "the project we have had as MAS is to be able to take control over the social organizations. In order to do that, you need to start from working at the districts level and, from there, you can start climbing. For FEJUVE's next congress, for example, we have the wish that we're going to take on FEJUVE's leadership. . . . At least, that's what I can tell you we'd like to happen" (Parra 2008).[18]

These testimonies reveal a deliberate plan to penetrate the structure of social organizations and their networks and, through this strategy, to consolidate MAS's influence in the city. Simultaneously, because the party rewards loyal leaders (or, at least, it is expected that the party rewards them), this strategy creates a situation in which authorities within social organizations perceive these entities as "a trampoline for launching oneself into a public administration position" (Morales 2008). This can be exemplified with the case of FEJUVE. The highest authority of this organization since 2004, Abel Mamani, was appointed as the water minister for Morales's government in 2006.[19] His appointment translated into the direct presence of FEJUVE in the government structure. FEJUVE's presence in the government, in turn, entailed growing capacities for the organization to negotiate corporativist demands, as it provided it the opportunity to manage the res publica. On the other hand, FEJUVE's presence in the government structure hindered the possibilities of open confrontation between the social organization and the government. In other words, the organization was neutralized. As an authority of FEJUVE put it, "we have lost considerable capacities for mobilization. Why? Because leaders have occupied ministries and other public offices. . . . They have received quotas of power. But the people can see what their real interests are and thus it is difficult to articulate the organization" (Huanca 2008).[20]

In the case of COR-El Alto, the linkage with MAS is more subtle and less direct. Like FEJUVE, this organization supports, albeit not exempt of criticism, the government and the process of social transformation sponsored by MAS. Unlike FEJUVE, COR has never been represented directly in the government apparatus; COR has not physically occupied spaces of power under the Morales government. But party operators have sought to infiltrate this organization, and they have established negotiations directly with the leadership. In Edgar Patana's words, "Former executives of COR have always had rapprochements with political parties. Since 2002 they have been courting MAS so that they could negotiate spaces of power, such as a candidacy for deputyship or something else. But we have never been 'organic' members of MAS" (Patana 2008).

In addition, Patana laments the lack of participation of workers in the government structure. In his words "as Alteños, as workers, and as members of COR, we are represented by absolutely nobody in the government" (Patana 2008). Patana further laments the presence of "neoliberal" ministers within the Morales cabinet "whose very presence in the government structure has been detrimental to workers' interest." His testimony echoes that offered by Román Loayza when he renounced MAS in April 2009. Taken together, their critical positions toward MAS reveal a detachment by MAS from the social organizations that brought it to power. MSM leader Sebastián Michel attributes this to the consolidation of a "bureaucratic MAS," that is, a group of individuals who, while being alien to social organizations, control MAS (and the popular organizations that shape it) from the top.

In sum, because popular organizations such as FEJUVE and COR have not become "organic" members of MAS, they have no say in defining its programmatic lines. Instead, their links to the party are predominantly driven by pragmatism and the negotiation of spaces of power within the government. By the same token, MAS has attempted to control these organizations from above and thus erode their independence and autonomy.

Conclusion

MAS's rise to power coincided with a regional trend toward the election of left-wing leaders to occupy the presidency. But the "leftist" governments currently in office in Latin America are far from homogeneous. Whereas some authors have classified the current lefts by using dichotomies (e.g., "good" vs. "bad" left, "populist" vs. "social-democratic" left, and so forth) others have rejected such taxonomies partially on the grounds that they fail to explain where

Bolivia actually fits therein. As has been shown in this chapter, Morales largely owes his power to social mobilization from below. Although he exhibits populist features, he is not cut from the same cloth as other leaders like Hugo Chávez and Rafael Correa, to whom Morales is routinely equated (Weyland 2009; Vargas Llosa 2007; Castañeda 2006; Schamis 2006). Because Morales's leadership is rooted in years of social mobilization from below, to which he is accountable, he is a populist of a different kind than Chávez and Correa. But as has also been shown, the operations of the accountability structures are somewhat complex.

The Bolivian left turn could be portrayed as an instance of autonomous bottom-up social mobilization, yet it is combined with top-down attempts of cooptation by a charismatic leader. Morales is himself a product of bottom-up mobilization, but through his ruling MAS he now attempts to use the state to control the social organizations that brought him to power (which, it should be noted, may not be an easy task). Recent studies have shown that due to its peasant origins, MAS operates with decentralized and bottom-up schemes of participation; however, the chapter suggests that this occurs predominantly in rural areas, where MAS adopts "collective decisionmaking processes which are characteristic of the syndical peasant union organizational traditions" (Zuazo 2008:26). In those settings, for instance, MAS utilizes mechanisms of horizontal democracy for electing candidates to public office and for holding them accountable, which highlights the originality of its horizontal and bottom-up features, and reflects the ideals under which MAS was conceived.[21] Notwithstanding its innovative features, in the urban settings examined in this article, which are critical in order to win government and ensure governability, MAS has not innovated much in terms of political practices, and it operates according to the logics of a populist machine. This relates to how politics have played out historically in these urban settings, which are relatively new environments for the party, and where MAS replicates top-down client-patron schemes of participation. A current challenge for MAS is to incorporate (or adapt) some of the more egalitarian and innovative forms of participation in rural areas into urban environments. It remains to be seen how MAS can build a bridge between the "new" practices in rural areas and the clientelist practices that are more prominent in the cities, and thus build healthier party-society linkages in urban settings.

This chapter has revealed a set of continuities with older national-populist political parties such as MNR and CONDEPA, in terms of strategies for the occupation of the territory and, also, in terms of its linkages with urban social organizations. In the process of structuring itself in the cities of La Paz and El Alto and pushing its base to the cities, MAS absorbed existing and decaying structures of older political parties and, along with this absorption, MAS has incorporated their militants and adopted these parties' logics of action as well as their political practices. As a result, one *masista* vice minister lamented that "what we are seeing in these cities [in La Paz and El Alto] is a process of *condepización* of MAS. Whether we like it or not, MAS has a logic of action that reflects the remnants of CONDEPA logic" (Morales 2008). Comparative studies between MAS and how older national-populist parties in Bolivia articulated themselves and practiced politics in urban spaces will reveal much about breaks and continuities among them.

Notes

Thanks to Eric Hershberg, Max Cameron, and Graeme Robertson for invaluable comments, guidance, and encouragement during every step of the writing of this chapter.

1. Morales won the 2005 presidential elections with 1,544,374 votes (53.7 percent of those who voted). Far behind Morales, the second place went to Jorge "Tuto" Quiroga, leader of right-of-center Democratic and Social Power (Poder Democrático Social, or PODEMOS). He obtained 821,745 votes, which represented 28.6 percent of those who voted. Information retrieved from Bolivia's National Electoral Court (Corte Nacional Electoral, or CNE) on 26 March 2009.

2. Morales's landslide victory allowed MAS to become government without having to configure broad coalitions with other parties. This meant he was able to appoint cabinet members from autonomous indigenous groups and other social movements. The configuration of heterodox alliances was a dominant feature in the Bolivian political arena during 1985–2005, and this was known as the "pacted democracy." From 1985 until 2005, this superstructure took the form of a series of gentlemen's agreements concluded among the main party leaders in an effort to configure "stable" governments. In practice, this restricted and illiberal system excluded an entire section of the Bolivian population from participation, while it guaranteed the implementation and maintenance of some of the most conspicuous neoliberal restructuring in the Latin American region.

3. Álvaro García Linera is a prominent sociologist and current vice president of Bolivia.

4. The MAS obtained eight senators and twenty-seven deputies in the 2002 elections. Although Morales and three other deputies of MAS were elected to congress in 1997 and gained congressional experience (institutional capital) since then, their roles during the first term (1998–2003) were closely linked to noninstitutional politics. In 2002, during his first term, Morales was expelled from congress after being accused of leading violent protests against government-sponsored coca eradication campaigns. This incident, however, only helped to boost Morales's popular support and explains, at least in part, why MAS performed so well in the 2002 elections. It was in these elections that *masistas* multiplied themselves in congress and when MAS assumed the role of congressional opposition.

5. Morales was ratified with 67.41 percent of the votes nationwide. It should also be noted that opposition prefects were ratified in Beni, Pando, Tarija, and Santa Cruz.

6. Moira Zuazo (2008) also found that when the district is large and its inhabitants are not closely linked to social organizations, there is a tendency toward the invitation of candidates by *dedazo*. The selection of candidates through mechanisms of direct democracy is not common in such areas. The same occurs with plurinominal deputies and with national senators, as most of them are "invited."

7. José Antonio Quiroga was invited to run as Morales's vice presidential candidate for the 2002 election. He declined the offer for personal reasons.

8. Cooperativist miners also demanded a deeper pension reform than the government was proposing and the lowering of the retirement age to fifty-five.

9. *Mallku* is the Aymara word for "condor." In addition, it roughly translates as "prince" or "leader."

10. The *compadre* Carlos Palenque died in March 1997, just a few months before the national elections. He was replaced by the *comadre* Remedios Loza. Although CONDEPA obtained a significant share of the votes in the 1997 elections, it ended in third place and became a partner of the Bánzer's coalition government for one year. This generated discontent in its constituency, which voted largely for the Movimiento Sin Miedo (MSM) in the municipal elections of 1999 in La Paz, and for MAS in the national elections of 2002.

11. According to many accounts, Bertha Blanco was the person who brought MAS to El Alto. Ms. Blanco has worked actively to build a masista structure in the city of El Alto. She is currently estranged from MAS.

12. Cristina Martínez is currently one *concejal* (out of two) for MAS in El Alto.

13. Although the *dirección departamental* has de facto capacities to discipline local branches, there are no formal bureaucratic mechanisms to regulate these processes.

14. This process is gradual, however, and party members cannot be elected to higher-level positions (regional, departmental, national) without first serving as presidents of a district. According to Samuel Guarayos (2008), "In order to be a president of a district, a candidate needs to prove its loyalty and needs to be approved by its territory. He then needs to have a minimum of four years of active militancy in MAS, and no experience as an authority in the 'neoliberal' parties that have massacred our people and have championed corruption."

15. Guzmán regarded this lack of accountability as "unfair and unfortunate" and lamented that such "unclear procedures" are detrimental to the internal democracy of MAS.

16. The speaker's name has been omitted to protect the interviewee's identity.

17. FEJUVE brings together residents and neighborhood associations of El Alto. COR is an organization of workers, which includes factory workers, teachers, journalists, and artisans, but is dominated by the *gremialistas* (street traders). Together with a third organization, the Federation of Gremialistas, FEJUVE and COR possess an impressive mobilizational strength in the city. Despite the importance of the Federation of Gremialistas to the political life of El Alto, this section only focuses on FEJUVE and COR and does not make direct claims with regard to the links between MAS and Gremialistas. However, all my interviewees in El Alto concurred in pointing out the similarities between the examined organizations and the Gremialistas in regard to their linkages to MAS.

18. MAS's attempts to control social organizations are often restrained by the internal rules of those organizations. For example, in the case of FEJUVE, there are elections to renew its leadership body every two years. But these elections stipulate a rotation system that impedes authorities from perpetuating in power. This system, which is rooted in Aymara principles of rotation, is basically a system of shifts: a representative of the southern part of the city is elected for a period of two years and cannot be elected for a consecutive term. She cannot be replaced by another resident of the south; a representative of the northern part of the city needs to replace that candidate. Because this acts as a barrier to restrain party ambitions, many masista leaders openly recognize that one of their goals is to modify the statutes of social organizations like FEJUVE.

19. Abel Mamani was FEJUVE's highest authority since 2004. He played a leading role during the revolts of June 2005 in El Alto, which led to the resignation of Carlos Mesa. Mamani's appointment as a minister was resisted by FEJUVE, whose authorities claimed that "Mamani utilized FEJUVE to satisfy his personal purposes without consulting the bases" (Huanca 2008). FEJUVE's response to his appointment also shows a rejection of Morales's practice of inviting authorities without consulting the bases.

20. Eventually, however, Mamani was expelled from the government under (still unproved) charges of corruption.

21. However, this should not lead us to fall into a quick idealization of MAS in rural areas as these areas are not exempt from top-down client-patron practices.

7

Constituent Power and the Caracazo: The Exemplary Case of Venezuela

Jon Beasley-Murray

There are only two problems with the notion of a Latin American "left turn": first, it isn't left; second, it isn't a turn. Talk of a left turn, or even left turns in the plural, revives the hoary old opposition between "left" and "right," between governments of contrasting ideological stripes, and posits some kind of almost inevitable swing between the two. Elections are the proof of political change. Everything is to be read in the urns: the electoral victories of Venezuela's Hugo Chávez, Brazil's Lula, Bolivia's Evo Morales, and so on herald some new epoch in Latin American politics. But the left, we are told, must beware of botching its opportunity or the pendulum will inevitably drift back toward the right. So now what counts is state policy and implementation: the difference that the left in power can make, the changes it can enforce in what is still a manifestly unequal and divided social structure. For instance, the BBC heralded the presidential victory of Paraguay's Fernando Lugo, one of the newest members of the "left turns" club, by commenting on "the complex and monumental task" he faces "of bringing change to a country weighed down by decades of corruption, poverty, and inequality" (Painter 2008). It is as though the burden for change fell solely on Lugo's shoulders. Or as though, more broadly, the project of the left in power really was, as Benjamin Arditi puts it in Chapter 8 of this volume, "to change the status quo."

All this talk of left turns and what comes next ignores the fact that the electoral successes are themselves the result of prior changes; the status quo has *already* shifted. The self-styled left is less the agent of change than its beneficiary. At best, its victories at the polls are the symptom of deeper changes that are taking place elsewhere. Lugo's accession to power (as well as that of Chávez, Lula, and Morales) is reaction rather than action; it is not in itself an event. The problem with the vast majority of the discussion of the Latin American left turns is that it confuses symptoms with causes. Analytically and also politically, it substitutes constituted for constituent power.

In what follows I offer an alternative account of contemporary Latin American politics, with the stress on constituent power and so on the relationship between multitude and state, rather than that between left and right. I begin with a discussion of the concept of constituent power, particularly as it is theorized by Antonio Negri (1999). I then discuss the broader processes that lie behind the so-called left turns, stressing the social insurgencies or *jacqueries* (popular revolts) to which the left as much as the right has been forced to respond. I spend some time on the particular case of the Venezuelan Caracazo of February 1989, both because it is one of the first such revolts that initiates the current constitutional moment and because it reveals the elements of the process with special clarity. In this sense, Venezuela is not one pole at the far end of a leftist continuum that supposedly ranges from social democracy to populism. Rather, I treat the Venezuelan model as an ideal type and suggest that the constituent processes in other countries simply follow it more or less closely. And yet, in each case, the insurgencies that initiate the contemporary left turns are embedded in complex national and regional histories. I show how the Caracazo emerged from a whole history of protests and transformations in everyday life in which constituent power is a matter of habit. Finally, I return to the present and to the so-called left turn of Hugo Chávez to consider how chavismo relates to this longer and broader account of the multitude and constituent power.

Over the course of this chapter, then, I move from the theoretical to the sociological and the historical, and from the general to the particular. That, however, is merely a convenient mode of presentation. What is interesting and exciting about the processes that have given rise to the Latin American left turns is the how they force us to rethink and rework some of the fundamental concepts of political theory. Too much discussion of contemporary Latin American politics has tried to corral it within a tired set of oppositions, not least those between left and right, or between social democracy and populism. Yet if there is something excessive about developments in the region over the past twenty years, it is also because they refuse to fit well within conventional categories. They break the frame of political representation. We see new societies in formation, and our tools to describe them still lag behind. Our challenge, as always, is to try to catch up with the creativity and innovation exhibited by the multitude of ordinary men and women throughout Latin America.

Constituent Power

The purported opposition between left and right passes over the prior distinction between constituent and constituted power. Indeed, the binary between left and right tends to ignore the question of power altogether; it makes politics a matter of ideology or policy, of the *content* that is to fill institutional *forms* that are taken for granted. By contrast, constituent power concerns the shape those forms will take. It concerns the institutions that structure the republic, and the powers that are to be accorded to them. For what is finally at stake in the succession of social mobilizations that have shaken Latin America over the past three decades, and in the variety of responses to those mobilizations on the part of elected regimes (be they of the right or the left), is the institutional legacy of creole republicanism.[1] With Latin America on the verge of celebrating the two-hundredth anniversary of the foundation of independent states, the postcolonial settlement has been challenged and found wanting. In response, we see an effort to refound the republic. Here, then, I agree with someone such as Freya Schiwy, who argues that we are in the presence of a profound challenge to the entire postcolonial system of governance (Schiwy 2008). The so-called left turns are not simply a reaction against a failed neoliberalism, and still less the expression of periodic political fashion. They are the indication of a profound political transformation. Where I disagree with Schiwy is in the notion that this is limited to what she calls a "*rescate cultural*" or even a "movement of cultural *reconstitución,*" some kind of return to a pre-Columbian past. Though the expression of constituent power may, and indeed must, draw on older traditions and historical traditions, Schiwy's own case study of Bolivia shows that it is also distinguished by its search for novelty, its creativity and invention, rather than by the rehabilitation of past political forms. Any new social structures to emerge from the current conjuncture will be post-postcolonial, rather than a turning back of the political clock. For the preeminent characteristic of constituent power is that it is active and expansive, rather than reactive or defensive. Indeed, it is *constituted* power that reacts to the insistent pressure of a multitude it can never fully contain.

Constituent power is the power to make constitutions, to shape the institutional and juridical order that will subsequently regulate society. By contrast, constituted power is the regulative power encoded in and exercised by such institutions. Hence it is that constituent power is primary, for it preexists and gives rise to the power exercised in making or preserving the law. Constituent power is the ground of politics, law, and indeed normativity as such. In Carl Schmitt's words, "Prior to the establishment of any norm, there is a fundamental *political decision of the constitution-making power*" (Schmitt 2008:77, emphasis in the original). So constituent power also exists prior to and beyond the rule of law. As Hans Lindahl observes, Schmitt's move "to recover the primacy of constituent over constituted power . . . aims to rescue the primacy of democracy over the rule of law" (Lindahl 2007:21). And Negri likewise stresses the fact that constituent power is "the motor or cardinal expression of democratic revolution" (Negri 1999:11). Yet none of this has much in common with liberal democracy. For liberalism, the debate about the best form of government is already anticipated and short-circuited; from the perspective of constituent power, however, everything is still up for grabs. Indeed, the fact that it precedes the rule of law, that it trumps all laws, means that constituent power can be reminiscent of dictatorship. Though it is the power exercised by the people or, given that the "people" are a subsequent construction, by the diverse multitude that preexists the institution of sovereignty, it is also the power to decide on the exception, the power to suspend the constitution. Schmitt argues that "the distinctive position of a 'constitution-making' assembly, which convenes after a revolutionary elimination of the preexisting constitutional laws, is best designated a 'sovereign dictator'" (Schmitt 2008:109). No wonder that the exercise of constituent power can prove controversial! The expression of constituent power, and the establishment of constituent assemblies, in countries such as Venezuela and Bolivia has been quickly stigmatized by its opponents as a sign of the breakdown of democracy, rather than its renovation. We can, however, distinguish between constituent power and dictatorship if we insist that constituent power is fundamentally positive, in that it creates: it is constitution making. Dictatorship as the concentration of state power in a single office, on the other hand, is fundamentally negative, in that it withholds: it is constitution suspending. Insofar as constituent power suspends or interrupts an established constitution, such as the decayed institutions of the creole republic, it is to gain the freedom to invent new habits and new forms of life.

Constituted power is a delegated power: it is the result of the articulation, mediation, or, better, *capture* of a force that both anticipates and exceeds it. Hence the power that a political order exercises is always derivative, and that order is itself the creation of constituent power. In the words of Abbé Sieyès, "in each of its parts a constitution is not the work of a constituted power but a constituent power. No type of delegated power can modify the conditions of its delegation" (Sieyès 2003:136). For Sieyès, the task of the constituent assembly was to harmonize these two modalities of power: to ensure that government was well constituted. But the very notion of good constitution presupposes a distinction between the constituent and the constituted; it assumes that the two are not necessarily or normally in harmony. Indeed, the split between them is at the heart of what Martin Loughlin and James Walker term the "paradox of constitutionality": that the people, the presumed subject of power, are denied access to it; "the power they possess, it would appear, can only be exercised through constitutional forms already established or in the process of being established" (Loughlin and Walker 2007:1). The tension between constituent and constituted power is inevitable, as the constitution can never fully account for the power that gives rise to it. There is always something left over. As Damian Chalmers notes, then, "constituent power signifies, first, the idea of political and legal surplus" (Chalmers 2007:295). Hence it is absolutely true that constituent power appears as "excess." But this is far from the "anarchy" imputed to it. There is nothing anarchic about constituent power and certainly not in the vulgar sense of anarchy as unpatterned, formless, or chaotic. It is constituent power that gives rise to form, because it is endlessly and creatively form making. Constituted power is an attempt to arrest this creativity.

The fiction of a social pact or contract is presented as the resolution of the tension between constituent and constituted power. Rather than true resolution, however, the notion of a pact is the means by which the state tries to call an end to democratic insurgency. The state imposes the notion of a primordial contract upon society, as mythical presupposition to guarantee its own legitimacy. The premise of the social contract is that constituent power is somehow exhausted, that constitution making is over, that the rule of law has replaced democratic insurgency. The social contract suggests that the constitution is fixed. The contract aims to secure sovereign right, to confine constituent power only to the mythic moment of revolutionary foundation, and to banish any subaltern excess to beyond the pale. It institutes hegemony as the only political game in town. Should the excessive passions and desires of constituent power return, as the repressed inevitably do, they are stigmatized as antipolitical and irrational, violent confrontation or atavistic recalcitrance. Any reminder of the primordial creativity that gives rise to social order is pathologized as an obstacle to progress. And in a similarly strange reversal, contractualist consensus, the provisional truce negotiated by a sclerotic constituted power, is presented as the only way to get things done. Now, however, the Latin American social compact is in disarray. Hence the drive to refound the republic and, more broadly, to rethink the political, not as left versus right but again and more fundamentally as what takes place in the gap between constituent and constituted power.

The constituent moment that has given rise to the Latin American left turns is an opening. It is a recognition that, in Benjamin Arditi's words, "political history has no closure" (Arditi 2008:73). Or, more precisely, political history is always forced open by the reinvigoration of constituent power. In response, constituted power is an effort to close things down, albeit by offering new forms of inclusion, new forms of representation in response to the urgings of the multitude. The interplay between constituent and constituted power is constant. Nothing takes place in a void, and even the most spectacular of social explosions of the past few decades builds on years of more ordinary, everyday resistances and struggles. Each national and regional history has its own particularities. At the same time, however, we have seen an extraordinary resonance across different contexts that has made it possible to think, however briefly, that everything and anything is possible.

Jacqueries

It is impossible to agree with the widespread contention that the current wave of radical efforts to "refound" republican institutions began with the election of Hugo Chávez and his Fifth Republic Movement. Again, this is to confuse symptoms with causes, effects with events. If we are to understand this constituent moment as a whole, we need to look at the insurgencies that have, in almost every case, preceded the electoral triumphs of the so-called left. To put this another way, we need to go beyond the polls that are no more than symptoms of broader movements; we need, in Arditi's words, to "think outside the box and put the electoral benchmark on hold" (Arditi 2008:68). Fetishizing electoral success and governmental policies leads to a grievous reduction of our conception of the political. These successes are the outcomes of a long series of social mobilizations that date back at least to the Venezuelan Caracazo of 1989, and that include also the Argentine disturbances of 2001, the Bolivian water and gas conflicts of 2000 and 2003–2004, and the protests around Paraguay's Ycuá Bolaños supermarket fire of 2004. Any narrative of contemporary Latin American politics that does not include this almost unprecedented conjunction of social insurgencies would be partial at best. If the region is indeed now moving toward a post-neoliberal epoch, rather than simply experiencing yet another swing of the electoral pendulum, it is thanks to these mobilizations rather than to the left-wing political cadre who are their beneficiaries. That cadre now claims to represent the forces that, almost as an afterthought, propelled the left into power in so many countries. But again I agree with Arditi that such claims to representation hardly exhaust the political.

Still, these social mobilizations are apparently stubbornly resistant to analysis, which is perhaps why they have been so consistently bracketed from so many accounts of contemporary Latin American politics. They seem so new, so different, and so disturbing. It is no doubt easier to stigmatize them as "criminal or delinquent," and so to deny them any political importance, rather than to acknowledge how they challenge us (and have challenged the Latin American left) to rethink the political.

Michael Hardt and Antonio Negri suggest resurrecting and renovating the old concept of the "jacquerie" to conceptualize these apparently spontaneous and disorganized uprisings. As they point out, this term has been used to describe everything from "the ferocious sixteenth- and seventeenth-century European peasant uprisings" to "race riots, various forms of urban rebellion, food riots, and so forth" (Hardt and Negri 2009:236). Of course, there is a long tradition of such brief rebellions in Latin America. Incidents such as the Caracazo have in some senses their precursors in the so-called austerity riots or anti–International Monetary Fund (IMF) riots, especially in the wake of the regional debt crisis of 1982. As John Walton documents, food riots, strikes, and social disturbances shook cities in Peru, Argentina, Ecuador, Bolivia, Panama, and elsewhere from the late 1970s in reaction to the economic and social impact of neoliberal reforms. These protests were frequently unheralded, violent, and surprisingly successful: in Walton's words, "stunned governments frequently rescinded or ameliorated the policy" that had sparked the protest. "Subsidies were restored, rate hikes canceled, and compensatory wage increases granted" (Walton 2001:321). In some cases, as in Haiti and the fall of Duvalier in 1986, such protests of moral outrage and indignation even helped to topple existing regimes. Moreover, both these protests and the subsequent social insurgencies of the 1990s and 2000s also (as I will show in more detail for the Venezuelan case) need to be seen within an even longer history of urban disaffection that spans the twentieth century. Latin America's urban masses, in particular, have long undergone a sort of training in periodic protest. And as Hardt and Negri put it, "despite their brevity and discontinuity, the constant reappearance of these jacqueries profoundly determines not only the mechanisms of repression but also the structures of power itself" (Hardt and Negri 2009:237). They indicate, we might say, the insistent pressure of constituent power, a constant low-level dissatisfaction with the conventional terms of political participation that only sometimes erupts in spectacular fashion. They become almost habitual.

To locate the origin of Latin America's constituent moment in 1989 and the Caracazo is, then, in some ways rather arbitrary. We could perhaps just as well point to the riots that broke out in São Paulo in April 1983. Or, in a somewhat different register, we could look at the hybrid "micropolitics" of the same period in Brazil that brought together issues of class, gender, sexuality, and race in a heady brew that Félix Guattari and Suely Rolnik describe as a "molecular revolution" (Guattari and Rolnik 2008). This micropolitics was parallel but not reducible to the organizing around Lula's presidential candidature that eventually paid off in the election of 2002. And yet 1989 is as good a date as any. This is a year that has, of course, been celebrated for marking the fall of the Berlin Wall, the end of the Cold War, the triumph of liberal capitalism, and, in Francis Fukuyama's turn of phrase, even the "end of history." With the benefit of hindsight, however, we can see that the rather more interesting events of that year took place in the West rather than the East. The fall of actually existing socialism in Eastern Europe ushered in neoliberalism rather than liberalism: a rampant free market and massive deregulation with gangster-style business practices and a clutch of football-club-owning millionaires.

Across the globe in Latin America, and far less fêted by the international press than events in Europe later in the year, a brief insurgency in Caracas already offered clues to neoliberalism's demise. The Caracazo ended almost as soon as it had begun and could easily be written off (insofar as it was noticed at all) as a marginal anomaly. At the time, Venezuela was probably the region's most stable democracy, a shining example of robust continuity by comparison with, say, Argentina, Chile, or Brazil, as these latter countries nervously emerged from dictatorship. Indeed, the inauguration of Venezuelan President Carlos Andrés Pérez was trumpeted as a beacon for the rest of the hemisphere. But in fact the demonstrations that broke out only a few weeks later were perhaps the first of the social ruptures that indicated the end of Latin America's social pact. For in the end, what makes the Caracazo such a clear illustration of Latin America's constituent moment is the way it so dramatically shattered the spectacle of constituted power. It was a revolt in which the political and the economic, or protests against political and economic regimes, came together in a new way. In this sense it also anticipated, for instance, the Argentine protests of 2001 that were both immediately economic (prompted by, among other things, the devaluation of the peso) and inescapably political, or rather a wholesale attack on political representation.

The problem posed by the jacquerie, Hardt and Negri suggest, is the question of political organization and political institutions: "the central program must move from resistance to proposition and from jacquerie to organization—but that is an extremely difficult task, whose obstacles we must face head on" (Hardt and Negri 2009:246). And indeed, it is this that has been the central problem facing the left governments that have come to power more or less directly in the wake of the series of jacqueries that have shaken Latin America in the past couple of decades, and that have forced a rethinking of the nature and form of political institutions. Most discussion of the so-called left turns has refused to "face head on" the difficulties of this transformation of constituent into constituted power; again, they have been too concerned with the conventional (and secondary, if not wholly irrelevant) issue of the difference between left and right. This is in part because analysts have chosen to bracket off the social insurgencies that have, in almost each and every instance, presaged a subsequent turn at the ballot boxes. Again, however, it is in Venezuela that the distinction between jacquerie and subsequent regime has been clearest, and that the problem of organization has been most sharply debated and contested. It is for this reason that Venezuela is far from being some kind of outlier, or one pole in a continuum that stretches from the Chávez phenomenon on the far left (or even "populist") end of the spectrum to (say) the anemic social democracy still peddled by Chilean concertación. No, it is more edifying to see Venezuela as the norm, of which other cases, such as the Chilean one, are more or less pale deviations. Indeed, the reason that Bachelet's election was indeed heralded as part of the selfsame so-called left turn was precisely because, however little she promised to change governmental policies (her election was in policy as well as party political terms more about continuity than change), as a woman, a single mother, and a former torture victim in this deeply conservative, Catholic, and still-traumatized country, she offered a reshuffling, however mild, of the protocols for political representation. Yet the problems that plagued her administration (above all, perhaps, the student demonstrations that arose shortly after her term began, in 2006) were also about the failures of the political system's representational mechanisms and, as such an echo, however distant, of what was most clearly at work in Venezuela. In short, and allowing for the myriad differences between (say) Chile and Bolivia, Nicaragua and Brazil, Venezuela remains the ideal typical case for any understanding of the region's politics. It is not exceptional; it is exemplary.

Where I disagree with Hardt and Negri is their suggestion that the governments put in place following this series of Latin American jacqueries (for which the Caracazo is emblematic and exemplary) in fact resolve the problems of organization that these uprisings highlight. In fact, it is when writing with Giuseppe Cocco that Negri most clearly stakes out this position, with the claim (with reference particularly to Argentina and Brazil) that what we are seeing is the emergence of a "constituent New Deal [that] organizes the strength of the subaltern classes such that they are presented, nationally and internationally, as multitudes—that is, no longer as objects of representation but as subjects" (Hardt and Negri 2009:226, 227). I am skeptical about the radicalism of either Lula or the Kirchners, or even Morales or Chávez. Indeed, the 2006 squabble between Néstor Kirchner and his Uruguayan counterpart Tabaré Vásquez over a paper mill polluting the River Uruguay, which divides their two countries, showed that both were still happy to make populist moves in defense of national sovereignty. Likewise, and for all their internationalist gestures, the governments of Brazil, Bolivia, and Venezuela are no less dedicated to upholding constituted power. In short, even the most progressive governments now in power in Latin America promote police management more than political mobilization; in reconstructing a social pact shattered by almost thirty years of social mobilization they are set on once more shoring up the façade that is constituted power. Out of the ruins of their inevitable failure, however, we may perhaps see something more interesting and more hopeful emerge. Or even in the ruins themselves: for as I hope to show, the Caracazo itself presented already at least some features of what can only be called common sense—a sense of the common. It was far from the sheer chaotic unleashing of repressed energy; within the tumult, the seeds of an alternative, if carnivalesque, social logic became apparent.

The Caracazo

In the electoral campaign of late 1988, early 1989, Carlos Andrés Pérez had run as a populist, drawing on the memory of his previous regime in the late

1970s, when the country thrived on the high price of the oil that it exported. But this was the last gasp of Venezuelan populism, to which the country would never again return. For on returning to power, he soon announced a packet of drastic neoliberal reforms. One of the consequences of these policies would be a dramatic jump in the costs of public transportation. On the morning of 27 February 1989, commuters on the outskirts of Venezuela's capital refused to pay the higher prices demanded of them. This was the comparatively mundane beginning to the Caracazo. It began with a move for auto-valorization: a refusal of the prices imposed from above, and the values that they implied.

Within hours, protest spread all over the capital city and across the country in what was an apparently "anarchic movement, without direction, totally spontaneous, in no way preconceived by any subversive organizations" (Giusti 1989:37). By midmorning, people had built barricades and were stopping trucks, above all those thought to carry food, to empty them of their merchandise, as well as looting shops and malls. Outrage was provoked by the discovery that shopkeepers had hoarded goods in anticipation of imminent price rises. In Caracas, the main squares and highways were blockaded. Cars were set alight. Motorcycle dispatch riders spread news, communicated rebellion, and ferried personnel (López Maya 2003:125). A protest against bus fares had turned into a general revolt against neoliberal structural adjustment. Moreover, the riot took on colors of carnival as the police were both powerless to intervene and, in some cases, even sympathized with the movement and helped to ensure that the plunder took place with some order and just distribution between young and old, men and women. Groceries and clothing were taken to those who were unable to participate in the pillage themselves, and large sides of beef and pork were carved up and shared out. A barter economy flourished and "looting dissolved momentarily money's ability to regulate collective life." In the end, an estimated one million people took part in the disturbances, "in effect erasing state control of the street" (Coronil and Skurski 1991:317, 291). That night, even as tanks started to roll in to put down what was by now a full-scale insurrection, in the poor barrios high up on the hills overlooking Caracas "a party was underway, with champagne, steak, and imported whisky, all products of the looting" (Ojeda 1989a:43). Salsa and merengue music blared from stolen hi-fi equipment. Common unrest had become shared celebration.

The state was slow to react. The president was traveling and only half aware of what was going on, told "that nothing out of the ordinary was happening" (López Maya 2003:134). It was not until the afternoon of the following day that a government official even tried to address the nation. When eventually the minister of the interior appeared on television, halfway through his appeal for calm he "was overcome by nervous exhaustion and rendered speechless on camera. Disney cartoons replaced him without explanation." The state was quite literally struck dumb by events. It failed to articulate even the thinnest of hegemonic fictions. The social pact was almost completely ruptured. And it was completely shattered by the government's eventual response. For when the state finally moved, it moved with force against its own citizenry. A state of exception was declared, the constitution suspended, freedom of the press curtailed, and a curfew imposed. As F. Coronil and J. Skurski observe, the "traditional language of populism" was abruptly abandoned. Indeed, Pérez was now a president "without a people" (Coronil and Skurski 1991:321). The multitude had taken its place. With the state's representational strategies bankrupt, massive repression was unleashed. For the next few days, the center of Caracas was a war zone. "Caracas was Beirut": a city at the epicenter of a civil war (Ojeda 1989b:33). Up to a thousand people were killed as firefights rang out downtown and the military fired artillery rounds almost indiscriminately at tower blocks, seeking out snipers but also in fear at what might lie within. In the words of one journalist, "behind that silent cement the multitude is hidden. Thousands of eyes observe our movements" (Giusti 1989:75).

The real fear provoked by the social mobilization of February 1989 was less anarchy than the glimpse of an alternative, almost unimaginable social order. The protests revealed elements of creativity and self-organization— incipient and undeveloped, to be sure, but further elaboration of the networks that emerged in the uprising was soon cruelly curtailed. Clearly, the most spectacular effect of the Caracazo was the way it comprehensively undermined the myth of any social pact that allegedly sustained the legitimacy of either Pérez's government, or indeed the Venezuelan social order as a whole. But it would be a mistake to see the disturbances as simply negative, simply reactive. The Caracazo was an expression of constituent power in that it presented the seeds of alternative political and social structures; it suggested that "another world" was possible, even though that alternative as yet had no name. Indeed, in that the events were led by no party and spurred by no slogans, the Caracazo seemed to resist representation altogether: its constituent potential was far from solidifying into some constituted mold.

Old Mole

1989 heralds a new moment in Latin America's political history, but its relation to that history is complex. The upsurge of discontent and violence that spoiled the triumphalism of Venezuela's new government was surprising and unheralded, but it also drew on a long if almost subterranean tradition. It appeared to come from nowhere, but is better understood as Marx's "old mole" of revolution, which burrows underground only to surface dramatically at the most unexpected of moments (Marx 2005:198). Yet however embedded the

Caracazo was in both a tradition of social rebellion and also in the everyday practices of ordinary Venezuelans, the other surprise was that it seemed to lead to no determinate outcome. The mole returned underground almost as soon as he had poked his head above the surface. The country entered a period of latency; it was a long time before the trauma of social protest found political articulation. But this only goes to show that that articulation, when finally it arrived, was arbitrary. It was symptom rather than direct product. It is true that in the end the "left turn" in Venezuela, and indeed throughout Latin America, claimed to be able to respond and give form to the upheavals to which they were belatedly reacting. Chávez (and Morales, and Kirchner, and Lula) appeared to give voice to the energies and desires that had undermined the previous social order. But the gap between protest and project, between constituent and constituted power, demonstrates that in no way does the one follow naturally from the other. Another world is still possible.

Venezuela had been the prime Latin American example of a pacted democracy. Pérez's presidential inauguration was to have cemented the country's position at "the 'center' of world democracy," paraded before an unprecedented gathering of world leaders from 108 countries (Ojeda 1989b:33). Having avoided the political violence that had blighted so much of Latin America, and relishing its oil wealth, the country had long been regarded as an "exceptional democracy," exempt from the conflicts that afflicted the rest of the region; it was put forward as "a model democracy for Latin America" (Ellner and Salas 2006:xiii). Its success apparently demonstrated the benefits and viability of a formal social pact, embodied quite literally the "Pact of Punto Fijo" of 1958. Venezuela's major political parties had agreed to defend the constitution and to respect electoral results; they had established a minimum common program and a promise to share power with electoral rivals; and they had incorporated elements of so-called civil society, such as labor unions and professional associations. It was under the auspices of *puntofijismo* that, in the subsequent three decades, the country became known for baseball and beauty queens rather than coups or revolutions. But the Pact of Punto Fijo broke down in the Caracazo. The "fixed point" was overwhelmed by the tidal surge of an irrepressible multitude, and then by the state's vicious abandonment of even the pretence of hegemony.

The trigger for the Caracazo was no more (and no less) than habit. Commuters were accustomed to paying one price for public transport; they protested when they were suddenly forced to pay another. In response to the shock doctrine of neoliberal reform, the Venezuelan population took violent umbrage. The uprising was an expression of an instinct for self-preservation or survival. But the impulse to demonstrate also drew on traditional habits, a hidden tradition to which politicians and political scientists had been blinded in their celebration of prosperity and peace. Margarita López Maya emphasizes the continuities between the 1989 rebellion and previous moments of social protest: a 1902 British and German blockade of Venezuela's ports, for instance, had provoked "protests whose protagonists were multitudes whose organization and leadership were unknown." Further disturbances accompanied the death of the dictator Juan Vicente Gómez in 1935 and ran on into 1936. General José López Contreras, Gómez's successor, tried to convert the multitude that had expressed its displeasure into a people with which the state could negotiate (López Maya 2000:78, 84). Slowly, this project of converting multitude into people was realized. Over the course of the 1940s and 1950s, despite outbreaks of protest in 1945 (marked by a particularly "festive tone") and 1948, not to mention January 1958 with the fall of the country's last dictatorial regime, gradually "the protagonism of the multitude gave way to that of social and political organizations" (López Maya 2000:87, 85).

In short, Venezuela's rapid modernization and urbanization in the first half of the twentieth century had been characterized by a series of multitudinous protests and demonstrations. But these were eventually absorbed and disarmed by so-called civil society. The Pact of Punto Fijo, then, was itself the culmination of a long process of state reaction to this ever-present multitude. In the thirty years of exceptional democracy that followed, "the political institutions of mediation first replaced the multitudes and then excluded them from the political system." But old habits die hard. The Caracazo revealed their continued presence, now more expansive and stronger than ever. Since 1989, "the multitudes have taken to the street once more" (López Maya 2000:101, 104).

The Caracazo was both new and old. It was old in that it was the resumption of habits of protest long dormant, yet never entirely forgotten. It was the return of affects long repressed, yet never fully eliminated. And yet the Caracazo was also new: it was a watershed in Venezuelan history and, moreover, for Coronil and Skurski part of a "worldwide reordering of body politics" (Coronil and Skurski 1991:299, 334). A sign of its novelty, and of the way it fractured the frame of political and social representation, was the fact that for a long time nobody even knew what to call it. The events "disrupted established interpretive schemes, resisting the efforts of official and opposition forces to fix them with a name." They were "27-F" or *los sucesos* (the events); "the disturbances" or *el sacudón* (the big jolt); a "social explosion," a *poblada* (popular uprising), or *el masacrón* (the big massacre); or they were simply "the war" (Coronil and Skurski 1991:311). Language could not contain what had taken place. It would take some time before a politician arose who could give voice to the energy that had burst out in the Caracazo, who could claim (for the time being at least) to have tamed the old mole. But rather than taming it, perhaps Hugo Chávez merely forced it underground once again.

Chávez to the Rescue

If we imagine Chávez coming to the rescue, we must ask what he came to save. Surely, as much as he claims to channel the historic discontent of those long marginalized by the pact of Punto Fijo, and before that by the entire postcolonial settlement of the creole republic, equally his purchase on power is based on the promise that only he can ensure Venezuela's continued governability. Rather than a force of disorder, Chávez implicitly presents himself as the sole assurance that the country is not to disintegrate in violent conflagration. He reacts to the Caracazo with the claim that only he can prevent its reoccurrence. He invokes the grievances and desires of those who have repeatedly found themselves excluded from the country's political system, so as to better capture and mold them within structures that bear the imprint of constituted power. Chávez is the epitome of constituted rather than constituent power, but also the demonstration of the former's dependence upon the latter. He resurrects politics in the Schmittian sense of friend versus enemy (*chavista* versus *escuálido*) so as to ward off another, more fearful politics for which such names would make no sense at all, an unnameable politics of those who (still) have no given name. For all the resentment and vituperation of the Venezuelan middle class, in some sense Chávez arrives on the scene to save *them*. His intervention consists in reconstructing the political scene itself, in refounding the institutions that provide its frame and backdrop. Chávez comes to the rescue of the Venezuelan social pact.

Very much on the sidelines of the events of February 1989, a small group of young military officers were trying as hard as anyone else to make sense of what had happened. The Bolivarian Revolutionary Movement (Movimiento Bolivariano Revolucionario or MBR) was a clandestine organization, founded in 1982, that brought together would-be revolutionaries who had sworn fidelity to a vague set of ideals based loosely on the Enlightenment political philosophy of Simón Bolívar. They became convinced that the only way to achieve significant change in Venezuela was through a coup d'état. Not much had come of their plotting, however, and the Caracazo with its sudden explosion of violence in the streets took them, as much as anyone else, by surprise: they "felt aggrieved that the moment and the opportunity that they had been half expecting had passed them by without any possibility of taking action." Before their eyes they felt they saw something like an emerging historic movement threatening the old order, but these young Turks were in no position to impose any kind of hegemonic leadership; they were "not remotely prepared" (Gott 2001:47, 43). The most disappointed of all at the MBR's failure to seize this opportunity would have been the movement's founder: a young army lieutenant who spent the morning of February 27 lying ill in bed. His name was Hugo Chávez Frías.

Chávez's insight was the recognition that the Caracazo was an expression of constituent power. In its wake, he and his group accelerated their plans to take over the state, and began putting "forward the argument for a constituent assembly as the only path out of the trap" of a now bankrupt puntofijismo (Chávez, Harnecker, and Boudin 2005:32). Three years later, in February 1992, they finally acted. Yet their attempted coup was a short-lived failure. Rebel forces took provincial cities but, in Caracas, Chávez was unable to detain President Pérez as planned, and he found himself surrounded and cut off in the city's historical museum. He confessed later that "the civilians didn't show up" (quoted in Gott 2001:69). The people were missing. Forced to turn himself in, the would-be coup leader asked only for a minute of airtime on national television so as to tell his allies elsewhere that they too should surrender. It was this brief broadcast that made his name, as Chávez declared to the country that "for now" the attempt to overthrow the regime had failed. On TV, speaking directly to the nation without the mediation of the MBR or any other organization, at last Chávez found his métier. Though he would soon be jailed for his leading role in the conspiracy, in the space of an instant, with a two-word phrase evoking change to come, he had identified himself with a messianic promise.

By 1994, Chávez was pardoned and released (Pérez had been impeached for corruption and thrown out of office). No longer a clandestine organization, the MBR focused on "its fundamental political strategy of demanding the convocation of a National Constituent Assembly" (López Maya 1998:90). In the buildup to the 1998 presidential race, it was transformed into a political party: the Movement for the Fifth Republic (Movimiento Quinto Republica, or MVR). Running on a manifesto to build a new republic, Chávez was handsomely elected into power, winning 56 percent of the vote. A constituent assembly followed in 1999, and a new constitution was approved in December of that year. The constitution called for a one-time "mega election" in which all elected officials, from city council members to president, would have to stand to be relegitimated. On 30 July 2000, as over 33,000 candidates competed for more than 6,000 posts, in a stroke the election "eliminated the country's old political elite almost entirely from the upper reaches of Venezuela's public institutions" (Wilpert 2007:22). The old guard had gone; but in each electoral race a new guard took its place. The old pact had ruptured; a new pact, in which the state would now appeal directly to the multitude over the airwaves, had just begun.

Ever since, and throughout his regime, Chávez has appealed to this constitutional transformation as the foundation and anchor of his "Bolivarian Revolution." Millions of copies of the document itself were printed and distributed throughout the country, and the president has been accustomed to carrying it with him at all times and to gesturing to and with it during his political speeches. It is symptomatic that, in reaction, one of the first (and indeed very few) acts of the brief government of Pedro Carmona, installed for forty-eight hours after the soon-reversed coup of 2002, was to declare that the name of the country itself, which the first words of Article One of Chávez's constitution had declared to be the "Bolivarian Republic of Venezuela," was to be once more simply the "Republic of Venezuela." Symbolically, this was the Carmona regime's attempt to overthrow the constituent process. So the multitude that came into the streets that April to reinstate their president were also seeking to put that process back on track. But Chávez, too, was forced to react and adjust. His government took a very different tone thereafter, as if in somewhat belated recognition of the debt he owes the multitudes who have now twice very visibly provided the force that propelled him to power. Some of that reaction has taken the form of a radicalization (a turn toward the discourse of socialism); but other aspects of that reaction have been more literally reactionary, not least in the attempt to rewrite the constitution in such a way as to consolidate the state apparatus. For the antichavista scaremongering around the constitutional referendum of 2007 did indeed have a point: the proposed reforms were another instance of constituted power folding back on constituent power. It is therefore significant that the measures failed to be approved, and mostly because of the widespread abstention on the part of many who would otherwise support the Bolivarian Revolution. That exodus even from the plebiscitary structure of chavismo demonstrates that the multitude refuses to be seen as a *plebs*, as a people to whom the premier can appeal if and when he wants. For the multitude is always destined to betray the people, to refuse the contract offered it.

Conclusion

This is no swing between right and left. In Venezuela as throughout Latin America, it is clear that the impetus behind these badly named "left turns" has been overwhelmingly constitutional. They are impelled by a series of rebellions whose target is the entire political order and its representational system. They come into office almost by default, as the representational fiction of the creole republic collapses around their heads. And the policy differences between them (nationalization or privatization, free trade or tariffs) are secondary to the shared goal of recreating constituted power, relegitimizing the political system. So Chávez's repeated referenda, his incessant retweakings of the political rules that he himself has put into place, are not so much an expression of a process that has gone off the rails, still less the sign of some personal megalomania, as a return to the political baseline. It is the constitution that is still at stake in the ongoing viability of the Bolivarian republic. And across Latin America, the "left turns" continue to be about a conflict between the subterranean power of a constituent power that is closer to the surface than ever, and a constituted power that is more or less frantically trying to reinvent liberalism for these post-liberal times. Or as Raúl Sánchez and Yann Moulier Boutang put it, in the wake of the absolute "refusal of the coloniality of power," Latin America has become "the revolutionary frontier of politics" thanks to the reemergence of a multitude and its "forceful moments of constituent power" (Sánchez and Boutang 2009:36, 39). What remains to be seen is whether the new forms of governability and new forms of subordination incarnated by leaders such as Chávez, Kirchner, Morales, and Lula, will manage to keep the old mole underground for much longer (*Colectivo Situaciones* 2006; Zibechi 2009). My wager is that, despite setbacks such as the more recent episodes in Honduras (which failed precisely because it was an attempt at mobilization from the top down), we haven't seen the last of the multitude and its constituent power. And perhaps next time the immanent social logics of common, carnivalesque redistribution and auto-valorization will prove somewhat more durable. Perhaps.

Note

1. I thank Max Cameron for first suggesting this observation.

8

Arguments About the Left:
A Post-Liberal Politics?

Benjamin Arditi

When Hugo Chávez was elected president of Venezuela, the left governed only in one other country, Cuba. Since then, there has been a tectonic shift in Latin American politics. Left-of-center coalitions are now in office in more than half a dozen countries and many observers speak of a pink wave or left turns in the region. This article seeks to shed some light on this process. It outlines criteria of theoretical and practical reason to address what it means to speak of the left in this juncture and looks at ways of characterizing its resurgence. Winning elections is the undisputed benchmark to assess the left turns. It is also restrictive because the ongoing changes in the region seem to go beyond the fortunes of short-term coalitions. This is why I propose to supplement the standard benchmark with additional criteria. The main one is the success of the left in redefining the parameters of the political and ideological center. In the final section, I focus on what I see as the most innovative aspect of these turns, namely, their challenge to the conventionally liberal understanding of politics. A post-liberal political scenario is emerging as actors experiment with various formats and sites of engagement alongside the liberal sphere of electoral representation. It is not a Manichean either/or situation; ongoing insurgencies are weary of liberal politics but are nonetheless contaminated by them. My conclusion is that we are bound to see more rather than less hybridity in this post-liberal scenario.

What Makes the Left Turns Leftist?

Let me begin by stating the obvious: there has been a shift to the left in Latin American politics. The political landscape is now populated by the likes of Hugo Chávez, Evo Morales, Cristina Kirchner, Tabaré Vásquez, Lula da Silva,

Daniel Ortega, Rafael Correa, and Fernando Lugo instead of Alberto Fujimori, Carlos Menem, Carlos Andrés Pérez, and Gonzalo Sánchez de Lozada. It is also commonplace to speak of the elusiveness of the signifier *left*. Understanding what the term stands for has become more difficult ever since mainstream socialist and left-of-center organizations started to adopt a market-friendly outlook and to phase out the language of class warfare, national liberation, internationalism, strict Westphalian sovereignty, state ownership, and so on. The irony is that both claims are true, but they cannot be true together without forcing a performative contradiction. For how can we speak of a turn to the left if we are unsure about what counts as the left?

One way to circumvent this difficulty is to say that it worries academics more than it does leftist parties and movements. The latter will go on with their business without pondering much about what the label entails, particularly because the left-right spectrum does not seem to play a significant role in the making of political identities among the citizenry. This might be the case, but the time and effort that political warriors have spent shoring up their progressive credentials and lambasting the right suggests that the question might not be irrelevant for them either. Besides, even if the term left (or right) has lost much of its political purchase among voters, the fact that we continue to use it is significant in itself. This is reminiscent of something P. Worsley once said about populism: "since the word *has* been used, the existence of verbal smoke might well indicate a fire somewhere" (Worsley 1969:219).

A second option is to make the meaning of the left dependent on the evocative force of the term, which is what the bulk of academics, journalists, and politicians do anyway when they speak of left turns. A series of policies, gestures, speech patterns, and friendships prevalent in a group or in the practices of its visible leaders appear as leftist because, at some point, they have been classified as such. Although this makes things easier, the fact that the referents are far from unequivocal can create all sorts of difficulties. The anti-imperialism and concomitant defense of sovereignty and nonintervention that once dominated the left's imaginary is waning. We used to associate anti-imperialism with resistance to US interventionism, whether as a principled defense of the Cuban and Nicaraguan revolutions or as the demand of self-determination from Guatemalans and Chileans after the elections of Jacobo Arbenz and Salvador Allende. It also meant opposition to capitalism, particularly in the context of the Leninist characterization of imperialism as the highest stage of capitalism. However, as Lomnitz put it, in light of the changes in Latin America's position in the international economy, today's "anti-imperialism is not anti-capitalism so much as a politics of reconfiguration of regional blocks" (Lomnitz 2006). Also, the idea of sovereignty in the strong Westphalian sense is languishing. One reason for this is that global processes prevent the nation-state from being the sole—and often even the main—locus of decisions affecting the polity.

Another is that self-determination clashes with another regulative idea that became part of the discourse of the Latin American left after the difficult years of the 1970s: the acknowledgment that hiding behind nonintervention can function as a ruse to justify the worst governmental excesses in matters of human and other rights.

A third possibility is to use typologies; these can be helpful in classifying the left turns by providing us with an image of thought to reduce complexity and to organize the field of experience. An example of a felicitous typology is U. Beck's distinction among globalism, globality, and globalization. These terms designate the neoliberal ideology that reduces globalization to free markets and financial flows, the experience of living in a world where the decline of closed spaces has been happening for a long time, and the processes of interpenetration of national states as a result of the operation of transnational actors and the supranational condition of contemporary politics, correspondingly (Beck 2000). This allows us to understand how one can endorse something like a politics of globalization while resisting globalism. Castañeda's distinction between good and bad left is an illustration of a more contentious typology. He defines the left as "that current of thought, politics, and policy that stresses social improvements over macroeconomic orthodoxy, egalitarian distribution of wealth over its creation, sovereignty over international cooperation, democracy (at least when in opposition, if not necessarily once in power) over governmental effectiveness" (Castañeda 2006:32). The binarism of this definition foreshadows the one at work in his typology. Castañeda pits the right, modern, democratic, accountable, sensible, and market-friendly left—which is virtually a clone of the one governing in Chile—against the wrong, populist, authoritarian, corrupt, state-centered, and irresponsible one of Chávez, Morales, Andrés Manuel López Obrador, Ollanta Humala, Néstor Kirchner, and now presumably his wife, Cristina Fernández de Kirchner. The political intent of this normative distinction between right and wrong left is to provide a guiding criterion for the foreign policy of the United States and like-minded governments toward left-of-center coalitions in the region: don't pick fights that are not worth fighting, offer incentives to those who move closer to the proper left, and contain those who refuse to give up their wrong ways.

Some might find it useful to modify and improve Castañeda's distinction by redefining who or what counts as the right and wrong left or by adding shades of gray and expanding the number of lefts to three, four, or more. I see little scholarly advantage in doing so, given that it leaves the motive of the distinction untouched, namely, the intent of sorting leftist governments according to their commitment to electoral democracy and a certain synchronicity with the images of rationality and modernity derived from the Washington Consensus. This circumscribes the left to a liberal perspective, which is nothing to frown about except for the fact that it makes the qualifier *left* superfluous.

A Minimal Conceptual Framework
for Specifying the Political Left

All this tells us that we need to say something about what the left stands for if
we want to discuss the left turns. For this I propose two overlapping sets of criteria. One provides us with a minimal conceptual grid to frame the term: the
left aims to change the status quo, it is the torchbearer of equality and solidarity, and what passes for either of these is verified through polemics. These are
criteria of theoretical reason that highlight the context dependency of the signifier *left;* they avoid pegging it to this or that project of change and/or representation of equality and solidarity by leaving the actual filling of change,
equality, and so on, to the polemics among political players themselves. The
other set of criteria focuses on the praxis of left groupings and constitutes a
supplement of practical reason: the identity of these political groupings shifts
in accordance with the hits and misses of their projects, their changing adversaries, and the representations they make of themselves.

Criteria of Theoretical Reason

I begin with the conceptual grid. First, the left turns have to do with the political left as it manifests itself through speech and action in concert in the public
sphere, whether in government or in opposition, through its political parties or
through other types of organizations. Some may want to include the academic
left of people like us, who make a living by teaching and preaching about progressive values and ideas, or even the broadly defined cultural left, whose
work, identity, and lifestyle is broadly considered part of the left because of a
shared taste in music, films, literature, or newspapers (Rabotnikof 2004). This
is understandable given that, in Latin America teachers, writers, and artists
often join political movements and intervene in very public polemics on current
affairs, so the frontiers between the various lefts are fluid. But to include them
we need to add a proviso: the cultural and the academic left start to count as political only when they match their normative preference for progressive values
and proposals with an existential investment. The latter consists of taking a
public stand in controversies and/or working for the advancement of a political
group and its projects with the intention of changing the world.

There are many ways to understand what it means to change the world
and how different another world must be before we can call it "other," but at
least we can agree that the motivation to do so has to do with the acknowledgment that the one we live in has too many injustices. Hence the second criterion: the left is the torchbearer of the Cinderella values of the French
Revolution, equality and solidarity (which replaces the gender-specific original, *fraternity*). This is a crucial difference with liberals, who took individual

freedom as their driving force and remained relatively indifferent to the systemic inequalities of capitalist accumulation while accepting a tradeoff between market individualism and solidarity. The left considers liberty to be part of its heritage but believes that without equity it is precarious; like Rousseau, it sees in inequality the seeds of dependency and subordination that will eventually make a travesty of freedom. This is why the left gathers those who seek to improve on existing thresholds of egalitarianism and solidarity through critical thought and collective action. It makes normative claims about the desirability of greater social justice and of open discussion of public affairs. It is not particularly relevant whether this pursuit is channeled through mainstream institutions of liberal democratic states—parties, legislatures, and executive branches of government—or through other sites of intervention that are starting to demarcate a post-liberal setting for politics (more on this in the final section). Echoing Karl Marx, all this happens in circumstances that are not of the left's choosing and within the constraints imposed by the strategic relationships with others, the available resources, and a particular time frame.

There is, of course, no hard referent or authoritative judge to determine what counts as equality, solidarity, or participation in critical debates, or how the various strands of the left conceive and combine each of these elements, or what kind of tension between them they are willing to tolerate. All we have is a plethora of singular cases. This is where the third criterion enters the scene: equality, solidarity, and participation have no relevant political existence outside efforts to singularize them in polemical cases. Polemics occurs within the coordinates of a given horizon of possibilities, contending forces, and alternative projects and policies. This creates a scenario of continual verification where what passes for the left enters into the equation and therefore reinforces the claim that there is no such thing as a unitary left and that left politics is largely context-dependent.

Criteria of Practical Reason

Now we can turn our attention to what I described earlier as a supplement of practical reason. It is that the Latin American left, whether as a concept, an identity, or a set of practices inventoried under that name, has been continually shaped by three sets of interlocking factors. One is the historical experience resulting from the hits and misses or the successes and (mostly) defeats of the past half century or so. Another is the strategic relationship with a changing outside, be this the oligarchy, the forces of imperialism, military rule, or electoral and everyday adversarial politics with other groups in liberal democratic settings. The third factor is the manifold representations of the left in manifestos, pamphlets, and theoretical writings that try to make sense of the other two and address the classical questions of who we are and what we are fighting for.

These elements are interwoven in the itinerary that goes from insurrectional to electoral politics and from popular fronts to broad-based coalitions, as well as in the post-liberal angle of left politics. If the 1960s were the glory days when the enthusiasm generated by the Cuban Revolution and Che Guevara's guerrilla experience in Bolivia boded well for the socialist shape of the future, the 1970s and a good deal of the 1980s are the lost decades for the left. After some initial success in Chile with the election of Salvador Allende in 1970, a string of right-wing coups and the concomitant militarization of state responses to popular protests marked a period of political defeat, persecution, exile, and demobilization. The unexpected effect of this defeat is that it prompted a significant number of political groups either to reassess their misgivings about electoral democracy or to broaden their appeal beyond workers and the peasantry. The academic and partisan literature addressing this reassessment is copious, and the left matched its cognitive shift with a decisive drive to get rid of military governments and to construct or reconstruct democratic regimes. The new enemy was not so much the ruling classes or imperialism but authoritarian rulers, and the tacit agreement was that property relations would not be touched in a transition, all of which explains why the socialist agenda was either downplayed or deferred. Eventually the tide turned toward multiparty democracy. This is partly because of the efforts of anti-authoritarian forces but also because, by the mid-1980s, repressive regimes were facing growing isolation and opprobrium: anticommunism was virtually bankrupt as an ideological currency to justify the brutality of governments or to obtain support from the United States and the tacit acquiescence of the international community. The wave of transitions stretches from the election of Jaime Roldós in Ecuador in 1979 to the defeat of the Partido Revolucionario Institucional (PRI) in Mexico in 2000.

However, the conservative revolution spearheaded by Ronald Reagan and Margaret Thatcher in the 1980s outflanked the left by championing ideas and policies that eventually became an article of faith among multilateral organizations and an index of what sound economic practice was about. By the time the Washington Consensus had become the unofficial blueprint for economic reforms—and *liberalization, deregulation, free trade,* and *privatization of state enterprises* the familiar words of order of the 1980s and 1990s—most in the parliamentarian left were already coming to terms with the need to adjust social policies to monetary stability and fiscal discipline. Trust in the state as the gatekeeper of sovereignty through its ownership of natural resources, industries, and services was undermined by the drive to court foreign direct investment and expand international trade. Neoliberalism served as shorthand for the corpus of ideas behind these reforms. Perhaps the only significant blip in this imaginary of markets (and elections) is the emergence of the Zapatistas in Chiapas, Mexico, in 1994, the same day that the North American Free Trade

Agreement, or NAFTA, was born. They promoted four themes that are now part of the left's political agenda: the dignity and empowerment of indigenous peoples, the critique of neoliberal policies, the discussion of alternatives to electoral democracy, and the call to reenact internationalism and solidarity on a planetary scale.

Things did not go as planned for advocates of neoliberal policies, either. By the mid-1990s, the certainties of the navigational map charted by the Washington Consensus were being reassessed as the unfulfilled promises of empowerment and material well-being piled up. Multilateral institutions that consistently downplayed claims that things might be going wrong began to acknowledge the need to factor the social dimension into the economic matrix and thus ease the pressure on governments to reduce public debt at all costs. The region's governments faced the destabilizing mix of modest growth with strong inequality and electoral politics with widespread social protests. In countries like Ecuador, El Salvador, Guatemala, Mexico, and Peru, the *remesas* (remittances) sent back by migrants who found their way into the United States or Europe to work mostly as *indocumentados* (undocumented workers) have become a lifeline for their economies. Virtually everywhere—including Chile, the showcase of market-driven economic growth in the region—the excluded express their disaffection and real anger in the ballot box and in the streets. Protesters include the *piqueteros* and middle-class victims of the *corralito* (2001 bank closing) in Argentina, *cocaleros* (coca growers) in Bolivia, *sem terra* (landless) in Brazil, students and Mapuches in Chile, and impoverished peasants in Paraguay. The fall of President Fernando de la Rúa in Argentina in December 2001 is the iconic moment of this backlash against politics and politicians associated with the failures of neoliberal adjustment policies, encapsulated in the chant, "Que se vayan todos, que no quede ni uno solo" (All of them must go, not a single one can stay). It is not by chance that the Latin American Studies Association chose to discuss what comes after the Washington Consensus as the general theme for its scholarly meeting of 2007.

"Que se vayan todos" was significant for another reason too, one that exceeds the boundaries of Argentine politics. As is well known in Argentina, the discontented middle classes, unionists, and the bulk of the piqueteros and *asambleistas* (assemblyists) that had vilified the political class in 2001 began to address demands to the state and eventually participated in the general elections of 2003. One interpretation of this change of heart is that the chant was not meant as a rejection of political representation or as the celebration of the multitude in action. It was instead a more conventional accusation directed to a political class that failed to do something about the misery resulting from the privatization and adjustment policies of the 1990s. There is an element of truth in this, but it overlooks the fact that "Que se vayan todos" also expressed the enthusiasm for another way of doing politics. Many of those coming together

in the protests, assemblies, and neighborhood meetings of 2001 were motivated by the belief that there was something fundamentally wrong with representation and that it was worth experimenting with alternatives like exodus,
multitude, self-government, recall, and so on. A similar experimentation took
place in the Guerra del Agua in Cochabamba, Bolivia, in 2000, the resistance
of Atenco to the construction of the new international airport of Mexico City
in 2002, or the Guerra del Gas in Bolivia in 2002–2003. There is a long et
cetera of cases like these. What is noteworthy is that in all of them, the resistance to neoliberalism converges with efforts to move beyond the liberal framework of participation. "Que se vayan todos" functions as shorthand for this
convergence, as a symptom of the post-liberal dimension at work in the left
turns alongside elections and partisan representation.

The certainties of the economic and political commonsense of the 1980s
and 1990s were also undermined by the deafness of the main political player
in the region. Whatever interest the United States had in Latin America virtually disappeared after 9/11, except on questions of trade, in matters it considers of national security—like immigration and drugs—or during occasional
panic attacks triggered by electoral results in countries like Bolivia and
Venezuela. The US war on terror and subsequent invasion of Iraq simply increased its estrangement, probably because the neoconservatives who became
the ideological driving force of the Bush administration were more interested
in asserting the global power of the United States by reshaping the Middle East
than by strengthening hemispheric relations. Of course, the geopolitical presence of the United States or the financial muscle that gives it unrivaled voting
power in the International Monetary Fund (IMF) allows it to play a role in
major policy decisions. But the years of relative disregard for the region have
taken their toll. The failure of the United States to win support for its preferred
candidate during the election of the secretary-general of the Organization of
American States (OAS) in 2005 is one example of this. Another is the strong
presence of China in the region. Its investments and long-term trade agreements with Venezuela, Argentina, and Brazil have enabled China to extend its
political presence in a region that the United States saw as its natural zone of
influence (Romero and Barrionuevo 2009:1, 15).

Taken together, the failures of governments to tackle demands for symbolic
and particularly material goods, the intellectual and political retreat of orthodox
neoliberal policies, and the vacuum created by the aloofness of the United States
in the region creates a setting conducive for the resurgence of the left. In the familiar parlance of detective television shows, they provide it with a motive and
an opportunity to succeed. This resurgent left has more diverse tonalities than its
predecessors, and it is difficult capture them simply by drawing from the familiar categories of social democracy and populism. But we can agree at least that
the term *left* applies to collective actions that aim to change the status quo be-

cause another, less oppressive and more just and egalitarian world is deemed possible and necessary. Drawing from this discussion, we can identify the set of markers that shape the bulk of the Latin American lefts today:

• Contrary to what transpires from a red-menace rhetoric dressed as a critique of populism, this left is not enthralled by a Marxist political script. This is partly because of the aforementioned criteria of theoretical and practical reason: it sees equality, solidarity, critical thought, or the questioning of the status quo as context-dependent variables, not ideological set pieces.

• The bulk of the left is now less hostile toward private property and the market and has warmed up to accepting cohabitation with them, yet it confronts the orthodoxy that only a decade ago was heralded as the embodiment of economic rationality.

• In opposition to the ideology of the minimal state and a zero-sum game between a big, wasteful, incompetent state and the vital and efficient private sector, for the left, the state remains crucial for regulating markets and pursuing redistribution policies, even if some strands advocate a politics of exodus from the state.

• The left is suspicious of the US ambition to fashion a unipolar world with itself at the helm, which is consistent with its anti-imperialist tradition, but it is quite happy to negotiate trade agreements with it if these are advantageous to their countries.

• Even if multiparty electoral democracy—the heart of the liberal conception of politics—is a fixture in the imaginary of the left, so is the experimentation with post-liberal formats of political participation.

Left Turn(s) With and Without the Electoral Benchmark

Having looked at what we mean by the *left*, the next step is to examine what could allow us to speak of left *turns* in Latin American politics. If we measure the success of the left in terms of actual alternatives to liberal governance and market-driven economic policies, the results are fuzzy everywhere except in Venezuela and, to a lesser extent, in Bolivia. Both countries are blessed with vast reserves of oil and gas at a time when the price of such commodities has hit record heights thanks to factors like the war in Iraq and the appetite of the Chinese for energy resources to fuel economic growth in the years leading to the financial crisis of 2008. F. Panizza discusses this in a lucid interpretation of the resurgence of left-of-center parties in Latin America by saying that it is doubtful whether the left has come closer to developing an alternative to the status quo beyond opposing the neoliberal agenda and contributing to frame a post–Washington Consensus agenda (Panizza 2005b:718, 727–728, 730). Lomnitz shares this view, explaining that "the new left is not revolutionary and anti-capitalist; it is pro-regulation. It will continue to turn to developmentalism if there is no concerted effort to promote alternative models" (Lomnitz 2006).

The difficulty of generating clear policy choices is quite real but it need not be such a worrisome sign given that alternative policies usually arrive after a new paradigm or imaginary gets a foothold in the public imagination. Thatcher and Reagan's neoliberal worldview rested on fairly simple sound bites, such as never trust tax-and-spend politicians, the state is an inefficient economic agent, competition gives you better and cheaper services, adjustment policies are tough but inevitable, wealth will eventually trickle down and make everyone more prosperous, and so on. People often forget that their actual policies were developed on the go after they were elected, and once they were applied they were not always successful or even consistent. The many casualties of the adjustment policies of the 1980s and 1990s are still waiting for the realization of the much-heralded trickle-down effect, and economists have long pointed out that under Reagan's watch the United States amassed the largest public deficit on record before this dubious honor was bestowed on George W. Bush.

Alternatively, if we measure success in terms of winning elections, the left did very well in countries like Chile, Bolivia, Brazil, Ecuador, Nicaragua, Paraguay, Uruguay, and Venezuela, despite the differences in their political forces, policies, and styles of government. Some would include Argentina under Kirchner and Fernández de Kirchner as well. The left has also done well in Mexico and Peru, where it positioned itself as a major political player—often indispensable to get major legislative and policy decisions off the ground—without becoming government. Governing is a critical marker of success; it opens up a new political scene and provides important resources to officeholders, which is why the left should strive to be the winning force.

But what about places where the left has not done particularly well, whether in terms of forming a government or in terms of having a strong presence in the legislatures? Should we exclude them from the debate about left turns? The commonsensical response is yes, as winning elections is the prevalent criterion for judging these turns. I agree with this, but not wholeheartedly, as common sense—which is the commonplace turned into sound judgment—might be often right, yet it is also restrictive in terms of imagining alternatives to the given. That is why we should think outside the box and put the electoral benchmark on hold for a moment to contemplate other empirical and conceptual indicators. This will allow us to include experiences that normally do not qualify as indicators of left turns and provide us with a more complex picture of these turns.

Before discussing this I want to make it clear that I do not mean to minimize the importance of elections but to highlight that they are not the only democratic way to foster changes. There are—there have always been—other ways of doing so, from demonstrations to sit-ins and road blockades, and from civil disobedience to the right to rebellion theorized by the very liberal John Locke. Also, the ability to affect decisionmaking processes and enforce binding agreements does not depend solely on electoral results. Governing empowers the left, but it also is, or can be, a humbling experience. Hence, the extra leverage the left acquires when in government it is bound to be challenged continually in electoral and other arenas. Adversaries will try to put limits on what it can do and very likely they will modify its agenda, as Chávez learned when his constitutional amendments were rejected in the December 2007 referendum and had to go through another referendum in 2009 to finally prevail. Just like Nietzsche once said, resistance is already present in obedience because one never surrenders individual power; we can take as a rule that those who lose a contest—be it an election, a war, a public debate, or what have you—are defeated but not necessarily disarmed. The governing Partido Acción Nacional (PAN) in Mexico can dismiss Andrés Manuel López Obrador and the Partido de la Revolución Democrática (PRD) as sore losers after PAN's razor-thin and much-disputed electoral win in 2006, but they know very well that the defeated have surrendered nothing and that the struggle goes on.

Resistance to authoritarian rule in the Southern Cone in the 1970s and 1980s shows us how one can have a degree of political success without winning elections. Recall that people in those countries had been developing alternative spaces, relationships, and identities by setting up independent trade unions, student organizations, or nongovernmental organizations (NGOs) long before the repressive governments were repealed. The same can be said about aesthetic experimentation: the arts, the media, literature, theater, and music thrived outside the rigid aesthetic languages favored by authoritarian governments. These acts of resistance were changing things by undermining the demobilizing perception that all resistance to the regime was futile and by reminding authorities that they could not impose their decisions at will.

Those who participated were neither unafraid nor paralyzed by repression. In a way, they practiced their freedom despite the state because they were already acting as citizens, even if citizenship was a legal fiction wherever there was an Alfredo Stroessner, Augusto Pinochet, Humberto Castelo Branco, Jorge Videla, or any of their many military and civilian epigones in government. For those who challenged the order of things, citizenship was a practice of liberation rather than an appeal to a legal status recognized by the state, even if the goal was to make it a statutory right rather than a risky exercise of defiance. Freedom was not perceived simply as a prize to be cashed in a post-authoritarian future because people were already enjoying a sense of freedom as they struggled for it. This performative dimension is less heroic but equally present in liberal democracies. There, to borrow a line from J. Grugel, the impact of social or political activism "lies in the capacities to put arguments in the public domain; to build coalitions for change; to provide resources for other groups; and to make connections across and within civil society" (Grugel 2005:1073).

Whether in repressive scenarios or in more gentrified settings, the left can succeed in modifying public policies, legislation, or budget allocations—and therefore partake in governing in the Foucaultian sense of structuring the possible field of action of others (Foucault 1982:207–209)—without winning an election because the constituent force of political performativity is at work anytime, anywhere.

We have seen that Panizza is not fully convinced that the public policies pursued by the left managed to provide us with alternatives to market-driven economies. Yet he also states that the ideas of the left are part of an emerging post–Washington Consensus agenda, which amounts to acknowledging that the left has had some measure of success in setting up alternatives to neoliberalism. I would take this a step further and argue that the agenda-setting capacity of the left reflects an important shift. This time it is not the transit from revolution to electoral democracy discussed earlier, but from a defensive to a proactive stance, in this case one that seeks to shape the invisible ideology that gives an aura of reasonableness to the political center. Here I draw from something V. Armony mentions about the shift to the left. He states that "the discontent with the status quo and the desire for social change are framed by a narrative that presents itself as an alternative to the pro-market reform narrative . . . [and] *defines the current ideological center in Latin America*" (Armony 2007, emphasis in the original). What is at stake in what he says is not the development of a centrist politics but the constitution of a new discursive center of reference for politics and the leading role of the left in this process. For Armony, the left *already is* the new center.

We can build on this observation to reinforce the idea that the left turns are wider than what the electoral benchmark suggests. In the 1980s and 1990s, the right dictated the parameters of the center or, more precisely, it advocated the part about endorsing markets and public sector reforms. I underline this because people often forget that the other key components—human rights, ideological pluralism, and multiparty democracy—were secured despite and not because of the right. These were demands spearheaded by the left and by all those who sought to undo authoritarian rule at a time when the right was happy to endorse the anticommunist ideology that served first as an alibi for repressing progressive forces and then to pursue a neoliberal agenda. The Chilean referendum of 1988 is such a clear example of this. In voting for the "yes" option, the right was committing itself to another eight years of Pinochet's rule and showed that it was quite comfortable with an authoritarian project with economic liberalization even if this meant downplaying human rights, democracy, or equality. So, if the center of reference of the post-authoritarian years is seen as a brainchild of the right, it is only because it succeeded in placing politics under the mantle of economic reforms and subsequently capitalized on the erroneous perception that to dispute the centrality of the market was to put into question electoral democracy, too.

The current standard of what constitutes the center is more clearly a creation of the left. On the one hand, it has had an impact on the political and cultural dimensions of the center. A scenario traditionally dominated by educated middle-aged white or *mestizo* men is now populated by a growing number of women and indigenous people whose credentials do not always include higher education degrees. The left has spearheaded their causes and their claims long before the right even discovered gender difference and ethnic diversity. Additional indicators of the left's impact on this renewed sense of what the center stands for are the drives to denounce and punish corrupt politicians, to politicize questions of cultural and ethnical exclusion, and to conduct ongoing experimentation with new participatory channels that deepen the liberal format of politics or step outside it. On the other hand, the new center has a socioeconomic dimension that includes strengthening the state to regulate markets and curb the excesses of privatization (particularly in the case of water, energy, and communications), increasing social expenditures for redistribution purposes, and critically examining IMF's policy guidelines and their rejection if considered detrimental to the national interest.

Latinobarómetro (2007) registers this shift in the configuration of the political center, particularly with regard to the relation between state and market. Despite the marked differences among Latin American countries, the one coincidence that the study reports is the centrality of issues of inequality and discrimination in the electoral agenda. In virtually all eighteen countries covered by the study, people are increasingly disenchanted with the market and believe that only the state can provide lasting solutions to their problems. This is why the study states that "the only consensus in the region is the consensus about the Washington Consensus—it didn't solve the problems and we need to find an alternative to it" (Latinobarómetro 2007:8, 9; also commentary by Zovatto 2007). The 2008 report confirms this tendency by saying that at a global level, "those who until recently advocated unfettered competition are now presiding over the largest state intervention in contemporary economic history" (Latinobarómetro 2008:6). The neoliberal economic narrative and the one-size-fits-all policies of its *pensamiento único* is waning. Its focus on monetary policy, markets, and the reduction of public deficits at the expense of the state and social welfare was an article of faith among many politicians and economists in the region. Today, in contrast, the state is being vindicated as the only actor capable of regulating the unchecked financial markets that were responsible for the current crisis, and governments are embarking on an expansive fiscal policy to jump-start aggregate demand and reduce inequalities, even if it generates short-term deficits in public finances. What is remarkable is that this has not sparked a wave of nostalgia for authoritarian rule. Quite the opposite: people demand more democracy even if experiences such as the *asambleas barriales* (neighborhood assemblies), the *fabricas recuperadas* (recuperated factories), or the Guerra del Agua (Water War) show that democracy is not always confined to its electoral dimension. When respondents ask for more rather than less democracy, they are obviously vindicating the symbolic dimension of democracy, that is, asking for more participation, but they are also grafting onto it the material dimension of public policies that enhance the well-being of the dispossessed. To quote Latinobarómetro, "there is ample evidence that the meaning of democracy in Latin America has an economic component that democracies in other parts of the world did not have" (Latinobarómetro 2008:7).

What can we infer from all this? That in a setting marked by new cultural referents and by the retreat of market orthodoxy, the right has to move closer to a discursive configuration coded by the left to expand its electoral and social base. This resignification of the center enables us to interpret the current turn to the left in Latin American politics as the establishment of a new political and ideological common sense as well as the winning of elections and success in advancing a given set of policies. Just as the neoliberal drive of Thatcher and Reagan triggered a cognitive shift before it was able to come up with specific policies, the left is already succeeding in transforming the accepted coordinates of what is politically reasonable and desirable. It must now use its imagination to consolidate this success by developing visionary policies and institutions to tackle the challenges and dreams of the people of the region. The left may fail in its efforts to modify the distribution of wealth and privileges to benefit the poor and excluded, yet, even if it does, the left turns are already achieving two things. One is that they have managed to reintroduce questions of equality, distribution, and inclusion into the political agenda. This opens up a chance for political invention to give substance to what the Economic Commission for Latin America and the Caribbean (ECLAC) used to call economic growth with equity. The second is that connecting the turns to a resignification of the political center instead of pegging them to the vicissitudes of electoral processes makes it possible to imagine the duration of their effects after Chávez, Morales, Correa, Kirchner, and others have left the political stage.

Post-Liberalism to Come as a Politics of the Left

Now I move to the final topic of this article. We can group the bulk of the recent literature on the left according to whether it focuses on mainstream or on alternative politics. This may be a disputable simplification, but it also reduces complexity and helps us move on with the argument. Mainstream interventions usually concentrate on political parties and movements as well as governance because they look at the left in national or local executive and legislative bodies. Those dealing with alternatives to the status quo tend to discuss nonelectoral political initiatives and to view the left as a force of resistance, opposition, and change. They also differ in terms of citations: names like Guillermo O'Donnell, Philippe Schmitter, Juan Linz, Alan Knight, Scott Mainwaring, Adam Przeworski, and Manuel Antonio Garretón appear often in the first group and those of Antonio Gramsci, Antonio Negri, Paolo Virno, Gilles Deleuze, Ernesto Laclau, and John Holloway as well as those from subaltern studies are more salient in the second. Mainstream and alternative themes and citations rarely mix in the literature, which is a shame because there is so much room for hybridity. A post-liberal setting of politics includes hybrid and other possibilities.

Post-Liberalism: Political History Has No Closure

Let me say a few words of caution about post-liberalism. The current wave of left politics still draws its inspiration from the socialist imaginary, whether in its cultural orientations, the enactment of distributive demands, or the general vindication of the dignity of those who are excluded because they are poor, indigenous, or women. Yet, unlike their Leninist predecessors, the left tends to demand equality without necessarily seeking to abolish capitalism, international trade, or liberal citizenship. This is not because it is content with cosmetic changes to disguise the misery and frustration created by the imposition of markets and neoliberal policies in places where a level playing field for competition is nonexistent. It is because the left has a much more layered relationship to the liberal tradition that prevents us from seeing it simply as antiliberal. As we saw earlier, the left does not necessarily reject markets as a matter of principle, and though elections might have lost some of their appeal among the young and the excluded, they remain a significant part of leftist politics. If anything, the liberal heritage in matters of civil rights and electoral participation has to be defended from its authoritarian and elitist liberal enemies. I say this even if the left also acknowledges that partisan competition is in no great shape and needs reforming, and some have important objections to representation and the state in the name of the plurality and singularities of the multitude.

The left, then, is more post-liberal than antiliberal. The prefix does not suggest the end of liberal politics and its replacement with something else, yet it is clear that the *post* of post-liberal designates something that cannot be fully contained within the liberal form. These two remarks give us the necessary elements to specify what we mean by post-liberalism. First, it means that there is a series of political phenomena that take place in the borders of liberalism and their status vis-à-vis liberalism cannot be decided outside a disagreement or polemic. Supranational politics that involve players that are neither sovereign states nor multilateral organizations, the *usos y costumbres* that guide everyday life in local communities, autonomous municipal governments, the *presupuesto participativo* (participatory budgeting), and the demands for radical changes in patterns of participation and redistribution are some examples of politics in the borders of liberalism. And second, post-liberalism indicates that our understanding of democracy does not stop at the gates of its liberal incarnation. The emergence of sites and formats of political exchange that go beyond territorial representation has loosened the connotative link between electoral and democratic politics. C. B. Macpherson (1965) formulates this very well when he recounts how the adjective *liberal* came to precede the name *democracy*. He reminds us that the compound expression *liberal democracy* is a relatively recent occurrence because the liberal state existed long before it became democratic with the addition of universal suffrage. Its democratization was accompanied by the liberalization of democracy, as this was a democracy embedded in the society and the politics of choice, competition, and the market. This occurred, he says, after many decades of agitation and organization by those who were denied a voice in running public affairs (Macpherson 1965:6–11). The link between the two components is a result of struggles and of the hits and misses of political projects, not the expression of natural affinity, which is why the liberal take on democracy might be a great achievement but not the crowning of political history. If it were, the left's scope for inventiveness would be restricted to an endless fine-tuning of the inherited institutional setting. We can take Macpherson's arguments one step further by proposing post-liberalism as an image of thought of the politics and democracy to come of the left, one that includes electoral contests but is not reducible to them.

By describing it as a politics "to come" I do not mean to say that post-liberalism is a future politics that is not yet here but eventually will be or an ideal waiting for its eventual realization. It is not a question of waiting for Godot but of taking seriously what Jacques Derrida meant by this when he spoke of justice, democracy, or hospitality to come. These are *always* to come because, regardless of whether we think we have already settled what we mean by democracy or justice, different people at different junctures are bound to reopen the question and embark in polemics to reframe their meaning. This "to come" is also informed by what Slavoj Žižek's calls "enacted utopia." Unlike the standard rendering of utopia as an idealized nonplace, the "enacted" variant is used to indicate that the shadow of the future is already at work here and now because "we *already are free fighting for freedom, we are already happy while fighting for happiness*, no matter how difficult the circumstances" (Žižek 2002:559, emphasis in the original). As we have seen, this is precisely what happened throughout the resistance to authoritarian rule in South America: citizenship was not a statutory right but many acted as if they were free citizens. Taken together, Derrida's to come and Žižek's enacted utopia provide us with a particular understanding of the "futurality" of post-liberalism to come: it does not mean waiting for an arrival but, rather, recognizing something ongoing before it "formally" arrives. Put differently, the "to come" of post-liberalism designates something that is already happening: it is an invitation to partake in a future that has already begun to occur. For the same reason, this "to come" cannot be absent from liberal democratic polities, either. There is no relation of pure exteriority between them: post-liberalism welcomes elections and representation, and the liberal state must coexist with the presupuesto participativo, *municipios autónomos* (autonomous municipalities), and *usos y costumbres*. To cut to the chase, in the device called "left turns," liberalism is what we are but also what we are gradually ceasing to be, whereas post-liberalism is a symptom of what we are in the process of becoming, an index of our becoming other (Arditi 2003, 2007a). In what follows, I describe briefly some aspects of this post-liberalism.

Electoral and Supranational Politics Plus Empowerment Through Social Citizenship

The classical locus of democratic citizenship in liberal thought is characterized by three basic features: the recognition of people as equals in the public sphere, the voluntary nature of participation, and the political demand for citizen empowerment as the right to participate in the selection of public authorities within the territorial borders of the nation-state. Post-liberalism challenges this in several ways.

One pertains to the nature of electoral participation. Schmitter (2006) proposes a series of reforms that are part of a post-liberal democracy, such as offering a small payment for voting (which should not be confused with buying votes), which runs counter to the idea of voluntary participation. This reward for voting is a means to increase voter turnout and functions as a modicum of substantive equality—something dear to the left—by compensating the very poor for the personal expenses incurred when participating in elections. Another proposal consists of reciprocal representation among countries with high levels of trade or strong migratory flows. Each of them would elect two or three senators with full voting rights in the senate of the other to promote legislative projects and introduce issues of concern for their home country in the political agenda of their neighbor. A third proposal is an ingenious way to allocate public funding for political parties. In addition to following the standard criterion—pegging the amount to past electoral performance—citizens themselves would have a voucher and assign it to the party of their choice. If they are not happy with available options, their vouchers will go to fund new parties (Schmitter 2006). All three reforms are feasible without necessarily increasing the amount of public funding currently set aside for political parties.

Another challenge to liberalism is the expansion and legitimization of politics outside the physical enclosure of the nation-state carried out by actors below the governmental level. The literature on this topic is copious. People like Richard Falk, Robert Keohane, Stephen Krasner, and R. B. J. Walker speak about the difficulties of Westphalian sovereignty, whereas Ulrich Beck, David Held, and Andrew Linklater have championed a theoretical framework for supranational politics using the label of *cosmopolitan* democracy and citizenship. At present, this cosmopolitanism is less a set of actually existing institutions than it is a description of a set of informal practices and a project of political reform. There is no recognized instance to validate citizenship rights outside the state, so the cosmopolitan variant remains in a legal and political limbo analogous to Hannah Arendt's "right to have rights," regardless of membership to a state. Yet there is already an ad hoc practice of supranational politics spearheaded by nongovernmental actors who do not wait for governments or international agencies to authorize them or grant them rights to act beyond the territory of their nation-states. Their initiatives have a performative dimension in the sense discussed earlier when commenting on resistances to authoritarian rule in the Southern Cone: they are already transforming the idea of citizenship by engaging in cross-border political exchanges. There are abundant examples—the transnational advocacy networks in Latin America studied by M. E. Keck and K. Sikkink (1998), fair-trade initiatives seeking to introduce a modicum of equality in North-South commerce, the activism of those energized by the World Social Forum of Porto Alegre, and protests like those against the World Trade Organization in Cancún. The cosmopolitanism of these initiatives caters to the internationalism of the left and reverberates with its motto of solidarity—now across frontiers—inherited from the French Revolution.

A third aspect of post-liberalism involves actions, demands, and proposals of social empowerment as a way to be political and democratic while focusing on redistribution instead of participation in the selection of public authorities. What comes to mind here is the Guerra del Agua in Cochabamba in 2000, the movement of *fabricas recuperadas* in Argentina, the initiatives of NGOs and social organizations seeking to modify the agenda and policy debates to develop a MERCOSUR Solidario, and the proposals for a presupuesto participativo in cities from Porto Alegre to Rosario and Buenos Aires. As in the case of the "Que se vayan todos," the common thread in these cases is the opposition to neoliberalism and the search for channels of participation in addition to those offered by liberalism. Social citizenship is one way. I do not understand this in the classical socialist sense of the self-government of producers or in terms of T. H. Marshall's (1950) third-generation rights to health, education, housing, and the like—which remain inoperative despite being enshrined in most constitutional texts in Latin America. Social citizenship refers instead to modes of expression of the popular will that seek a voice in the allocation of public resources rather than in the designation of public authorities. It opens up a possibility of engaging in political and democratic exchanges apart from—or alongside—electoral citizenship. Social and electoral citizenship supplement each other and it would be a mistake to see them as mutually exclusive formats of collective action. C. Offe and P. Schmitter speak of "secondary citizenship" or a second tier of politics to refer to this mode of empowerment associated with organized interest groups (Offe 1984; see also Schmitter 2006). These groups bypass electoral representation without necessarily restricting themselves to functional or corporative representation (Schmitter 2006; Arditi 2003, 2007b).

Hybrid Politics: Multitude, Citizens, State

The final aspect of post-liberal politics I wish to mention refers to interventions that do not have the state or political system as their primary targets. Politics outside the electoral mainstream is nothing new. I am not thinking of the obvious examples of armed insurgencies or the experiences of extra-parliamentarian parties and movements but of civil society—often a misnomer—as a site of political agency and invention. O'Donnell and Schmitter describe its contemporary history in the concluding volume of the *Transitions from Authoritarian Rule* quartet. They speak of the "resurrection of civil society" as an outcome of mobilizations carried out by social movements and organizations (O'Donnell and Schmitter 1986). These mobilizations may not be enough to precipitate regime change, but they contribute to expanded freedoms and to legitimized independent groups. The doings of these nonpartisan groups tells us that politics—in Carl Schmitt's sense of a capacity to distinguish friends from enemies and, if necessary, the disposition to confront the latter—goes beyond the designated sites and actors portrayed by the liberal tradition, if only because in authoritarian settings there is often no functioning party or electoral system.

For O'Donnell and colleagues this is a temporary state of affairs because parties take over as soon as there is an opening for their reentry into the public scene. Yet these events leave traces—a palimpsest of memories, inscriptions, and experiences—of the healthy state of political drives outside territorial representation. And they do not fade away respectfully with the arrival of partisan electoral machineries and their state-savvy image. Quite the opposite: nonpartisan political performances have become a regular fixture of politics through the stubborn presence of urban, indigenous, and other movements and initiatives, which tells us that what the literature calls "the resurrection" of civil society is much more than an interregnum between authoritarian and democratic rule. As Latinobarómetro points out, today "Latin America is mobilized as never before. Yet it is a non-conventional mobilization because it does not always conform to the regular participatory channels of society. . . . Participation happens outside political parties and is not formulated as institutional claims or through the formation of associations" (Latinobarómetro 2008:75, 77). In other words, it is not so much that electoral participation has waned but that there has been a surge in political mobilization outside the traditional arenas for expressing claims and formulating demands. This is yet another reminder that equating electoral politics with politics as such is simply erroneous, even if one must be suspicious about the embellished narratives of activists who see politics outside the mainstream as inherently closer to the democratic spirit.

Let me say more about this nonelectoral politics that includes but exceeds transitional moments. Carlo Donolo (1982) refers to it as homeopathic politics—when the social is "cured" by the social—and contrasts it with the usual allopathic politics in which demands made by society are processed by a formally external instance like the political system and addressed as policies or legislation. Homeopathic politics has a family resemblance to exodus and the politics of the multitude, though there are differences, as advocates of the multitude believe we need to develop nonstate strategic options because the state and representation are contrary to the singularity of the multitude—either people or multitude, says P. Virno (2004:23). The very un-Leninist title of J. Holloway's book—*Change the World Without Taking Power* (2002)—is quite eloquent in depicting the discontent of part of the left with the state and conventional politics. His main referent is the Zapatista experience; he proposes a critique of the "power over" of representative politics because it inevitably leads to domination and vindicates instead the "power to" characteristic of autonomist drives, particularly in the Zapatista experience he takes as a key political referent for his thought. Beasley-Murray addresses this discontent from the standpoint of the multitude. He sees the Caracazo of 1989 in Venezuela as the first post-neoliberal insurgency and the true inaugural gesture of the left turns in Latin America. This was, he says, a "violent, disorganized, and radical" form of political action that "marks an excess that has yet to be expunged from the Latin American political scene. . . . It demonstrated the bankruptcy of *Punto fijismo*, and so of the country's post-war social democratic consensus that was premised on a liberal contract and radical subalternization" (Beasley-Murray 2007; also see Hernández 2004). Insurgencies like this, he adds, are instances of constituent power, of a power to found anew that puts representation into disrepute.

Holloway and Beasley are on to something when they speak of nonelectoral ways to change the given. Both "power to" and the exodus advocated by Virno as a politics of the multitude point toward modes of acting consistent with the performative dimension of politics. Both coincide in that it is possible to transform the given without seizing state power and without focusing on political representation. This helps to counteract the sense of disempowerment among those who have a taste for public involvement but are weary of the hierarchies, real or perceived corruption, and homogenizing drives among political parties and other organizations. Their formal status as citizens recedes in the absence of channels of participation and exposes them to the experience of being functional denizens in their own polities. Nonelectoral—and often nonstate—ways to change the status quo are an attractive option for them.

I sympathize with these views but also have some reservations. One wonders how far to generalize the Zapatista experience Holloway takes as a political paradigm and to what extent it is feasible to implement policies of redistribution by shunning political parties and the state (or "power-over," as he calls them). Also, Beasley-Murray might overplay the novelty of the Caracazo and other insurgencies like the Zapatista uprising, the Argentinean mobilizations of December 2001, or the Bolivian gas protests. Novelty is undermined by their complex and more nuanced relationship with the past. The author himself seems to acknowledge this when he states that these insurgencies "built on and learned from the movements that had preceded them" (Beasley-Murray 2007). Whether because of links with the past or because of contamination with other political forms, the multitude is always a hybrid—as is, of course, any other political form, including liberalism. One indication of the hybrid nature of these insurgencies is the shift in the position of many asambleas barriales as well as of the piqueteros. The latter appeared in the Argentine political landscape in 1997–1998 and together with the asambleas were some of the protagonists of the events of 2001. Some saw in this the multitude in action insofar as the "Que se vayan todos" was an affirmation of a politics of exodus from representation. But we have already mentioned that most of the piqueteros and participants in the fábricas recuperadas made demands to the state and, in the general elections of 2003, went to the polls to support Néstor Kirchner and in 2007 voted Cristina Fernández de Kirchner into office. The fact that a critique of representation coexisted with electoral and partisan politics in the midst of these insurgencies reconfirms the hybrid nature of their political practice.

And then there is the vexing question of the state. Let us concede that the state in Latin America is generally bigger than it needs to be and far weaker than those who occupy positions in its various apparatuses would like it to be. The range of resources it can command is generally modest and it has a limited capacity to implement agreed-on policies—even more so in a world system of complex interdependence, where so many variables are beyond the reach of the will and the endogenous policies of domestic actors. This imposes important constraints to what the left or any other political force can achieve by simply seizing state power. Yet the state matters, whether as an instance of regulation or of redistribution of wealth. There is a need for an agency capable of enforcing compliance with binding agreements—counting on the good faith of the contracting parties is not always a wise premise—and making sure that those who earn more actually comply with a progressive taxation policy.

The state has a comparative advantage over other social agents in matters of taxation, the emission and validation of means of payment, contracting loans, or reaching agreements with other states. Without the state, it is less likely that one will be able to enforce an initiative like the Tobin Tax, which is designed to protect domestic financial markets from the destabilizing effects of international speculation and develop alternative sources of income to fund environmental and development projects. Neither would it be easy to reverse the rush toward quick bilateral trade agreements and seek instead broad regional agreements among Latin American countries to negotiate better deals, let alone separate property rights from trade agreements and reject the Agreement on Trade-Related Aspects of Intellectual Property Rights (known as TRIPS) when they involve drugs that are critical for public health. The state is better equipped than others to tackle these kinds of things.

Žižek (2007) underlines the state's importance in caustic remarks about leftist intellectuals who are reticent about "grabbing state power" and choose instead to withdraw to create spaces outside its control: "What should we say to someone like Chávez? 'No, do not grab state power, just withdraw, leave the state and the current situation in place'?" (Žižek 2007). On the contrary, for Žižek the state must be used to promote a progressive agenda and the mobilization of new forms of politics. He is right, even if the dismissal of non-state alternatives is unfair: these, too, are ways to transform the given.

The point is that a post-liberal politics of the left refuses to perceive contamination between the multitude and representation as something particularly problematic. It is less a case of incongruous politics than one of hybridity. Besides, today's multitude is different from its seventeenth-century precedent in at least one respect: it is no longer a phenomenon resisting the centralizing drive of emerging national states but is set against existing state apparatuses. This means that, unlike the Spinozist multitude, the contemporary one bears traces of the state, and therefore a political strategy aiming to establish a zero-sum game between multitude and state would be simplistic and misguided. Beasley-Murray (2007) accepts this implicitly when he describes social insurgencies as the direct precedent of the left turns in Latin America. The Caracazo, he says, is the starting point of insurgencies of a new type "directly linked to an electoral vehicle that followed it, but demonstrably autonomous and irreducible to that vehicle." I interpret this not as a simple discontinuity between an originating force and the consequences of its actions but as a way to explain the manifestation and perseverance of the cause in its effects. If these insurgencies can maintain autonomy while relating to representation in manifold ways and if, as seen earlier, this relationship explains at least in part the left turns, then one has to conclude that the novelty and distinctiveness of their politics must not be confused with a relation of pure exteriority with the state, parties, and elections. Recent experience shows that even if these insurgencies and representation follow different paths, they still contaminate one another and engender hybrid forms.

I believe we will be seeing many more of these hybrid constructs among the left as it embraces more decisively a post-liberal politics. Experimentation is ongoing, and it has a potentially risky side related to the role of violence. There is unease about political violence. On the left, many prefer to distance themselves from it—especially when leaders cannot control it—even when they realize that violence is a side effect of transformative action. The default response of the media and conservative pundits is to latch on to what they perceive as instances of violence as proof of the destructive aims of radical protest. The usual examples are rallies in which the Círculos Bolivarianos mobilize Caracas slum dwellers, the cutting of roads by piqueteros in Argentina, the kidnapping of local authorities by the people in Atenco near Mexico City, and so on. For its critics, violence seems to be such an unliberal thing to do, contrary to the rule of law and the accepted procedures of the liberal state.

This is only partly true. I am not referring only to the selective amnesia of those who overlook the act that violence has been exercised primarily by those who want to maintain an exclusionary status with racist strands and a marked capacity to remain insensitive in the face of the suffering of the underdogs. Violence is actually constitutive of any order, even the juridical order. As Jacques Derrida famously put it, if the law must be enforced, then force is constitutive of law and not an accident that could happen to it or not (Derrida 1992). Some might retort by saying that legitimate violence exercised by the state is acceptable, but subversive violence is not. Although this argument has its merits, very liberal societies are proud to celebrate acts of violence that helped them make them what they are. For example, to call the Boston Tea Party a party is either a misnomer or a desire to dignify the exploits of people who gathered in 1773 with the intent to destroy property for political reasons. To be consistent, José Bové and the Confédération Paysanne's razing of a McDonald's restaurant in France in 1999 should be called the Millau Burger Party instead of being portrayed as proof that critics of globalization lack proposals and that all they can do is resort to wanton destruction of property. So, let us agree that violence per se is nothing to celebrate, and that force and violence are part of politics and one should expect violence to make a sporadic appearance in the left turns.

Note

This is an updated, revised version of an article that appeared in *Latin American Research Review* 43, no. 3 (2008):59–81.

Part 3

Issues of Political Economy

9

Inequality and
the Incorporation Crisis:
The Left's Social Policy Toolkit

Luis Reygadas & Fernando Filgueira

This chapter is organized around three main ideas: (1) in recent years Latin American countries experienced a profound incorporation crisis created by the combination of electoral democracies and the shortcomings (and achievements) of the Washington Consensus (WC) era; (2) the "shift to the left" in Latin America represents the political expression of this incorporation crisis; and (3) left-leaning governments are trying to confront this crisis with diverse policies aimed to reduce inequalities.

Inequality is an inherent characteristic of contemporary societies. Yet, there exist both good and bad inequalities. Inequalities may also be functional or dysfunctional for economic and social development. Unfortunately, Latin America finds itself plagued by bad inequalities—of human capital, wealth stemming not from innovation but from monopolies or inter-elite political exchanges, exclusionary or two-tiered welfare systems characterized by the fragmented coverage of goods and services—and high levels of these inequalities at that. The problem is that the level and forms of modern-day inequalities in Latin America are simply irreconcilable with any possible avenues for human development, among other reasons because they are incompatible with economic development.

In a way, inequality has expanded into a wide range of social, economic, and political dynamics that have effectively thwarted the formation of virtuous cycles between the different fields of development. As such, economic inequality militates against the formation and reproduction of institutionalized and broad-based, representative political systems. Inequality that exacerbates the skewed distribution of economic and political power adversely affects the struggle against rent-seeking access to and management of public goods and of such resources as property. Economic inequality makes it profoundly complex to construct models of social security to which different strata pledge their loyalty, and inequality impedes the formation of alliances that sustain universal basic welfare programs and tax systems that facilitate their financing through state revenues. The struggle against inequality requires enduring, stable public policies that can redefine fiscal and social pacts. For this to be achieved, the functioning of democracy, its character, stability, and ability to represent as well as delay, defer, and aggregate demands, is key.

Although electoral democracies have prevailed and overtly authoritarian regimes have diminished since the 1990s, it is likewise possible to observe at least four processes that were eroding the faith in the stability, character, and substance of democratic regimes:[1]

1. Many countries in the region confronted political crises of enormous magnitude, some of which were rechanneled with few major problems by democratic means, whereas others embarked on perilous roads of plebiscitarian democracies and constitutional authoritarianisms. The challenge of managing the crises can be termed liberal stability of democracy. At the root of this challenge is found a very significant lack of representation of current party systems in many Latin American countries.

2. Indeed, in a substantial number of countries there has surged a rising climate of citizen apathy, disinterest, and distrust in democratic mechanisms, and, in some cases, an open preference for nonpartisan and nonelectoral channels of expressions of citizenship. This challenge can be synthesized in the idea of a lack of representation and participation and the problem of social and political alienation of the masses.

3. The paradox of democracy in the second half of the twentieth century is that while it signified distributive alternatives and alternatives for genuine power, democracy was profoundly unstable. This problem can be defined as the absence of significant alternation. Although this loss of significant alternation is also found in many countries of the North, it rests on levels of incorporation that are fundamental to social and civil citizenship that are lacking in Latin America. The apathy or anomie felt by the peoples of Latin America with regard to democratic politics responded in good measure to this absence of substance in alternation, while another part of the explanation rested in the extremely high levels of poverty and inequality that mark Latin American societies.

4. The majority of Latin American countries exhibit levels of inequality and poverty that almost two decades of democracy have failed to overcome in any meaningful way: in many cases poverty has increased—or has persisted at appalling new heights—and in almost all instances inequality has intensified. This poses a dual challenge to the democratic future of the region: the challenge of strengthening or, rather, constructing the social pillars of democracy and that of demonstrating to the citizenry a certain social function of democracy.

At the dawn of the new millennium reality has changed, and although some of the risks are present or hidden, it is clear that the mapping outlined above has changed considerably. The shift to the left in Latin America represents the political expression of what was termed in the forties and fifties in political sociology an "incorporation crisis." Such crises occur when the need for cooperative interaction in markets and polities and the pressure from below in terms of economic, political. and social demands are not being met by the political, social, and economic patterns and institutions of incorporation and regulation. In short, the issue pervades the region, and many people are excluded and feel excluded. It is also an inclusion crisis.

In the forties and during the postwar period this notion was applied mostly to help explain the emergence of populist leaders, movements, and parties in Latin America. The emergence of a modern working class, the increasing demands of an already small but vocal middle class, and the need to make room for large masses of rural migrants in regimes that remained highly elitist politically, limited economically—regarding their incorporation into modern labor markets—and socially exclusionary created political and social tensions in the 1940s and 1950s. The popular and at times populist shift that dominated Latin American politics in these years was its clearest political expression. Yet what the literature called "populism" in those times expressed a wide array of policy and political responses less homogeneous than a single label suggests. This is also true of present-day shifts.

Latin America has been facing a second crisis of incorporation or inclusion and has recently borne its first political offspring. This is a shift that is born of two parents and sustained by a contingent road companion. The mingling that gave birth to the new political realities is that of uninterrupted electoral democracies and the shortcomings (and achievements) of the WC era. The road companion that sustains and feeds this shift in the region is external and economic in nature: the commodity boom that propelled much of the regional economy during the several years prior to the 2008 global crisis.

But this political offspring is only taking the first unsteady steps toward a full-blown developmental shift. The four critical policy areas in which this offspring will be tested are (1) the welfare regime it creates, (2) the tax systems that are put in place to sustain it, (3) the regulatory model for domestic markets (especially labor markets), and (4) the model of development it chooses regarding the global marketplace. These four critical choices exist today because a major change in the legitimate menus has occurred both at the political and policy level in the region. With the WC and its extensions—regarding social policy—these four issues were supposed to be settled. Indeed WC discourse stated plainly that tax systems should be indirect and neutral, welfare policies targeted and based on markets for those who could afford it, tariffs nonexistent and subsidies slashed, and labor relations as decentralized and with as little role for the state as possible. We will focus on the challenges and emergent options regarding the welfare regime, but in doing so we will necessarily touch upon the other critical dimensions that have today a wider menu of legitimate options than in the nineties. We will also try to show how different countries combine the instruments to combat inequality and social exclusion in distinct portfolios of politics and policies.

This chapter surveys the policies crafted by the governments of Argentina, Bolivia, Brazil, Chile, Ecuador, Nicaragua, Uruguay, and Venezuela. These governments have initiated a wide array of measures, encompassing some similar to those taken up by right-wing and centrist governments (conditioned transfers) and others that emulate the politics of the Cuban socialist government (literacy campaigns, health projects), going through tax reforms, temporary employment programs, development incentives, recognition policies of minorities, and so on. This diversity suggests that dichotomies that separate the left into two currents, one traditional or populist and the other modern or social democratic, are ineffectual and unhelpful (Castañeda 2006; Bartra 2007). Reality appears to be more complex, as there are more than two lefts, and in each country there has been a range of diverse policies and no coherent and monolithic agenda. This heterogeneity reflects ideological debates and is the expression of the recent histories of each country, of social alliances, of the correlation of forces, and of resources that governments possess to combat inequality. Indeed, there has been an increase in participation and an expansion of the public policy menu in almost all of Latin America. Yet in each country, this has been produced through diverse leadership types; different forms of politics, representation, and participation; and the pursuit of markedly distinct policy packages. The divergence of models that are present within the left in the region is related to the presence of national configurations that combine in distinct ways the development of the previous phases of incorporation (the ISI and WC eras). The evolution of the types of international economic insertion, models of production and regulation, and systems of political representation and incorporation affects the form that party systems take in the new juncture and shapes the direction that emerging leftist governments stamp on the struggle against inequality and social exclusion.

In order to move toward a typology that contributes to the understanding of the similarities and differences of the actions that leftist governments have taken, we propose grouping them around three main strategies, each of which brings to light a different principle of equalization. The first strategy is the liberal one, which centers on equality of opportunities and includes programs for conditioned transfers and the formation of regulated markets of public services. The second strategy is the social democratic one, which stresses the equality of capacities and pushes for universal rights, tax reforms, and development programs. The third strategy is the radical populist one, which emphasizes the equality of results and promotes social campaigns, the redistribution of wealth, and strong state intervention in the economy.[2] Elaborating on these three strategies, Table 9.1 shows the full repertoire of equalization policies employed by leftist governments.

The Liberal Strategy: Conditioned Transfers and Privatization of Public Services

The liberal strategy argues that inequality is the result of differences in the assets of individuals and that the full functioning of market mechanisms is the best means by which to reduce such inequalities while stimulating actors to be productive, which would lead to the growth of wealth generated for the benefit of the whole of society. This approach advocates eliminating or reducing to a minimum subsidies and regulations, which are viewed as deleterious in that they foster dependent, rent-seeking, and opportunistic behaviors. In addition, education is regarded as a cornerstone of the struggle against inequality, since through education individuals can realize their potential and compete in markets. This is based on the principle of free competition: according to this principle, on a level playing field there would be equality of opportunity. State intervention must be reduced to a minimum and directed toward the most impoverished sectors.

During the 1980s and 1990s, many centrist and right-wing governments promoted this liberal strategy. By contrast, many of the actions taken by leftist governments can be interpreted as efforts to move away from this approach. Nevertheless, in many cases they have adopted similar measures. Among these the most notable are cash transfer programs geared toward the poor as well as the creation of quasi markets in the social arena.

Conditional Cash Transfer Programs

In Latin America, centrist and right-wing governments have been the main actors to initiate cash transfer programs directed toward the poor. (Honduras: PRAF II in 1990; México: PROGRESA in 1997 and Oportunidades since 2001; Brazil: PETI in 1998, Bolsa Alimentación in 2000, and Bolsa Escolar in 2001; Ecuador: Bono Solidario in 1998 and Bono de Desarrollo Humano beginning 2003; Nicaragua: Red de Protección Social in 2000; Colombia: Familias en Acción in 2001) (Serrano 2005:72–73). The majority of these cash transfer programs are conditioned transfers: families commit to children's attendance in school and agree for mothers to receive medical checkups. These funds or programs combine the cash nature of traditional social security transfers, the targeted and conditional nature of liberal-inspired systems, and the multisectoral emphasis of integrated social programs.

Table 9.1 Repertoire of Equalization Strategies Used by Left Governments in Latin America

	Strategies		
	Radical populist: *misiones*, subsidies, price controls, nationalizations	Social democratic: tax reforms, universal rights, development promotion	Liberal: Privatizations, conditional cash transfers
Argentina	• Subsidies • Wage rise • Taxes on agricultural exports • Currency control	• State-driven demand	• Plan Jefas y Jefes de Hogar Desocupados (Unemployed Heads of Households Plan)
Bolivia	• Literacy and health campaigns • Renationalization of oil and natural gas • Agrarian revolution • Wage increase	• Widening of labor and social rights • Tarifa de la dignidad (subsidized electricity)	
Brazil	• Land redistribution • Minimum wage increase	• PAC (Acceleration and Growth Program) • Social and Economic Development Council • Microfinance and microdevelopment	• ProUni (educational voucher) • Market-oriented pensions reform • Family Grant and Zero Hunger
Chile		• AUGE (universal access with explicit guarantees) • Chile Grows with You • Pensions reform (2008, Bachelet) • Subsidy to low-income students	• Chile Solidario • Fiscal responsibility, light tax reform • Educational vouchers • Pensions reform (Lagos) • Privatization of public services • Labor-market liberalization
Ecuador	• "Emergency declarations" • Price control • Subsidies to flours, fertilizers, domestic gas, and fuel • Wage increases for public employees	• Spinning development • Nurturing development • 5-5-5 credits and youth microfinance • Tarifa de la dignidad (electricity) • Progressive tax reform (proposal)	• Human Development Bonus • Housing Bonus
Nicaragua	• Literacy campaigns • Health and education renationalization • Citizen Power Councils	• Free education and health • Progressive tax reform (proposal) • Economic associations for small and medium entrepreneurs	• Hunger Zero (livestock animals)
Uruguay		• Equity Plan • Tax reform • "Jobs for Uruguay" • Wages councils • Structural reforms in health and education	• PANES (National Attention Plan for Social Emergency)

continues

Table 9.1 continued

	Strategies		
	Radical populist: *misiones*, subsidies, price controls, nationalizations	Social democratic: tax reforms, universal rights, development promotion	Liberal: Privatizations, conditional cash transfers
Venezuela	• Missions: literacy, health, education • Centralized control in Petróleos de Venezuela • Nationalizations: oil, telephones, cement, steel, communications • Subsidies, price controls, and wage increases • Community councils	• Shifts reductions • Universal rights recognition in education, health, and social security • Local development projects • Cooperatives	

As accepted tools in the repertoire of social policies in the region, recent leftist governments have reassumed, extended, or launched cash transfer programs directed toward the poor. In many instances, these programs have increased the amount of assistance, providing more benefits and extending coverage. That is to say, such transfer programs have meant incremental change without profound policy change (Antía 2008). In Brazil, the Lula government pushed for the Fome Zero (Zero Hunger) and Bolsa Família programs, which in 2005 covered more than seven million families. In efforts to combat extreme poverty in Chile, the Chile Solidario program combined cash transfers with promotional components, psychosocial support, personalized attention, and extending coverage to 250,000 families (Serrano 2005:51–52). Ecuador saw the government of Rafael Correa double the amount of the Bono de Desarrollo Humano (Human Development Bond) from $15 to $30 per month, increase coverage to include the disabled, and double the Bono de Vivienda (Housing Bond) from $1,800 to $3,600 (Ramírez y Minteguiaga 2007:98). In Nicaragua under Daniel Ortega, the government implemented the Hambre Cero (Zero Hunger) program, under which livestock animals were distributed to the central female members of poor households.

A variant of conditioned transfers are programs of monetary support for the unemployed. In Argentina, where the unemployment rate came to surpass 20 percent, the government developed far-reaching programs aimed at the unemployed. Amid a severe economic and political crisis, the Plan Jefas and Jefes de Hogar Desocupados (Unemployed Heads of Households Plan) was put into action, and in 2003 it covered almost two million people, overwhelmingly surpassing previous programs of a similar nature (Golbert 2004:23–25). Repayment requirements such as community work were established, yet it has proven to be quite a challenge to ensure their fulfillment. Initially, the project sought to be a universal and temporary program, but it became permanent and did not achieve universal coverage, having reached only approximately 70 percent of the unemployed. This limitation gave rise to projects being implemented in a clientelistic fashion through intermediaries (approximately 15 percent going to *piquetero* organizations and the rest channelled through political brokers). The plan was born out of a context of great social mobilization and, unlike other transfer programs that use a language of paternalism or human capital formation, bases itself on a discourse of social justice.

In Uruguay, a program called PANES (Plan de Atención Nacional a la Emergencia Social, or the National Plan for Attention to Social Emergency) was established and put into effect in 2005 by President Tabaré Vásquez in order to address pressing issues not necessarily associated with unemployment. In addition to the Citizen Income Program (providing monthly transfers of $56 to eligible families), PANES included other aspects, including temporary employment (Work for Uruguay), nutrition, emergency health, education in a critical context, and housing for the homeless (Svalestuen 2007). Moreover, PANES adopted a discourse of the right to inclusion, and was a temporary program, to be replaced in 2007 by the Plan de Equidad (Equity Plan).

Through these actions, leftist governments in Latin America have demonstrated inertia with respect to similar programs that are being instituted by other political forces, without completely breaking from their residual, paternalistic, and clientelistic character. The novelty rests in the increased coverage and amount of support; other aspects are included and, in some cases, a language of economic and social rights is employed. Yet, results from the conditioned transfer programs are mixed (Franco and Cohen 2006; Villatoro 2007). While they are effective in ensuring that resources are channelled to the poorest sectors, they carry the risk of stigmatizing beneficiaries, who are compelled to maintain their "culture of poverty" in order to retain their status as candidates to continue to receive the assistance (Hevia 2007). Another limitation lies in the opportunity costs, as resources cease to be used for other programs that could generate more effective results. In the case of Brazil, Lena Lavinas has documented a tradeoff between income transfer programs and public investment in social infrastructure (housing, sanitation, health, education), which means that while the Bolsa Familia has raised the income of the poor, it has halted or diminished their access to various basic needs (Lavinas 2009).

Finally, it is important to highlight the relative significance of these programs in the fiscal structure of the Latin American social states. Beyond the fact that these programs have captured the greater part of general, technical, and academic attention, they represent no more than 1 or 2 percent of GDP and, in general, do not constitute more than 10 percent of total social expenditures in Latin American countries (CEPAL 2005). More recently, less attention has been paid to the transformations in education, health, and social security, the central pillars of social policy.

Quasi Markets in Education, Health, and Social Security

Another element of the liberal strategy has been the fostering of quasi markets in the social sphere. The prototypical case is the social reforms of the Concertación governments in Chile. The pension system has been reformed to link pension levels to performance in the labor market, education vouchers have been introduced to increase competition between schools, and the labor market has been liberalized. These and other measures have spurred economic growth and have contributed to reducing poverty in Chile more than in any other country in Latin America, but they have not had the same success in the realm of inequality. Chile remains among the most unequal countries in the region, with a Gini coefficient of 0.57. In Brazil it was the government of Fernando Henrique Cardoso that initiated market reforms in health and education, but the Lula government has continued these and adopted new measures of a liberal nature, such as the reform in the pension regime and the ProUni program, which grants an education voucher to facilitate the admission of low-income students and minorities into private universities (Turra 2007:84, 93).

* * *

Why have some leftist governments carried on with liberal strategies and continued targeted antipoverty programs and quasi-market models instead of combating inequality through universal programs more attuned to their ideology? It is probably due to a combination of various factors: (1) institutional inertia, given that these governments had found these mechanisms in effect and could continue and broaden them with relative facility, without having to make any grand structural reform; (2) adaptation and learning, since some specialized programs and, particularly, some of the logic of quasi markets have proven useful or at least adaptable as strides toward more structurally distributive practices, as in the case with PANES in Uruguay, health care and education "vouchers" in Chile, and Bolsa Família in Brazil; (3) resource limitations: targeted programs are less costly than universal ones; (4) political convenience: they grant great legitimacy at a low cost; and (5) limited opposition, since such specialized programs are endorsed by centrist and right-wing forces because they do not contradict neoliberal politics and appear more like residual measures than as rights that could be demanded from the state. These have been some of the easiest strategies to pursue with few resources and even fewer political costs. Other options more attuned with the programmatic line of the lefts, such as a progressive tax reform, an extensive overhaul of health and education systems that would guarantee universal rights, or a redistribution of wealth on a massive scale would all require greater political power and substantial economic resources, as will be seen in examining the following strategies.

The Social Democratic Strategy

The strengthening of a social democratic alternative is a novel phenomenon in Latin America (Lanzaro 2007). Historically, other lefts—nationalist, populist, or socialist—have had greater relevance. There is considerable controversy over whether the governments of Tabaré Vásquez, Ricardo Lagos, Michelle Bachelet, or Lula da Silva can be considered social democratic. They exhibit many differences from European social democracies, since they do not base themselves on the same class alliances nor in the same institutions of the social state, and since populist styles of political leadership are more prominent in Latin America. Nonetheless, the growth of the middle class throughout the twentieth century, ideological readjustments after the fall of the Berlin Wall and globalization, and, above all, the consolidation of party systems and electoral participation of the left during the most recent decades created the conditions for the strengthening of social democratic tendencies, which are more gradualist and committed to representative democracy and the rules of the market.

In relation to the struggle against inequality, a social democratic strategy would be characterized by the gradual construction of more egalitarian institutions by means of moderate regulation of the market and an emphasis on the equalization of capacities. Under this strategy, attempts in recent years to establish universal social policies, tax reforms, and development promotion policies have featured prominently.

Toward a New Universalism?

One of the historic demands of the left is to guarantee the universal exercise of economic, social, and cultural rights by creating a citizenship framework that grants equality of access to basic needs. Generally, left-leaning governments employ a discourse of universal rights, but they are still far from achieving them. Nevertheless, there have been actions oriented in this direction.

The Equity Plan (Plan de Equidad), launched in September 2007 by the Uruguayan government, appears to be the most articulated policy on universal social rights. It has replaced PANES, yet it combines the assistentialist and short-term elements of the latter with an intent to reconstruct and modernize the social state. Proposals for reforms in the health and education systems are especially noteworthy and, together with tax reforms and extended pension coverage, they seek to create a network of basic services and social protection for all citizens, available from infancy to death. The Equity Plan includes measures that can yield a considerable impact on the reduction of inequalities, chief among them a system of noncontributory social assistance that would encompass 95 percent of families living below the poverty line, substantial expansion of early childhood education, the extension of retirement benefits, and a series of actions to improve the quality of education at all levels. The design of the plan aims toward a social democratic strategy of basic universalism and gradual extension of noncontributory social assistance (Andrenacci and Repetto 2006; Filgueira et al. 2005).

In Chile, there has been a slide, although slow and zigzagging, from liberal positions toward a more social democratic orientation. Since the Lagos period (2000–2006), the discourse of rights has been effectively incorporated into the design of social programs. In the area of health, the Acceso Universal con Garantías Explícitas system (Universal Access with Explicit Guarantees, or AUGE) was established to determine illnesses and pathologies to be treated universally, along with rights pursuable in court (Serrano 2005:38; Waissbluth 2006:42–46). Subsequently, the Bachelet government instituted the Chile Crece Contigo (Chile Grows with You) program, a comprehensive child protection system that covers the period from pregnancy up to four years of age. The system is universal in scope and targets assistance to the 40 percent of the population that is most vulnerable. The view is that by achieving greater equity in this crucial phase of the life course one can aspire to greater equality of capacities for future development in the educational system and labor market. In 2008, congress approved a reform in the pension system, which guarantees a basic retirement of $136 monthly, to be increased to $170 in 2009. This constitutes a step toward introducing a moderate decommodification in a pension framework in which the liberal model continues to prevail.

In Nicaragua free education and health services have been established, but they operate in very precarious conditions (Téllez 2007). In Venezuela, there is constitutional recognition of universal rights in the areas of education, health, and social security, although it remains to be seen whether an institutional architecture that can ensure lasting access to basic needs will be created.

Tax Reforms

Tax reforms are a key component of social democratic strategies in pursuit of equality, although this area has gained relatively little ground in Latin America. In Uruguay, a tax reform that included greater progressivity of direct taxes was approved in 2006, although its critics point out that it has taxed incomes but has not touched inheritances or business profits. Daniel Ortega announced his intention to carry out a progressive tax reform in Nicaragua, but he has not yet been able to do so. In Ecuador a tax reform is projected that would increase direct taxes of the highest income-earning sectors from 25 percent to 35 percent.

To date none of the leftist governments in the region has achieved a social alliance that would allow for a sweeping tax reform to provide the state with resources to embark upon broad and enduring social programs that would substantially reduce income inequalities. In most cases, the tax burden represents only a meager percentage of the GDP, and is distributed in a regressive form. In cases where the proportion is greater, social expenditure tends to be high but not particularly progressive. This is because countries with greater tax revenues tend to be those with higher spending in social security, which is generally the least progressive of social expenditures.

An endemic problem across Latin America is that public income transfers are very limited (an average of 5.7 percent of GDP) and that many of them include regressive features. This is particularly evident in the case of pensions, social security, and expenditures for secondary and university education. Cash transfer programs have been much more progressive, but their total amount and coverage are limited and represent on average only 1.4 percent of GDP (Lindert, Skoufias, and Shapiro 2006:2). Nevertheless, there is a clear trend with regard to taxes which, taking into account more recent data, would tend to confirm increments in the overall tax burden with an emphasis on diverse types of direct taxes, including levies on exports (Filgueira 2007).

Other redistributive measures of modest scale but of broad political impact have entailed the application of criteria of progressivity in setting fees for public services. In Bolivia and Ecuador "dignity tariffs" (*tarifas de la dignidad*) have been introduced in electricity service, whereby high consumption sectors are charged higher fees while low consumption sectors are subsidized.

Policies for the Promotion of Development

With the emergence of leftist governments, the neoliberal taboo that long restricted and demonized state actions of development promotion has been breached. Perhaps the Correa government in Ecuador is the one that has placed the most emphasis on development promotion programs. The government has established a multiyear development plan for 2007–2010, created the Subsecretariat for the Social and Solidarity Economy, increased investment for small infrastructure projects, created the 5-5-5 microcredit program ($5,000 dollars over five years with five percent interest), pressed forward a microcredit program for youths, and endorsed the formation and consolidation of small and medium-sized business through the programs, "Spinning Development," which manufactures school uniforms, and "Feeding Development," which supports small milk producers.

In Brazil, the government has designed the PAC (Accelerated Growth Program), created the Economic and Social Development Council, given subsidies for private sector initiatives in infrastructure projects, and fostered collaboration between the state and business through PPPs (Public-Private Partnerships) (Turra 2007:95–97). In Argentina, demand was stimulated to contribute to the economic recovery of the country following the 2001–2002 crisis. In Nicaragua, associations for small and medium-sized businesses have been formed, while local development projects and microcredit programs have been promoted in Bolivia, Chile, Uruguay, and Venezuela.

An interesting novelty regarding old-style developmentalism is that in some instances more participatory and decentralized modalities are introduced to local development programs. For example, in Uruguay NGOs participated in the implementation of PANES and then in the Equity Plan; In Brazil and Ecuador the social economy is being promoted through participatory schemes, while in Bolivia community and family economic initiatives are being supported.

The great challenge for the social democratic strategy in the area of equality is the transition to systems of universal education, health, and social security that transcend the residual and welfare focus of conditioned transfers and the discretional and clientelistic character of social campaigns, as well as the fragmented, stratified, and corporatist character of the old health and social security systems. Thus far, none of the leftist governments in Latin America has managed to decidedly gain ground in this area. They have been confronted with opposition by unions and with middle- and upper-class resistance to reforms in the social security system and to extensive tax reforms that would confer financial feasibility and equity to welfare systems.

In the eyes of many Latin Americans, social democratic positions do not differ dramatically from liberal policies, in that the former make many concessions to privileged sectors and carry out their social programs all too slowly. That is why they may view other more radical options with sympathy.

The Radical Populist Strategy

After what Raphael Correa has dubbed "the long neoliberal night," we observe in various countries across Latin America a greater state presence in the control of the economy and a renewed emphasis on income distribution. A distinctive characteristic of some of the recent left-leaning governments is their radical stance on the capture and distribution of wealth, in particular in a context in which incomes have risen extraordinarily due to high prices of primary products (petroleum, natural gas, metals, agricultural products). They consider the best mechanism of equalization to be state intervention in order to redistribute wealth and offset the disparities created by the markets. Under this strategy, measures such as social campaigns, export taxes, subsidies, price and wage controls, and nationalization stand out as defining features.

Social Campaigns

A number of governments in Latin America have organized intensive campaigns to combat poverty and exclusion of marginal urban and rural populations. The paradigmatic case is that of Venezuela, although there have been similar policies followed in Bolivia, Ecuador, and Nicaragua. The government of Hugo Chávez, which is sustained by high petroleum prices, has channelled substantial resources into civic-military campaigns designed as "missions," among them Misión Robinson, which promotes adult literacy education for two million people; Misión Robinson II, which advocates primary education completion for the recently literate; Misión Ribas, which equips adults with secondary education and college preparatory studies; Misión Sucre, which offers support for middle- and low-income university students; Misión Barrio Adentro, which advances modules of primary health care; Misión Sonrisa, which provides dental care; Operación Milagro, which grants free vision correction operations; Misión Alimentación, which ensures accessible and low-cost food security; and Misión Zamora, which presses for delivery of land, financing, training, and other services to campesinos (Lander 2007:54–57). Not unlike cash transfers, social campaigns seek political legitimacy, but they do so through different mechanisms. They do not have a residual or targeted character, but rather are strategic programs that have been endowed with abundant resources and cover a broader range of benefits and services, including nonmonetary aspects. In addition, social campaigns have fostered instances of popular organization, in particular the formation of over 20,000 Communal Councils. Although some of the actions of social campaigns are similar to those of antipoverty policies of more moderate governments, they are accompanied by a radical discourse that creates other meanings and generates other expectations. Margarita López Maya, an intellectual critic of chavismo, points out that many Venezuelans, who before were excluded from social and political participation, "now feel like complete citizens" (adapted from Robinson 2008:12; original: "*ahora se sienten como ciudadanos completos*"). Lastly, their civic-military character is not based on the old institutions of the Venezuelan state. A new institutionality is being created, directed by the presidency, and with a corporatist and clientelistic character.

Millions of Venezuelans have benefited from literacy, health support, and popular nutrition programs. However, these social programs have two serious limitations. On the one hand, they are not sustained by an efficient state or economy, but on a petroleum bonanza that disguises the inefficiency of an administration plagued by corruption and managed by criteria of political profitability. On the other hand, despite the revolutionary rhetoric, the social policies of the Chávez government seem to follow an assistentialist logic. This is not only reflected in the names of some programs with clear military and religious resonance ("Missions," "Operation Miracle," "Operation Smile"), but also in the content and form of the programs, which appear as handouts that the all-powerful president bestows on the poor, particularly on those who are loyal to him (Gratius 2006). There is also heated controversy over the efficiency of the missions in reducing poverty and inequality. Proponents of the missions point out that the social benefits are laying the foundations for a new social policy that will guarantee universal social rights (Lander 2007:57). But critics argue that any benefits are offset by the persistence of unemployment, shortages of basic goods, and increasing inflation. While acknowledging that poverty has decreased from 54 percent of the population in 2003 to only 27.5 percent in 2007, they stress that this is owing to the rise in GDP triggered by the increase in petroleum prices, and note further that the Gini coefficient has risen from 0.44 in 2000 to 0.48 in 2005 (Rodríguez 2008a).

Bolivia, Ecuador, and Nicaragua have initiated social campaigns similar to those in Venezuela, with assistance from the Cuban and Venezuelan governments, but with fewer resources and a more limited scope. In Bolivia, the literacy campaign initiated in 2006 has already achieved its first great success: in March 2008 it was announced that the department of Oruro had become the first district free of illiteracy, and that the country was expected to soon reach its goal of eradicating illiteracy nationwide. Health campaigns have been organized in rural and marginal areas, while a land distribution program has been initiated in an effort to propel an agrarian revolution based on family and community agriculture (Orellana 2006; Stefanoni 2006). In Ecuador "Emergency Declarations" have been made to attend to social problems outside existing institutional capacity, which is tied to the political logic of winning support for the Constituent Assembly (Ramírez and Minteguiaga 2007). The Correa government has also embarked upon a literacy campaign that in March 2008 resulted in the Amazonian province of Pastaza being proclaimed the country's first illiteracy-free zone. In Nicaragua, the government of Daniel Ortega has also launched a literacy campaign and has stimulated the formation of "Citizen Power Councils" as institutions of direct democracy through which various social programs can be advanced (Robinson 2008). These entities have been met with opposition from the legislature, which has tried to limit their reach and responsibilities and called attention to their clientelistic and authoritarian character (Téllez 2007).

Export Taxes

One of the limitations of the neoliberal framework was that the most dynamic activities in the new export model enjoyed numerous fiscal benefits: exemptions, very low tax rates, and subsidies. Clear examples would be fiscal facilities for *maquiladora* enterprises in Mexico and Central America or the low taxes on primary commodity exports in South America. By contrast, several left-leaning governments have pressed for taxes on exports. For instance, in Bolivia the government of Evo Morales inverted the percentage of taxes on hydrocarbons. Previously, businesses were left with 82 percent of the profits and paid 18 percent in taxes, whereas today a tax of 82 percent has been levied on their activities. This has been framed as a project of "Amazonian-Andean Capitalism," which seeks to transfer surpluses from the production and export of hydrocarbons toward the family and community economy (Stefanoni 2006). In Argentina the Duhalde government established a withholding tax on 35 percent of the value of agricultural exports, and this was continued by the government of Néstor Kirchner. In the case of Venezuela, the high price of petroleum has provided the Chávez government with abundant resources that have served to finance social programs and to assist like-minded governments and organizations abroad. In Ecuador, from the time he was minister of the economy, Rafael Correa pressed for the reorientation of petroleum earnings toward social expenditure, a policy that has continued since his rise to the presidency. As a result, social spending in the country increased by 15 percent, rising from 5.3 percent of the GDP in 2006 to 6.1 percent in 2007 (Ramírez and Minteguiaga 2007).

The policy of heavily taxing exports contributes to the popularity of left-leaning governments, but has also faced much resistance by sectors of the middle classes, domestic business, and transnational corporations. In Bolivia, this has merged with conflicts between the government of Evo Morales and the provinces where the majority of gas is produced and where demands for regional autonomy have multiplied. In Argentina, the government of Cristina Fernández de Kirchner modified the withholding system for agricultural exports by introducing a flexible, price-dependent scheme, which raised taxation levels significantly: in the case of *soya* it climbed from 35 to 44 percent and at times to 48 percent. This generated a series of intense protests by agricultural producers, supported by sectors of the middle class, culminating on 12 July 2008 in an historic vote in the senate that, in a huge political setback, rejected the president's proposal. In Venezuela and Ecuador, there have likewise been protests against export taxes. Often, to decree a tax on exports is more painless than constructing consensus around a tax reform over the long haul. It is an easy and attractive measure that is often accompanied by a discursive egalitarianism: wealthy exporters are taxed in order to give to the poor. Yet, there may be a downside in that it punishes the most productive sectors of the economy, leaving rent-seeking and speculative capital untouched (Novaro 2008). A stable coalition has yet to take shape to guarantee continuity of the export taxes. Finally, the success of these policies has been associated with high international prices of petroleum, gas, soya, minerals, and other primary commodities, which makes their long-term sustainability uncertain, particularly in light of the economic crisis that descended upon the region during the second half of 2008.

Subsidies, Price Controls, and Wage Increases

Some leftist governments are directly intervening in the functioning of the economy through price and wage controls and the establishment of key subsidies. The government of Evo Morales has brought about significant increases in salaries, from 11 percent in 2006 to 7 percent in 2007 (Moldiz 2007:172). In Ecuador, Rafael Correa established wage increases for public servants, teachers, doctors, and domestic servants; raised incomes of retirees; and maintained the universal subsidy of domestic gas and gasoline. There are state efforts to block price increases, while flour, fertilizers, and public transportation have also been subsidized. Correa also proposed to regulate bank profits through the proposed Law of Financial Justice, but failed to obtain approval in congress (Ramírez and Minteguiaga 2007). In Argentina, the state intervened in setting some prices and salaries, as well as the exchange rate. Although the Lula government has intervened less in the Brazilian economy, it has followed a policy of increasing the minimum wage, which rose by 40 percent between 2002 and 2006 (Turra 2007:92). In Uruguay there was likewise a wage increase in 2006, though it resulted not from direct intervention by the government of Tabaré Vásquez, but rather through pressure on the Wage Council (a tripartite institution for negotiation), which resulted in an increase of 10.4 percent in wages and a rise in 11.5 percent in household income, while unemployment dropped to 10 percent, the lowest rate since 1998 (Chasqueti 2007:250–251).

Subsidies and price and wage controls have been most extensively applied in Venezuela. Especially noteworthy are price controls on basic goods, but there are also subsidies for many other products and services, including an enormous subsidy on gasoline and imports and foreign travel, as well as a controlled exchange rate. These measures have bolstered the egalitarian discourse of the Chávez government, but their actual efficiency in reducing inequalities is questionable, since middle and upper sectors also benefit, while unemployment persists: 2002 and 2004 saw the highest open unemployment rates in Latin America in Venezuela, which continue to be in the double digits (OIT 2007). Venezuela also has the most elevated inflation rate in all of Latin America, in addition to suffering shortages of basic goods and hosting a flourishing black market in dollars (Rodríguez 2008a).

Nationalization of Enterprises

In some cases, the new left-leaning governments have nationalized enterprises and resources, undoing the privatizations of the neoliberal era. Petróleos of Venezuela never ceased to be a state enterprise but had acquired a certain level of managerial independence, which has since been reduced by Chávez in efforts to augment its contribution to political and social programs. In 2007, the government bought 82 percent of the shares of the Caracas electrical company and took over the principal telephone service provider. In 2008 several cement companies were taken over and there were threats to nationalize the banks, the leading steel enterprise, telecommunications firms, and large hospitals.

In Bolivia, the nationalization of hydrocarbons has been one of the great debates of the new century and one of the major campaign promises of Evo Morales. In May 2006 he issued the "Heroes of Chaco" decree, as a result of which the state, through the oil company Yacimientos Petrolíferos Fiscales Bolivianos, came to exercise control over hydrocarbon supplies by imposing on private enterprises a tax of 82 percent on the profits. The Morales government has similarly recovered the Vinto Metallurgical Company and the telecommunications company ENTEL, and is not ruling out the nationalization of enterprises in the mining, railway, and telecommunications sectors (Moldiz 2007:170–171).

The nationalization of enterprises and other radical policies instrumented in Venezuela, Bolivia, Ecuador, Argentina, and Nicaragua are framed in what can be called leftist radical populism, which in Arditi's terms (Chapter 8 in this volume) has a "post-liberal" orientation, wherein the importance of institutions of representative democracy are circumscribed by strong executives (authoritarianism of Chávez, plebiscitarian presidency of Correa, charismatic leadership of Evo Morales, Caesarism of the Kirchners or Daniel Ortega) and by forms of direct democracy (constituent assemblies, community councils, plebiscites, etc.). This form of governing is not all too different from that associated with some populisms of the center or right in the region, but what distinguishes it is that, in economic matters, calls for strong state intervention in the regulation of markets and in the social sphere lead to widespread reliance on subsidies and redistributive measures.

The radical populist strategy has been the most ambitious response to the incorporation crisis created by the failures of neoliberalism in Latin America. Compared to the other two strategies, radical populism operates more swiftly and more aggressively to confront hegemonic sectors, reduce privileges, and deliver more resources to excluded groups. Nonetheless, it is a strategy with enormous risks and costs: it has concentrated power in the executive, sparked intense political confrontations, and there are doubts as to its economic viability in the medium term, beyond the boom of primary commodity prices.

Diverse Ways to Face the Incorporation Crisis

The policies that leftist governments have followed in the struggle against inequality can be understood as distinct attempts to resolve the incorporation crisis. There are not merely two ways to solve this problem, but various. Moreover, none of the governments has been limited to just one course of action, but has relied instead on an assortment of diverse policies. Yet, the combinations and emphases are different. If two of the most contrasting cases are compared—Chile and Venezuela—one immediately notices an immense diversity in the policies of the left-leaning governments. At the extreme, closest to liberalism, is Chile, where market policies have carried much weight. Much emphasis is placed on fiscal discipline and economic efficiency, although in recent years there have been a number of actions oriented toward social democracy and the politics of recognition. At the other extreme, nearest to radical populism, is Venezuela, which has constructed a brand of "revolutionary assistentialism"—increasingly authoritarian and clientelistic, with a radical and confrontational rhetoric, characterized by civic-military missions, millions in transfers of oil surplus toward social programs, and increasing state intervention in the economy. In between, there are many hybrid variants. Uruguay began with a conditioned transfer plan, but is shifting toward a social democratic program of tax reform and universal social rights. Brazil has allocated considerable resources to conditioned cash transfer programs, which overlap with developmentalist strategies. In Argentina, export taxes and cash transfers to the unemployed have stood out prominently, complemented by policies of economic regulation to stimulate growth. In Ecuador, development promotion measures are the most exemplary characteristic, but this has coincided with cash transfers, redistributive policies, subsidies, price and wage controls, and literacy campaigns. Bolivia has carried out literacy and health campaigns, but the most relevant features are the high taxes on hydrocarbons and the policies of inclusion of the indigenous population. Nicaragua has likewise deployed social campaigns and stimulated local institutions of direct democracy, but has also proposed a progressive tax reform.

Examining all the cases as a whole, what we see is a tendency toward the demercantilization of social policies and a shift in emphasis. In the era prior to the left turns, targeted programs to combat inequality and the introduction of market criteria in the operation of health, education, social security, and labor relations prevailed. Now that the left turns have emerged, the question of inequality is at the forefront, and many ways to circumscribe and regulate the market through state intervention, some more radical than others, are being promoted.

To date, none of the recent left-leaning governments in Latin America has experienced a significant reduction in social inequalities. In no country has an extensive and progressive tax reform been realized, and in no country have education, health, and social security systems been reformed with a clear sense of equity. In addition, in many cases clientelism and political polarization persist, while recent economic growth is tenuous and very much dependent on the high prices of primary commodities. At the same time, the question of inequality has embedded itself in the center of the public agenda, and perhaps there are better prospects than ever before for the formation of more egalitarian welfare regimes. Its medium-term success will depend as much on the strength of left-leaning governments to construct education, health, and social security systems that would guarantee a basic threshold of well-being for the whole population as on their ability to consolidate democracy, achieve sustainable economic growth, and create a broad political and social pact.

The future of the state in Latin America will hopefully be the history of its future democratic struggles. Never before has the region known such hegemony of democracy and such an expansion of basic political incorporation measured in terms of clean, periodic, and free elections where all or most of the adult population can and does vote. In this single fact perhaps rests the greatest hope for social citizenship in Latin America. Furthermore, the recent backlash against neoliberal reforms and the electoral victory of left-leaning political parties across most of the region suggest that there is new space for maneuvering. But, as the last twenty to thirty years of economic and social policy crises and reforms have shown (1970–1990), such a future might well be forestalled by the constraints posed by global capitalism, the beliefs and interests of its financial gatekeepers, the defense of patrimonial privileges of the middle classes, and by the frailty of Latin America's tax systems and their political basis of support.

Yet there is room for moderate optimism. After almost two decades of the failed prescriptions imposed on previous social states, political realities and technical possibilities are coming together and may shape a renewed and improved road for the creation of true welfare regimes. This would be the best answer to the second incorporation crisis in Latin America. There is, of course, a more distinct pessimistic outcome: the increasing disappearance of the state not just as provider of social security, but its disappearance as a basic provider of public goods in general (security, basic services, judicial systems, public infrastructure, etc.). In its place, a sort of neofeudal order could emerge with market solutions for the rich, retreating but still regressive corporatism for a shrinking middle class, and a large excluded population orphaned of any form of basic state protection.

Structural conditions and political actors—both national and transnational—will be key in defining the future paths of the Latin American states. For the first optimistic road to inclusion, it is necessary that elite-based and popular-based political parties reach a historic compromise. Such compromise can only be reached if both previously elite and popular-based parties are capable of redefining their leadership regarding their old and new constituencies. Indeed, one of the major problems facing the political systems of Latin America is that left- and right-leaning parties tend to privilege the representation of constituencies from the old developmental model, rather than the current new constituencies that emerged from the breakdown of the import substitution model and the emergence of the new export-oriented model.

Political will, however, will not only be needed at the domestic level, with parties that address broad interests rather than narrow lobbies and financial interests, but also at the transnational level, requiring a more drastic humbling of elected representatives as to their responsibility and future action regarding twenty years of misguided development schemes of the social state. Neither social emergency funds, nor fiscally restrictive budgets, nor defensive and regressive corporatism, nor even less private market-oriented solutions to social security have proven adequate for the immense challenge of incorporation that lies ahead for the states and peoples of Latin America.

Notes

1. By 1996, these perceptions of democratic incompleteness abounded in political analyses. In compiling select bodies of literature on democracy, Collier and Levitsky (1997) identified more than 550 adjectives modifying the notion of democracy.

2. There exists a fourth strategy, that of recognition, which centers on equity and calls for affirmative action measures for sectors that have traditionally been excluded, such as indigenous peoples, blacks, women, and so on. Due to limitations of space, we will not analyze this fourth perspective.

10

Macroeconomic Policies of the New Left: Rhetoric and Reality

Juan Carlos Moreno-Brid & Igor Paunovic

In the past ten years, Latin America has witnessed the election of left-of-center governments in various countries of the region,[1] with an electoral platform based on explicit and firm rejection of the Washington Consensus's decalogue on macroeconomic policies and reforms. Once in office, all of them are implementing economic strategies that combine orthodox and heterodox elements, thus departing from the neoliberal toolkit centered on downsizing the state and severely restricting its intervention in economic matters in favor of market mechanisms. However, neither their rejection of the Washington Consensus nor their departure from previous policies could be characterized as homogenous and uniform. Their actual policies differ to some degree, depending on the type of economic problems they inherited from previous governments, policy space they have, and the objective they pursue.

To what extent do the policies and programs of the contemporary left constitute a new agenda for development? Regardless of their novelty, will they be effective in helping to place the region on a path of robust and sustainable long-term economic expansion with a more equitable distribution of income and wealth? Or are they doomed to be just one more series of well-intended but frustrated populist experiments that will sooner or later push these countries into economic crisis, recession, and rampant inflation? Acknowledging that it may certainly be too early to fully answer these questions, the purpose of this chapter is to identify key elements to gauge whether and in what ways the economic projects and results of left governments in South America differ considerably from those of governments from the rather opposite side of the ideological spectrum in our region.

The Roots of the Leftward Shift in Latin America

Several contributions to this volume consider the sociopolitical underpinnings of the contemporary shift to the left, whereas this chapter will first concern itself with the economic factors that have given rise to such a remarkable turn of events in the region. We find two main economic reasons behind the recent surge of leftist governments in Latin America. The first, and likely most important, is the disappointing results of the reforms inspired by the Washington Consensus. Indeed, these liberal reforms—financial liberalization, deregulation, privatization, and opening up of the capital account—failed to trigger a phase of high and sustained expansion. In fact, the rate of economic growth, as well as the evolution of productivity in the region, was highly disappointing in comparison with the performance achieved during the four decades of import substitution industrialization, in which the state played a leading role in supplying investment and shaping the composition of production. Significantly, Latin America's performance in the aftermath of the reforms also pales in comparison with that of other developing economies, particularly those of East Asia.

Indeed, during the period when these reforms were fully in place—from the mid-1980s to the late 1990s—Latin America's growth was very slow, lagging behind that of the developed world as well as that of many developing regions. In addition, its rate of GDP expansion has been very volatile, and subject to major collapses: The Mexican financial crisis of 1995 was followed by other crises in Brazil (1999), Argentina (2000–2002), Colombia (1999), Ecuador (1999), Venezuela (2002–2003), Uruguay (1999–2002), and the Dominican Republic (2003–2004). (See Table 10.1.)

Moreover, few jobs were created in the labor market during these years, and the vast majority of them were in the informal, low-productivity sector in which workers enjoyed limited or no social protection. Social spending also failed to keep up with burgeoning demand from a population suffering the consequences of the opening of economies to global competition and the regionwide turn toward fiscal austerity, which included, among other measures, the removal of an array of subsidies that had dampened the effects of the region's notorious income inequality.[2]

Given such lackluster social and economic performance, it should come as no surprise that, at the end of the twentieth century, 205 million people lived in poverty in Latin America (close to 40.5 percent of the total population), with 79 million of them suffering conditions of extreme poverty. Such proportions were actually not very different from the ones registered in 1980. And, not unrelated, Latin America continued to be the most unequal region in the world. Its average Gini coefficient (0.55) was higher than that of Africa and East Asian newly industrial countries: Malaysia, Philippines, and Thailand (with a

Table 10.1   Economic Growth, Inflation, and Fiscal Balance, 2003–2007

	GDP Growth Rate					
	2003	2004	2005	2006	2007	Average
Argentina	8.8	9.0	9.2	8.5	8.7	8.8
Bolivia	2.7	4.2	4.4	4.8	4.6	4.1
Brazil	1.1	5.7	2.9	3.7	5.4	3.8
Chile	3.9	6.0	5.6	4.3	5.1	5.0
Colombia	4.6	4.7	5.7	7.0	8.2	6.0
Mexico	1.4	4.0	4.2	4.8	3.2	3.5
Peru	4.0	5.1	6.7	7.6	8.9	6.5
Uruguay	2.2	11.8	6.6	7.0	7.4	7.0
Venezuela	−7.8	18.3	10.3	10.3	8.4	7.9

	Inflation Rate					
	2003	2004	2005	2006	2007	Average
Argentina	3.7	6.1	12.3	9.8	8.5	8.1
Bolivia	3.9	4.6	4.9	4.9	11.7	6.0
Brazil	9.3	7.6	5.7	3.1	4.5	6.0
Chile	1.1	2.4	3.7	2.6	7.8	3.5
Colombia	6.5	5.5	4.9	4.5	5.7	5.4
Mexico	4.0	5.2	3.3	4.1	3.8	4.1
Peru	2.5	3.5	1.5	1.1	3.9	2.5
Uruguay	10.2	7.6	4.9	6.4	8.5	7.5
Venezuela	27.1	19.2	14.4	17.0	22.5	20.0

	Fiscal Balance[a]					
	2003	2004	2005	2006	2007	Average
Argentina	0.3	2.0	0.4	1.0	0.6	0.9
Bolivia	−7.9	−5.7	−3.5	0.3	8.0	−3.2
Brazil	−2.5	−1.3	−3.6	−2.9	−2.0	−2.5
Chile	−0.4	2.2	4.6	7.7	8.8	4.6
Colombia	−4.7	−4.3	−4.5	−3.8	−3.0	−4.1
Mexico	−1.1	−1.0	−1.1	−1.8	−2.0	−1.4
Peru	−1.8	−1.3	−0.7	1.5	1.8	−0.1
Uruguay	−4.6	−2.5	−1.6	−1.0	−1.7	−2.3
Venezuela	−4.4	−2.0	1.6	0.0	3.0	−0.4

Source: Authors' elaboration based on official data.
Note: a. Fiscal balance refers to the central government of each country.

Gini coefficient of 0.46). As a result of mediocre economic performance and a lack of opportunities, many countries in Latin America have acute problems of migration. In 2000–2005, for example, Mexico had the highest rate of emigration in the world.[3]

The second reason for the revived fortunes of the Latin American left is the dramatic improvement that the region has experienced recently in its terms of trade, a development that resulted from the booming expansion of some Asian economies that sharply increased their demand for Latin America's raw materials, energy, cereals, and grains. This windfall gain brought about a vast increase in fiscal revenues as well as in the supply of foreign exchange to many Latin American countries with a comparative advantage in highly sought-after natural resources. This phenomenon dramatically did away with two key components that historically limited economic growth in these countries: the fiscal and balance of payments constraints. And, in turn, the boom in commodity prices augmented the degrees of freedom available for governments to implement heterodox economic policies, thereby freeing them from the conditionality imposed by international financial institutions.

Although the Chinese–Latin American and Indian–Latin American flows of trade and foreign investment are still relatively small (USD 40 billion and 6 billion, respectively), their increasing trends augur a change for our region that reflects a more multipolar world economic order. The surge in South-South foreign direct investment is an important element in this regard. Economic ties with China, India, and other Asian countries may become more important for some South American countries given the US economic slowdown and the continued need of the above-mentioned Asian countries to tap key natural resources worldwide to sustain their own economic expansion. As we argue in the last section of this chapter, the current global crisis threatens to change these trends and is creating a new set of conditions whose effects on Latin American economies have not yet become entirely clear.

These factors[4] favored and enabled the resurgence of heterodox economic policies in Latin America advocating, in particular, a larger role for the state in the economy, including a critical view of privatization and of the role of international financial institutions such as the International Monetary Fund (IMF) and the World Bank. Alongside the electoral advances of left-of-center parties in Argentina, Bolivia, Brazil, Chile, Costa Rica, Ecuador, Nicaragua, Panama, Peru, Uruguay, and Venezuela, we have witnessed a drastic reduction in the reliance on IMF financial resources in the region as countries are benefiting from windfall gains due to favorable terms of trade and by tapping other sources of funds with no policy conditionality attached to them.

On Populist Macroeconomic Policies

Traditionally, the left-of-center parties in Latin America had been labeled by mainstream economists as populist, in the sense that their macroeconomic policies were not sustainable. There is a wide variety of interpretations of "populism." Indeed, populist is a category frequently used, typically in ideologically charged, pejorative ways to characterize—usually a priori and with no precise definition—the economic policies of any leftist government. However, populism must be clearly defined in order for it to have an analytical value. In this chapter, and in our work in general, "economic populism" is defined as a set of policies that, on the one hand, are geared to improve social or economic conditions of a majority or to boost the economy's rate of expansion and, on the other hand, they are marked by:

- a surge of fiscal or external imbalances that cannot be maintained or, in other words, financed in the medium or long run; and
- a persistent and continuous intervention of the government—through, for example, direct control of prices or rationing quantities in key markets in an excessive and unsustainable form, be it in terms of their time duration or of the scale of their actions.

When so defined, the assessment of whether an economic regime or agenda should be categorized as a populist one clearly depends on the analysis of expectations of fiscal sustainability of the policies implemented. It also depends on a judgment of how excessive or adequate government interventions are in specific markets. Such interventions may include controls and regulations, nationalizations, and even expropriations.

In addition, an assessment of the fiscal sustainability of any macroeconomic strategy in Latin America—or for that matter any less-developed country—depends on the estimated forecasts of the evolution of its terms of trade. In cases when a significant improvement may reasonably be assumed to be permanent, then certain policies may not be considered populist. When improvements are temporary, similar regimes and strategies may be judged as yet another set of experiments of a populist nature soon to have dismal consequences on the inflation and growth paths of the economy.

The present decade's turn to the left in the region has revived the debate on the validity of this type of labeling. Critics contend that their economic policies are ultimately doomed to failure, arguing that sooner or later they will bring about bloated government deficits and inflation, scaring away investors and pushing the economy into a crisis. The presidential elections in Brazil in 2002 were perhaps the strongest expression of that indiscriminate labeling. Indeed, when leftist candidate Luiz Inácio Lula da Silva was ahead in the polls and then went on to win the election, investors pulled billions of dollars out of Brazil, bringing about a substantial increase in the country's interest rates compared to the benchmark measure of US Treasury bonds. Their fears proved unfounded and, though it took some time, Lula's leftist government gained the trust of foreign and domestic investors alike.

However, for the left-of-center governments in general, the issue of sustainability has never really gone away. The rhetoric of the left, with its emphasis on social justice and a more widespread sharing of the benefits of economic growth, must be reconciled with the reality of a fiscal and an external constraint. The potential gap between them must be always taken into account in order to avoid, on the one hand, a social and political crisis and, on the other, hyperinflation and an economic crisis. Such a gap has continued to provide ammunition to the ideological opponents of left-of-center governments. The reality, as always, has been more complicated than the simple black-and-white ideological labeling of left-of-center governments as populists. In the next sections we look at key elements of the economic performance of the new left governments, aiming to assess to what extent they may or may not be identified as populist experiments under the definitions applied above.

The Stylized Facts: Macroeconomic Performance of Left-of-Center Governments in Latin America, 2003–2007

On closer inspection of the macroeconomic results of the left-of-center governments in Latin America in the present decade, one finds substantial heterogeneity and a lack of a unique, distinctive pattern or tendency in economic performance, policy design, and implementation. Most important, as outlined below, there is no evidence that left-of-center governments are generally paying less attention to maintaining fiscal discipline and low inflation than their ideological counterparts. It is worthwhile to compare the results of the left-of-center governments with those of their more conservative counterparts, to get a clearer picture on the issue of sustainability and the macroeconomic performance of these two groups. Thus, we present here several important macroeconomic indicators for both groups of countries.

We analyze the performance of medium and large Latin American economies in the period 2003–2007. Left-of-center governments throughout that period include Argentina, Brazil, Chile, and Venezuela. We also analyze the performance of Uruguay from 2005 under Tabaré Vásquez, and of Bolivia from 2006 under Evo Morales. We do not take into account the performance of Ecuador under Rafael Correa, Nicaragua under Daniel Ortega, or Guatemala under Alvaro Colom, as they have been elected too recently for sufficient data to be available at the time of this writing. We compare the macroeconomic results in these countries to those in Bolivia (2003–2005) and in Colombia, Mexico, Peru, and Uruguay (2003–2004).

The comparison of macroeconomic results with respect to growth of GDP of these two groups of economies points to a conclusion that they do not differ substantially. The left-of-center group has, on average, recorded somewhat better performance with a rate of economic growth of 6.2 percent for that period, while the conservative group has recorded 5.4 percent. It seems that the bout of prosperity that has affected Latin America in the last five years has not had any discernible pattern regarding the political orientation of the governments.

In both groups there are economies with high growth rates and those with much lower ones. Among leftist governments, Argentina with 8.8 percent on average and Venezuela with 7.9 percent are the best performers. Brazil, on the contrary, has had an average growth rate of only 3.8 percent. That rate is only slightly higher than Mexico's (3.5 percent), the worst performer in the other group. Peru and Colombia's growth rates, driven by high mineral and oil prices, have been steadily improving, averaging 6.5 percent and 6 percent, respectively.

The other indicator generally used to assess the macroeconomic performance is the rate of inflation. On that front, left-of-center governments have been less successful, but not by much. The data indicate that, on average, they have recorded an 8.8 percent inflation rate from 2003 to 2007. The average for the group, however, masks a wide heterogeneity that goes from a low of 3.5 percent on average in Chile to 20 percent for Venezuela. Indeed, when we exclude Venezuela, the average of the group falls to 6.5 percent. This is not that different from the result for the group of other Latin American economies (5.1 percent). The significance of Venezuela in terms of GDP growth and fiscal result is not that important (see Figure 10.1).

We find particularly interesting the comparison of the two groups of economies with regard to their fiscal results. The argument about whether a leftist macroeconomic policy is sustainable or not hinges on the notion of fiscal profligacy. Populist governments embark on a spending spree that is not matched by a commensurate increase in fiscal revenue, leading to high fiscal imbalance, widening of current account deficit, monetary financing of fiscal deficits, and high inflation. This accumulation of macroeconomic disequilibria inevitably results in economic instability, capital flight, and a deep economic crisis.

This scenario, however, is completely absent from the recent macroeconomic experience of the left-of-center governments in Latin America. What is more, their fiscal results have been far superior to those of more conservative governments. The first group as a whole has recorded a small fiscal surplus equivalent to 0.3 percent of GDP in the period. Paradoxically, the more conservative group of governments, which are supposedly more inclined to have a responsible macroeconomic management, have on average recorded a fiscal deficit equivalent to 3 percent of GDP in the same period. It is also worth emphasizing that none of the latter have, on average, had a positive result during that period.

Figure 10.1   Comparison of Macroeconomic Performance of Left-of-Center and Other Governments in Latin America, 2003–2007

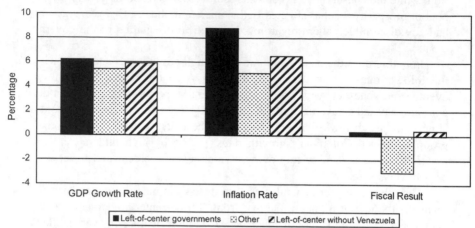

Source: Authors' elaboration based on official data from ECLAC.

Note: Left-of-center governments are in Argentina, Bolivia (2006–2007), Brazil, Chile, Uruguay (2005–2007), and Venezuela; other governments are in Bolivia (2003–2005), Colombia, Mexico, Peru, and Uruguay (2003–2004).

Preliminary Conclusions

Hence, the left-of-center governments have passed the litmus test of the populist thesis much better than their more conservative counterparts. The main reason for that is the apparent ability of the left-of-center governments to raise the tax burden in their economies. The most prominent examples are Argentina and Venezuela, whose tax burdens in the period 2003–2007 increased from 23.4 percent of GDP to 29.2 percent and from 11.9 percent to 17 percent, respectively. The same trend could be seen in Brazil with an increase equivalent to 4.1 percent of GDP over the period, with Chile and Uruguay experiencing increases of 2.7 percent and 1.7 percent, respectively. The respective data for Peru is 2.7 percent, for Colombia 2 percent, and for Mexico a meager 0.2 percent of GDP. One source of that increase is more abundant revenue from economic activity. As the pace of economic growth picked up, revenue from taxes also increased, in some cases more than proportionally. Another source is better tax administration. Most governments in the region have streamlined tax collection systems, making it more difficult to avoid paying taxes.

Finally, in some countries new taxes have been introduced, contributing to the strengthening of the fiscal position. The case in point is export tax on agricultural products in Argentina, which proved to be a highly controversial tax since it has been levied mainly on wealthy landowners. The basic idea of the tax is that sectors that benefit from globalization and from booming global demand should shoulder some of the adjustment cost of lagging sectors. In other words, payments of taxes should be based on the ability to pay. This brings back the idea of justice and equity as one of the principles of taxation. That differs considerably from the situation in Mexico and Central American countries where some sectors of the economy are exempted from paying taxes (e.g., in-bond offshore assembly plants, tourism, mining, etc.), in order to attract foreign direct investment. In these countries most tax revenue comes from lagging sectors, while more dynamic sectors are precisely those that enjoy generous tax incentives. Consequently, the elasticity of tax revenues with respect to GDP is probably smaller there than in countries where dynamic sectors are taxed at least proportionally.

In addition to tax revenues, there has been an increase of non-tax revenues in many countries since prices of minerals, oil, and, recently, some agricultural products have steadily increased over the period. That has benefited all exporters of commodities, irrespective of their governments' political orientation. However, an additional source of fiscal revenue is a redistribution of royalties in favor of governments. As we noted before, this has been a feature exclusively of left-of-center governments' economic policies. This source has played a significant role in the cases of Venezuela and Bolivia, and is likely to do so in Ecuador as well. In contrast, the conservative governments of Peru and Colombia, equally dependent on exports of natural resources, have opted not to follow this route. As a result, their fiscal revenue did not improve nearly as much as that of Bolivia and Venezuela.

Left-of-center governments in Latin America have been more active on another front of great importance, namely, the reduction of foreign indebtedness. As mentioned before, they have been particularly sensitive to the issue of external vulnerability and have also tried to increase their maneuvering room with such strategies as, among others, paying off in advance their IMF debt. In addition, their improved fiscal position has resulted in less need to tap into international capital markets to finance fiscal deficits. Finally, the renegotiation of Argentina's foreign debt has dramatically reduced her foreign indebtedness indicators. (See Table 10.2.)

The data show that countries where left-of-center governments have been in power have on average reduced their foreign total debt[5] as a proportion of GDP by 38.2 percentage points from 2003 to 2007. Even if Argentina, whose reduction has been equivalent to 80.9 percentage points of GDP, is excluded, the rest has witnessed a 29.7 percentage point reduction. In contrast, the right-of-center group has seen only a 14.1 percentage point reduction in the same period.

It is also true that in some countries, notably in Argentina and Uruguay, previous governments had left their economies highly indebted. That's why

Table 10.2   Fixed Investment, External Debt, and Real Minimum Wage, 2000–2007

	Fixed Investment (percentage of GDP)					
	2000	2003	2004	2005	2006	2007
Argentina	16.2	12.9	15.9	17.9	19.5	20.5
Bolivia	17.9	13.9	13.2	13.4	14.0	15.1
Brazil	16.8	14.5	15.0	15.1	15.8	17.0
Chile	19.8	20.2	20.9	24.5	24.2	25.8
Colombia	13.0	16.0	17.4	19.9	21.8	24.8
Mexico	21.4	19.7	20.5	21.1	22.1	22.6
Peru	20.2	17.8	18.3	19.2	21.2	24.0
Uruguay	13.2	8.1	9.5	10.4	12.3	12.1
Venezuela	21.0	14.1	17.9	22.4	25.7	29.8

	External Debt (percentage of GDP)					
	2000	2003	2004	2005	2006	2007
Argentina	54.5	127.8	111.8	62.1	50.7	46.9
Bolivia	80.2	95.3	86.2	80.2	54.8	40.8
Brazil	33.6	38.9	30.3	19.2	16.1	15.2
Chile	49.2	58.2	45.5	38.0	32.5	33.0
Colombia	38.4	41.4	34.7	26.6	25.1	22.1
Mexico	23.3	18.9	17.3	15.2	12.3	12.2
Peru	52.5	48.2	44.8	36.1	30.6	29.3
Uruguay	44.3	98.4	87.7	68.7	54.7	52.9
Venezuela	31.1	48.4	38.8	31.9	24.4	23.2

	Real Minimum Wage (2000 = 100)					
	2000	2003	2004	2005	2006	2007
Argentina	100	84.0	123.8	171.1	193.2	219.6
Bolivia	100	116.9	112.0	106.3	111.1	109.7
Brazil	100	117.4	121.4	128.5	145.3	154.8
Chile	100	108.3	111.3	113.4	116.3	118.5
Colombia	100	102.0	103.8	105.0	107.9	108.6
Mexico	100	100.4	99.1	99.0	99.0	98.3
Peru	100	102.2	106.9	105.1	112.0	111.7
Uruguay	100	77.7	77.5	131.9	153.2	159.6
Venezuela	100	83.3	92.7	103.7	113.9	114.4

when leftist governments were elected there was a sense of urgency to try to reduce foreign indebtedness to more sustainable levels. However, this only reinforces the conclusion that left-of-center governments have been more active than their conservative counterparts in bringing down the foreign debt.

The improved general economic conditions in the last five years in Latin America have resulted in a more dynamic investment activity across the board. However, in the economies where the governments have a political orientation toward the left, the results have been somewhat better, probably reflecting their concern that only with a higher rate of economic growth would it be possible to resolve longstanding problems like poverty, exclusion, informality, and inequality. From 2003 to 2007, the fixed investment[6] has, on average, increased 6 percentage points of GDP in these countries. In the other group, the increase has been less pronounced, equal to 3.8 percentage points of GDP. Even if we exclude the exceptional 15.7 percentage point increase in Venezuela, the former group has fared somewhat better with a boost of 4 percentage points. This is of greatest importance for future economic growth since fixed investment enlarges their productive capacity.

Last, we compared real minimum wages in these two groups of economies. Consideration of minimum wage rates is relevant to an understanding of wage levels more generally, as movements of minimum wages usually drive rates at higher rungs in the labor market. In the period analyzed, there is no general pattern regarding real minimum wages in countries with the left in power. There have been huge increases in Argentina and Uruguay where they more than doubled in the 2003–2007 period. However, a substantial part of that is only a recuperation of what was lost during the recession of 1999–2002. In Venezuela and Brazil, real minimum wages have increased by one-third, which is more or less in line with the increase of GDP. Finally, in the cases of Chile, where they increased less than 10 percent, and Bolivia, where they are still below the level recorded in 2003, real minimum wages have lagged substantially behind the increases in GDP. This heterogeneity shows that no general policy to radically change the distribution of income exists in countries with leftist governments.

The conservative governments, in turn, have followed the path of Chile and Bolivia. Real minimum wages were slightly lower in 2007 than in 2003 in Mexico, in spite of a steady stream of moderate growth in economic activity. In Peru and Colombia, economies with some of the highest rates of GDP growth in Latin America recently, real minimum wages have increased 9.3 percent and 6.5 percent, respectively, from 2003 to 2007. To illustrate the lag real minimum wages have witnessed in these two countries, it is worth mentioning that the GDP accumulated an increase of 32.3 percent in the case of Peru and 30.2 percent in Colombia during the same period.

In the macroeconomic results obtained so far by the Latin American leftist governments examined above, little, if any, evidence could be seen of a populist trait as defined in this chapter. Regarding economic growth, these governments have been somewhat more successful than their more conservative counterparts. The opposite is true regarding the inflation rate. Moreover, fiscal management being the crucial test of macroeconomic policy sustainability, the leftist governments actually seem to have been much more prudent than the other group.

This conclusion, however, must still be taken with a grain of salt in the sense that for many of the new left governments in the region (as well as for those closer to center or right of it), their fiscal strength heavily depends on commodity export revenues whose terms of trade have improved at spectacular rates in recent years. Bolivia, Venezuela, and Argentina are cases in point. For them, it seems safe to argue that the continuation of their strongly expansionary economic policies would have hardly been sustained if not for the surge in their terms of trade. It remains to be seen how these governments will react in response to the adverse effects of the current recession and financial distress of the US economy on the rest of the world and, particularly, on Latin America's exports.

Special attention should be paid to Argentina in this regard, given the government's emphasis on price and wage controls as the main tool to curtail inflation and guarantee the domestic availability of certain grains. In addition, the current government's attempts to tamper with the calculations of the official price indices have not helped investors' perceptions regarding its fiscal prudence, the transparency of its economic strategy, and its impact on inflation. Venezuela's drive to nationalize key industries is also worth a careful monitoring. To the extent that the government does have enough highly qualified managers, administrators, and engineers, such drive may be sustainable. Otherwise, it may sooner or later run up against bottlenecks in human resources and lead to major inefficiencies, inflation, and fiscal crisis.

To state our position clearly in these matters, we believe that none of these governments can currently be described as populist but certainly run the risk of being so in the future. Whether this shadow falls or not depends partly on the evolution of the international markets for agricultural commodities and minerals, but also on the ability of these new left governments to put in place an industrial policy that builds up a solid manufacturing base—or for that matter a service sector—able to compete successfully in the world as well as in their domestic markets against their international competitors.

Going Beyond the Populist–Nonpopulist Dichotomy

In our opinion, a more fruitful way to analyze macroeconomic policies of the contemporary left in Latin America is to place them in the broader economic context in which they operate. This allows a better understanding of their binding constraints and degrees of freedom, and leads to identifying the links with a more general set of governments' social and political objectives. We propose two indicators, one related to the policies regarding the productive sector and the other related to the issue of growth and redistribution.

The first indicator for assessing the macroeconomic policies of the new left has to do with their policies toward the productive sector. Do they intend to change the position of their enterprises in the global value chain or not? Do they rely on exports of commodities or try to diversify their export base? Paradoxically, when one poses the problem in these terms, Ecuador, Venezuela, and Bolivia are much closer to Peru, Colombia, and Mexico than to Brazil or Chile.

These latter countries have put no small amount of effort into diversifying their productive structures and their exports. They are moving away from the traditional specialization in production and exports of natural resources through a conscious effort that was, in the past, termed an active "industrial policy." Successful development of the biofuel industry based on sugarcane, the development of a sophisticated technology for offshore drilling of oil, or the production of top-of-the-class mid-range civilian aircraft are some of the examples of Brazilian advances. Chile has become the second most important exporter of salmon in the world in less than two decades, has developed production of first-class fruits and vegetables for export, and has successfully fomented its wine-producing industry. In contrast, Bolivia and Venezuela are hardly doing anything to move beyond the existing specialization pattern. It seems that Argentina and Uruguay are in between these two extremes. In the case of Uruguay, and certainly in the case of Ecuador, it is probably too early for some firm conclusions on this subject.

The second indicator for assessing the macroeconomic policies of the new left is closely related to the first and has to do with the main thrust of their economic policies. Is the direction of economic policies mainly toward redistribution of existing rents, or is it toward the provision of incentives to produce more and to increase productivity? Is there an attempt to weaken or to strengthen the state's cooperation with the private sector?

In our opinion, the main thrust of economic policies in Venezuela, Bolivia, and Ecuador is in the direction of redistribution of existing rents. All three have concentrated on the objective of changing the political balance of power using the state as the main instrument. In effect, their most important political project is to change the constitution, that is, to change the basic rules of the game. As a result, economic policies in general have not been geared toward strengthening public and private sectors' cooperation, but to a more confrontational relationship. As was mentioned before, these governments have successfully renegotiated distribution of rents with foreign investors and are attempting to do the same domestically.

In contrast, Brazil, Chile, and Uruguay have been enhancing public-private partnerships and have mainly adopted economic policies that stimulate production and competitiveness. The primary direction of their policies is toward finding cooperative solutions that would increase involvement of the state in economic affairs but without alienating the private sector. Again, Argentina is somewhat in between these two positions.

Macroeconomic policies are closely related to and determined by that broader context. Those economies that fail to move beyond the existing specialization pattern based on exports of commodities will suffer boom and bust cycles typical of countries that experience the resource curse. Their macroeconomic policies will tend to be procyclical, benefiting from high prices of commodities and suffering when they diminish. In contrast, economies that succeed in diversifying their productive structures and exports will be less vulnerable to swings in international prices of commodities, so their macroeconomic environment will be more stable.

Furthermore, those countries oriented mainly toward a redistribution of existing rents will gradually undermine the ability of their economies to produce and to export since confrontational policies discourage private sector investment. That would increase their macroeconomic vulnerability, especially in cases where the distributional conflict continues without a resolution. Episodes of capital flight on a massive scale in the past are reminders of what could happen if confrontational policies continue. More cooperative policies that try to foment complementarities and synergies between public and private sectors are more likely to result in strengthened and more sustainable macroeconomic results.

Postscript

The current global crisis, arguably the biggest since the Great Depression, is likely to be the most important test of the sustainability of the new left's macroeconomic policies, and actually of the policies implemented in the whole region. As the period of high international prices for commodities comes to a close, the vulnerabilities inherent in the macroeconomic management in the previous period will be revealed.

Three general observations could be made, even though the full extent of the crisis is not known at the time of this writing. First, Latin American economies in general are better prepared to withstand the crisis than at any point in the last three decades. Foreign reserves are relatively high, the level of external debt relative to GDP is much lower than was the case only five years ago, and several countries have recorded fiscal and external surpluses after having achieved rather low and stable rates of inflation. Poverty has decreased to register its lowest incidence in nearly fifteen years and employment has been on the rise. These elements should give, in principle, more policy space to adopt countercyclical macroeconomic policies if the situation gets worse. Certainly this possibility is conditioned on the extent to which fiscal revenues have increased as a proportion of GDP.

Second, unlike during the 1980s, the main imbalances in Latin America this time around have been produced by the private sector. As the public sector has behaved rather responsibly in macroeconomic terms in recent years, the likelihood of government defaults is relatively low. However, corporate defaults, especially in cases where they have been involved in derivatives and where they have currency mismatches, are much more likely. Banks and corporations have contracted huge amounts of foreign debt because the interest rates abroad during a considerable period were much lower than domestically, and the exchange rate risk premium was low. As credit lines have been mostly cut off recently, they are now experiencing growing difficulties in obtaining financing and in rolling over their obligations.

Third, if the current crisis proves to be long and deep, even the best-positioned economies with a relatively low level of macroeconomic vulnerability could succumb to the indiscriminate retreats of capital from emerging markets caused by the contraction of external demand (affecting exports, services, and family remittances) and declining terms of trade. The deterioration in the global economy and worsening financial conditions in that scenario will affect every country in the region. The plight of the Brazilian real and of the Chilean peso, both losing value in excess of one-third in relation to the US dollar in a period of just two months—not to mention the collapses in their stock markets—is an omen of what could come later. The outflow of capital is driving down their stock markets and putting pressure on their currencies at a time when the demand for their exports has diminished substantially. However, if the crisis does not drag on for too long, economies like Brazil and Chile, with sounder fundamentals—both in terms of fiscal strength and international competitiveness—have a better chance to weather it without severe long-term consequences for their output and employment growth possibilities.

Notes

The opinions here expressed are the authors' own responsibility and do not necessarily coincide with those of the United Nations. An earlier version of this chapter was presented at "Latin America's Left Turns," a workshop held at Simon Fraser University, Vancouver, Canada, 18–19 April 2008.

This chapter presents the most recent results of our joint research program on the economic performance and policies of the left-of-center governments in Latin America in the past ten years. Some of our previous contributions on this topic may be found in Moreno-Brid and Paunovic (2006) and Moreno-Brid and Paunovic (2008).

1. The term "new left" is not used here in the European sense of the last thirty years, but only as a way to identify the left-of-center governments that have arrived to power in the last ten years in Latin America.

2. See also Stallings and Peres (2000) and Weller (2001).

3. For a more detailed discussion of the problem of migration in Mexico, see Pardinas (2008).

4. Besides the two economic factors—fiscal and balance of payments constraints—there are also political considerations that played a role in the shift toward the left in Latin America that are explored in greater detail in other chapters of this volume. On the one hand, many traditional conservative political parties were seen as unable to respond to the growing popular demand of the electorate in favor of a shift in policies to address the increasingly worrisome job and economic concerns of the majority of Latin Americans. In addition, another political element behind Latin America's shift to the left is the radical change in the geopolitical priorities of the US government after the 9/11 attacks. Indeed, after that date, Latin America appeared to swiftly fade away among the US government's priorities. An indicator of such loss of priority in the US agenda is the weakening of all the efforts to establish a Free Trade Area of the Americas. This goal, once the flagship project to strengthen economic ties between the US and the region, has practically been abandoned. Recently, in the process leading up to the presidential elections in the United States, there have been signs of a revived interest in Latin America, as free trade and migration have been topics in the debates among potential candidates. But notwithstanding this, the US relationship with Latin America does not seem to be a center of political concern.

5. We use that indicator since it includes the outstanding debt contracted with the IMF.

6. This term refers to investment in fixed assets, that is, in assets that are expected to last more than one year (machinery, land, buildings, vehicles, etc.).

11

Foreign Investors over a Barrel: Nationalizations and Investment Policy

Paul Alexander Haslam

"Mission accomplished, mission accomplished for the Bolivian people." With these words, Evo Morales announced the conclusion of negotiations with ten foreign oil and gas companies that increased the state's share of the value of production to 82 percent and its ownership stake to a majority. "With these contracts we want to resolve the economic problems of the country . . . we feel sovereign over our resources without expelling anyone, this is nationalization without compensation" (*La Razón*, 29 October 2006). It was, as the Ministry of Hydrocarbons described it, the "new form of 21st century nationalization, for the era of globalization" (*La Razón*, 14 December 2006). Morales together with Venezuela's Hugo Chávez have taken the most dramatic steps toward the nationalization of strategic sectors, although, in a less audacious fashion, new left governments in Argentina and Chile have also acted to increase the fiscal pressure on foreign investors. These manifestations of "back to the future" policies, until recently considered obsolete relics of the import-substitution era, appear to be a direct challenge to the neoliberalism consolidated throughout Latin America over the last twenty-five years—and mark an important change in attitudes and policies toward foreign investors in the region. The encouragement of foreign direct investment (FDI) inflows, the liberalization of regulations for establishment and operation, and the explicit recognition by governments of investors' rights to stability and predictability of the rules of the game were key pillars of John Williamson's Washington Consensus policy prescriptions and broadly accepted practice throughout Latin America in the 1990s (Williamson 2002).

The role of FDI policy as a cornerstone of the Washington Consensus makes it an ideal case to investigate the extent to which the new left in Latin America has departed from neoliberalism and why. Three key dimensions of policy changes on FDI will be investigated: (1) domestic legislation and international treaties that define the rights and obligations of foreign investors vis-à-vis the government; (2) regulation of the activities of multinational corporations (MNCs) by state agencies; and (3) state-firm bargaining and nationalizations. This chapter focuses on the changes in FDI policy under the left-leaning governments of Argentina (2003 to the present), Boliva (2006 to the present), Chile (2000 to the present), and Venezuela (1998 to the present). The selection of cases gives us a wide range of variation in governmental approaches to foreign investors among countries that ostensibly share a leftist political orientation. However, it is important to underline that Argentina and Chile show a kind of response that is categorically distinct from the more radical approaches in Bolivia and Venezuela. Nonetheless, I believe it is possible to articulate a broad hypothesis that accounts for this variation without falling into the trap of attributing different policy choices to the particular ideologies of specific leaders.

It is hypothesized that the following economic factors give policymakers a wider range of choices (in terms of regulating and pressuring firms):

1. Since the end of the 1990s, there have been objective changes in the relative bargaining power of states and firms that favor states. These changes are related to both sectorally specific conjunctures like rising oil prices and regional dynamics of integration and investment.
2. The new left has contributed to a change in policymaker perceptions regarding the economic spillovers of FDI and, most importantly, the opportunity costs of aggressively regulating foreign firms.

However, the range of economic policy choice is also circumscribed by the following political factors:

1. The nature of the fundamental economic class alliance upon which stable rule and economic development depends
2. Institutional path dependency inherited from the neoliberal period. Path dependency may be based on legislation or treaties that sought to constitutionalize liberal economic principles.

To a certain extent, the choice to regulate foreign investors can be seen as a tradeoff between the political-economic incentives and costs of regulation. Argentina and Chile are countries where the objective bargaining power of the state has improved relative to firms and where the new left has introduced changes to the way the contribution of FDI to development is perceived. These changes have fomented a reconsideration of the investment policy dating from the neoliberal period. However, the pressure to change is blocked to a certain extent by the broader continuity of the neoliberal economic class alliance underlying stable rule and the path dependence of rules inherited from the neoliberal period. In contrast, the more radical departure in FDI policy in Bolivia and Venezuela would be due to similar changes in bargaining power and perceptions (enhanced by the size of the petro-economy of these countries), combined with weaker political constraints. In these cases, the weaker political constraints have permitted Evo Morales and Hugo Chávez to break with the legal path dependence of the neoliberal period and constitutionalize their own vision of the appropriate relationship between foreign firms and society.

Investment Policy and Development in Latin America

Foreign investors have played an important role in the development (or, depending on one's viewpoint, exploitation) of Latin America since at least the end of the nineteenth century. At this time, and during the early years of the twentieth century, government policy followed classical liberal precepts resulting in few restrictions on the entry and operation of foreign firms and investors. It was not until the beginning of the import-substitution period that state regulation, and particularly nationalization, of foreign enterprises appeared on the political radar. Bolivia's nationalization of Standard Oil's assets in 1937, the first nationalization of a US company in Latin America, set off a chain reaction throughout the region.

Although nationalization has attracted the attention of most commentators, investment policy needs to be understood more broadly. Investment policy represents a stance by governments on how foreign investors can best contribute to economic growth and development. Notwithstanding some of the current arguments about the embeddedness of foreign investors in East Asia, which have not been practiced in Latin America (Evans 1995; Kohli 2004), the choices open to the governments of the region have been along a continuum between an ideally liberal environment with few regulations and an ideally interventionist environment in which the state actively manages the contribution of FDI to development—including nationalizing it. In Latin America, since 1930, these choices have been cyclical with many countries opting for increased regulation of foreign investors in times of wealth and growth, and liberalization in times of crisis. Policy options typically include a complicated set of legal instruments, bureaucratic oversight, and political bargaining that may be broken down into three distinct policy categories:

- Domestic legislation and international treaties that define the rights and obligations of foreign investors vis-à-vis the government
- Regulation of clearly defined elements of the activities of MNCs, such as taxation, by the state agencies authorized to do so (within the parameters of existing domestic legislation and international treaties)

- State-firm bargaining over major issues of ownership, control, and extraction of surplus from the enterprise. Despite some overlap between this category and the regulation cited above, state-firm bargaining is distinguished by the possibility that extra-legal pressures could be brought to bear on the firm, and is normally associated with more interventionist forms of regulating FDI.

Within each category, however, policy may be either more interventionist (statist) or more liberal (free market). The statist approach, typical of import-substitution industrialization, has generally identified the country's natural comparative advantages and state-created competitive advantages as the principal causes of foreign direct investment inflows. It asserts that governments need to channel FDI into priority sectors and pressure firms to increase their contribution to development. Much of the literature produced in the 1970s and early 1980s described (and even celebrated) the ability of the interventionist state to channel FDI into its development priorities through a variety of techniques including high tariffs, performance requirements, fiscal incentives, subsidies, regulation, and obligatory joint ventures or creeping national ownership (Adler 1988; Bennett and Sharpe 1985; Gereffi 1983; Evans 1979; Kronish and Mericle 1984; Moran 1974). Thus, the state sought to manipulate and channel the behavior of transnational corporations in ways that maximized their contribution to economic development, while the MNCs sought to minimize any government intervention that conflicted with their strategy and profitability. This perspective does not reject the possibility of compatible interests between the state and the firm, but tends to view interests as more heterogeneous and therefore potentially in conflict (Vernon 1971). The dominant theoretical approach within this paradigm has been the theory of the "obsolescing bargain" that suggested that states would, over time, increase their bargaining power relative to firms as they learned how to regulate and manage the industry. As the bargain—the original terms enjoyed by the firm when it entered the country—obsolesced, the state would eventually extract more surplus from the firm. Although many elements of this theory, particularly the idea that the bargain always obsolesces in favor of the state have been questioned (Beamish 1988; Bierstecker 1987; Kobrin 1987), a broader "political bargaining model" remains relevant (Eden, Lenway, and Schuler 2005).

The liberal position, dominant prior to the Great Depression, and during the first major crisis of the Latin American ISI economies in the mid-to-late 1950s (Moran 1974), and again during the neoliberal period (post–mid-1970s in Argentina and Chile, post-1982 elsewhere), has typically argued for the stability of the rules of the game (policy framework) as the key motivating factor behind FDI inflows. In correspondence with the theory of endogenous growth, it has generally viewed the contribution of FDI as greatest when least constrained. In other words, local economic spillovers are enhanced when firms' choices are driven by their global strategy rather than by government policy. Similarly, the liberal position tends to believe in a broad harmony of interests between firm and state (Dunning 1991; Luo 2001; Moran 2005; Safarian 1999; Stopford and Strange 1991).

The advent of neoliberalism and the observable absence of state-firm bargaining in the 1990s led some theorists to assert that bargaining no longer defined the multinational enterprise–host country relationship (Dunning 1991; Luo 2001:402–403). Governments and firms were viewed as increasingly interdependent in realizing wealth and competitiveness in the global marketplace (Stopford and Strange 1991:24–25). In this perspective, the state became a "market player" or "competition state" where its principal role was to facilitate business success by providing key legal knowledge and physical infrastructure, but not through direct intervention in the economy (Cerny 1990:230; Safarian 1999:108). Neoliberal governments in Latin America during the 1990s legislated in conformity with this perspective in the expectation of increased FDI flows and developmental spillovers: liberalizing foreign investment legislation, legally restricting the permissible range of state interference with foreign firms, reducing government regulation, and privatizing state-owned enterprises.

One important caveat, of great importance for the subsequent discussion, needs to be added. Just as all public policies tend to serve multiple political and economic objectives, so too with investment policy. It is important to remember that the original wave of privatization and investment liberalization that brought foreign companies back to Latin America in the late 1980s and early 1990s was not just about choosing the "right" policies for growth and development. It clearly played a signaling role: broadcasting to the world that Latin America, after the ravages of the debt crisis and hyperinflation, was open for business. Second, foreign investment was viewed as necessary (indeed, the only possible source of capital) to modernize industrial and public service infrastructure in a context where governments were fiscally handicapped by enormous debt burdens. Third, privatizations were often used to strengthen the *cúpula económica* (economic elite) through requiring alliances between domestic and foreign capital, and buying the political support of crucial veto players in the business sector for economic liberalization and the leaders that implemented them (Manzetti 1999:81–83; Silva 1996:182–189; Fazio 1997; Schamis 2002).

However, the issue of which perspective (interventionist or liberal) is the correct one remains unresolved in the academic literature. For example, recent case study research into high-tech sectors in Mexico has come to opposite conclusions on a similar set of facts. Theodore Moran found that reducing the restrictions on MNCs would help better integrate subsidiaries into the global competitive strategy of their parent companies, resulting in increased firm size, the use of the latest technology and managerial techniques, and greater developmental spillover effects on the local economy (Moran 1998:46, 162). In contrast, Kevin Gallagher and Lyuba Zarsky underline the enclave nature and limited spillovers of FDI in high-tech Mexican industry (Gallagher and Zarsky 2007). In this respect it is not possible to say, objectively and without qualification, that it is necessary for new left governments to bargain with foreign companies in order to meet policy goals such as growth with equity. We can say, however, that new left policymakers believe that it is necessary to actively channel FDI for developmental purposes in accordance with the interventionist perspective on state-firm relations.

The Policy Framework

The legal framework that governs FDI in a given country is principally determined by the national statutes on FDI and international agreements such as bilateral investment treaties; the investment chapters of bilateral and subregional trade agreements and common markets; and multilaterally negotiated agreements. Both national legislation and international treaties lay out the obligations of host states toward foreign investors regarding the definition, admission, establishment, operation, and withdrawal of foreign-owned companies, as well as specify dispute settlement procedures. Legislation may also establish obligations for the firm including taxation levels, certain percentages of national ownership, employment of nationals, right to government subsidies, links to subcontractors, or standards of financial reporting and good corporate governance and behavior for the foreign investor—although such restrictions were rare in the neoliberal period.

As previously indicated, the liberalization of FDI inflows was a cornerstone of neoliberalism. The neoliberal policy framework established relatively free conditions of access for MNCs, as well as stable and predictable rules. Across the region, liberal investment rules were adopted in the late 1980s and early 1990s. Both Chile and Argentina predated the trend as the foundational dictatorships of Pinochet and Videla adopted DL600 in 1974 in Chile and similar legislation in 1976 in Argentina (revised in 1993). These statutes were echoed, in the 1990s, at the international level through the ratification of bilateral investment treaties (BITs) and free trade agreements (FTAs) with investment chapters. Such statutes typically included national treatment for foreign investors, few (if any) sectoral exemptions, full access to state subsidies, standards of treatment and compensation for expropriation meeting or exceeding international customary law, and, in the case of BITs and FTAs, guaranteed access for MNCs to international investor-state dispute settlement tribunals.

The initial adoption of these foreign investment regimes may be interpreted as a response to the poor economic conditions, fiscal crisis of the state, and sharp decline in FDI inflows that accompanied the pervasive social crises experienced in the early 1970s. In this context, and again in the early 1990s, restoring foreign capital inflows was desperately needed to balance the national accounts, restore growth, and modernize crumbling infrastructure. It was reasonable to expect that liberalization of FDI rules would enhance investor confidence, as it had in the past. In both Argentina and Chile, maximizing FDI inflows was an important part of the neoliberal project. In Argentina, during the 1990s, the need to modernize infrastructure and to compensate for persistent current account deficits caused by the convertibility exchange rate regime drove a liberal policy. In Chile, the massive financial resources needed to access its untapped mineral wealth produced a similar dependence.

Under the new left in Argentina and Chile, the domestic legislation has remained untouched and therefore exhibits continuity with the neoliberal period. Even FDI legislation passed by Hugo Chávez in 1999 retains the liberal mark of the legislation it replaced. The major change in Venezuela was to carve out new exceptions to the legislation—particularly those found in the Hydrocarbon Law. The new legislation, perhaps in a tacit recognition of future interventionism, allowed companies to subscribe to legal stability contracts (CEJs) if they met certain conditions such as creating fifty new jobs and transferring technology (CONAPRI 2006).

In addition to reforming and liberalizing domestic statutes, neoliberal governments sought to constitutionalize these changes by implicating their countries in a web of international treaties to protect investment. Such legal frameworks were to provide stability and security for foreign investors by limiting the range of legitimate government interventions in their affairs and providing for compensation and access to binding international arbitration should these norms be violated (Vandervelde 1998:632). Developing country governments tended to view liberal legislation as signaling devices in their efforts to attract foreign capital. As Jeswald Salacuse and Nicholas Sullivan put it: "a BIT between a developed and a developing country is founded on a grand bargain: a *promise* of protection of capital in return for the *prospect* of more capital in the future" (Salacuse and Sullivan 2005:77). However, there is only mixed and inconclusive evidence that BITs encourage FDI inflows (Egger and Pfaffermayr 2004:801; Halward-Driemeier 2003:11; Tobin and Rose-Ackerman 2005:31; Neumayer and Spess 2005:1582). Such treaties are also controversial due to their effects on governmental policy autonomy, particularly regarding fears that they constitute a corporate bill of rights that handicaps governmental efforts to protect social programs and the environment (Shadlen 2008). Furthermore, BITs typically remain valid for fifteen to twenty years after they have been denounced by either signatory, making it difficult for governments to escape their implications.

Since the rise of the new left in Latin America, there has been a clear and unambiguous decline in the appeal of these instruments—but the level of rejection varies by country. Although Chile has signed fewer BITs since the government of Ricardo Lagos assumed office in March 2000, it has continued its aggressive strategy to diversify its integration into world markets with a series of bilateral investment treaties and free trade agreements that include investment protection. The BITs (Dominican Republic, Spain, Switzerland) and many of the FTAs (Colombia, South Korea, Peru, United States) signed in this period follow the pattern of "neoliberal" treaties of the mid-1990s. Argentina has demonstrated waning enthusiasm for, but not complete repudiation of, investment treaties—signing an additional two after 2003 (Panama and Albania). Argentina's disenchantment with liberal investment agreements is undoubtedly enhanced by the forty-two known international arbitration cases brought by investors against the republic relating to its devaluation of January 2002. Among other new left governments, the panorama of these instruments is complicated and somewhat contradictory. In Uruguay, the administration of Tabaré Vásquez signed in 2004 a state-of-the-art liberal BIT with the United States including all of the typically contested provisions. Departures in this agreement from the neoliberal versions of the investor-state dispute settlement mechanism that permitted greater transparency and state oversight of disputes were, ironically, the consequence of the US Bipartisan Trade Promotion Authority Act of 2002 and primarily motivated by concerns of the US Congress about safeguarding US regulatory policy from challenges by foreign investors—not the result of pressure by the Latin American new left (Gantz 2003:687; Kantor 2004:384, 388–389, 395). Even Venezuela under Chávez signed liberal BITs with France (2002) and Italy (2001), although it must be noted that his government's principal interest lies in solidarity agreements that privilege state-state cooperation and investment by state-owned enterprises.

Therefore, in terms of the content of international investment agreements and investment provisions of free trade agreements, there is little indication of policy change between neoliberal and new left periods. However, this statement needs to be qualified, as several of these countries have sought to undermine the reach, impact, and utility of these agreements to disgruntled investors, using both extra-juridical and legal means. Argentina refused to conclude new agreements with increased rates with privatized public service providers suffering under the January 2002 devaluation law if they had cases before the International Centre for the Settlement of Investment Disputes (ICSID), the principal forum for international arbitration of investor-state disputes. The new oil exploitation contracts concluded between Venezuela and nationalized foreign oil companies expressly deny recourse to international arbitration in the case of an investment dispute (all disputes are to be handled by domestic courts). The Chávez administration also announced that any company bringing a suit against it in international arbitration would not be eligible for future contract tenders. Bolivia withdrew from the jurisdiction of ICSID,

Figure 11.1   Number of Bilateral Investment Treaties Concluded, 1987–2007

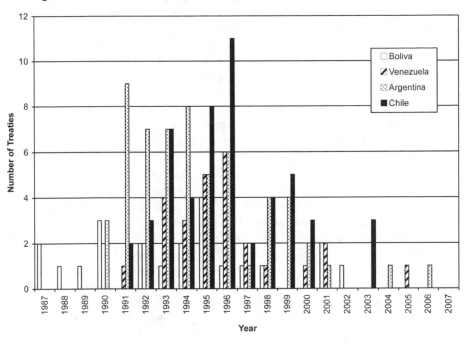

Source: United Nations Conference on Trade and Development, *Investment Instruments Online, Bilateral Investment Treaties (BITs): A Compilation* (Geneva: United Nations). www.unctad.org/Templates/Page.asp?intItemID=2344&lang=1.

effective November 3, 2007. This seemed to be a largely symbolic move, as the investors protected under Bolivia's BITs have other international arbitration options in those agreements—namely, recourse to ad hoc arbitration or dispute settlement through the International Chamber of Commerce. Nonetheless, such actions may be seen as part of broader moves by Argentina, Bolivia, and Venezuela to retain the legal framework for investor protection, while threatening reprisals for using it. It should be noted, however, that Ecuador has gone even further than its new left neighbors, repudiating nine BITs in 2008 and denouncing the ICSID convention in July 2009—as required by article 422 of its new constitution (UNCTAD 2009:6).

Furthermore, although the content of those few investment treaties has not changed, the increased salience of solidarity agreements and promotion of joint ventures between the state-owned enterprises of new left governments represents an important sea change. The opening of Mercosur to Venezuela may be viewed in these terms. More interesting is Chávez's ALBA

(Alternativa Bolivariana para las Américas), which grew during 2004–2009 to include nine countries as full members (Antigua and Barbuda, Bolivia, Cuba, Dominica, Ecuador, Honduras, Saint Vincent and the Grenadines, Nicaragua, and Venezuela) in addition to sectoral integration agreements involving the Caribbean Community. Such agreements principally agree on friendly relations, trade liberalization, and cooperation toward economic, political, and social (particularly health and education) objectives. However, they also have implications for investment. The Venezuela, Cuba, Bolivia agreements facilitate joint ventures between state-owned enterprises; exempt state-owned, mixed-ownership, or private enterprise (in the cases of Venezuela and Bolivia) from taxes on profits; and institutionalize technology transfer, particularly from Venezuela in the petroleum sector. Strictly speaking, the ALBA accords are not about foreign investment, but rather direct state-state cooperation resulting in the reconstruction or creation of new state-owned enterprises and joint ventures in the extraction, processing, and commercialization of natural resources, media, and financial sectors. The statist bias is most clearly illustrated in Venezuela's commitment to develop the capacities of Bolivian mixed or state-owned firms to process natural resources (ALBA 2006). But Venezuela has also leveraged its state-owned enterprises to buy out third-party private firms and extend state control over its own and other economies. In September 2009, a company linked to the Venezuela (PDVSA)–Nicaragua (Petronic) joint venture Albanisa purchased all the assets of the Swiss multinational Glencore in Nicaragua (*Latin America Weekly Report*, 19 November 2009:14). In this respect the ALBA agreements facilitate the investment promotion and cooperation through state-owned enterprises throughout the hemisphere.

Regulation, Taxation, and State-Firm Bargaining

In Chile and Argentina, the principal changes to the rules that govern foreign investors have been through the renegotiation of contracts with private providers of public services (Argentina) and the increase of the tax burden on the mostly foreign firms that operate in the large-scale mining sector (Chile).

Argentina: Renegotiation of Contracts with Privatized Utilities

The renegotiation of public service contracts of the privatized firms (those privatized during the neoliberal 1990s) and, most importantly, the renationalization of a handful of firms, has raised questions regarding the extent to which the new left government of Néstor Kirchner was seeking to redefine the relationship between the state and foreign investors. It is difficult to generalize to broader policy trends regarding the importance of the renegotiations because they were the direct result of the exceptional economic situation and legal state of emergency that was in effect in Argentina following the devaluation of 2002. Although in some aspects the contractual renegotiations did not appear to be a significant departure from past practices, it is worth noting the change in state priorities revealed in the course of the renegotiations, and the progressive (although largely unintentional) nationalization of some public utility sectors, particularly water and sanitary services.

The renegotiations themselves were the direct result of the political-economic crisis that enveloped Argentina in December 2001 and the devaluation of January 2002. The Public Emergency and Reform of the Exchange Regime Law of 6 January 2002 (No. 25.561) took Argentina off its decade-long "convertibility" regime that had pegged the Argentine peso to the US dollar at a value of 1:1 and dictated the "pesofication" of the national economy—including the conversion of all public service rates to pesos at the rate of 1:1 and the nullification of any indexing clauses in public service contracts. Bearing in mind the massive devaluation of the Argentine peso falling to 4:1 against the US dollar, eventually stabilizing at around 3:1, this meant a significant reduction in the revenue collected through public service rates. The legislation also set out a framework for renegotiating these rates with the mostly foreign companies operating public services. In the meantime however, companies were forbidden from reneging on their contractual obligations (infrastructure investments, extension of service, etc.) (Azpiazu and Bonofiglio 2006).

A Unit for the Renegotiation and Analysis of Public Service Contracts (UNIREN) was created to bring this negotiation process to a conclusion (Decree 311/03). Public service contract targets were frequently renegotiated with private firms under neoliberalism, although many of the major regulatory challenges that opposed organized interest groups (particularly consumers) to firms were resolved by regulatory agencies in a way that tended to benefit firms over consumers (i.e., lower reductions in prices than stipulated in original contracts, monopoly extensions, unfulfilled coverage targets, increased tariffs) (Abdala 2001:11–13). However, the willingness of the state to do some hard bargaining with foreign firms—up to the point of rescinding concessions—does appear to be a qualitative break from the neoliberal period. Argentina made the successful conclusion of negotiations with foreign firms dependent on the withdrawal of their claims before international commercial arbitration tribunals such as ICSID (*Página/12*, 16 February 2006). Furthermore, the focus of negotiators on keeping rates down (or minimizing increases), when the governing law suggested that both consumer prices and firm profitability were to be considered, was also a major change from past practices.

However, success in the compression of prices for consumers (which undermined the profitability of firms) appears to have shifted the burden onto industrial and commercial users, and meant the state has had to compensate for the loss of revenue through subsidies (in rail services, for example) and through transferring private external debt to the public sector (Azpiazu and Bonofiglio 2006:34; *Página/12*, 26 March 2006). Indeed the continuity with the import-substitution era is striking, when in the name of populist concerns, state-owned firms kept rates down but persistently ran deficits and underinvested in infrastructure. Indeed, this arrangement (in the absence of later renegotiations on rates) may well foreshadow the state stepping in to finance infrastructure investment on a continuing basis, while private firms operate the service.

Another particularly important outcome from the renegotiation process has been the renationalization of privatized firms, usually justified in terms of their failure to comply with the terms of their concession contracts (particularly regarding investment and extension of services). As of January 2007, there were four cases of such renationalizations at the national level, the most important being Correos Argentinos S.A. (mail) and Aguas Argentinas S.A. (water and sanitation).

The case of the French multinational, Suez, and Aguas Argentinas S.A. has drawn the most attention. Suez's contract was rescinded for unfulfilled obligations, and the privately owned firm renationalized as AYASA (Aguas y Saneamientos Argentinos S.A.), 90 percent owned by the state and 10 percent owned by its workers. There are good reasons to doubt that this is the beginning of a trend in Argentina. Minister of Planning Julio de Vido, who oversaw the renegotiation of contracts, and Chief of Cabinet Alberto Fernández both asserted that the nationalization of Aguas Argentinas was not the beginning of a nationalization drive (*Página/12*, 2 April 2006; 26 March 2006). Furthermore, reports suggest that the renationalization was principally the consequence of Suez's abandonment of its concession (due to the calculation it could do better through an arbitral ruling) rather than reflecting a new policy direction. As D. Azpiazu and N. Bonofiglio put it, the nationalizations in Argentina seemed to be "a response to the 'lack of interest' of foreign capital to continue in this sector rather than a strategic reestablishment of the state as provider of basic public services" (2006:49).

Chile: Changes to Mining Royalty Legislation

After a failed attempt by some prominent members of the Concertación to increase the tax burden on foreign mining companies in 1997–1998, the subject of taxing foreign mining companies was relaunched in early August 2002 under the Socialist Party–led Concertación government of Ricardo Lagos (see Haslam 2007:1174–1177). On 5 August, the Ministry of Mining released its

figures on the contribution of the privately owned mining sector to public finances. The figures revealed that only two mining companies had paid taxes
in the last ten years (the Australian firm Escondida and the South African
Mantos Blancos). Minister of Mining Alfonso Dulanto commented that there
was "space" for a more significant contribution, especially considering that the
government estimated that the average rate of profit for the *gran minería* was
25 percent (*La Tercera*, 6 August 2002). Although the government continued
to deny that it was in fact interested in changing the rate of taxation on the
mining sector, the debate was officially launched.

The proposal to create a mining royalty on sales quickly gathered steam
and appeared to garner wide support in congress and among the population as
a whole, including in the moderate right-wing party, the Renovación National
(RN), which had lobbied on behalf of mining companies to defeat a similar
proposal in 1997–1998. Public opinion surveys suggested the royalty was supported by 67 percent of Chileans (*La Tercera*, 21 April 2004). By mid-June
2003, in the context of copper prices returning to and exceeding historical av-
erages, the government announced that it would be pursuing the legislation of
a 3 percent mining royalty. The Lagos administration also decided to advance
the royalty as a change to the dictatorship's Organic Constitutional Law on
Mining Concessions (1982), requiring a 4/7 majority in Congress and thus
forcing the opposition to bear the brunt of either approving or rejecting it during an electoral calendar.

However, the royalty law was defeated in the lower house on 21 July
2004 when the moderate right-wing opposition largely abstained from voting,
and again in the senate on 10 August 2004. Intensive lobbying by foreign
firms was cited by one of the Concertación's prominent supporters of the royalty, Congressman Antonio Leal (*La Tercera*, 24 July 2004). The royalty was
relaunched in November 2004 and submitted to congress in December, this
time as a change to taxation laws (not a constitutional reform) requiring only
a simple majority held by the government Concertación. The legislation proposed a 4 to 5 percent tax on operational profits of companies producing over
50,000 tonnes. Furthermore, the government viewed the royalty "tax" as less
disruptive of "private property rights" and the contract law of DL 600 (*La
Tercera*, 19 November 2004). The legislation, nonetheless constituted a step
back from the royalty, in terms of the abandonment of the principle of compensating the state for the exploitation of nonrenewable resources, and was
viewed as such by Christian Democratic partners of the Concertación (*La
Tercera*, 16 December 2004). Royalty II, as it was known, passed the lower
chamber in March 2005 with significant support from across the political
spectrum, including the far-right Union Democrata Independiente (UDI). The
Chilean case points to the importance of the institutional legacy of the dictatorship both in terms of the constitutionalization of the Mining Law, and the

overrepresentation of the right in Congress—which made changing the legislation much more difficult.

Bolivia and Venezuela: Nationalization on the Cheap

Despite the tinkering on the margins of the neoliberal model in Argentina and Chile, it is in the Andes where the largest steps were taken in terms of nationalization—reminiscent of the distant past. Evo Morales announced the nationalization of oil and gas on 1 May 2006 in a theatrical performance of sovereignty that saw the armed forces occupy fifty-six oil and gas installations throughout the country. Subsequent announcements of nationalizations included a metallurgical firm, railways, private pension funds, the telephone company Entel, and power generation, transmission, and distribution. The new constitution (2008) called for the nationalization of all basic services, including potable water, sewage, electricity, domestic gas service, telecommunications, and integrated public transport (*Business News America*, 13 October 2008).

But even here, nationalization—particularly in oil, gas, and mining—does not mean what it used to in comparison to the big expropriations of Latin American history such as Standard Oil in Mexico in 1938 or Anaconda and Kennecott in Chile in 1970. In those cases, there was total expropriation of foreign assets, expulsion of the foreign company, and often, failure to pay compensation. Morales changed the concession system to one in which other companies provided services to the state oil company Yacimientos Petrolíferos Fiscales Bolivianos (YPFB), which would control the entire value chain from exploration to commercialization. Companies would also be taxed at a higher rate, rising to 82 percent of the wellhead value of production in the mega-fields of San Alberto and San Antonio (operated by Petrobrás, Repsol YPF, and Total). In practical terms, this meant YPFB would take a majority stake in all existing oil and gas companies by both confiscating the publicly held pension fund shares of the "capitalized" *petroleras* (those companies that had been partially privatized) and negotiating the purchase of additional shares with all the companies (including those entirely privately operated) up to 51 percent. In addition, the Decree Law envisaged the "refounding" and transformation of YPFB from a rubber-stamping secretariat to a company that operated in all stages of the hydrocarbon industry.

The nationalization implemented by Morales in Supreme Decree 28701 was nationalization on the cheap that sought control and rent and recognized the contribution of private capital to development. The appropriate historical referent in Latin America is not, therefore, the celebrated nationalizations that resulted in the creation of Pemex or Codelco, but the

"Chileanization" of Chile's copper companies (the purchase of majority shares and increase in taxation rates) that occurred under Eduardo Frei's Christian Democratic government in the late 1960s. This also points to the broad appeal of nationalist claims over natural resources—that goes beyond the left. Morales, strictly speaking, was implementing the Hydrocarbons Law No. 3058 of 2005, itself the product of the July 2004 binding referendum on the recuperation of hydrocarbon resources conducted by Carlos Mesa's government.

Furthermore, it is not clear to what extent such nationalizations represent a return to state-sponsored industrialization of the past, or whether they are simply an attempt to capture more rent along the entire value chain. The refounding of YPFB and its implication in joint ventures and industrialization projects (the nationalization of Vinto, Petroandina, and Petrosur) suggest an activist state reminiscent in some ways of Peter Evans's triple alliance (1979). But the triple alliance was fundamentally about industrialization, not redistribution; the nationalizations in Bolivia also seem to privilege redistributive goals and have been publicly justified in terms of obtaining more resources to invest in education, health, and programs to improve the people's quality of life (*La Razón*, 12 June 2006). In this respect, it remains to be seen whether state participation in nationalized industries will become productive (in the sense of building technical and managerial capacity and channelling profits into productivity and capital investment) or whether it will assume a rentier character.

The Venezuelan approach to nationalization is very similar to the Bolivian. The nationalization of foreign oil firms took the form of a migration from operational contracts to new joint ventures with PDVSA (Petróleos de Venezuela, S.A.). In these new joint ventures, PDVSA gained a 60 percent controlling stake, taxes and royalties were significantly increased, drilling rights were reduced (in geographical scope), and investors were denied access to international arbitration of investor-state disputes. Since the announced nationalization of oil and gas, Chávez moved to nationalize companies in other strategic sectors of the economy including electricity generation and distribution, telecommunications, cement and construction, iron and steel, petrochemicals, banking, and oil services.

What is particularly interesting about the Chávez experiment (and is shared by Bolivia) is the methodical constitutionalization of reform that undermines the future possibility of private sector–led development of strategic sectors, particularly hydrocarbons. The constitutional reforms of 1999 permitted Chávez to reiterate that the ownership of oil resources were vested in the republic—which reflected a change from the previous formulation that it rested in the state. It was thought that the "republic" reference would make it more difficult for a future government to treat hydrocarbons as an alienable (privatizable) resource. In addition, Chávez codified a constitutional guarantee for the role of the state in the production and commercialization of hydrocarbons (*El Universal*, 21 July 1999). These changes make it impossible, without constitutional reform, to privatize, even partially, the country's hydrocarbon resources, as occurred during the *apertura*. The state's command over hydrocarbons was further legalized through the Organic Hydrocarbons Law of 2001 that set the tax and royalty regime for foreign investors in the sector, and the 1999 Investment Promotion and Protection Law that carved out hydrocarbons as an exception to the protections offered in that legislation. Investors were also denied recourse, in the new contracts concluded with PDVSA, to international investment arbitration and must settle any investment disputes in domestic courts. It is worth noting that the constitutional guarantees essentially permit the state to abrogate any investment contract in the hydrocarbon sector without compensation.

In general, investors in most sectors have been willing to negotiate their nationalization—meaning the purchase of a majority stake by the government—and the governments of Bolivia and Venezuela have paid compensation that has been considered adequate in most cases. Recourse to international arbitration by nationalized companies has been relatively rare; Venezuela has faced eight ICSID disputes in 1998–2008, fewer than the number brought against the United States in the same period (ICSID 2009). Although the long-term impacts of such extensive nationalization programs have yet to be seen, it is worth noting that private investment in exploration and exploitation continues—Repsol YPF, Gazprom, and Total all signed investment commitments with the Bolivian government in 2009 (*Business News America*, 9 October 2009).

Discussion

In some ways, the continuity with the policies of the neoliberal era—in terms of the content of international agreements and relatively minor contract and taxation changes in Argentina and Chile—is striking. Even the nationalizations in Bolivia and Venezuela, although extensive, are less radical than past practices in the region. This would seem to indicate minor tinkering on the margins of the neoliberal model, but such a conclusion would be misleading. This is because the most important transformation brought by the new left is in the realm of perceptions regarding foreign investment and its role in society. The new lefts, even in Argentina and Chile, have rejected the more extreme neoliberal arguments about the natural harmony of interests between firms and the government and the "opportunity costs" of regulating it. This has opened a space to put more pressure on foreign investors, which is more in line with the historic predictions of the obsolescing bargain model. In this interpretation, it is not the policy changes of the new left that are mysterious and require explanation; it is rather the self-restraint and unwillingness of neoliberal governments to pressure multinationals that is the historical aberration.

Change: Perceptions, Discourse, and Willingness to Bargain

Certainly, the new left has rejected the more extreme positions of the neoliberal period regarding the contribution of foreign investment to the national economy, particularly the alleged harmony of interests produced by efficiency-maximizing firms and the endogenous growth strategy. On the one hand, this is revealed in public discourse on the role and contribution of foreign investment to national development. In Argentina, high-ranking political figures, including then-president Néstor Kirchner, repeatedly accused Spanish multinationals of sacking the country. Even in Chile, there was (by Chilean standards) an aggressive public discourse, including remarks by high-ranking figures such as Minister Nicolás Eyzaguirre, that sought to paint mining multinationals as evading taxes and not contributing sufficiently to the country's economic development. The government released figures showing the small contribution of mining firms to national receipts. And at one point in the debate over royalties, the minister tried to use the threat of royalties to force the mining companies to renounce other tax concessions of DL600 (in exchange for dropping the royalty) (*La Tercera*, 9 January 2004).

Indeed, companies are much more likely to be subjected to explicit and implicit political bullying as new left governments maneuver to get desired economic outcomes from the private sector. Bad deals during past privatization processes, failure to fulfill contractual investment commitments, or noncompliance with regulatory norms have been invoked to justify the nationalization of particular firms. Government audits of investment plans have been used to ensure firms continue to invest in a context of regulatory uncertainty in the gas and mining sectors in Bolivia. *Business News America*'s reporting on a bid to take over a Chilean construction firm suggested that the Venezuelan government, "usually bases its decision to nationalize companies on what it calls operating irregularities. It has therefore become common practice to inspect companies in an effort to find weak spots—which may include low wages—before announcing their nationalization" (*Business News America*, 9 June 2009). The renewed activism of the state and its willingness to intervene has served to make the private sector much more attentive to government expectations.

In this respect, the new left has broken with the neoliberal discourse that asserted that any and all foreign investment was good for development and that spillovers were naturally occurring. In its place, a more critical perspective has taken hold, generally favorable to FDI, but recognizing that the state can be more active in regulation, setting investment requirements, and higher taxation. As Evo Morales put it—they want investors as partners in economic development.

Perhaps most importantly, there has been a change in perceptions regarding the "opportunity cost" of regulating FDI and making changes to the rules of the game, such as increased levels of taxation or regulation. The neoliberal argument that changing the rules of the game (in any minor fashion) would result in lower FDI inflows has been definitively dismissed by new left politicians. Argentina is a good example of this phenomenon, which brings together both subjective and objective factors in the interpretation of the opportunity cost of regulation. Argentina of the 1990s, with fresh memories of hyperinflation and economic stagnation, handicapped by the convertibility regime and a general inability to cut government spending or earn sufficient export revenue, was dependent on large capital inflows (particularly FDI) to balance its current and capital accounts. In this context, Argentine policymakers and the general population were convinced that the stability of the rules of the game, particularly convertibility, was the cause of the country's economic renaissance. Any changes to the rules, it was argued, would undermine their reputation as a good business climate, the massive capital inflows on which the country depended, and the Argentine recovery as a whole.

In post-crisis (and post-neoliberal) Argentina, the illusion that the stability of the rules was the sole cause of prosperity was definitively dismissed. Following the devaluation, many economic rules were changed, and the economy had nowhere further to fall. This opened up an immense freedom regarding changes to public service contracts, nationalizations, and hard bargaining (with firms, international debt creditors, the IMF, etc.). Objectively speaking, the devalued exchange rate meant that dependence on FDI inflows en masse was reduced and, subjectively speaking, the fear of breaking the rules was banished. Argentina's post-2002 recovery could not be attributed to stability of the rules of the game, but instead Argentina's comparative advantages resulting from its sizable domestic market and abundance of natural resources.

Beyond perceptions of the role and contribution of FDI to development, it must be underlined that the conditions have changed since the early 1990s (broadly in line with the predictions of the obsolescing bargain model) to permit more pressure on foreign firms. Interestingly, these factors (unlike perceptions) are unrelated to the emergence of the new left per se—which raises the difficult question of how much policy change has to do with the new left, and how much has to do with changing objective conditions. This is clear in the Argentine example above, where overall dependence on FDI inflows was reduced following the 2002 devaluation.

But it is also evident in the reasons for the success of Royalty II in Chile and the failure of the prior attempt to change the tax regime for large-scale mining, the Villarzú proposal of 1998. The low price of copper in large part frustrated the 1998 proposal and increased the political opposition to it. In contrast, the Royalty II legislation was written to work at $US 0.93c/tonne of copper, and by late 2005, the price was at historic highs of $US 1.50. Furthermore, in the intervening years, with few new discoveries of major deposits, fears developed that the mining boom could soon reach its end, leaving the country economically devastated, as had the collapse of the nitrates economy in the 1930s. Getting the most out of the current mining boom became, objectively speaking, much more important.

These structural changes are even more evident in the hydrocarbon-producing economies, namely Bolivia and Venezuela. Increases in petroleum and gas prices made the economic opportunity cost (in terms of lost state revenue) of not renegotiating contracts to be unacceptably enormous. The political opportunity cost in economies with dire social problems was equally unmanageable. Only a diehard neoliberal would have refused this conjuncture. And in fact, neoliberal politicians made the first moves in Ecuador (Palacios revoked a concession operated by Occidental Petroleum) and Bolivia (Carlos Mesa's 2005 Hydrocarbon Law). The state of the industry in these countries is also different from the early 1990s when the lack of investment by state-owned firms in natural resource extraction and lack of financing options (due to the debt crisis) necessitated the use of private capital to expand and modernize production. In Bolivia, some $US 3.5 billion in foreign investment in exploration increased the country's proven and probable reserves from 5.7 trillion square feet in 1997 to 48.7 in 2006 (*La Prensa*, 2 May 2006). Now that infrastructure has been modernized and, most importantly, production increased as the result of private investment, it makes good political sense to change the rules of the game to capture more rent. In the long term, if public investment in exploration and exploitation declines, the pendulum may once again swing toward liberalization.

Furthermore, where the state has been willing to nationalize single firms within a broader sector dominated by private enterprise—the state can put economic pressure on private companies by establishing more competitive market conditions. In Venezuela, for example, the creation of Cantv (telephony) and a mobile handset manufacturing joint venture with a Chinese firm has permitted the government to serve the bottom of the pyramid market in cellular telephones, as well as move into direct competition with private firms in the provision of cable television services (*Business News America*, 2 July 2009). This competition is likely to put pressure on private sector firms to reduce costs to the consumer.

Another element that is not given sufficient credit in improving the bargaining power of states relative to firms is the dynamism of the regional integration process. The existence of a bloc of new left governments also makes a difference to the real and perceived opportunity costs of acting. Chávez and the recognized technical competence of PDVSA made a difference by offering to fill the gap of lost expertise, technology, and capital should foreign investors quit. Sympathetic governments reduced the fallout from nationalization. In contrast to past periods of nationalizations, US companies are less implicated in the region as investors and as targets of these nationalizations. The major investors affected by Bolivia's nationalizations were Petrobrás (Brazil), Repsol YPF (Spain), and Total (France). These governments have been much more supportive of Bolivia's actions than US administrations were of comparable policies in the past. Brazilian and Spanish governments expressed consternation and concern over the nationalizations, but Spain nonetheless signed a cooperation accord in August 2006 promising 60 million euros in aid and forgiveness of 100 million euros in bilateral debt (*La Razón*, 3 August 2006). Just days after the nationalizations, in an emergency meeting held in Puerto Iguazú, Morales was able to convince Argentina and Brazil to pay more for the gas they imported from Bolivia and work toward energy infrastructure projects linking South American to Bolivian gasfields. It is also important to recognize that Bolivia has emerged as the most important country in the geopolitics of energy in South America. Petrobrás in Bolivia supplies São Paulo with 60 percent of its energy needs, while Argentina's gas reserves are expected to run out within ten years (*La Prensa*, 6 and 7 May 2006). In this context, price and majority ownership may be less important issues than guaranteeing the long-term supply necessary to fuel the Southern Cone's growing economies (*La Prensa*, 22 May 2006).

This is classic state-firm bargaining theory; it has nothing, intrinsically, to do with the new left. What the new left has contributed is the ideological justification for nationalization, namely redistribution, and subjective changes in the interpretation of opportunity costs. The left has proved itself willing to see if they can capture more of the surplus created by private firms. They have shown that the neoliberal emperor has no clothes, that investment decisions by private enterprise are not driven by unconditional devotion to the stability of the rules of the game, but by fundamentals: is there mineral in the ground, at what price can it be extracted, at what price can it be sold, are there more profitable opportunities (in the long and short term) elsewhere?

Continuity: The Force of the Law
and the Weight of the Economic Elite

Although the change in perceptions and objective conditions would seem to herald a perfect opportunity for renewed state-firm bargaining, in fact the actual policy changes we have seen in Argentina and Chile are, for the most part, tinkering on the margins of the neoliberal model. It is only in Bolivia and Venezuela that more extensive changes and nationalizations have occurred. Two possible explanations for this divergence present themselves: the path dependence of the law and the weight of domestic political and economic coalitions.

The debate in Chile regarding the modification of taxation on mining companies is particularly illustrative. The debate about options was framed by the difficulty of changing the law created by the dictatorship and confirmed through the democratic government's internationalization drive in the 1990s. The preferred option, changing the dictatorship's Mining Concession Law (1982) to permit a royalty on sales, was rendered impossible through the qualified majority required. Royalty II, simply a change to tax laws (the prerogative of the state), was runnerup by default. The choices in the Chilean government were thus highly circumscribed by the *constitutionalized* legal and political framework inherited from the dictatorship.

This was not the case in Argentina, where the rule of law was less independent and more politicized, and where the executive faced fewer congressional political obstacles. Nonetheless, the Argentine response was also circumscribed by its international (if not domestic) legal obligations resulting from its BIT program of the 1990s. Bolivia and Venezuela are more extreme points on this continuum, where Morales and Chávez's strong domestic support permitted them to not only undermine the constitutionalization of neoliberalism, but establish their own vision of the state-society relationship through constitutional, institutional, and legal reform.

Another reason for the continuity in investment policy seen in Argentina and Chile is the continuing strength and political salience of the economic coalition that supported and benefited from neoliberalism, namely, the mega-conglomerates known as *grupos económicos*. It is also important to remember that the choice of FDI policy in Latin America has rarely been determined by the merits of the state-failure versus market-failure debate alone, but has been intimately connected to political coalition building, namely, the use of rents to reward supporters, and the discipline of liberalization to weaken opponents. Neoliberal governments used the excess profits from privatization and deregulation to build and cement new political alliances with the elite segments of the private sectors. As a result, in both Argentina and Chile there are not other political-economic alliance possibilities. Domestic conglomerates are well internationalized and integrated with foreign companies, and there would be little support from the grupos for policies that alienated their partners. These political-economic constraints help explain policies that tinkered with the model without changing it, and that limited policy to the capture and redistribution of surplus to the political support base of these respective governments.

Indeed, one may well ask if the more radical departures from neoliberalism in Bolivia and Venezuela are due to the different political and economic support coalitions behind the election of Evo Morales and Hugo Chávez. The unique position of the state as exploiter of hydrocarbons in relatively undiversified economies has meant the potential for vast independence (or relative autonomy) of the state from the local and foreign private sectors. These situations are not comparable to the more industrialized and diversified economies of Argentina and Chile.

This chapter has discussed the extent to which new left governments in Argentina, Bolivia, Chile, and Venezuela have elaborated policies on FDI that may be considered distinct from the neoliberal period. Overall, the chapter has demonstrated a bifurcation between the greater continuity in domestic and international legal frameworks governing investment in the Southern Cone economies and the constitutionalization of change in the two Andean countries. However, in all four cases, change has been less radical than past experiments with nationalization, as the private sector retained a role, usually through a minority shareholding position, in many of the nationalized firms. Also, in all cases, new left politicians have departed from perceptions of the neoliberal period regarding the natural spillovers of foreign investment and the opportunity cost of regulating and bargaining with them—and have shown that they are willing to put political and economic pressure on firms in order to attain their policy objectives. Objective conditions have also changed, according to the predictions of the obsolescing bargain model, and governments find themselves in a stronger position relative to firms than during the 1990s. This combination of changes in subjective and objective factors in the state-firm relationship has opened the door to increased regulation and even nationalization of firms across Latin America. The contrast between the Southern Cone and Andean experiences is explained in large part by the constraints in Argentina and Chile that resulted from the legal path dependence of the neoliberal model and the dominant economic forces in those economies. Nonetheless, state-firm relations have undergone a transformation throughout the region since the rise of the new left.

Part 4

Conclusion

12

Latin America's Left: The Impact of the External Environment

Eric Hershberg

The "pink tide" sweeping Latin America is composed of governments, oppositional currents, and social movements of considerable heterogeneity, and one message of this book is that efforts to generalize across countries or to craft neat typologies frequently obscure as much as they reveal about social forces, political processes, and development strategies. Nor has the literature generated convincing frameworks for projecting the likely fortunes of the Latin American lefts, both those segments that occupy seats of power and those that challenge the political order from outside the halls of government. This concluding chapter considers the external context in which progressive forces must pursue their aspirations, taking as its point of departure the notion that domestic factors alone cannot account for both the origins and potential trajectories of the multiple currents that comprise Latin America's contemporary left. The environment that the left faces today is a reflection of a series of uneven yet significant breakdowns of hegemony, in the international as well as the domestic arenas: long-entrenched features of the economic, political, and ideological landscape have been disrupted, yet alternatives remain less than fully defined or consolidated.

For scholars analyzing Latin America, the pink tide is quite striking for a number of reasons; three are worth mentioning, given our assertion that what is in play amounts to no less than a series of hegemonic crises. First, critics of the third wave transitions in Latin America long lamented their conservative bias. According to one prominent current of this argument, the frequently pacted nature of transitions from authoritarian rule carried with it a risk of encouraging a "freeze" in social and economic relations, imposing a powerful bias against redistributive policies (Karl 1987; Hershberg 1989). Another line of argumentation, developed most compellingly by William Robinson, has portrayed the emergence of representative democracy—polyarchy- -as a reflection of a transnational alliance between domestic elites and US interests willing to allow for political voice so long as they felt confident that the left would not challenge underlying socioeconomic relations of inequality (Robinson 2006). Contemporary developments put this assessment in question and, indeed, upon careful review, it is unclear whether the sort of pacts described in the seminal work of O'Donnell and Schmitter were as widespread or as enduring as was commonly assumed.[1] Here, too, the putative inability of fledgling democracies to effect redistributive reforms is perhaps gainsaid by the performance of Latin American political systems since the turn of the new century. While this is in part a reflection of internal dynamics, I argue in this chapter that the external climate exercises considerable influence as well.

Second, even where today's left governments advocate "refounding" the state through constituent assemblies charged with drafting new constitutions, a phenomenon described in this volume by Maxwell A. Cameron and Kenneth Sharpe as typical of the Andes, the pronounced shift to the left is taking place entirely within constitutional means. One is tempted to observe that, whereas political scientists analyzing the third wave envisioned regime change without state transformation, what we are witnessing today in the Andean countries are attempts to carry out state transformation without regime change. Venezuela may well represent a case of regime change from democracy to semi-authoritarianism—and in Central America the Nicaraguan case defies simple categorization—but as a general rule the agenda of this strand of the Latin American left has come to entail transforming democracy through varying combinations of redistribution, symbolic reorientation, and post-liberal forms of political incorporation. While this agenda emerges from domestic pressures, once again, events are being driven by and will be shaped by trends that transcend the national level.

Finally, analysts of hemispheric affairs have frequently concluded that the presence of the United States as regional hegemon powerfully constrained Latin American countries from pursuing autonomous courses of action with regard both to economic policies (e.g., toward foreign investors and property rights, maintaining orthodox macroeconomic policies, and effecting debt repayment) and international alliances. With regard to the former, Paul W. Drake has written eloquently about the influence of US economic ideas in the region from the times of the Kemmerer commissions of the 1920s through the neoliberal decades of the 1980s and 1990s (Drake 2006). As for the latter, from World War II onward, Latin America figured prominently in US Cold War strategy, with repeated interventions rationalized in terms of the imperative of preventing Soviet influence in the hemisphere. The presence of the United States loomed large: Latin America, to use Greg Grandin's phrase, became the "Empire's Workshop," a laboratory for superpower intervention in third world settings around the globe (Grandin 2006). Yet whereas the weight of the Colossus to the North once seemed to limit the range of development projects available to Latin American countries, today, in the aftermath of the Cold War and the advent of the War on Terror, there are increased opportunities for autonomy and for deviation from ideologies, practices, and alliances espoused by Washington.

Typically, explanations for the rise of the variegated left and its diverse trajectories both inside and outside government focus on domestic variables, and these are undeniably central. Frustration with the performance of democratic systems during a period of neoliberal predominance, rejection of incumbents associated with that poor performance, and the configuration of new alliances among social actors long excluded from power are among the key factors addressed in this book and in the broader literature. Yet today as in the past, key features of an evolving international context shape the character of progressive forces throughout the region as well as the opportunities and constraints that they encounter.[2] In an ambitious attempt to explain the durability of Latin American democracies established during the so-called third wave that began three decades ago and that swept Latin America from the 1980s into the 1990s, F. Hagopian and S. A. Mainwaring (2005) underscore the significance of the international context. In so doing they go beyond the boundaries established by much of the literature on democracy's performance, and complement L. Whitehead's earlier work on how the international environment influenced the process of democratization itself, that is, the phase of transition rather than that of democratic governance (Hagopian and Mainwaring 2005; Whitehead 2001).

Inspired by these contributions, this concluding chapter identifies several of the most salient developments in the international system and explores their consequences for the particular characteristics of the left in different settings and their prospects for effecting sustainable political and economic change. This focus on the external dimension aims to fill an important gap in our thinking about the future of Latin American societies, polities, and economies, complementing the conventional focus on the significance of domestic conditions. A recurring theme throughout the analysis is that hegemonic structures that once constrained opportunities for development in Latin America have broken down in recent years. To use Robert Cox's terminology, this implies a shift in the constellation of ideas, institutions, and material capabilities within the region (Cox 1996). This shift has eroded the capacity of institutions to provide mechanisms to deal with conflict that are accepted as legitimate because they can express leadership in terms of general interests. For Cox, hegemony can usefully capture features of world order, provided it rests upon a supportive foundation of social forces and forms of state.

Embedded liberalism at the time of the creation of the Bretton Woods institutions, followed by neoliberalism under the Washington Consensus, represented successive attempts to establish hegemonic orders in the postwar period. The widely recognized failure of the Washington Consensus, accentuated in glaring fashion by the global financial turmoil beginning with the Asian financial crisis and later the collapse of the subprime markets in the United States, creates the prospect of a counterhegemony. Although no such counterhegemonic order has yet to appear on the horizon, today's economic, political, and security environment has changed in ways that open possibilities for the various currents of the contemporary pink tide.

Four Features of the International Context

In an insightful volume published in 1995, Barbara Stallings and collaborators identified several key features of "a new international context" for development, and traced how these were playing out across Latin America, Africa, Southeast Asia, and East Asia (Stallings 1995). This chapter takes a similar approach to understanding how the international context today—quite different from that which prevailed when Stallings and her colleagues prepared their study more than a decade ago—is shaping trajectories of change in Latin America. The changes that concern us encompass economic, geopolitical, and ideological domains. Taken together, they present a novel set of opportunities for the left to gain influence, to articulate alternative visions of democratic development and, in some instances, to implement economic development strategies encompassing policies that were off of the agenda during the last quarter of the twentieth century.

The following sections of the chapter analyze four international contextual variables and explore their impacts in distinctive settings. Our focus is on (1) Latin America's growing integration into the world economy; (2) the worldwide boom in—and subsequent collapse of—commodity prices; (3) the end of the Cold War and weakening of US influence, accompanied by strengthened diplomatic capabilities within Latin America; and (4) ideational shifts and contagion effects. The analysis considers the significance of these trends for development strategies pursued by Latin American governments, particularly those that can be situated on the left of the political spectrum, for which distributive equity as well as growth, subaltern empowerment as well as stable governance, are taken as integral to democratic change.

Growing Integration into the World Economy

The years following Latin America's "lost decade" of the 1980s witnessed an abandonment of inward-oriented development strategies and growing integration into the world economy. Although degrees of integration were uneven across different sectors as well as across countries and both inter- and intranational subregions, there was little dissent from the principle that Latin America's fortunes lie in engagement with global markets along what came to be known as neoliberal lines. Reforms undertaken as part of the adjustment and restructuring processes reflected an environment in which the United States and international financial institutions allied with it exercised powerful influence over economic dynamics throughout Latin America. This was an era during which Margaret Thatcher's famous dictum that "There is No Alternative" gained widespread acceptance among policy elites across the region, and sometimes within the electorate as well, and the reforms eliminated or severely curtailed many of the mechanisms used historically by Latin American states to reduce inequalities, such as subsidies for basic consumer goods and services and protection for inefficient producers from competition from abroad. At the same time, by reducing inflation, facilitating access to cheaper imports, and promoting greater efficiency in public expenditures, market-oriented reforms did away with some of the phenomena that most adversely affected the poor. Overall, however, the shift to a new model did not overcome Latin America's longstanding inequalities. Quite the contrary: as Reygadas and Filgueira demonstrate in their contribution to this volume (Chapter 9), they exacerbated disparities between rich and poor, prolonging Latin America's status as the world's most "lopsided continent."[3]

The encounter with globalization signaled engagement with a set of processes that to this day are shaping development strategies and outcomes, imposing constraints in some instances and opening opportunities in others. It is useful to distinguish three key dimensions of Latin America's encounter with globalization: integration with global financial flows, opening to international trade, and linkages to global production networks.[4]

First, financial integration in the wake of the international debt crisis carried with it continued vulnerability to external shocks, as was seen repeatedly throughout the 1990s and into the present decade. Mexico's so-called tequila crisis of 1994, the Brazilian financial crisis of 1998, and, most catastrophically, Argentina's meltdown in 2001 were emblematic of the pitfalls of exposure to the whims of global financial markets. The downturns that accompanied these crises had significant negative impacts on the most vulnerable segments of the population, exacerbating inequalities through their effects on both labor markets and public expenditures. But as the global economy is being buffeted today by a crisis that began in the US financial sector, Latin American countries are arguably less vulnerable to fickle financial flows than was the case at the turn of this century. In countries such as Brazil and Chile, governments of the left have opted to follow orthodox macroeconomic policies in part as a means to minimize vulnerability to external financial trends. The consequences for the prospects for more equitable development are noteworthy.

Moreover, several Latin American countries have paid down international debt significantly, even while the regionwide average remained at a steady level of 38 to 40 percent of GDP between 1981 and 2005 (Wade 2006:123). Figures vary widely across countries: at 63.6 percent of GDP, Argentina's public debt in 2006 stood at double the level of a decade earlier, and that of Brazil had increased by nearly half, from 10 percent to 15 percent of GDP. Similarly, Colombia increased its foreign indebtedness from 15 percent of GDP in 1990 to 37 percent in 2000 and 45 percent in 2006. By contrast, Chile witnessed an impressive decline, from 84 percent in 1990 to 25 percent in 2006, and Venezuela, too, saw its debt decline by roughly half, from 47 percent in 1996 to 24 percent a decade later. Mexico, like Colombia, a country where the left did not achieve state power, experienced a drop in indebtedness by roughly half within that same period (CEPALSTAT, n.d.). There has been, then, highly uneven performance, and there appears to be no strong correlation between left governments and the record with regard to public indebtedness.

Thanks in large measure to ambitious efforts to maintain fiscal surplus, however, Latin American governments have been able to reduce vulnerability by accumulating substantial foreign currency reserves, which reached 3.7 percent of GDP in 2007 (ECLAC 2007b:57). The increase in reserves from 2006 to 2007 alone was nearly 30 percent, although CEPAL notes that, because these are denominated primarily in US dollars, the region's exposure to dollar devaluation is dangerously high (ECLAC 2007b:69).[5] The maintenance of fiscal surpluses, reduction in debt, and accumulation of reserves may have served as a brake on the recessionary implications of the worldwide financial crisis, particularly to the degree that they have made possible countercyclical policies designed to stimulate demand and sustain employment. Regardless of their position on the left-right spectrum, governments that can draw on these assets have better prospects for maintaining economic stability and limiting the adverse impacts of international financial shocks, impacts that would affect the poor disproportionately. Indeed, the widespread implementation of orthodox policies during the years preceding the financial crisis would seem to have opened the door to pursuit of Keynesian responses to the current situation. Even if applied in only piecemeal fashion, the fact that countercyclical policies are so prominent on the agenda testifies to the declining salience of neoliberal doctrines that prevailed across the region throughout much of the past quarter century.

Turning to a second dimension of economic integration, Latin American countries failed over the past two decades to increase their share of global trade, but their trade profile has changed significantly, in ways that may reduce vulnerability, foster increased rates of growth, and separate the region's fortunes from those of the US. The vision of a single hemispheric trade regime along lines favored by the United States from the 1990s onward has not been realized: what we see instead is a hodgepodge of bilateral and subregional accords, alongside a healthy diversification in South America of trade patterns both within the region and toward Europe and Asia. This diversification offers some degree of protection from external shocks, as countries can withstand declines in trade with particular partners to the extent that others sustain or increase their level of interaction.[6] Especially noteworthy are the connections between natural resource–based sectors in numerous countries and the Chinese industrial juggernaut, which arguably has replaced the United States as the key determinant of export performance for much of South America.

The contemporary landscape is highly uneven and replete with contradictory trends. Interestingly, some of the pink-tide governments in South America have opted to pursue a dual strategy, encompassing participation in regional blocs alongside bilateral accords with the United States, the European Union, and Asian counterparts. Most notable among these is Chile, but Uruguay, as well, has entered into a bilateral agreement with Washington.[7] Mexico's economy is ever more integrated with that of its partners in NAFTA, and for Central American countries and the Dominican Republic, implementation of the Central American Free Trade Agreement (CAFTA) reinforces the existing trend toward ever closer economic integration with the United States.[8] In both Central America and Mexico, the bulk of trade and foreign direct investment is in the manufacturing sector, whereas in South America, by contrast, natural resources and services represent more significant portions of the total (ECLAC 2008). The fact that the governments associated with the pink tide in Central America (Guatemala, Nicaragua, Honduras under Zelaya, and, now, El Salvador) have criticized CAFTA but shown no inclination to exit or even revise the accord testifies to the degree to which that subregion remains inextricably tied to, and dependent upon, its trade relations with the United States.

The two principal trading schemes put forth as alternatives to Washington's bilateral arrangements—its proposed Free Trade Association of the Americas (Mercado Común del Sur, or Mercosur) anchored by Brazil and Argentina and the ALBA promoted by Venezuela—aim primarily to promote intraregional trade or, in the case of the former, to provide a platform for collective negotiation in the global trade arena. Thus, debates are taking place on the left with regard to trade focus on strengthening Mercosur and ALBA, and on the relative merits of one or another of these two frameworks. Most distinctively, and of significant import for some currents of the pink tide, the Venezuela-led ALBA envisions a system of reciprocal exchange in which the relative levels of development of different partners are taken into account, with an express goal of facilitating the flow of resources from wealthier to poorer countries. Participation in ALBA involves exchange of goods and services according to pricing schemes that are socially determined rather than set by market mechanisms (Tockman 2008). The existence of ALBA, and related Venezuelan-initiated schemes for international economic cooperation, provides significant opportunities for reducing poverty and inequality in relatively underdeveloped countries that form part of the pink tide. Whether this will endure in the event of a contraction in the Venezuelan economy provoked by an eventual decline in oil prices remains to be seen and, of course, the very existence of ALBA would be called into question in the event that Hugo Chávez were removed from office, through legal or extralegal means.[9]

If Latin America's performance has been modestly positive with regard to finance and trade, domains in which the hegemonic frameworks envisioned by the United States have been eroded, little progress has been made to significantly upgrade the region's position in global value chains that, organized by transnational firms, constitute the drivers of the contemporary world economy (Dicken 2003). Degrees of success have varied: Chile has made important advances across several sectors, continuing to emphasize natural resource endowments but adding knowledge-based inputs that have enabled it to upgrade its position along several significant value chains. Brazil has done well in numerous industries, notable among them aircraft manufacturing, agro-industry, and mining. Innovations in the Uruguayan software industry are impressive, and Argentina continues to develop agro-export capabilities based on technological innovation. These modest successes offer prospects for expanded employment—and quality jobs—as well as opportunities for sustained growth. Advances are evident beyond the pink-tide countries as well. Mexico, for example, has made meaningful strides in sectors that benefited from NAFTA—auto parts and components are an especially clear example—though linkages to domestic firms have been disappointing, as has the overall record in terms of productivity and technological upgrading. Similarly, thanks in part to the impact of a flagship investment by Intel Corporation, Costa Rica became integrated over the past decade into the global electronics industry, albeit at a relatively low position in terms of local value added (Paus 2005).

But these success cases are not reflective of the regional norm, which is deeply troubling to the extent that the central economic challenge facing Latin American countries—and firms and communities—is whether they will be able to upgrade their value-added activities in ways that will better position them to succeed in an ever more globalized economy. As Moreno-Brid and Paunovic argue in their contribution to this volume (Chapter 10), absent higher productivity levels, the region will remain excessively dependent on imports of technology-intensive goods and services and will fail to make inroads in competitive markets that have the potential to generate high-quality jobs. It is the domestic domain that will shape degrees of success in meeting this demand imposed by participation in the global economy, and here the response by left governments remains tentative and insufficiently coordinated.

There are some intriguing developments. As suggested above, in the Southern Cone and Brazil and in isolated cases elsewhere, governments are making substantial investments in technical training and in provision of support for local and national producers' associations, particularly of the latter's efforts to boost capability for innovation. Whether in agro-industry in Brazil and Chile or software in Uruguay, in this part of South America the engagement of left governments with the private sector has facilitated efforts to increase competitiveness.[10] If there is some ground for optimism in the Southern Cone, however, considerable skepticism is in order concerning whether pink-tide governments in Andean economies, relying heavily on hydrocarbon and mining exports, are taking appropriate measures to boost the capabilities of the domestic productive sector. There have been nominal efforts to promote import substitution in Venezuela, Ecuador, and Bolivia (and Cuba), and to explore possibilities for new forms of property arrangements (e.g., cooperatives) that might stimulate growth as well as a degree of redistribution. But evidence of productivity-enhancing interventions is limited, despite some rhetoric in that direction, particularly in Venezuela (and Cuba). To the extent that government policies in this respect are timid, the region will be missing an historic opportunity to translate what may prove to have been just a fleeting moment of commodity-based prosperity into sustainable, innovation-driven economic advance.

In sum, to date the record of Latin American economies in adapting to the growing integration of the world economy remains disappointing, yet there are signs that the past decades' hegemonic frameworks for adapting to globalization are in decline. And there do seem to be modest differences between left governments and those not part of the pink tide. First, several countries within the pink tide have maintained fiscal surpluses and thus reduced their exposure to external financial shocks. Second, there has been a diversification of trade partnerships and an interest in forging commercial alliances distinct from or in addition to those involving the United States and principles of comparative advantage rather than reciprocity. Third, there is evidence of modest yet uneven commitment to boosting productive innovation in order to better link economies to promising niches in global value chains. Prospects for sustaining economic growth and improving distribution of resources will hinge in large measure on further advances in these domains.

Shifts in Terms of Trade: The Boom in Commodity Prices and the 2008 Collapse

For much of Latin America, continued lagging in productivity seemed of diminished prominence over the past five years due to the boom in commodity prices, which enabled countries blessed with natural resources to substantially increase the benefits derived from participation in the global economy. Rising commodity prices boosted GDP growth rates to levels unknown for the past quarter century, as beginning in 2003 the region's economies expanded at a steady clip of over 4 percent per year and in some countries reached double digits. Overall, the export prices of Latin American products more than doubled between 2002 and the first half of 2008. ECLAC reports that

> The prices of the leading export commodities of Latin American economies such as crude petroleum and petroleum products, copper, soy beans, coffee, and oil seed, which represented a quarter of total exports of goods in 2005, increased by 143%, 123%, 26%, 104%, and 40% respectively between 2002 and 2006. As a result, on average the purchasing power of Latin American exports has risen by roughly 60% between 2002 and 2006. (Caldentey and Vernengo 2008:10)

In contexts where state revenues are derived significantly from export taxes, this offers an important opportunity for increasing public investment in both social and material infrastructure, a consideration that is especially important given the continued failure of Latin American states to impose reasonably progressive income tax regimes. Alongside substantial increase in exports since 2000, there has been a sharp increase in imports, but the overall figures, showing a roughly equal increase across the region, mask sharp differences by country. Between 2000 and 2007 Bolivia doubled its imports but increased the value of exports by three-and-a-half times, and both Brazil and Chile achieved gains of nearly equal importance (ECLAC 2008). These figures highlight the impact of rising commodity prices up until 2008, which propelled a remarkable improvement in Latin America's terms of trade. As reported by ECLAC:

> Between 2003 and 2007, Latin America's terms of trade showed a cumulative improvement of 19%. However, change is afoot in the factors that have been conducive to regional terms of trade. In 2006, there was a 5.9% improvement in the merchandise terms of trade, while this figure dropped to 2.2% in 2007. Although the improvement in terms of trade has been smaller in 2007, countries such as the Bolivarian Republic of Venezuela, Bolivia, Chile, and Peru have nonetheless made striking gains thanks to increases in the prices of their raw materials. Generally speaking, it is the terms of trade of Central American countries that continue to be far less favourable. (CEPAL 2007:65)

Whereas dependency theory's contention that developing countries suffer inexorably deteriorating terms of trade is put in question by the cycle that seems to have come to a close during the second half of 2008, the minimal improvements in merchandise terms of trade suggest that concerns about technological backwardness remain as justified as ever. Moreover, as noted in a recent paper by Caldentey and Vernengo, a majority of Latin American countries witnessed a decline in their terms of trade even over the course of the recent boom: the improvement was highly concentrated in exporters of petroleum and petroleum derivatives (Caldentey and Vernengo 2008:12). Beyond this, the reliance on commodity exports is troubling in developmental terms, for at least three reasons. First, primary sector activity is least conducive to the creation of significant numbers of high quality jobs, which by all accounts is paramount for the region's capacity to reduce inequalities in a sustainable fashion. Second, while a rise in commodity prices generates substantial increases in revenue for states that rely heavily on export taxes, it diminishes pressure to enact equity-oriented reforms of historically regressive tax systems. Finally, and perhaps most importantly, the cascading financial crisis that began in the United States during mid-2008 and that subsequently swept developed and developing economies alike had a sharp and unanticipated downward impact on commodity prices, jeopardizing the recent success in achieving adequate growth levels and expanding social investment. Indeed, despite the modest rebound experienced during mid-2009, the still unfolding crisis provides a stark reminder that reliance on high prices for commodities is a recipe for continued vulnerability.

It is largely owing to increases in commodity prices that Latin American governments managed to increase substantially their expenditures on social programs, which in per capita terms expanded on a regionwide level by 10 percent between 2002 and 2005 (CEPAL 2007:2). Yet here, as well, performance has been uneven across the region and across cases in which the left holds office, and whether recent gains can be sustained in the current recessionary context is among the most pressing questions confronting governments throughout the region.

Weakening US Hegemony Accompanied by Strengthened Diplomatic Capabilities Within Latin America

It has become commonplace to note that Latin American affairs became of steadily diminishing importance to US foreign policy during the Bill Clinton and George W. Bush administrations (Hakim 2006). This trend, lamented in some quarters and celebrated in others, was driven in part by Washington's distraction with the War on Terror and the ongoing debacle in Iraq and elsewhere in the Middle East and Southern Asia. It stems as well from the enduring effects of the end of the Cold War, during which Latin America appeared to US policymakers as a crucial space for containing the putative Soviet threat.[11] Whereas a decade ago the demise of the Soviet bloc appeared to matter most for the prospects of the Latin American left by having removed a potential referent for an alternative development paradigm, and thus fueling the contention that "there is no alternative" to the free market approach espoused by Washington and International Financial Institutions (IFIs), today its importance lies in its having opened space for alternatives to emerge without being labeled national security threats by domestic or US detractors.

That greater space has signified challenges to US hegemony is evident in numerous arenas that foster room for maneuver for governments associated with the pink tide. In the Andes, the sorts of measures that once would have provoked sharp denunciation and even intervention from Washington—nationalizations of transnational enterprises, ambitious agrarian reform proposals, and rejections of US security priorities—have developed with scant resistance from Washington. Not even the emergence of a "Bolivarian axis" can be portrayed with any seriousness as a vital threat to US security: this is so despite a few half-hearted attempts by Bush administration officials to link Hugo Chávez to "international terrorism" (particularly in light of growing evidence of his support for the Fuerzas Armadas Revolucionarias de Colombia [FARC] and his increasingly friendly ties with Iran) and Russia's recent return to the region as a supplier of military hardware to Venezuela.[12] Most significantly, the US-driven National Security Doctrine that shaped Latin American military institutions and provoked countless coups against even mildly reformist governments during the second half of the twentieth century has been rendered obsolete by the disappearance of a Soviet referent.

Meanwhile, small states once heavily dependent on the United States have benefited from increasing Venezuelan loans and aid, which now dwarf the sums provided by the United States and the international financial institutions in which it exercises considerable sway. By some accounts, growing Chinese investment further diminishes the influence of the United States over policy regimes in Latin America. The incipient Bank of the South, initiated by Venezuela but now including Brazil among its principal sponsors, offers the prospect of development aid for the most impoverished countries in the region without imposing the conditionality attached to agreements reached with the traditional IFIs. That the latter are now virtually absent from the region, no longer needed in light of many governments' full coffers combined with Venezuelan largesse, further testifies to the diminished influence of the United States over Latin American economic policies. Today's security environment provides a moment of greater latitude to pursue unorthodox economic policies.

No less indicative of Washington's declining sway is the growing autonomy of Latin American governments in the diplomatic arena. Evidence of this development first emerged perhaps in the decisions by Chile and Mexico to reject US lobbying at the United Nations to authorize the Iraq war, and the ability of the region's governments to thwart the candidacy of Washington's preferred choice for secretary-general of the OAS. The growing influence of regional actors acting independently of the United States was highlighted as well by the categorical regional opposition to the 2002 coup that briefly ousted Hugo Chávez from the Venezuelan presidency, a position that contrasted sharply with the tacit endorsement by the United States and that proved more influential to boot. Similarly, in 2008 it was Latin American governments, particularly those of Brazil and Chile, that, operating through the Rio Group of Latin American nations, defused a tense confrontation between Ecuador and Washington's foremost ally in the region, Colombia, over the latter's incursion into Ecuadorian territory in pursuit of FARC guerrillas. The strike was criticized across the region and led Ecuador, Venezuela, and Nicaragua to break diplomatic ties with Bogota. Perhaps most importantly, the United States has been incapable of challenging the emergence of intraregional alliances not beholden to Washington's preferences. The December 2008 addition of Cuba to the Rio Group, and the latter's strong condemnation of the continuing US embargo against that country, provides an especially stark illustration of Latin America's newfound diplomatic mettle (Barrionuevo 2008).

The South American Community of Nations (Unión de Naciones Suramericanas, or UNASUR), a political project aimed to facilitate gradual convergence of the Andean Community, Mercosur, and Chile, and meant to link coordinate efforts of countries in the region with regard to a range of political and developmental objectives, was established at a 2004 summit of Latin American heads of state. Perhaps the most noteworthy instance of UNASUR taking a leadership role in hemispheric affairs emerged in 2008, when the Moneda Declaration, unanimously approved by all twelve members of the Union and promoted in particular by the Brazilian Foreign Ministry, sought to defuse the escalating conflict between the leftist Bolivian government and the conservative opposition, which had received substantial funding and logistical support from Washington. The resolution combined unambiguous backing of Evo Morales's government with strong warnings for its detractors. The message was that the opposition remains internationally isolated and must bear in mind that countries in the region are unwilling to countenance violent actions intended to destabilize and eventually overthrow the Morales government or divide the country along regional lines (Zibechi 2008). It is difficult to overestimate the potential significance of the expanded autonomy of Latin American governments for the ability of progressive governments in the region to withstand challenges not only from the United States, but also from the most recalcitrant segments of the domestic elite.[13]

A final example of expanded intraregional cooperation is the Bolivarian axis, anchored by Venezuela and encompassing to varying degrees and in various ways Cuba, Bolivia, Ecuador, and Nicaragua, with more or less embedded ties to several Caribbean islands. This opens up significant alternatives for pink-tide governments to elaborate novel approaches to development strategy. One need not consider the extreme case of Cuba, afforded much greater room for maneuver by its ties to Venezuela, at the same time that it contributes health and literacy workers to support *misiones* in Venezuela and Bolivia, to establish the significance of Venezuelan leadership in creating an alternative paradigm for development in a context of declining US influence.

Ideational Shifts

If during the 1980s and 1990s the worldwide trend was toward confidence in markets, what John Williamson termed a "universal convergence," today there is growing awareness of their limits.[14] Even before this past year's rediscovery of the virtues of Keynesianism, defenders of the so-called Washington Consensus had come to recognize the important role to be played by states in coordinating markets and building capabilities needed by citizens to survive and even thrive in those markets. Thus the emphasis in development policy circles on human capital investments and social policy, both of which are preoccupations that have come to be shared across the political spectrum.

But here as well, ideational shifts are very important. Chapters in this volume by Reygadas and Filgueira (Chapter 9), Moreno-Brid and Paunovic (Chapter 10), and Haslam (Chapter 11), all testify to some of the changes. In the realm of social policy, there is a rethinking of principles of targeting as opposed to universal benefits, with the latter opening space for the introduction of elements of classical social democracy in the Southern Cone and Brazil (B. Roberts 2008). Rethinking the basic components of social policy extends to some circles that continue to accept many of the provisions of the Washington Consensus, but there is a growing universe of opinion that rejects these provisions much more broadly. The result is the increasing salience of new models for distributing resources to the needy (e.g., *misiones*), for handling relationships with MNCs (e.g., nationalizations or, sometimes, renationalizations), or for allocating property rights (e.g., land reforms, experiments with cooperatives of various sorts, etc.). We are also witnessing an opening of space for discussion of industrial policies, which were off the agenda for nearly two decades and, for that matter, even for provision of basic subsidies and imposition of price controls. Governments of the pink tide today encounter a far less constrained set of options for policy innovation in social affairs, international economic relations, and market governance.

Finally, beyond the economic sphere there is the near universal acceptance of democracy as the sole basis for legitimate rule, albeit with differing notions of what democracy entails. This has both external and internal dimensions. With regard to the former, opponents of leftist governments encounter a terrain highly adverse to any efforts to undermine or overthrow democratically elected governments.[15] At the domestic level, too, as noted earlier, even the most radical plans for refounding the political order must remain within the confines of democratic legitimation. Having said that, what is meant by democracy varies widely. Where institutional mechanisms for representation have been weak, efforts to forge elements of direct democracy are more widespread than in countries where those institutions are more consolidated. Even in the Andean countries where the left's detractors criticize its heavy-handedness and plebiscitarian tendencies—and in Venezuela the resort to semiauthoritarian instruments—the governments in question are pursuing reforms through formally democratic mechanisms. It is here that the aforementioned quest to transform states without abandoning democratic regimes stands out most strikingly. As we will discuss below, this is an instance where trends in the international environment, ideational in nature, intersect in important ways with domestic factors in shaping the prospects of the pink tide across Latin America.

Contagion effects are a further instance in which the domestic domain is insufficient to understand ideational shifts and in which challenges to the long prevailing hegemonic order are evident. The diffusion of ideas plays an important role in determining both the mobilizational dynamics of progressive social movements and the development strategies pursued by pink-tide governments: that Latin American countries are experimenting with new ideas is a reality that shapes widespread understandings of what is possible and what is desirable. Although I refer here to Latin American "countries," implying "governments," it could be argued that this is just as much the case at the level of social movements: the Argentine *piqueteros* and the intellectuals allied with them derive lessons from their understanding of Mexico's Zapatistas and, in turn, influence left antichavistas or Bolivians disillusioned with the Morales government's distancing itself from insurgent movements (Holloway 2002). In a quite separate domain, another ideational shift of great importance concerns the politics of recognition. Bolivia is the case that stands out most strikingly, but popular forces have picked up on this across the Americas, where citizenship has come to be understood in post-liberal terms (Yashar 2005). Collective as well as individual rights are increasingly acknowledged as sources of legitimacy and as appropriate ends to be pursued through progressive development strategies. These are cases, it bears noting, where specifically Latin American trends constitute external factors influencing events inside particular countries.

Concluding Reflections: Domestic Determinants of the Lefts' Prospects

External factors matter for governments and movements that constitute Latin America's pink tide, and those that prevail at this juncture reflect the onset of a post-hegemonic order. The idea of a neoliberal world order can no longer be taken for granted. There is no configuration of states, social forces, and international institutions that provides the basis for leadership in a neoliberal direction that can command wide assent. The rise of insurgent social movements, the refounding of states, as well as neoliberal institutions' loss of influence and ideas bespeaks a profound hegemonic crisis. Whether a counterhegemony is possible remains to be seen. This of course depends on trends inside as well as outside the region.

We have seen that the impact of external dynamics is mediated by the internal context. Three aspects of this stand out. First, we must consider the structure of domestic economies and the comparative and competitive (dis)advantages that this establishes for generating growth and distributing its fruits. Second, and not unrelated, are the social/coalitional underpinnings of governments and opposition. And, third, there are the characteristics and capabilities of political leadership and of political and economic institutions. None of these three factors are static, nor are they resistant to change. But part of a coherent development strategy is to create internal conditions conducive to sustainable wealth creation and ongoing redistribution. Just as comparative advantages can be created, so too can coalitions be built and institutions established and strengthened. The capacity of pink-tide governments to spearhead such processes of internal transformation will be as important as the external environment for determining success or failure. Indeed, they will determine whether domestic forces are able to take advantage of opportunities opened up by external context.

Just as democracy has ebbed and flowed in Latin America over the past century, the fortunes of progressive forces have varied. Glimmers of hope, often tantalizingly brief, have alternated with frequently protracted periods of pessimism. Today we are witnessing a moment of flourishing, but the historical record suggests that it would be imprudent to predict an enduring pink tide. The external environment may change unpredictably—as the crisis that began during 2008 makes abundantly clear—and the configuration of domestic interests and their preferences is certain to evolve as well. But whether our focus is on government or on civil society, leftist currents in Latin America have the capacity to influence the constraints and opportunities in which they operate. As Gramsci noted nearly a century ago, picking up on insights that Machiavelli articulated hundreds of years earlier, political success rests upon *virtú* as well as *fortuna*. Whether the various currents of the Latin American left will have the wisdom to take advantage of good luck and the foresight to adapt to adverse conditions will go a long way in determining their staying power and their capacity to effect enduring change. No less than the future of social justice and robust citizenship depends on it.

Notes

This chapter draws on material presented at a May 2008 workshop at the University of Aalborg, Denmark, and at the June 2008 meeting of the Canadian Association of Latin American and Caribbean Studies. I am grateful to participants in these sessions for comments. Maxwell A. Cameron provided insightful suggestions in response to an initial draft. Luis Moncayo provided valuable research assistance.

1. For the centrality of pacts for transitions, see O'Donnell and Schmitter (1986).

2. It bears mentioning that exogenous factors also frame conditions encountered by governments that are not part of the pink tide.

3. The term comes from Hoffman and Centeno (2003).

4. Considerations of space preclude our analyzing the consequences of another feature of globalization, namely, the increasing reliance on the flow of remittances by migrants working abroad. This is particularly relevant for the growing migrant populations from Central America, Mexico, and the Caribbean in the United States.

5. Of course, during the second half of 2008 the dollar has appreciated considerably, in contrast to the trend of the preceding period.

6. The latter is not assured, however. Preliminary data show that Argentine and Brazilian exports declined by roughly one-third during the last quarter of 2008 compared to the previous year.

7. Interestingly, this is contested within the governing Frente Amplio, and the leading candidate to replace Tabaré Vásquez in the 2009 elections, José Mujica, has called for withdrawal from the bilateral deal with the United States in favor of a more strictly regional approach.

8. Throughout the isthmus, attitudes toward CAFTA have been a key cleavage separating right and left, with social movements mobilizing their constituencies in unsuccessful efforts to stymie the accord. Significantly, however, once in power, neither the Sandinistas in Nicaragua nor the Colom government in Guatemala has shown any inclination to withdraw from the treaty. For this reason, and all the more so in light of Central America's reliance on migrant remittances, the likelihood of continued dependence on US economic circumstances is greater than that for South America.

9. Though data remain difficult to come by, this appears to have been meaningful for Bolivia under Evo Morales. It is clearly crucial for understanding the recent good fortunes of the Cuban economy, though examination of this phenomenon lies beyond the scope of this paper. For analysis of the implications for Cuba or the "Bolivarian matrix," see Monreal (2006).

10. This and the following paragraph draw heavily from information contained in ECLAC (2007a).

11. See, however, G. Pope Atkins's contention that the decline in Latin America's importance to US Cold War strategy actually occurred earlier (Atkins 1989:41–47).

12. Interestingly, the insignificance of Russian military ties to Venezuela was acknowledged in January 2009 by none other than US Defense Secretary Robert Gates.

13. At this writing the resolution of the crisis in Honduras remains uncertain, but it is notable that Latin American diplomacy, articulated through the OAS and the mediation of Costa Rican President Oscar Arias, was unable to achieve restoration of President Manuel Zelaya after his ouster in a coup d'état. That the State Department, rather than the OAS, managed to reach a shaky deal for his return to power suggests that the Colossus of the North may indeed retain singular influence in some parts of the region.

14. The Washington Consensus was first articulated in Williamson (1990).

15. For a discussion of how this has influenced strategies of opposition to the Morales government in Bolivia, see Eaton (2007).

References

Abdala, Manuel A. (2001) "Institutions, Contracts and Regulation of Infrastructure in Argentina." *Journal of Applied Economics* 4: 217–254.

Adler, Emanuel (1988) "State Institutions, Ideology, and Autonomous Technological Development: Computers and Nuclear Energy in Argentina and Brazil." *Latin American Research Review* 22, no. 3: 50–90.

ALBA (2006) "Acuerdo para la aplicación de la alternativa Bolivariana para los pueblos de nuestra América y el tratado de comercio de los pueblos." *Alternativa Bolivariana para las Américas.* www.alternativabolivariana.org/index.php (accessed 19 January 2010).

Albó, X. (2006) "El Alto, La Voragine de Una Ciudad Unica." *Journal of Latin American Anthropology* 11, no. 2: 329–350. doi: 10.1525/jlca.2006.11.2.329.

Albro, R. (2007) "Indigenous Politics in Bolivia's Evo Era: Clientelism, Llunkerío, and the Problem of Stigma." *Urban Anthropology* 36, no. 3: 28–43.

Alenda, S. (2003) "Dimensiones de la Movilización en torno a Conciencia de Patria: Hacia un modelo explicativo de un caso de neopopulismo boliviano." *Revista de Ciencia Política* 23, no. 1: 119–135.

Altman, D. (2006) "(Algunas) reformas institucionales para el mejoramiento de la calidad de la democracia en Chile del siglo XXI." In *Desafíos democráticos*, ed. C. Fuentes and A. Villar, 49–86. Lom Ediciones.

Alto, H. D. (2007) "El MAS-IPSP Boliviano." In *Reinventando la nación en Bolivia*, ed. K. Monasterios, P. Stefanoni, and H. D. Alto. La Paz: Plural Editores.

Andean Democracy Research Network (2008) "Bolivia Between Referenda: From Recall to Ratification of a New Constitution." Centre for the Study of Democratic Institutions, The University of British Columbia. Flash Report. http://blogs.ubc.ca/andeandemocracy (accessed 18 January 2010).

Anderson, B. (1991) *Imagined Communities: Reflections on the Origin and Spread of Nationalism*, revised ed. New York: Verso.

Andrenacci, L., and F. Repetto. (2006) *Universalismo, ciudadanía y Estado en la política social latinoamericana.* BID-INDES. Washington, DC: Mimeo.

Antía, F. (2008) "Transformaciones del estado social: ¿hacia una nueva fase de reformas en Chile y Uruguay?" *Revista Debates* 2, no. 1: 123–149.

Arbona, J. M., and B. Kohl (2004) "La Paz-El Alto." *Cities* 21, no. 3: 255–265.

Arditi, B. (2003) "The Becoming-Other of Politics: A Post-Liberal Archipelago." *Contemporary Political Theory* 2, no. 3: 307–325. doi: 10.1057/palgrave.cpt .9300100.

Arditi, B. (2007a) "Ciudadanía de geometría variable y empoderamiento social: una propuesta." In *Ciudadanía y desarrollo humano*, ed. F. Calderón, 123–148. Buenos Aires: Siglo XXI-PNUD.

Arditi, B. (2007b) *Politics on the Edges of Liberalism*. Edinburgh: Edinburgh University Press.

Arditi, B. (2008) "Arguments About the Left Turn(s) in Latin America: A Post-Liberal Politics?" *Latin American Research Review* 43, no. 3: 59–81. doi: 10.1353/lar.0.0061.

Armony, V. (2007) "The 'Civic Left' and the Demand for Social Citizenship." Prepared for workshop "Left Turns? Progressive Parties, Insurgent Movements, and Alternative Policies in Latin America," Peter Wall Institute for Advanced Studies, University of British Columbia, Vancouver, 25–27 May 2007.

Arnson, C. (2007) "Introduction." In *The "New Left" and Democratic Governance in Latin America*, ed. C. Arnson and J. R. Perales. Washington, DC: Woodrow Wilson International Center for Scholars.

Arnson, C. (2009) *La "nueva Izquierda" en America Latina: derechos humanos, participacion politica, y sociedad civil*. Washington, DC: Woodrow Wilson International Center for Scholars.

Atkins, G. P. (1989) *Latin America in the International Political System*, 2nd ed. Boulder, CO: Westview.

Azpiazu, D., and N. Bonofiglio (2006) "Nuevos escenarios macroeconómicos y servicios públicos." *Realidad Económica* 224 (November–December): 32–68.

Barrett, P., D. Chavez, and C. Rodriguez-Garavito (2008) *The New Latin American Left: Utopia Reborn*. London: Pluto.

Barrionuevo, A. (2008) "At Meeting in Brazil, Washington Is Scorned." *New York Times*, 17 December. www.nytimes.com/2008/12/17/world/americas/ 17latin.html.

Bartra, R. (2007) *Izquierda, democracia y crisis política en México*. México: Nuevo Horizonte.

Beamish, P. (1988) *Multinational Joint Ventures in Developing Countries*. London: Routledge.

Beard, C. (1913) *An Economic Interpretation of the Constitution of the United States*. New York: Macmillan.

Beard, C. A. (1986) *An Economic Interpretation of the Constitution of the United States*. New York: Free Press.

Beasley-Murray, J. (2007) *Insurgent Movements*. Prepared for workshop "Left Turns? Progressive Parties, Insurgent Movements, and Alternative Policies in Latin America," Peter Wall Institute for Advanced Studies, University of British Columbia, Vancouver, 25–27 May 2007.

Beasley-Murray, J. (2008) "Fear of Heights: Bolivia's Constituent Process." *Radical Philosophy* 148 (March/April): 2–6.

Beasley-Murray, J. (n.d.) "Postface: April 13, 2002." *Posthegemony*, forthcoming.

Beasley-Murray, J., M. A. Cameron, and E. Hershberg (2009) "Latin America's Left Turns: An Introduction." *Third World Quarterly* 30, no. 2: 319. doi: 10.1080/01436590902770322.

Beck, U. (2000) *What Is Globalization?* Cambridge: Polity.

Bennett, Douglas C., and Kenneth E. Sharpe (1985) *Transnational Corporations Versus the State: The Political Economy of the Mexican Auto Industry.* Princeton: Princeton University Press.

Beverley, J. (2009) "¿Existe un giro neoliberal en Latinoamerica Hoy?" *LASA Forum* XL, no. 1 (Winter).

Biersteker, T. J. (1987) *Multinationals, the State and Control of the Nigerian Economy.* Princeton, NJ: Princeton University Press.

Blanco, B. (2008) Advisor, Indigenous Parliament. Interview. 14 August.

Blanco Muñoz, A. (1998) *Habla el Comandante.* Interview. Caracas: Catedra.

Business News America (13 October 2008) "Morales Assures Cooperatives Will Be Respected Under New Constitution." www.bnamericas.com (downloaded from Factiva database, document WBNA000020081013e4ad003jv).

Business News America (9 June 2009) "ANALYSIS: The Real Reasons Behind the Nationalization of Construction Firms." www.bnamericas.com (downloaded from Factiva database, document WBNA000020090609e569002jp).

Business News America (2 July 2009) "Cantv Looks to Launch DTH, IPTV." www.bnamericas.com (downloaded from Factiva database, document WBNA 000020090702e57200231).

Business News America (9 October 2009) "YPFB Maintains That Country Is Open to Foreign Investment." www.bnamericas.com (downloaded from Factiva database, document WBNA000020091009e5a9001e2).

Caldentey, E. P., and M. Vernengo (2008) *Back to the Future: Latin America's Current Development Strategy.* Working Paper 07/2008. New Delhi: International Development Economics Associates. www.networkideas.org/featart/aug28/back2future.pdf (accessed 18 October 2008).

Cameron, M. (2009) "Latin America's Left Turns: Beyond Good and Bad." *Third World Quarterly* 30, no. 8: 331–348. doi: 10.1080/01436590903321836.

Cammack, P. (1997) "Cardoso's Political Project in Brazil: The Limits of Social Democracy." *Socialist Register* 33: 241.

Canache, P. (2006) "Urban Poor and Political Order." In *The Unraveling of Representative Democracy in Venezuela*, ed. J. L. McCoy and D. J. Myers, 33–49. Baltimore: Johns Hopkins University Press.

Cardoso, F. H. (1993) "The Challenges of Social Democracy in Latin America." In *Social Democracy in Latin America*, ed. M. Vellinga, 274–275. Boulder, CO: Westview.

Caribbean, U. N. E. C. F. L. A. A. T. (2008) *Social Panorama of Latin America 2007* (Pap/Cdr.). UN.

Carlin, R. E. (2006) "The Socioeconomic Roots of Support for Democracy and the Quality of Democracy in Latin America." *Revista de ciencia política* (Santiago) 26, no. 1. doi: 10.4067/S0718-090X2006000100003.

Castañeda, J. (1993) *Utopia Unarmed: The Latin American Left After the Cold War.* New York: Knopf/Random House.

Castañeda, J. G. (2006) "Latin America's Left Turn." *Foreign Affairs* 85 (May/June): 28.

Castañeda, J. G., and M. A. Morales (2008) *Leftovers: Tales of the Latin American Left*. New York: Routledge.

Castiglioni, R. (2005) *The Politics of Social Policy Change in Chile and Uruguay*. New York: Routledge. http://openlibrary.org/b/OL3296102M/politics_of_social_policy_change_in_Chile_and_Uruguay (accessed 22 March 2010).

Castro, F. (2008) "Lula." *La Jornada*, 25 and 30 January, 6 February.

Cavarozzi, M. (1993) "The Left in South America: Politics as the Only Option." In *Social Democracy in Latin America*, ed. Menno Vellinga, 146–162. Boulder, CO: Westview.

Centeno, M. A., and F. López-Alves (2001) *The Other Mirror*. Princeton, NJ: Princeton University Press.

CEPAL (2005) *Panorama Social de América Latina 2004*. Santiago, Chile: CEPAL.

CEPAL (2006) *Shaping the Future of Social Protection. Access, Financing and Solidarity*. Santiago, Chile: CEPAL.

CEPAL (2007) *CEPAL News*, 2. Santiago, Chile: CEPAL.

CEPALSTAT (n.d.) "Database and Statistical Publications. Public Finance: Public Debt." www.eclac.org/estadisticas/bases (accessed 26 October 2008).

Cerny, P. G. (1990) *The Changing Architecture of Politics: Structure, Agency and the Future of the State*. London: Sage.

Chalmers, Damian (2007) "Constituent Power and the Pluralist Ethic." In *The Paradox of Constitutionalism*, ed. Martin Loughlin and Neil Walker, 291–315. Oxford: Oxford University Press.

Chasqueti, D. (2007) *Uruguay 2006: éxitos y dilemas del gobierno de izquierda*, 249–263. Santiago, Chile: Revista de Ciencia Política.

Chávez, H. (2005) *Foro Social Mundial: El Sur, Norte de Nuestros Pueblos Desde El Gimnasio Gigantinho*. Porto Alegre, Brasil, 30 January 2005. www.mre.gov.ve/Noticias/Presidente-Chavez/A2005/Discurso-030.htm (accessed 15 March 2008).

Chávez, H. (2006) "Act for the People's Anti-Imperialist Struggle." VI World Social Forum, 27 January. www.chavezinenglish.org/2006/WSF2006.html (accessed 15 March 2008).

Chávez, H. (2008) "Rise Up Against the Empire: Address to the United Nations." *CounterPunch*, 15 March. www.counterpunch.org (accessed 15 March 2008).

Chávez, H., M. Harnecker, and C. Boudin (2005) *Understanding the Venezuelan Revolution: Hugo Chavez Talks to Marta Harnecker*, illustrated ed. New York: Monthly Review.

Colectivo Situaciones (2006) "¿Hay una 'nueva gobernabilidad'?" http://194.109.209.222/colectivosituaciones/articulos_23.htm (accessed 20 January 2010).

Collier, D., and R. Collier (1991) *Shaping the Political Arena: Critical Junctures, the Labor Movement, and Regime Dynamics in Latin America*. Princeton, NJ: Princeton University Press.

Collier, D., and S. Levitsky (1997) "Research Note: Democracy with Adjectives: Conceptual Innovation in Comparative Research." *World Politics* 49, no. 3: 430–451. doi: 10.1353/wp.1997.0009.

Collier, R. B., and D. Collier (2002) *Shaping the Political Arena: Critical Junctures, the Labor Movement and Regime Dynamics in Latin America*, new ed. Notre Dame, IN: University of Notre Dame Press.

CONAPRI (2006) "Marco legal para las inversiones (Caracas, January 2006)." *Consejo Nacional de Promoción de Inversiones*. www.conapri.org (accessed 19 January 2010).

Coronil, F., and J. Skurski (1991) "Dismembering and Remembering the Nation: The Semantics of Political Violence in Venezuela." *Comparative Studies in Society and History* 33, no. 2: 288–337.

Cox, R. W. (1996) *Approaches to World Order*. Cambridge: Cambridge University Press.

Cufré, D. (2006) "Se acabaron los aumentos indiscrimados de tarifas." *Página/12* (March).

Cullel, J. V. (2004) "Democracy and the Quality of Democracy." In *The Quality Of Democracy: Theory and Applications*, ed. G. O'Donnell, J. V. Cullell, O. M. Iazzetta, and J. V. Cullel, 93–162. Notre Dame, IN: University of Notre Dame Press.

Dahl, R. A. (1956) *A Preface to Democratic Theory*. Chicago: University of Chicago Press.

Datanalisis (2008) *Escenarios: Informe Quincenal*. Caracas: Datanalisis Polling Firm.

Datanalisis (2009) *Escenarios: Informe Quincenal*. Caracas: Datanalisis Polling Firm.

Dávila, M. (2005) *Health Reform in Contemporary Chile: Does Politics Matter?* M.A. thesis, University of North Carolina.

Declaración Final, XIV Encuentro del Foro de São Paulo (2008) Presented at the São Paulo Forum meeting, Montevideo, Uruguay.

Declaración Final, XV Encuentro del Foro de São Paulo (2009) Presented at the São Paulo Forum meeting, Ciudad de México.

D'Elia, Y., and L. F. Cabezas (2008) *Las Misiones Sociales en Venezuela*. Caracas: Instituto Latinamericano de Investigaciones Sociales.

de Rato, Rodrigo (2007) *International Monetary Fund (IMF)*. Presented at the 37th Washington Conference of the Council of the Americas, Washington, DC, 2 May.

Derrida, J. (1992) "Force of Law: The 'Mystical Foundation of Authority.'" In *Deconstruction and the Possibility of Justice*, ed. D. Cornell, M. Rosenfeld, and D. G. Carlson, 3–67. New York: Routledge.

Dicken, P. (2003) *Global Shift: Reshaping the Global Economic Map in the 21st Century*, 4th ed. New York: Guilford.

Do Alto, H. (2006) "Un Partido Campesino-Indígena en la Ciudad: Liderazgos Barriales y Facciones En El Movimiento al Socialismo (MAS) en La Paz, 2005–2006." *Bolivian Studies* 13: 63–86.

Do Alto, H. (2007) "El MAS-IPSP Boliviano." In *Reinventando la nación en Bolivia: Movimientos Sociales, Estado y poscolonialidad*, ed. Karin Monasterios, Pablo Stefanoni, and Hervé Do Alto. La Paz, Bolivia: Plural Editores.

Donolo, C. (1982) "Sociale." *Laboratorio Politico* 2: 103–120.

Drake, P. W. (2006) "The Oxymoron of Polyarchy." In *The Hegemony of US*

Economic Ideas in Latin America, ed. E. Hershberg and F. Rosen. New York: New Press.

Drake, P. W., and E. Hershberg (2006) *State and Society in Conflict*. Pittsburgh, PA: University of Pittsburgh Press.

Dunning, J. H. (1993) *The Globalization of Business*. London: Routledge.

Dunning, John H. (1991) "Governments and Multinational Enterprises: From Confrontation to Cooperation?" *Millennium Journal of International Studies* 20, no. 2: 225–244.

Eaton, K. (2007) "Backlash in Bolivia: Regional Autonomy as a Reaction Against Indigenous Mobilization." *Politics Society* 35, no. 1 (March): 71–102. doi: 10.1177/0032329206297145.

ECLAC (2007a) *Economic Panorama of Latin America*. Santiago, Chile: ECLAC.

ECLAC (2007b) *Preliminary Overview of the Latin American and Caribbean Economy*. Santiago, Chile: ECLAC.

ECLAC (2008) *Economic Survey of Latin America and the Caribbean 2008*. Santiago, Chile: ECLAC.

Economist, The (2006) "The Working Man's Statesman Gives a Rare Interview to *The Economist*." 5 March, 2–3.

Economist, The (2008) "Death in Venezuela: Deadly Massage." 17 July.

Eden, Lorraine, Stephanie Lenway, and Douglas A. Schuler (2005) "From the Obsolescing Bargain to the Political Bargaining Model." In *International Business and Government Relations in the 21st Century*, ed. Robert Grosse, 253–271. Cambridge: Cambridge University Press.

Egger, P., and M. Pfaffermayr (2004) "The Impact of Bilateral Investment Treaties on Foreign Direct Investment." *Journal of Comparative Economics* 32, no. 4: 788–804.

El Deber. (7 October 2006a) "La población minera continuó sangrando." www .eldeber.com.bo/2006/20061007/nacional_4.html (accessed 11 June 2010).

El Deber. (7 October 2006b) "Cambian al ministro de minería." www.eldeber .com.bo/2006/20061007/nacional_8.html (accessed 11 June 2010).

Eley, G. (2002) *Forging Democracy: The History of the Left in Europe, 1850–2000*. Oxford: Oxford University Press.

Ellner, S. (2008) "Las tensiones entre la base y la dirigencia en las filas del chavismo." *Revista de Economíca y Ciencias Sociales* 14, no. 1: 49–64.

Ellner, S. (2009) "La política exterior del Gobierno de Chávez: La retórica chavista y los asuntos sustanciales." *Revista de Economía y Ciencias Sociales* 15, no. 1: 115–132.

Ellner, S., and M. T. Salas (2006) "Introduction: New Perspectives and the Chávez Phenomenon." In *Venezuela: Hugo Chávez and the Decline of an Exceptional Democracy*, annotated ed., ed. S. Ellner. Lanham, MD: Rowman and Littlefield.

El Universal (21 July 1999) "Constituyente debe tocar el Petróleo." Patricia Ventura Nicolás. http://buscador.eluniversal.com/1999/07/21/pet_art_ 21204AA.shtml (accessed 21 February 2007).

Espósito, C., and W. Arteaga (2006) *Movimientos Sociales Urbano-Populares en Bolivia: Una lucha contra le exclusion social, politica, y economica*. UNITAS-Programa Desarrollo del Poder Local.

Evans, P. B. (1979) *Dependent Development: The Alliance of Multinational, State, and Local Capital in Brazil*. Princeton, NJ: Princeton University Press.

Evans, P. B. (1995) *Embedded Autonomy*. Princeton, NJ: Princeton University Press.

Fazio, H. R. (1997) *Mapa actual de la extrema riqueza en Chile*. Santiago: LOM Ediciones.

Filgueira, F. (1999) "Tipos de welfare y reformas sociales en América Latina: Eficiencia, residualismo y ciudadanía estratificada." In *Reforma do Estado e mudanc?a institucional no Brasil*, ed. M. A. Melo. Recife: Fundacao Joaquim Nabuco, Escola de Governo e Politicas Publicas, Editora Massangana.

Filgueira, F. (2007) *Cohesión, riesgo y arquitectura de protección social en América Latina*. Serie Políticas Sociales 135. Santiago, Chile: CEPAL.

Filgueira, F., C. G. Molina, J. Papadópulos, and F. Tobar (2005) *Universalismo básico: una alternativa posible y necesaria para mejorar las condiciones de vida en América Latina*. Montevideo: INDES.

Filgueira, F., F. Rodriguez, P. Alegre, S. Lijtenstein, and C. Rafaniello (2006) "Estructura de riesgo y arquitectura de protección social en el Uruguay actual: crónica de un divorcio anunciado." In *Dilemas sociales y alternativas distributivas en el Uruguay,* ed. F. Filgueira and D. Gelber. Montevideo: Universidad Católica del Uruguay.

Foucault, M. (1982) "The Subject and Power." In *Michel Foucault: Beyond Structuralism and Hermeneutics*, 2nd ed., ed. H. L. Dreyfus and P. Rabinow, 208–226. Brighton: Harvester.

Franco, R., and E. Cohen, ed. (2006) *Transferencias con corresponsabilidad*. Mexico: FLACSO Mexico.

French, J. D. (2000) "The Latin American Labor Studies Boom." *International Review of Social History* 45, no. 2: 279–308. doi: 10.1017/S0020859 000000146.

French, J. D. (2006) "The Labouring and Middle-Class Peoples of Latin America and the Caribbean: Historical Trajectories and New Research Directions." In *Global Labour History: A State of the Art*, ed. Jan Lucassen. Bern: Peter Lang.

French, J. D. (2008) *Understanding the Politics of Latin America's Plural Lefts (Chávez/Lula)*. Kellogg Institute Working Paper no. 355, pp. 7–8.

French, J. D., and A. Fortes (2005) "Another World Is Possible: The Rise of the Brazilian Workers' Party and the Prospects for Lula's Government." *Labor: Studies in Working-Class History of the Americas* 2, no. 3: 13–31. doi: 10.1215/15476715-2-3-13.

Gallagher, K. P., and L. Zarsky (2007) *The Enclave Economy: Foreign Investment and Sustainable Development in Mexico's Silicon Valley*. Cambridge, MA: MIT Press.

Gantz, D. A. (2003) "The Evolution of FTA Investment Provisions: From NAFTA to the United States–Chile Free Trade Agreement. *American University International Law Review* 19: 680–768.

García, M.-P. (2008) "La Praxis de los consejos comunales en Venezuela: ¿Poder popular o instancia clientelar?" *Revista de Economía y Ciencias Sociales* 14, no. 1: 125–152.

Garretón, M. A. (1989) "Popular Mobilization and the Military Regime in Chile: The Complexities of the Invisible Transition." In *Power and Popular Protest: Latin American Social Movements*, ed. Susan Eckstein. Berkeley: University of California Press.

Gereffi, Gary (1983) *The Pharmaceutical Industry and Dependency in the Third World*. Princeton, NJ: Princeton University Press.

Gill, L. (2000) *Teetering on the Rim*. New York: Columbia University Press.

Giusti, R. (1989) "Noche de queda." In *El Dia que bajaron los cerros*. Caracas: Editora El Nacional, Editorial Ateneo de Caracas.

Gobierno de Argentina (2007) *Proceso de Renegociación Contratos de Servicios Públicos*. Unidad de Renegociación y Analysis de Contratos de Servicios Publicos.

Golbert, L. (2004) *¿Derecho a la inclusión o paz social? Plan Jefas y Jefes de Hogar Desocupados*. Serie Políticas Sociales núm. 84. Santiago, Chile: CEPAL.

González, L. E. (1995) "Continuity and Change in the Uruguayan Party System." In *Building Democratic Institutions: Party Systems in Latin America*, ed. Scott Mainwaring and Timothy Scully. Stanford, CA: Stanford University Press.

Goodale, M. (2009) *Dilemmas of Modernity: Bolivian Encounters with Law and Liberalism*. Stanford, CA: Stanford University Press.

Gott, R. (2001) *In the Shadow of the Liberator: The Impact of Hugo Chavez on Venezuela and Latin America*. London: Verso.

Grandin, G. (2006) *Empire's Workshop: Latin America, the United States, and the Rise of the New Imperialism*. New York: Metropolitan.

Gratius, S. (2006) "La 'revolución' de Hugo Chávez: ¿proyecto de izquierdas o populismo histórico?" *Escenarios Alternativos* 3, no. 39.

Grugel, J. (2005) "Citizenship and Governance in Mercosur: Arguments for a Social Agenda." *Third World Quarterly* 26, no. 7: 1061–1076.

Guarayos, S. (2008) President MAS-La Paz dirección departamental. Interview. 28 July.

Guasch, J. L., and J. Laffont (2003) *Renegotiation of Concession Contracts in Latin America*. Finance, Private Sector, and Infrastructure Unit Policy Research Working Paper, No. 3011, pp. 1–48. Washington, DC: World Bank.

Guattari, F., and S. Rolnik (2008) *Molecular Revolution in Brazil*, new ed. Los Angeles: Semiotext(e).

Guzmán, O. (2008) Adviser, National Coalition for Change (CONALCAM); Militant, District 6 (Villa Copacabana). Interview. 26 August.

Hagopian, F., and S. P. Mainwaring (2005) *The Third Wave of Democratization in Latin America: Advances and Setbacks*. New York: Cambridge University Press.

Hakim, P. (2006) "Is Washington Losing Latin America?" *Foreign Affairs* 85 (January/February): 39.

Hallward-Driemeier, M. (2003) "Do Bilateral Investment Treaties Attract Foreign Direct Investment? Only a Bit . . . And They Could Bite." World Bank Policy Research Working Paper No. 3121.

Hamilton, N. (1982) *The Limits of State Autonomy: Post-Revolutionary Mexico*. Princeton, NJ: Princeton University Press.

Hardt, M., and A. Negri (2009) *Commonwealth*. Cambridge, MA: Belknap Press of Harvard University Press.

Harvey, R. (2000) *Liberators: Latin America's Struggle for Independence, 1810–1830*. London: John Murray.

Haslam, P. A. (2007) "The Firm Rules: Multinational Corporations, Policy Space and Neoliberalism." *Third World Quarterly* 28: 1167–1183. doi: 10.1080/01436590701507594.

Hawkins, K. A. (2003) "Populism in Venezuela: The Rise of Chavismo." *Third World Quarterly* 24, no. 6: 1137–1160. doi:10.1080/0143659031000163010.

Hawkins, K. A., and D. R. Hansen. (2006) "Dependent Civil Society: The Circulos Bolivarianos in Venezuela." *Latin American Research Review* 41, no. 1: 102–132. doi: 10.1353/lar.2006.0008.

Hernández, J. A. (2004) "Against the Comedy of Civil Society." *Journal of Gender Studies* 13, no. 1: 137. doi: 10.1080/13569320420001866532.

Heródoto, B., ed. (1989) *O Que Pensam Os Presidenciáveis: Luiz Inácio Lula da Silva. Partido dos Trabalhadores*. São Paulo: Harbra.

Hershberg, E. (1989) *Transition from Authoritarian Rule and Eclipse of the Left: Toward a Reinterpretation of Political Change in Spain*. Ph.D. diss., University of Wisconsin–Madison.

Hershberg, E. (2006) "Technocrats, Citizens and Second Generation Reforms: Considerations on Colombia's Andean Malaise." In *State and Society in Conflict: Comparative Perspectives on Andean Crises*, ed. Paul W. Drake and Eric Hershberg. Pittsburgh, PA: University of Pittsburgh Press.

Hevia, F. (2007) *El programa Oportunidades y la construcción de ciudadanía*. Tesis de doctorado, CIESAS.

Hochschild, H. (1998) "Sonami Forsees a Difficult Scenario for 1998." In *Minería Chilena, Directorio Minero de Chile 1998*, 86. Santiago, Chile: PuntoDiez S.A.

Hochstetler, K., and E. J. Friedman (2008) "Can Civil Society Organizations Solve the Crisis of Partisan Representation in Latin America?" *Latin American Politics and Society* 50: 1–32. doi: 10.1111/j.1548-2446.2008.00011.x.

Hoffman, K., and M. A. Centeno (2003) "The Lopsided Continent: Inequality in Latin America." *Annual Review of Sociology* 29, no. 1: 363–390. doi: 10.1146/annurev.soc.29.010202.100141.

Holloway, J. (2002) *Change the World Without Taking Power: The Meaning of Revolution Today*. London: Pluto.

Holston, James (2008) *Insurgent Citizenship: Disjunctions of Democracy and Modernity in Brazil*. Princeton, NJ: Princeton University Press.

Huanca, L. (2008) Executive, FEJUVE-El Alto. Interview. 13 August.

Hylton, F., and S. Thomson (2007) *Revolutionary Horizons: Past and Present in Bolivian Politics*. London: Verso.

Ibarra Güell, P. (2003) *Social Movements and Democracy*. New York: Palgrave.

ICSID (2009) Search ICSID Cases. *International Centre for Settlement of Investment Disputes*. http://icsid.worldbank.org/ICSID/FrontServlet?request Type=CasesRH&reqFrom=Main&actionVal=ViewAllCases (accessed 25 November 2009)

Kalyvas, A. (2001) "Book Reviews." *Constellations* 8, no. 3: 413–422. doi: 10.1111/1467-8675.t01-1-00248.

Kantor, M. (2004) "The New Draft Model US BIT: Noteworthy Developments." *Journal of International Arbitration* 21, no. 4: 383–396.

Karl, T. L. (1987) "Petroleum and Political Pacts: The Transition to Democracy in Venezuela." *Latin American Research Review* 22, no. 1: 63–94.

Keck, M. E. (1992) *The Workers' Party and Democratization in Brazil*, new ed. New Haven, CT: Yale University Press.

Keck, M. E., and K. Sikkink (1998) *Activists Beyond Borders: Advocacy Networks in International Politics*. Ithaca, NY: Cornell University Press.

Kobrin, S. J. (1987) "Testing the Bargaining Hypothesis in the Manufacturing Sector in Developing Countries." *International Organization* 41, no. 4: 609–638.

Kohli, A. (2004) *State-Directed Development*. Cambridge: Cambridge University Press.

Komadina, J., and C. Geffroy (2007) *El Poder del Movimiento Político. Estrategia, tramas organizativas e identidad del MAS en Cochabamba (1999–2005)*. La Paz, Bolivia: CESU; DICYT-UMSS; Fundación PIEB.

Kronish, Rich, and Kenneth S. Mericle, ed. (1984) *The Political Economy of the Latin American Motor Vehicle Industry*. Cambridge: MIT Press.

Lakoff, G. (2008) *The Political Mind: Why You Can't Understand 21st-Century American Politics with an 18th-Century Brain*. New York: Viking Adult.

Lander, E. (2007) "Venezuela: logros y tensiones en los primeros ocho años del proceso de cambio." In *Gobiernos de izquierda en América Latina. Un balance político*, ed. B. Stolowicz, 39–76. Bogotá: Aurora.

Lanzaro, J. (2007) "La tercera ola? de las izquierdas latinoamericanas: entre el populismo y la socialdemocracia." *Encuentros Latinoamericanos* 1, no. 1: 20–57.

Lanzaro, J. (2008) "La Socialdemocracia Criolla." *Nueva Sociedad* 217: 40–58.

LAPOP (2006) *Latin American Public Opinion Poll 2006*. Santiago, Chile: LAPOP Survey 2006. www.vanderbilt.edu/lapop.

La Prensa (2 May 2006) "Quince empresas bajo control." www.laprensa.com.bo/20060502/especial/especial02.htm (accessed 18 February 2007).

La Prensa (6 May 2006) "Bolivia y España inician negociaciones." www.laprensa.com.bo/20060506/negocios/negocios01.htm (accessed 18 February 2007).

La Prensa (7 May 2006) "Gobierno apuesta a mejora sustancial en precio del gas." www.laprensa.com.bo/20060507/negocios/negocios03.htm (accessed 18 February 2007).

La Prensa (22 May 2006) "De Vido llegará mañana para sellar alza en el precio del gas." www.laprensa.com.bo/20060522/negocios/negocios02.htm (accessed 18 February 2007).

La Razón (12 June 2006) "Evo dice que la fundición de Vinto volverá al Estado." www.la-razon.com/versiones/20060612_005570/nota_248_297088.htm (accessed 18 February 2007).

La Razón (3 August 2006) "España recibe garantías para sus inversiones." www.la-razon.com/versiones/20060803_005622/nota_248_315998.htm (accessed 18 February 2007).

La Razón (30 April 2009a) "Bajo Observación, Torrico sigue siendo influyente en el MAS."

La Razón (30 April 2009b) "Con apoyo de Gil, Loayza se enfrenta a Evo."

La Tercera (6 August 2002) "Minera Escondida, de la Anglo Australiana BHP Billiton, y Mantos Blanco, de Anglo American." www.latercera.cl/medio/articulo/imprimir/0,0,3255_5676_1607627,00.html (accessed 15 February 2007).

La Tercera (9 January 2004) "Presión a las mineras: una pésima señal." www
.latercera.cl/medio/articulo/imprimir/0,0,3255_5676_47667607,00 (accessed
15 February 2007).
La Tercera (21 April 2004) "Derecha se abre a royalty y analiza costo electoral de
oponerse." www.latercera.cl/medio/articulo/imprimir/0,0,3255_5676
_74280986,00.html (accessed 15 February 2007).
La Tercera (24 July 2004) "Diputado Leal: 'En la Cámara triunfó el lobby y perdió
el royalty.'" www.latercera.cl/medio/articulo/imprimir/0,0,3255_5664
_82985373,00 (accessed 15 February 2007).
La Tercera (19 November 2004) "Gobierno relanza royalty como impuesto para
facilitar aprobación." www.latercera.cl/medio/articulo/imprimir/0,0,3255
_5676_99582227,00 (accessed 15 February 2007).
La Tercera (16 December 2004) "Gobierno envía sin cambios impuesto minero
al Congreso." www.latercera.cl/medio/articulo/imprimir/0,0,3255_5676
_103498513,00 (accessed 15 February 2007).
Latinobarómetro (2007) *Informe latinobarómetro 2007.* www.latinobarometro.org.
Latinobarómetro (2008) *Informe latinobarómetro 2008.* November. www
.latinobarometro.org (accessed 9 December 2009).
Lavinas, L. (2009) "Pobreza Urbana no Brasil: trade-off entre investimentos sociais
e transferências de renda." In *Procesos de urbanización de la pobreza y nuevas
formas de exclusión social,* ed. A. Ziccardi. Buenos Aires: CLACSO.
Lazar, S. (2006) "El Alto, Ciudad Rebelde: Organisational Bases for Revolt."
Bulletin of Latin American Research 25, no. 2: 183–199.
Levitsky, S., and K. M. Roberts (forthcoming) "Latin America's Left Turn: A
Framework for Analysis." In *The New Left in Latin America.* Baltimore, MD:
Johns Hopkins University Press.
Lindert, K., E. Skoufias, and J. Shapiro (2006) *Redistributing Income to the Poor
and the Rich. Public Transfers in Latin America and the Caribbean.*
Washington, DC: World Bank.
Lindahl, Hans (2007) "Constituent Power and Reflexive Identity: Towards an
Ontology of Collective Selfhood." In *The Paradox of Constitutionalism,* ed.
Martin Loughlin and Neil Walker, 9–24. Oxford: Oxford University Press.
Linera, Á. G., M. C. León, and P. C. Monje (2004) *Sociología de los movimientos
sociales en Bolivia.* La Paz, Bolivia: Plural Editores.
Llanos, R. (2008) Former National Director, Bolivian Penitentiary Regime.
Interview. 6 August.
Loayza, R. (2008) Founding member of the MAS, former national deputy, and del-
egate to the Constituent Assembly. Interview. 22 July.
Lomnitz, C. (2006) "Latin America's Rebellion: Will the New Left Set a New
Agenda?" *Boston Review*, September/October. http://bostonreview.net/
BR31.5/lomnitz.php (accessed 18 January 2010)
López Maya, M. (1998) "New Avenues for Popular Representation in Venezuela:
La Causa-R and the Movimiento Bolivariano 200." In *Reinventing
Legitimacy: Democracy and Political Change in Venezuela,* ed. D. J. Canache
and M. Kulisheck. Westport, CT: Praeger.
López Maya, M. (2000) "¡Se rompieron las fuentes! La política está en la calle."
In *Venezuela siglo XX: visiones y testimonios,* ed. A. Baptista. Caracas:
Fundacion Polar.

López Maya, M. (2003) "The Venezuelan Caracazo of 1989: Popular Protest and Institutional Weakness." *Journal of Latin American Studies* 35, no. 1: 117–137. doi: 10.1017/S0022216X02006673.

López Maya, M. (2008) "Innovaciones participativas en la Caracas bolivariana: La MTA de la Pedrera y la OCA de Barrio Unión-Carpintero." *Revista de Economía y Ciencias Sociales* 14, no. 1: 65–94.

"Los colores de la izquierda" (2008) *Nueva Sociedad*, no. 217 (September–October).

Loughlin, M., and J. Walker (2007) "Introduction." In *The Paradox of Constitutionalism: Constituent Power and Constitutional Form*, ed. M. Loughlin and N. Walker. Oxford: Oxford University Press.

Lozada, M. (2004) "El otro es el enemigo: imaginarios sociales y polarizacion." *Revista Venezolana de Economía y Ciencias Sociales* 10, no. 2: 195–210.

Lozada, M. (2008) "¿Nosotros o ellos? Representaciones sociales, polarización y espacio público en Venezuela?." *Cuadernos Del Cendes* 25, no. 69: 89–105.

Lucassen, J., and J. D. French, ed. (2006) "The Labouring and Middle-Class Peoples of Latin America and the Caribbean: Historical Trajectories and New Research Directions." In *Global Labour History: A State of the Art*, 304–306. New York: Peter Lang.

Lula, L. I. (2005) *Discurso Do Presidente Da República, Luiz Inácio Lula Da Silva, No Ato Político de Celebração Aos 15 Anos Do Foro de São Paulo*, 4–5. Brasília: Presidência da República Secretaría de Imprensa e Divulgação.

Luna, J. P., and F. Filgueira (2009) "The Left Turns as Multiple Paradigmatic Crises." *Third World Quarterly* 30, no. 2 (March): 371–395. doi: 10.1080/01436590802681108.

Luna, J. P., and M. A. Seligson (2007) *Cultura política de la democracia en Chile*. Nashville, TN: Latin American Public Opinion Project.

Luo, Y. (2001) "Toward a Cooperative View of MNC–Host Government Relations: Building Blocks and Performance Implications." *Journal of International Business Studies* 32, no. 3: 401–419.

Macdonald, L., and A. Ruckert (2009) *Post-Neoliberalism in the Americas*. New York: Palgrave Macmillan.

Machaca, M. (2008) MAS deputy for El Alto. Interview. 18 August.

Machado, J. E. (2008) *Estudio de los Consejos Comunales en Venezuela*. Caracas: Fundación Centro Gumilla.

Mackinnon, M. M., and M. A. Petrone (1998) *Populismo y Neopopulismo en America Latina*. Buenos Aires: Eudeba. http://openlibrary.org/b/OL 12963221M/Populismo_y_Neopopulismo_en_America_Latina.

Macpherson, C. (1965) *The Real World of Democracy*, 2nd ed. Toronto: Canadian Broadcasting Corporation.

Mainwaring, S., A. M. Bejarano, and E. P. Leongomez (2006) *The Crisis of Democratic Representation in the Andes*. Stanford, CA: Stanford University Press.

Mainwaring, S., A. M. Bejarano, and E. Pizarro (2006) *The Crisis of Democratic Representation in the Andes*. Stanford, CA: Stanford University Press.

Mainwaring, S., and M. Torcal (2003) "The Political Recrafting of Social Bases of Party Competition: Chile, 1973–95." *British Journal of Political Science* 33, no. 1: 55–84.

Manzetti, L. (1999) *Privatization South American Style.* Oxford: Oxford University Press.

Marshall, T. H. (1950) *Citizenship and Social Class.* Cambridge: Cambridge University Press.

Marx, K. (2005) *The Eighteenth Brumaire of Louis Bonaparte.* New York: Mondial.

Mayorga, R. A. (2006) "Outsiders and Neopopulism: The Road to Plebiscitary Democracy." In *The Crisis of Democratic Representation in the Andes,* ed. S. Mainwaring, A. M. Bejarano, and E. P. Leongomez, 132–167. Stanford, CA: Stanford University Press.

McCarthy, M. (2009) "Herramientas de la Revolucion? (Tools of the Revolution?) The Case of the Mesas Tecnicas de Agua and Politicized Participatory Water Policy in Venezuela." Presented at the Congress of the Latin American Studies Association, Rio de Janeiro, Brazil.

McCoy, J. (2008a) "Democratic Transformation in Latin America." *Whitehead Journal of Diplomacy and International Relations* 9, no. 1: 19–29.

McCoy, J. (2008b) "Venezuela: Leading a New Trend in Latin America." *Revista: Harvard Review of Latin America* (Fall): 52–56.

McCoy, J. L. (2006) "International Response to Democratic Crisis in the Americas, 1990–2005." *Democratization* 13, no. 5: 756. doi: 10.1080/13510 340601010644.

McCoy, J., and F. Díaz (forthcoming) *Political Conflict in Venezuela: An Insider's Story of Third Party Intervention, 2002–2004.* Washington, DC: United States Institute of Peace.

McCoy, J. L., and D. J. Myers (2006) *The Unraveling of Representative Democracy in Venezuela,* illustrated 2nd ed. Baltimore: Johns Hopkins University Press.

Mechoulan, E. (2004) "Introduction: On the Edges of Jacques Ranciere." *SubStance* 33, no. 1: 3–9. doi: 10.1353/sub.2004.0004.

Melcher, D. (2008) "Cooperatavismo en Venezuela: Teoría y praxis." *Revista de Economía y Ciencias Sociales* 14, no. 1: 95–106.

Merino, M. A. G. (1989) *The Chilean Political Process.* London: Routledge.

Michel, S. (2008) Party authority, MSM. Interview. 4 August.

Michels, R. (1962) *Political Parties: A Sociological Study of the Oligarchical Tendencies of Modern Democracy.* New York: Collier.

Minería Chilena (1998) *Chilean Mining Compendium 1998.* Santiago: Editec Ltda.

Moldiz, H. (2007) "Bolivia: crisis estatal y proceso de transformación." In *Gobiernos de izquierda en América Latina. Un balance político,* ed. B. Stolowicz, 155–196. Bogotá: Aurora.

Molina, F. (2006) *Evo Morales y el retorno de la izquierda nacionalista.* La Paz, Bolivia: Ed. Siglo XXI.

Molina, F. (2007) *Conversión sin Fe. El MAS y la Democracia.* La Paz, Bolivia: Ediciones Eureka.

Molina, F. (n.d.) *Conversión sin Fe. El MAS y la Democracia.* La Paz, Bolivia: Ediciones Eureka.

Monreal, P. (2006) "Cuban Development in the Bolivarian Matrix." *NACLA Report on the Americas* 39, no. 4: 22–44.

Moore, B. (1966) *Social Origins of Dictatorship and Democracy: Lord and Peasant in the Making of the Modern World.* Boston: Beacon.

Morales, G. A. (2008) Vice-minister, Vice-ministry of Basic Services. Interview. 9 August.

Moran, T. H. (1974) *Multinational Corporations and the Politics of Dependence: Copper in Chile.* Princeton, NJ: Princeton University Press.

Moran, T. H. (1998) "The Changing Nature of Political Risk." In *Managing International Political Risk*, ed. T. H. Moran, 7–14. Malden, MA: Blackwell.

Moran, T. H. (2005) "How Does FDI Affect Host Country Development? Using Industry Case Studies to Make Reliable Generalizations." In *Does Foreign Direct Investment Promote Development? New Methods, Outcomes and Policy Approaches*, illustrated ed., ed. E. M. Graham, M. Blomstrom, and T. H. Moran, 281–313. Washington, DC: Peterson Institute.

Moreno-Brid, J. C., and I. Paunovic (2006) "The Future of Economic Policy Making by Left-of-Center Governments in Latin America: Old Wine in New Bottles?" *ReVista, Harvard Review of Latin America, David Rockefeller Center for Latin American Studies*, Harvard University.

Moreno-Brid, J. C., and I. Paunovic (2008) "What Is New and What Is Left of the Economic Policies of the New Left Governments of Latin America?" *International Journal of Political Economy* 37, no. 3: 82–108.

Moschonas, G. (2002) *In the Name of Social Democracy: The Great Transformation from 1945 to the Present*, rev. ed. London: Verso.

Movimiento al Socialismo (2004) *Estatuto Orgánico o Carta Fundamental.* La Paz, Bolivia: Imprenta Gravifal.

Movimiento al Socialismo (2006) *La Revolución Democratica: Diez Discursos de Evo Morales.* La Paz, Bolivia: Malatesta.

Muñoz, A. B. (1998) *Habla El Comandante Hugo Chavez Frias—Venezuela Del 4 Febrero 92 Al 6 De Diciembre 98.* Caracas: Universidad Central De Venezuela.

Negri, A. (1999) *Insurgencies: Constituent Power and the Modern State.* Minneapolis: University of Minnesota Press.

Negri, A., and G. Cocco (2006) *Global: Biopoder y Luchas en una America Latina Globalizada.* Buenos Aires: Ediciones Paidos Iberica.

Neumayer, Eric, and Laura Spess (2005) "Do Bilateral Investment Treaties Increase Foreign Direct Investment to Developing Countries?" *World Development* 33, no. 10: 1567–1585.

Novaro, M. (2008) "El capitalismo agrario y la captura de rentas." *Página/12.*

Núñez, D. (2008) Founding member of the MAS, former deputy for the MAS, and current cocalero union leader. Interview. 19 August.

Ocampo, J., and J. Martin (2003) *Globalization and Development: A Latin American and Caribbean Perspective.* Palo Alto, CA: Stanford Social Sciences.

O'Donnell, G. (1994) "Delegative Democracy." *Journal of Democracy* 5 (January): 55–69.

O'Donnell, G. (2004) "Human Development, Human Rights, and Democracy." In *The Quality of Democracy: Theory and Applications*, ed. G. O'Donnell, J. V. Cullell, O. M. Iazzetta, and J. V. Cullel, 9–92. Notre Dame, IN: University of Notre Dame Press.

O'Donnell, G., and P. C. Schmitter (1986) *Transitions from Authoritarian Rule: Tentative Conclusions About Uncertain Democracies.* Baltimore: Johns Hopkins University Press.

Offe, C. (1984) *Contradictions of the Welfare State.* London: Hutchison.

OIT (2007) *Panorama laboral 2007. América Latina y el Caribe.* Lima: Organización Internacional del Trabajo.

Ojeda, F. (1989a) "Beirut en Caracas." In *El Dia que bajaron los cerros,* 43–46. Caracas: Editorial Ateneo de Caracas. http://openlibrary.org/b/OL9193175M/El_Dia_que_bajaron_los_cerros_(Serie_Cuarto_poder).

Ojeda, F. (1989b) "Paz a punta de cañones." In *El Dia que bajaron los cerros,* 33–35. Caracas: Editorial Ateneo de Caracas. http://openlibrary.org/b/OL9193175M/El_Dia_que_bajaron_los_cerros_(Serie_Cuarto_poder).

Orellana, L. (2006) *Nacionalismo, populismo y régimen de acumulación en Bolivia. Hacia una caracterización del gobierno de Evo Morales.* La Paz, Bolivia: CEDLA.

Ortega y Gasset, J. (1994) *The Revolt of the Masses.* New York: W. W. Norton.

Oxhorn, P. (1995) *Organizing Civil Society.* University Park, PA: Pennsylvania State University Press.

Pagina/12 (16 February 2006) "Reunion con empresarios españoles: Quejosos pero optimistas." www.pagina12.com.ar/diario/elpais/1-63208-2006-02-16.html (accessed 23 February 2007).

Pagina/12 (26 March 2006) "Las privatizadas y el pragmatismo K," David Cufré. www.pagina12.com.ar/diario/economia/2-64769-2006-03-26.html (accessed 23 February 2007).

Pagina/12 (2 April 2006) "Reportaje a Julio de Vido, Ministro de Planificación: 'Se acabaron los aumentos indiscriminados de tarifas,'" Mario Wainfeld and David Cufré. www.pagina12.com.ar/diario/elpais/1-65087-2006-04-02.html (accessed 23 February 2007).

Painter, James (2008) "Paraguay's President Faces Huge Task," *BBC,* 15 August. http: //news.bbc.co.uk/2/hi/americas/7561219.stm.

Panebianco, A. (1988) *Political Parties: Organization and Power.* New York: Cambridge University Press.

Panizza, F. (2005a) "The Social Democratization of the Latin American Left." *Revista Europea de Estudios Latinoamericanos y del Caribe* 79: 100–101.

Panizza, F. (2005b) "Unarmed Utopia Revisited: The Resurgence of Left-of-Centre Politics in Latin America." *Political Studies* 53: 716–734. doi: 10.1111/j.1467-9248.2005.00553.x.

Pardinas, J. E. (2008) *Los retos de la migración en México: un espejo de dos caras.* Serie Estudios y Perspectivas No. 99, p. 62. Mexico D.F.: Comisión Económica para América Latina y el Caribe.

Parra, E. (2008) Coordinator, FNMCB-BC, and delegate to the Constituent Assembly. Interview. 14 August.

Patana, E. (2008) President, COR-El Alto. Interview. 21 August.

Patruyo, T. (2008) *El estado actual de las misiones socials: balance sobre su proceso de implementacion institucionalizacion.* Caracas: Instituto Latinamericano de Investigaciones Sociales.

Paunovic, I., and J. C. Moreno-Brid (2007a) "Global Imbalances and Economic Development: Economic Policymaking by Left-of-Center Governments in Latin America." *International Journal of Political Economy* (December).

Paunovic, I., and J. C. Moreno-Brid (2007b) "New Industrial Policies in the New Left of Latin America?" Presented at "Left Turns? Political Parties, Insurgent Movements, and Policies in Latin America," May 2007, University of British Columbia.

Paus, E. (2005) *Foreign Investment, Development, and Globalization: Can Costa Rica Become Ireland?* New York: Palgrave Macmillan.

Penfold-Becerra, M. (2005) *Social Funds, Clientelism and Redistribution: Chavez's "Misiones" Programs in Comparative Perspective.* Caracas: Instituto de Estudios Superiores de Administracion.

Peredo, A. (2008) National senator for the MAS. Interview. 12 July.

Postero, N. (2007) *Now We Are Citizens: Indigenous Politics in Postmulticultural Bolivia.* Stanford, CA: Stanford University Press.

Postero, N. (forthcoming) "The Struggle to Create a Radical Democracy in Bolivia." *Latin American Research Review,* special issue on "Actually Existing Democracies."

Provea. (2007) *Informe Anual Octubre 2006/Septiembre 2007 Situación de los Derechos Humanos en Venezuela.* October. www.derechos.org.ve /publicaciones/infanual/2006_07/index.html (accessed 26 March 2008).

Przeworski, A. (1991) *Democracy and the Market: Political and Economic Reforms in Eastern Europe and Latin America.* New York: Cambridge University Press.

Przeworski, A., and J. Sprague (1986) *Paper Stones: A History of Electoral Socialism.* Chicago: University of Chicago Press.

Quiroga, J. A. (2008) Author and editor of *Nueva Crítica y Buen Gobierno* magazine. Interview. 18 July.

Quispe, R. (2008) Party militant and local authority, District 6 (Villa Copacabana). Interview. 18 July.

Rabotnikof, N. (2004) "Izquierda y derecha: visiones del mundo, opciones de gobierno e identidades políticas." In *Reabrir espacios públicos,* ed. N. G. Canclini, 268–307. México: UAM-Plaza y Valdés.

Ramia, C., ed. (1989) *El día en que bajaron los cerros: El saqueo de Caracas,* 2nd ed. Caracas: Ateneo.

Ramírez, F., and A. Minteguiaga (2007) "El nuevo tiempo del Estado. La política posneoliberal del correísmo." *OSAL* VIII, no. 22: 87–103.

Ranciere, J. (1998) *Disagreement: Politics and Philosophy.* Minneapolis: University of Minnesota Press.

Regalado, R. (2007) *Latin America at the Crossroads: Domination, Crisis, Popular Movements and Political Alternatives.* Melbourne: Ocean Press.

Reid, M. (2007) *Forgotten Continent: The Battle for Latin America's Soul.* New Haven, CT: Yale University Press.

Revilla Herrero, C. J. (2006) *Visibilidad y Obrismo: En La Estrategia De La Imagen Del Movimiento Plan Progreso En La Ciudad De El Alto,* 1–25. Programa de Desarrollo del Poder Local de UNITAS en DNI—El Alto.

Reygadas, L. (2005) "Imagined Inequalities: Representations of Discrimination and Exclusion in Latin America." *Social Identities* 11, no. 5: 489–508. doi: 10.1080/13504630500407943.

Roberts, B. R. (2008) "Neo-liberal Social Policies and State-Society Relationships in Latin America: The Impact on Citizenship." Presented at the "New Latin American Development Strategies in a Changing International Economic and Political Context" conference, University of Aalborg, May.

Roberts, K. M. (1998) *Deepening Democracy? The Modern Left and Social Movements in Chile and Peru*. Stanford, CA: Stanford University Press.

Roberts, K. M. (2002) "Social Inequalities Without Class Cleavages in Latin America's Neoliberal Era." *Studies in Comparative International Development* 36, no. 4: 3–33. doi: 10.1007/BF02686331.

Roberts, K. M. (2006) "Populism, Political Conflict, and Grass-Roots Organization in Latin America." *Comparative Politics* 38, no. 2: 127–148.

Roberts, K. M. (2007a) "Latin America's Populist Revival." *SAIS Review* 27, no. 1: 3–15. doi: 10.1353/sais.2007.0018.

Roberts, K. M. (2007b) *Repoliticizing Latin America: The Revival of Populist and Leftist Alternatives*. Washington, DC: Woodrow Wilson Center Update on the Americas.

Roberts, K. M. (2007c) "Conceptual and Historical Perspectives." In *The "New Left" and Democratic Governance in Latin America*, ed. C. Arnson and J. R. Perales, 10–14. Washington, DC: Woodrow Wilson International Center for Scholars.

Robinson, W. (2006) "The Oxymoron of Polyarchy." In *Latin America After Neoliberalism: Turning the Tide in the 21st Century?* ed. E. Hershberg and F. Rosen. New York: New Press.

Robinson, W. (2008) "Transformative Possibilities in Latin America." *Socialist Register* 44: 141–159.

Rodríguez, F. (2008a) "An Empty Revolution: The Unfulfilled Promises of Hugo Chávez." *Foreign Affairs* 87, no. 2 (March/April): 49–62.

Rodríguez, F. (2008b) *How Not to Defend the Revolution: Mark Weisbrot and the Misinterpretation of Venezuelan Evidence*. Wesleyan University, Department of Economics. http: //ideas.repec.org/p/wes/weswpa/2008-001.html.

Rodrik, D. (1997) *Has Globalization Gone Too Far?* Washington, DC: Institute for International Economics.

Rojas, R. R. (2005) "On Chavismo: Interview with Yolanda Salas (Caracas, 7 September 2004)." *Journal of Latin American Cultural Studies: Travesia* 14, no. 3. doi: 10.1080/13569320500382641.

Romero, S., and A. Barrionuevo (2009) "With Cash, China Forges Ties to Latin America." *International Herald Tribune*, 17 April.

Rueschemeyer, D., E. H. Stephens, and J. D. Stephens (1992) *Capitalist Development and Democracy*. Chicago: University of Chicago Press.

Sader, E. (1987) "The Workers Party in Brazil." *New Left Review* 126.

Sader, E., and Consejo Latinoamericano de Ciencias Sociales, Instituto de Estudios y Formacion de la CTA (2008) *Posneoliberalismo en America Latina*. Buenos Aires: CLACSO; Instituto de Estudios y Formacion de la CTA.

Safarian, A. E. (1999) "Host Country Policies Towards Inward Foreign Direct Investment in the 1950s and 1990s." *Transnational Corporations* 8, no. 2: 93–112.

Salacuse, Jeswald W., and Nicholas P. Sullivan (2005) "Do BITs Really Work? An Evaluation of Bilateral Investment Treaties and Their Grand Bargain." *Harvard International Law Journal* 46, no. 1: 67–130.

Sánchez, R., and Y. M. Boutang (2009) "Laboratoire Amérique latine: hibridation, interdépendance, et pouvoir constituant." *Multitudes* 35 (Winter): 34–39.

Sandbrook, Richard, Marc Edelman, Patrick Heller, and Judith Teichman (2006) *Social Democracy in the Global Periphery: Origins, Challenges, Prospects.* Cambridge: Cambridge University Press.

Sartori, G. (1976) *Parties and Party Systems.* Cambridge: Cambridge University Press.

Sassoon, D. (1996) *One Hundred Years of Socialism: The West European Left in the Twentieth Century?* New York: New Press.

Schaefer, T. (2009) "Engaging Modernity: The Political Making of Indigenous Movements in Bolivia and Ecuador, 1900–2008." *Third World Quarterly* 30, no. 2 (March): 397. doi: 10.1080/01436590802681116.

Schamis, H. E. (2002) *Re-forming the State: The Politics of Privatization in Latin America and Europe.* Ann Arbor: University of Michigan Press.

Schamis, H. E. (2006) "Populism, Socialism, and Democratic Institutions." *Journal of Democracy* 17, no. 4: 20–34. doi: 10.1353/jod.2006.0072.

Schiwy, F. (2008) "Todos Somos Presidentes/We Are All Presidents." Presented at the workshop "Latin America's Left Turns? Political Parties, Insurgent Movements, and Alternative Policies," Simon Fraser University, Vancouver, 18–19 April.

Schmitt, Carl (2008) *Constitutional Theory.* Trans. and ed. Jeffrey Seitzer. Durham, NC: Duke University Press.

Schmitt, C. (1996) *The Concept of the Political.* Chicago: University of Chicago Press.

Schmitter, P. (2006) "A Sketch of What a 'Post-Liberal' Democracy Might Look Like." www.talaljuk-ki.hu/index.php/article/articleview/502/1/21.

Seligson, M. A., Latin American Public Opinion Project, and V. University (2006) *Auditoría de la democracia.* Nashville, TN: Latin American Public Opinion Project.

Seligson, M. A. (2007) "The Rise of Populism and the Left in Latin America." *Journal of Democracy* 18, no. 3: 81–95. doi: 10.1353/jod.2007.0057.

Serra, J., and J. R. Afonso (2007) "El federalismo fiscal en Brasil: una visión panorámica." *Revista de la CEPAL* 91: 29–52.

Serrano, C. (2005) *La política social en la globalización. Programas de protección en América Latina.* Serie Mujer y Desarrollo núm. 70. Santiago, Chile: CEPAL.

Shadlen, K. (2008) "Globalisation, Power and Integration: The Political Economy of Regional and Bilateral Trade Agreements in the Americas." *Journal of Development Studies* 44, no. 1: 1–20.

Sieyès, A. (2003) "What Is the Third Estate?" In *Political Writings*, ed. M. Sonenscher, 92–162. Indianapolis: Hackett.

Silva, E. (1996) *The State and Capital in Chile: Business Elites, Technocrats, and Market Economics.* Boulder, CO: Westview.

Silva, E. B. (1998) *The State And Capital in Chile: Business Elites, Technocrats, and Market Economics.* Boulder, CO: Westview.

Silva, J. (2008) National deputy for La Paz. Interview. 30 July.

Skocpol, T. (1979) *States and Social Revolutions: A Comparative Analysis of France, Russia and China.* Cambridge: Cambridge University Press.

Smith, P. H. (2005) *Democracy in Latin America: Political Change in Comparative Perspective.* New York: Oxford University Press.

Smulovitz, C., and E. Peruzzotti (2000) "Societal Accountability in Latin America." *Journal of Democracy* 11, no. 4: 147–158. doi:10.1353/jod.2000.0087.

Stallings, B. (1995) *Global Change, Regional Response: The New International Context of Development.* New York: Cambridge University Press.

Stallings, B., and W. Peres (2000) *Growth, Employment, and Equity.* Geneva: Brookings Institution Press.

Stefanoni, P. (2006) "De la calle al palacio: los desafíos de la izquierda boliviana." *Entre voces* 5: 69–72.

Stopford, J. M., and S. Strange, with J. S. Henley (1991) *Rival States, Rival Firms: Competition for World Market Shares.* Cambridge, MA: Cambridge University Press.

Svalestuen, G. (2007) *Un análisis del Plan de Atención Nacional a la Emergencia Social del Uruguay.* Masters thesis, Universidad de Bergen.

Téllez, D. M. (2007) "Nicaragua. Hasta dónde llegue el autoritarismo de este gobierno dependerá de nosotros." *Revista Envío* 305 (August): 1–7.

Ticona, F., and A. Apaza (2008) President and vice president, District 20 in La Paz. Interview. 1 August.

Tironi, E., and F. Agüero (1999) "¿Sobrevivirá El Nuevo Paisaje Político Chileno?" *Estudios Públicos*, no. 74 (Otoño): 151–168.

Tobin, J., and S. Rose-Ackerman (2005) "Foreign Direct Investment and the Business Environment in Developing Countries: The Impact of Bilateral Investment Treaties." Unpublished paper. http: //ssrn.com/abstract=557121.

Tockman, J. (2008) "An Analysis of Bolivia's New Framework for Social, Political and Economic Integration." Masters thesis, Latin American Studies Program, Simon Fraser University.

Toranzo Roca, C. (2008) "Bolivia, Nacionalismo Populista." Presented at the workshop "Latin America's Left Turns? Political Parties, Insurgent Movements, and Alternative Policies," Simon Fraser University, Vancouver, 18–19 April.

Torcal, M., and S. Mainwaring (2003) "The Political Re-Crafting of Social Bases of Party Competition: The Case of Chile 1973–1995." *British Journal of Political Science* 33: 55–84.

Torre, C. D. L. (2007) "The Resurgence of Radical Populism in Latin America." *Constellations* 14, no. 3: 385.

Torrico, G. (2008) MAS's deputy for La Paz and leader of the Satucos. Interview. 29 July.

Touraine, A. (1993) "Latin America: From Populism Toward Social Democracy." In *Social Democracy in Latin America*, ed. M. Vellinga, 297. Boulder, CO: Westview.

Turra, J. (2007) "Lula en Brasil: un gobierno en contradicción con su base social." In *Gobiernos de izquierda en América Latina. Un balance político*, ed. B. Stolowicz, 77–104. Bogotá: Aurora.

Ugarteche, O. (1998) *La arqueología de la modernidad: el Perú entre la globalización y la exclusión*. DESCO. http: //orton.catie.ac.cr/cgi-bin/wxis.exe/ ?IsisScript=BIBLIOPE.xis&method=post&formato=2&cantidad=1& expresion=mfn=040511.

UNCTAD (2006) *Trade and Development Report*. Geneva: United Nations Conference on Trade and Development.

UNCTAD (2009) *Recent Developments in International Investment Agreements (2008–2009)* (No. 3). IIA Monitor. New York: United Nations Conference on Trade and Development.

United Nations Development Programme (2004) *Democracy in Latin America: Towards a Citizens' Democracy*. Geneva: United Nations.

Van Cott, D. L. (2005) *From Movements to Parties in Latin America: The Evolution of Ethnic Politics*. New York: Cambridge University Press.

Van Cott, D. L. (2008) *Radical Democracy in the Andes*. New York: Cambridge University Press.Vandevelde, K. J. (1998) "The Political Economy of a Bilateral Investment Treaty." *American Journal of International Law* 92, no. 4: 621–641.

Vargas Llosa, Á. (2007) "The Return of the Idiot." *Foreign Policy* 160: 54–61.

Vellinga, M. (1993) "The Internationalization of Politics and Local Response: Social Democracy in Latin America." In *Social Democracy in Latin America: Prospects for Change*, ed. M. Vellinga. Boulder, CO: Westview.

Vernon, Raymond (1971) *Sovereignty at Bay: The Multinational Spread of U.S. Enterprises*. New York: Basic Books.

Vilas, C. (2006) "The Left in South America and the Resurgence of National-Popular Regimes." In *Latin America After Neoliberalism: Turning the Tide in the 21st Century?* ed. E. Hershberg and F. Rosen. New York: New Press.

Villatoro, P. (2007) *Las transferencias condicionadas en América Latina: luces y sombras*. Santiago, Chile: CEPAL.

Virno, P. (2004) *A Grammar of the Multitude*. New York: Semiotext(e).

Wade, R. (2006) "Choking the South." *New Left Review* 38 (March–April 2006): 123.

Wainfeld, M., and D. Cufré (2006) "Se acabaron los aumentos indiscrimados de tarifas." *Página/12* (April).

Waissbluth, M. (2006) *La Reforma del Estado en Chile 1990–2005. De la confrontación al consenso*. Santiago, Chile: Universidad de Chile.

Walton, J. (2001) "Power and Popular Protest: Latin American Social Movements." In *Power and Popular Protest: Latin American Social Movements*, updated and expanded ed., ed. S. Eckstein, 299–328. Berkeley: University of California Press.

Weisbrot, M. (2008) "Death in Venezuela: Deadly Massage." *The Economist*. www.economist.com/world/americas/displaystory.cfm?STORY_ID= 11750858.

Weller, J. (2001) *Economic Reforms, Growth and Employment: Labour Markets in Latin America and the Caribbean*. Santiago, Chile: United Nations Publications.

Weyland, K. (1996) "Neopopulism and Neoliberalism in Latin America: Unexpected Affinities." *Studies in Comparative International Development* 31, no. 3: 3–31.

Weyland, K. (2004) "Neoliberalism and Democracy in Latin America: A Mixed Record." *Latin American Politics and Society* 46, no. 1: 135–157.

Weyland, K. (2005) "The Growing Sustainability of Brazil's Low-Quality Democracy." In *The Third Wave of Democratization in Latin America: Advances and Setbacks*, ed. F. Hagopian and S. P. Mainwaring. Cambridge: Cambridge University Press.

Weyland, K. (2006) "Ambition vs. Success in Latin America's Left." *LILAS Portal.* University of Texas-Austin. www1.lanic.utexas.edu/project/etext/llilas/portal/portal079 (accessed 18 January 2010).

Weyland, K. (2007) "What Is Right About Latin America's Left?" Unpublished manuscript.

Weyland, K. (2009) "The Rise of Latin America's Two Lefts: Insights from Rentier State Theory." *Comparative Politics* 41, no. 2: 145–164.

Whitehead, L. (2001) *The International Dimensions of Democratization: Europe and the Americas*, revised expanded ed. Oxford: Oxford University Press.

Williamson, J. (1990) *Latin American Adjustment: How Much Has Happened?* Washington, DC: Institute for International Economics.

Williamson, J. (2000) "What Should the World Bank Think About the Washington Consensus?" *World Bank Res Obs* 15, no. 2: 251–264. doi:10.1093/wbro/15.2.251.

Williamson, J. (2002) "Did the Washington Consensus Fail?" Foreign Trade Information System. www.sice.oas.org/geograph/westernh/williamson.asp.

Wilpert, G. (2007) *Changing Venezuela by Taking Power: The History and Policies of the Chavez Government.* London: Verso.

Worsley, P. (1969) "The Concept of Populism." In *Populism—Its Meaning and National Characteristics*, ed. G. Ionescu and E. Gellner, 212–250. London: Macmillan.

WSF (2004) "Revised World Social Forum Charter of Principles, June 2001 Version." In *World Social Forum: Challenging Empires*, ed. J. Sen et al. New Delhi: Viveka Foundation.

WSF (2007) "Revised World Social Forum Charter of Principles, June 2001 Version." In *World Social Forum: Challenging Empires*, 2nd ed., ed. J. Sen and P. Waterman. Toronto: Black Rose.

XIII Foro de São Paulo (2007) "Something to Celebrate in El Salvador." *NotiCen: Central American and Caribbean Affairs*, no. 8 (February).

Yashar, D. J. (2005) *Contesting Citizenship in Latin America: The Rise of Indigenous Movements and the Postliberal Challenge.* Cambridge: Cambridge University Press.

Zago, A. (1992) *La Rebelión de Los Ángeles.* Caracas: Fuentes Editores.

Zakaria, F. (2003) *The Future of Freedom: Illiberal Democracy at Home and Abroad.* New York: W. W. Norton.

Zedillo, E. (2002) "Lula: The End of Latin American Populism?" *Forbes* 170, no. 13: 55.

Zegada, M. T., Y. F. Tórrez, and G. Cámara (2008) *Movimientos Sociales en Tiempos de Poder: Articulaciones y campos de conflicto en el gobierno del MAS (2006–2007).* La Paz, Bolivia: Centro Cuarto Intermedio; Plural Editores.

Zibechi, R. (2008) "CIP Americas Program—UNASUR Puts Out Its First Fire in Bolivia: Brazil Makes the Difference." 9 December. http: //americas.irc -online.org/am/5721 (accessed 16 December 2009).

Zibechi, R. (2009) "Autonomy or New Forms of Domination?" Americas Program, Center for International Policy. 18 February. http: //americas.irc -online.org/am/5877.

Žižek, S. (2002) "A Plea for Leninist Intolerance." *Critical Inquiry* 28, no. 2: 542–566.

Žižek, S. (2007) "Resistance Is Surrender." *London Review of Books* 29, no. 22. www.lrb.co.uk/v29/n22/zize01_.html.

Zovatto, D. (2007) "Informe Latinobarómetro 2007—Conclusiones principales." November. www.nuevamayoria.com/ES/ANALISIS/zovatto/071120.html (accessed 15 December 2007).

Zuazo, M. (2008) *¿Cómo nació el MAS? La ruralización de la política en Bolivia: Entrevistas a 85 parlamentarios del partido.* La Paz, Bolivia: Fundacion Ebert.

The Contributors

Santiago Anria is a doctoral student in the Department of Political Science at the University of North Carolina–Chapel Hill.

Benjamin Arditi teaches political theory at the Universidad Nacional Autonoma de Mexico in Mexico City. His most recent book is titled *Politics on the Edges of Liberalism: Difference, Populism, Revolution, Agitation.*

Jon Beasley-Murray is assistant professor in the Department of French, Italian, and Hispanic Studies at the University of British Columbia. His forthcoming book is *Posthegemony: Political Theory and Latin America.*

Maxwell A. Cameron is professor of political science at the University of British Columbia. His research and teaching focuses on comparative politics and democratization in Latin America. He recently edited a collection of papers on democracy in the Andes for the *Revista de Ciencia Política* (vol. 30, no. 1, 2010).

Fernando Filgueira, a sociologist, is a social affairs officer at the UN Economic Commission for Latin America and the Caribbean in Santiago, Chile. He has published several books and articles analyzing social policies, poverty, and development models in Latin America, the United States, and Europe

John D. French is professor of history and African and African American Studies at Duke University. An historian of modern Latin America with a specialization in Brazil, his most recent book is *Drowning in Laws: Labor Law and Brazilian Political Culture.*

Paul Alexander Haslam is an associate professor at the School of International Development and Global Studies at the University of Ottawa. His current research focuses on corporate social responsibility, the regulation of foreign direct investment, and state-firm relations in Latin America.

Eric Hershberg is director of the Center for Latin American and Latino Studies and professor of government at American University. A past president of the Latin American Studies Association, he has written widely on Latin American politics and society.

Juan Pablo Luna is assistant professor in the Instituto de Ciencia Politica at the Pontificia Universidad Catolica de Chile, where he teaches comparative politics and research methods. His extensive publications on Latin American politics encompass studies of political representation, party systems, and development alternatives.

Jennifer McCoy is professor of political science at Georgia State University and director of the Americas Program at the Carter Center in Atlanta. She has published extensively on Venezuelan politics and on democracy in Latin America.

Juan Carlos Moreno-Brid is senior economic affairs officer and research coordinator at the UN Economic Commission for Latin America and the Caribbean in Mexico City. He is the coauthor, with Jaime Ros, of *Development and Growth in the Mexican Economy: A Historical Perspective*.

Igor Paunovic is currently with UNCTAD working on the issues related to the least developed countries. Previously, he was chief of the Economic Development Unit of the UN Economic Commission for Latin America and the Caribbean in Mexico City.

Luis Reygadas is professor of anthropology at the Universidad Autonoma Metropolitana–Unidad Iztapalapa in Mexico City. A student of inequalities, work cultures, and cultures of capitalism, his most recent book is *La Apropriación: Destejiendo las Redes de la Desigualdad*.

Kenneth E. Sharpe is the William R. Kenan Jr. Professor of Political Science at Swarthmore College. His current research examines institutional and economic conditions that encourage—or corrode—character and practical wisdom in professionals and politicians and in everyday life more generally. His forthcoming book on the topic will appear in 2011.

Index

Acción Democrática (AD), 47, 99*n4*
Accountability: from within, 111–113; bottom-up, 113; constraints on power and, 110; deficits in, 8; democratic, 4, 6; forms of, 17; horizontal/vertical, 110; leadership, 26; mechanisms of, 86; within organizations, 110; political, 102; to the public, 110; societal, 110; state, 85
Alianza Popular Revolucionaria Americana (APRA), 38*n2*, 47
Allende, Salvador, 31, 77, 150
Anti-imperialism, 15
Argentina: bank closings in, 151; cash transfer programs in, 177; Chinese presence in, 152; consumer prices in, 220; currency devaluation in, 219; development promotion policies in, 183; economic growth in, 195*tab*, 198, 199; economic protests in, 134; equalization strategies in, 176*tab*, 177, 183, 186, 188; export taxes in, 186; external debt in, 201, 202*tab*, 238; financial crisis in, 194; fiscal balance in, 195*tab*; foreign investment in, 209, 210, 214, 215, 217; growth of consumption in, 7; income increases in, 187; incumbent cooptation patterns in, 33; inflation rate in, 195*tab*; investment in, 18, 202*tab*;

middle class in, 151; minimum wages in, 202*tab*; nationalization of enterprises in, 188, 218–220; Peronism in, 10, 38*n2*; *piqueteros* in, 5, 45, 151; populist left in, 25; protests in, 151; state bargaining power in, 210; tax burden in, 200
Asian financial crisis, 24
Asistencialismo, 7
Authoritarianism, 3, 6, 9, 14, 70, 150, 156, 158, 172; constitutional, 172; resistance to, 155; transition from, 65, 76
Autonomy: creation of spaces for, 75; embedded, 37; government, 108; increased opportunities for, 235; regional, 108; subaltern, 14

Bachelet, Michelle, 2, 9, 25, 32, 135, 180
Betancourt, Rómulo, 47
Blanco, Bertha, 116, 120
Bolívar, Simón, 84, 140
Bolivia: accountability structures in, 102; centralization of power in, 103, 110; cocaine economy in, 106; Conciencia de la Patria in, 102, 115, 116, 124*n10*; constituent assembly in, 72; constituent power in, 71–75; constitutional change in, 63, 71–75, 98*n2*; constitutional crisis in, 14; constraints on government, 28*tab*,

About the Book

This accessible, up-to-date look at Latin American politics explores how—and to what effect—diverse forces on the left have not only captured the imagination of vast swaths of the continent's population, but also taken hold of the reins of government.

The authors assess the multiple currents of Latin America's left turns, considering their origins, their relationships to political parties and social movements, and their performance in office. They also consider the challenges faced by such leaders as Hugo Chávez, Evo Morales, and Lula da Silva in efforts to address long-standing socioeconomic inequalities. Explicitly comparative and enhanced with solid empirical material, the book offers a thoughtful commentary on Latin America's changing political environment.

Maxwell A. Cameron is professor in the Department of Political Science at the University of British Columbia. He is author of *The Making of NAFTA: How the Deal Was Done* (with Brian Tomlin) and *Democracy and Authoritarianism in Peru: Political Coalitions and Social Change*. **Eric Hershberg** is director of the Center for Latin American and Latino Studies at American University. His publications include *Latin America After Neoliberalism: Turning the Tide in the 21st Century?* and *State and Society in Conflict: Comparative Perspectives on Andean Crises*.